THE CITY IN INDIAN HISTORY

The City in Indian History

Urban Demography, Society, and Politics

Edited by

INDU BANGA

MANOHAR

URBAN HISTORY ASSOCIATION OF INDIA

2026

First published 1991
Reprinted 2026

ISBN 978-81-85425-40-5

Published by
Ajay Kumar Jain *for*
Manohar Publishers & Distributors
4753/23 Ansari Road, Daryaganj
New Delhi 110 002

Printed and bound in India

To Professor Satish Chandra Misra
In Memorium

CONTENTS

PREFACE

Founded initially as 'Urban History Group' in 1978 at the conclusion of a UGC sponsored seminar on 'Urban History in India' at Guru Nanak Dev University, Amritsar, the Urban History Association of India has endeavoured since 1979 to promote urban studies by organising seminars and symposia and through the publication of its **News-letters**, occasional papers, and proceedings of seminars. Though mostly from the discipline of history, the members of the Association belong also to the disciplines of geography, economics, sociology, political science and town-planning. The Association has welcomed collaboration with other institutions for the attainment of its objectives, notably with the Indian History Congress, the Nehru Memorial Museum and Library, and the Indian Institute of Advanced Study, besides a number of universities. It has received financial support from the Indian Council of Historical Research for some of its programmes.

The City in Indian History is based on papers presented to a seminar on 'urban demography, economy and social structure', organised by the Association in 1987 jointly with the Nehru Memorial Museum and Library, and occasional papers published by the Association from time to time. The main body of this book, thus, consists of sixteen papers which cover the city in Indian history from pre-historic to modern times. These papers relate to conceptual, methodological and historiographical problems in the study of urbanisation, urban morphology, demography, society and politics on pan-Indian, regional and local levels. The bibliography given at the end of this volume is largely selected from the bibliographical entries published in the **News-letters** of the Association from time to time.

This volume also contains three short pieces on the late Professor Satish Chandra Misra by Professor S. Nurul Haṣan, Professor J.S. Grewal and Professor Dwijendra Tripathi; Professor Grewal wrote his note soon after the passing away of Professer Misra who was associated with the founding of the Urban History Group and the Urban History Association of India from the very beginning till his untimely demise in 1984, and made a very substantial contribution to all the programmes of the Association as a member, a Vice-President and a President. In fact, he symbolised the close association between the universities at Amritsar and Baroda in pursuit of new areas and new methods of historical research. This volume is dedicated to his memory.

In the publication of this volume as much as in pursuing the programmes of the Association, I have received much help from a number of individuals and institutions, and I would like to take this opportunity of acknowledging our debt to them. Among the institutions I may repeat the names of the Indian History Congress, the Indian Council of Historical Research and the Nehru Memorial Museum and Library as among the foremost institutions which have helped the Association as well as the publication of this volume in one way or another. The Manohar Publications have been extremely accommodating and helpful in seeing the publication of this volume through; Shri O.P. Sarna has prepared the maps with great care. I am thankful to all the contributors to this volume for revising their papers in the light of editorial suggestions. It is sad to mention that two of the contributors are no longer with us: Professor G.D. Sharma and Dr Kanchan Jyoti. Several of my colleagues at Amritsar and Chandigarh have been helpful to me at all stages of the preparation and publication of this volume, and I would like particularly to mention Dr Harish Chandra Sharma, my colleague at Amritsar, and Dr Reeta Grewal, formerly a student at Amritsar and now a colleague at the Panjab University, Chandigarh.

Above all, I feel happy to thank Professor J.S. Grewal who has been helpfully associated with the publication of this book as much as with all the programmes of the Association from its very inception.

Indu Banga
Secretary
Urban History Association of India

26 September 1990
Chandigarh

PROFESSOR SATISH CHANDRA MISRA AS I KNEW HIM

I

I first met Professor S.C. Misra in 1949 when he was a young research student of Benaras Hindu University who had been deputed to spend a few months at the Aligarh Muslim University. At the initiative of late Professor Mohammad Habib, young Satish Misra was appointed as Student Assistant, a post which carried great prestige. In the Staff Common Room I had the occasions to discuss many historical problems with him particularly those connected with the reign of Sher Shah on whose reign he was doing the research. I was deeply impressed by his learning as well as intellectual curiosity. He had by then acquired a good working knowledge of Persian and could discuss the problems of interpretation of source materials with mastery.

Although I kept in close touch with his academic activities, I had the opportunity to know of his work more intimately in many ways. Under his inspiring leadership Baroda became one of the major centres of medieval and modern Indian history. He always exercised intellectual leadership in the craft of historical research, emphasising particularly the importance of collecting source materials, sifting complicated and even conflicting pieces of evidence and interpreting the evidence as objectively as possible. He was totally free from constricting bias of any type. He continued to take a great deal of interest in all the newer trends of historical investigation and interpretation which were emerging in different parts of the world.

I was particularly impressed by the interest he took in medieval archaeology. One of the few leading scholars of medieval Indian history who realised the value of archaeology to fill in the gap of the medieval Indian history, he took concrete steps to organise the excavation of the medieval Gujarati town of Champaner. His labour proved to be immensely rewarding.

His sudden demise at a time when his studies had reached their most productive stage has been a great loss to Indian historical studies. Personally, he was a dear friend who was always so considerate. The place vacated by him in my personal life can never be filled.

2 July 1990 — **S. Nurul Hasan**

Raj Bhawan, Calcutta — *Governor of West Bengal*

II

In the untimely demise of Professor Satish Chandra Misra, the Urban History Association of India has lost its President, and a pioneer of urban studies in this country. He was a founder-member of the Urban History Group which developed into the Urban History Association of India. His Inaugural Address to the Association, published as its first Occasional Paper, shows his deep understanding of the processes of urbanisation and the importance of urban studies for the history of India.The Association, still in its formative stage, has suffered a grievous loss. We have to bear the unbearable.

The discipline of history in this country which recently honoured Professor Misra as the General President of the Indian History Congress has lost in him a dedicated craftsman. I came to know him first through *The Rise of Muslim Power in Gujarat* when I was in England. I wondered then why Indian researchers went to Cambridge, Oxford or London when this kind of work could be produced in India. I met Professor Misra a year later in Delhi as a fellow delegate to a seminar organised by the university. I found the opportunity to tell him what I had felt on reading his book. He wanted to know which particular part of the book I had liked best. I mentioned the introductory chapters. He was pleasantly surprised and did not hesitate to tell me that I was the first person to appreciate what he himself regarded as the best part of his work. It still remains the best shortest introduction to the establishment of Turkish rule in India.

We met frequently after this first personal acquaintance. Gradually, I came to know the historian in Professor Misra. His doctoral thesis was on Sher Shah, which is still unpublished. When I asked him why, he told me that it needed revision and that he was thinking of bringing it out in two volumes. When I read the thesis I could not help feeling that this was one of the best theses I had seen. Professor Misra's self-assessment was only a reflection of the distance he had covered between the time of his writing the thesis and my conversation with him. I was surprised to learn that this work was written by Professor Misra in his early twenties. He was certainly a precocious historian. But in his late fifties he felt happier with *The Muslim Communities in Gujarat* than with *Sher Shah*.

The historian in Professor Misra looked for new, undiscovered but meaningful, facets of the past. I recall the enthusiasm with which he obliged visitors to Baroda to see the site at Champaner being excavated.

This was no search for a lost Trojan city. Professor Misra saw the growth of medieval archaeology in his Champaner project. That dream is still a dream, but a beginning has been made towards its realisation.

In his personal conversations, Professor Misra used to say that history is an 'inferior' discipline. Those who heard it for the first time were surely surprised, if not really shocked. But this was only a way in which he expressed his appreciation of philosophy and literature. A scholar of classical Persian and Urdu, Professor Misra edited, among others, the *Mirat-i-Sikandari*, a sixteenth century Persian text, and the *Qissa-i-Ghamgin*, an eighteenth century Urdu text. He also enjoyed reading literature, Urdu poetry and English fiction, but only the best. He had in fact begun tapping literature as history.

Professor Misra's love for literature and philosophy made him only a keener and profounder historian. It is difficult to find a person, or a historian, with wider empathies or a more open mind. What do we know of the medieval mind? He would often pose the question. In due course I discovered that he was trying to grapple with the greatness of Akbar. He promised himself to complete the study during several succeeding summer vacations. He proposed also to write on 'two cultures' in medieval India. An unwary listener would respond on the assumption that perhaps Professor Misra proposed to write on the Muslim and Hindu cultures, but only to discover that these were not the categories of his thinking. His 'two cultures' related to the life of the privileged and the depressed. There were many other potential interests which Professor Misra cherished in a single lifetime which proved to be rather short.

Maintaining the highest standards of integrity in his professional capacities, Professor Misra was a warm personal friend for many, particularly those who showed some sense of dedication to impersonal values. Like the best of the Victorians he talked of things rather than persons. Not that he was a Victorian in any other sense of the term. He knew no barriers, social or intellectual. His conversation ranged round everything that related to human existence, with a benign smile on his grave philosophic face that symbolised the man. Those who knew Professor Misra rather closely saw in him an indulgent father and a quietly considerate and affectionate husband. His friends and his kith and kin have lost as much as the discipline to which he dedicated his life.

J.S. Grewal
Vice-Chancellor
Guru Nanak Dev University

15 October 1984
Amritsar

III

To write about a friend is as difficult as to write about oneself. And the task becomes still more difficult, if one were to write about so close a friend as the late Professor Satish Chandra Misra. Perhaps the best I can do is to recapitulate what drew us closer.

We were very different in many ways. Or so I thought when I first met Professor Misra in 1966 at Delhi where both of us were attending an annual session of the Indian Historical Records Commission. He was already a recognised scholar while I had completed my Ph.D. only recently; he had been a Professor in a prestigious university for quite some time past while the Indian Institute of Management where I was working was not very well-known then even in Ahmedabad; and he was chiefly interested in socio-political developments in medieval India while my own focus was on business history of modern India. He looked, as he always looked thereafter, older than his age, slightly drooping shoulders, a melancholy but serene countenance, and a strikingly graceful demeanour without a trace of artificiality. Withdrawn, shy, and reticent, he appeared to me – apparently much younger in age and more youthful in attitude to things and people – almost inaccessible and unfathomable. I had heard of him but knew little about his work and contribution and I am sure that he had no idea of my own background.

We, however, were drawn into conversation, perhaps because of the geographical proximity of the cities we lived in, in the course of which he asked me why I studied history. My answer – 'because I want to know myself as a part of my surroundings' – betrayed a characteristic presentist view of history which regards past as nothing more than a laboratory for the historian to conduct experiments to comprehend his present. This belief had been integral to my historical sensitivity, reinforced by my interaction with the liberal tradition of historical learning for which the University of Wisconsin, my *alma mater*, has been known. Articulating it so unreservedly, I was rather apprehensive that it might offend a medievalist whose own approach to history had been shaped in an age of positivistic historiography in India.

I was in for a pleasant surprise. Not only that he expressed sympathy for my position but also delivered a brief discourse in support with generous allusions to the writings of Kant, Croce, Collingwood, Carr and several other thinkers. A great deal of passion flowed from his observation, but there was absolutely no hint of pedantry although it was obvious that his views were rooted in great deal of erudition and practical experience with historical craftsmanship. What was most remarkable, however, was that his shyness and reticence, that had stood as a formidable barrier between us, vanished in thin air and I found myself face to face with a strikingly sharp mind generating great deal of inspiration but almost no feeling of awe.

The professional resonance I experienced in my first meeting with Professor Misra soon developed into a close personal friendship. Our meetings became more frequent and discussions longer. And as I knew him better, I realised that presentism for him was not merely a subject of intellectual discussion; it was a deep conviction. This perhaps is the reason why he never published and seldom talked about his Ph.D. thesis on Sher Shah which, while throwing fresh light on the career and exploits of this ruler, bore in some degree the imprint of the positivistic trend of the early fifties when it was originally written. In contrast, he regarded his *The Rise of Muslim Power in Gujarat* (Asia, 1963), and *The Muslim Communities of Gujarat* (Asia, 1964) better representatives of his approach to historical enquiry. Both these works are clearly cast in a presentist mould. The accent in the former, though primarily a political history of Gujarat from the end of the thirteenth century up to the middle of the fifteenth, is on the contribution of the Muslim rulers of Gujarat to the shaping of a composite Indian culture, and the latter traces the evolution of a typical Indian identity of various Muslim groups that have enriched the social fabric of Gujarat.

The underlying assumptions that informed these works and a number of essays Professor Misra wrote in the later years gradually developed in his celebrated thesis of 'indigenisation' to explain the process attending the formation of the Indian society – plural and yet integrated, variegated as well as unified, and individualised but basically coherent – through the long panorama of India's past. What he wished to stress was that the Indian identity all through its recorded history has been shaped by the interaction of myriad immigrating cultures which readapted and integrated themselves with their new milieu without losing their respective individualities so that the end product was a colourful social mosaic rather than a dull homogenised mass. Indigenisation and not assimilation, as is often stressed, has been the distinctive feature of Indian history. Professor Misra did not have the time to postulate this theory comprehensively but even in outline it serves to expose the pathetic myopia of approaches that fail to observe the essential India of the religio-cultural pluralities which have contributed to the rich varieties of our society reinforcing at the same time its organic unity. At a time when the disastrous consequences of such myopic visions for our nationhood are all too apparent, the urgency of projecting a proper and undistorted view of Indian history cannot be overstressed.

The comprehensive exposition of the 'indigenisation' thesis was not the only casualty of Professor Misra's premature death. During the closing years of his life he was deeply involved in an interpretative study of Akbar informed by the hypothesis that his regime was the forerunner of modern Indian state. He also could not complete his work on the foundations of Indian capitalism for which he had collected a mass of data. Both these projects belong to the period which is normally associated with the medieval Indian history. Professor Misra's presentist sympathy, however, sometimes led him into occasional forays in modern India as well. His most impressive exercise in this area was his work relating to the Rajkot Satyagrah of 1938 launched by Gandhi, about which little has been written. This was claiming all his attention but he had completed only two-thirds of the work when the end came. Going through these pages one regrets that the society would never have the benefit of this fascinating study.

Professor Misra's greatness as a historian lay not only in his personal scholarly accomplishments. He also made signal contribution to broadening the horizon of historical studies. He was among the first, if not the first, to emphasise the significance of regional history for comprehending the historical realities of a country of subcontinental dimensions. Likewise, his stress on urban history stemmed from his desire to unravel the mysteries of social mobility in India. He was very emphatic in his belief that many crucial aspects of modern Indian society cannot be properly comprehended without analysing the process of urban growth and its impact on socio-economic ethos and behaviour. While this could be debatable, there was something infectious in his passion for urban history which in no small measure contributed to the establishment of the Urban History Association of India. His most unique contribution, however, to broadening the scope of historical research was his plea to use literature for historical enquiries. A creative writer as the mirror of his times and the historian as an experimenter in the laboratory of the past have much in common, he used to stress.

These concerns naturally influenced his strategy to build the Department of History at the M.S. University of Baroda. When he assumed its leadership in the late fifties he had only a small group of colleagues, barely sufficient to carry on the routine teaching work. The resources of the university to expand the department were extremely limited and with his aristocratic disdain for hovering around the powers that be, Professor Misra waited patiently until the situation improved, when the University Grants Commission accorded to the department a status of special assistance in the late seventies. With much larger and a more competent team Professor Misra pushed his colleagues and students to undertake research in agrarian and urban development of Gujarat and analyse historically the compulsions on the creative writings of prominent litterateurs in Hindi and Gujarati. One of his most unconventional ventures to broaden the horizon of history was to study archaeologically the medieval city of Champaner in the vicinity of Baroda, now reduced to debris. To the best of my knowledge never before, or perhaps since, archaeology has been harnessed to unravel the mysteries of medieval history.

The presentist interpretation of history is deeply rooted in source material and informed by relevant theoretical constructs. All Professor Misra's works, including his Presidential Address to the Indian History Congress in 1981, bear witness to these basic props of the presentist approach. Besides, the Ph.D. programme mounted by his department made it incumbent on the students to familiarise themselves with the theories relevant for their subject matter and learn the languages in which the source materials were available. Professor Misra also launched a vigorous programme to translate some important Persian texts into English such as *Mirat-i-Ahmadi* and *Tarikh-i-Mahmudshahi*. He himself had earlier edited *Mirat-i-Sikandari* in collaboration with a colleague of his university.

All said and done, Professor Misra had succeeded in only mapping the soil, as it were, of the vast territory he wished to explore. While he gave a new direction to his department, most of his schemes were still in their infancy at the time of his death. It is now left to the inheritors of his legacy to proceed from where he left off.

Professor Misra is missed not only because he was a great and sensitive historian. More importantly, he was a man of great civility and culture who considered it beneath his dignity to lose temper even in the face of grave provocations. I still recall an occasion when, while chairing a session in a conference of historians at Mussourie, he continued to over look the behaviour of some participants who were frequently interrupting the proceedings without even bothering about the chairman's permission. When later in the day I protested against what I thought was his undue magnanimity, he replied without any trace of rancour: 'I understand what you are saying, but I cannot be rude to anybody'. Nothing, however, could have given a ruder shock to his innumerable friends and admirers – and even to his foes if he had any – than his sudden departure from the world. I wish I could some how convey to him this complaint I have been harbouring ever since he left us in 1984.

Dwijendra Tripathi
Professor
Indian Institute of Management

13 September 1990
Ahmedabad

URBAN HISTORY IN INDIA: POSSIBILITIES AND PERSPECTIVES

S. C. MISRA

I should begin by making an obvious point: urban history is not an independent discipline. Possibly, it cannot as yet claim to be an autonomous subdiscipline either, which social and economic history are. Rather, it should be regarded, especially in India, where urban historical studies are still in their formative stage, as an area in which historians may fruitfully work, and in which they may seek the collaboration of other historians and social scientists in related disciplines like geography, sociology, economics and political science.

An area of inquiry which proposes to study a certain facet of experience in space and time, needs a certain focus, a certain approach. This focus is all the more necessary in a field where several disciplines converge. Essentially, as its designation qualified by an adjective suggests, urban history is the study of urbanisation, of the expansion of urban centres in the span of time, the factors which promote and retard such growth, and the ecology which towns generate in several related dimensions: in the natural environment, in the economic system, in political apparatus, in societal network, and even in the minds of men living in towns.

The town has emerged in history with two primary characteristics: first, a high density of population concentrated within a limited space and secondly, a predominantly non-agricultural, particularly non-cultivating nature of its population. This men-space ratio and occupational heterogeneity, with their consequential relationships, have formed the primary basis for differentiation between the city and the village.

Obviously, the urban centre comes into being within a rural setting. The rise of towns has been described as a revolution in human history, the starting point of civilisation and history, but it is a revolution which could not have and has not come about without an agrarian base, and without serving as a subordinate factor in an economic activity which was generated in the villages.

In an economy which is primarily agrarian, the rural-urban continuum is thus of paramount importance. The Indian town in many cases is an extension of the village, carrying over the same social unities and attitudes; the 'peasant urbanites' are no new feature in Indian history. Urban economic activities were an extension of those initiated in the villages. The linkages are so close and so pervasive that it is myopic, misleading, to see the town apart from the region which brought it into being or sustained its economic activity.

The historical novelty of the town, its uniqueness, its spatial and social dimensions, the concentration of diverse economic, social and political activities in it – the fact of its becoming the hub of civilisation – led to the rise of contrasting attitudes. There was a tendency in austere and puritanical modes of thought to conceive of the city as the den of evil, corrupting the pristine spirit of man, weaning him away from simple, godly life into the snares of temptation. In more sophisticated terms, the city was seen as a parasitic growth on the rural countryside, siphoning away its surplus, draining its manpower, without recompense for the village. An equally misleading view was to glamorise the city and place it sharply in contrast with the 'primitivism' characteristic of the village. In most languages, probably, there are words which have connotations unfavourable to the ruralite and complimentary to the urbanite. Such attitudes, like prejudices, have a hardy life; they persist.

It is not necessary here to stress the error which follows from exaggerating the dichotomy between the village and the town. Certainly, the nature of concentration and economic activity makes differentiation like this possible, even imperative: cultural variations follow. To exaggerate the corruption of the town and the simplicity of the village, the prasitism of the town and the helplessness of the village, and to negate the mutual dependence of either, is to take an extreme, if not an ideological, position.

Given this interdependence, in fact the total dependence of the town on the region which it serves, the role of the town in the evolution of society and civilisation can be understood in its proper perspective. No one has expressed it more eloquently than Lewis Mumford:[1]

> The city, as one finds it in history, is the point of maximum concentration for the power and culture of a community. It is the place where the rays of the many separate beams of light fall into focus, with gains in both social effectiveness and significance. The city is the form and symbol of an integrated social relationship; it is the seat of the temple, the market, the hall of justice, the academy of learning. Here in the city, the goods of civilisation are multiplied and manifolded; here is where the human experience is transformed into visible signs, symbols, patterns of conduct, systems of order. Here is where the issues of civilisation are focussed; here too the ritual passes on occasion into active drama of a full, differentiated and self-conscious society.

The city can indeed be seen as 'the matrix and the carrier, the mirror and the stage of that form of organised and social living which historically may be recognised as civilisation'. The city, though not an entity in itself, is 'an index value, indicating, measuring and summarising the civilisation'.[2] It is the one end of a continuum at the other end of which stands the village. It cannot exist without this vital support; nor can, except in primitive, subsistence cultures do village settlements exist without the town.

The social transformation which brought the town into existence, was of course, due to the surplus which was created by sedentarisation and agriculture. Urbanisation thus is contingent on a relatively advanced mode of production, on a relationship between the economic organisation of society and the level of technical theory (technology), which in turn determine the rate, the volume and the direction of resource utilisation.

It is neither possible nor necessary here to indicate the several approaches to the growing urbanisation in societies and the functions which the towns serve. Max Weber in his classic study emphasised what appears to us today a Eurocentric view, stressing its key role in the transition to a capitalist economy in Europe. Pirenne saw the market function of the town as a lever in its growth.

In problem-oriented history, the approach would itself be contingent on the question asked. The numerous facets of urban history can therefore hardly be spelt out. I should, however, like to make one distinction which

[1]Lewis Mumford, *Culture of Cities*, London 1938, 3.

[2]Paul Meadows, 'The City, Technology and History', *Urbanism, Urbanization and Change: Comparative Perspectives*, Addison Wesley, London 1976, 16.

I think is of some importance. In India and elsewhere, there is a considerable amount of literature on towns which may be called 'biographical', i.e. the biography of a town. In an earlier age, such studies were undertaken as a labour of love, the tribute of proud, devoted citizens to their city. In more recent times, they have been supported by city authorities and other public bodies. The biographical approach is primarily narrative and descriptive, tracing the history of the town through time, pausing on noteworthy events, noteworthy persons, and places of historical interest.

In Indian urban literature, there is a considerable literature of this nature on different towns, particularly old historical centres. The earliest probably is Sir Syed Ahmad's classic work on Delhi; Mohammed Latif studied Agra and Lahore. In Indian languages, there are similar studies: I know of four in Gujarati: on Ahmedabad, Surat, Khambhat and Bharuch. There are also others. Most Gazetteer volumes contain such histories, the District Gazetteer in detail, the Imperial Gazetteer in brief.

Far be it from me to minimise the importance of such pioneer and detailed studies. They have preserved much of what has subsequently been lost, especially old traditions, townslore, even landmarks. They help us in understanding what the town was in the minds of its citizens. Since a number of such studies were written in the colonial era when these towns were in a depressed state, they also reflect the sadness of the nostalgic citizens for the age gone by.

Nevertheless, it is necessary to distinguish urban history from urban biography. Urban history would be based on a core of questions which are to be answered by the study undertaken. It would be analytical and based on a conscious hypothesis, a hypothesis which is amenable to modification, even rejection on retrospect, but which furnishes the starting base for the inquiry.

II

Urban studies in India are growing rapidly in all social sciences. The economists undertake detailed surveys of growing towns; the sociologists study neighbourhoods, 'rural urbanites', urban elite; and for political scientists interested in psephology and local government, the town is a base.

This interest has emerged as a necessary corollary of the accelerated pace at which urbanisation has occurred in India after World War II, more particularly with the industrialisation which followed the Second Plan. Acute urban problems, overcrowding, slum growth, pollution, inadequate transport, and lately urban violence – factors like these have led to the spotlight being turned on the towns, especially the bigger ones. The census surveys, with their multifarious queries and concentration on population and occupational profiles, have also served to develop interest in urban problems. By now, urban planning and regional studies increasingly attract the attention of social scientists and policy framers.

Significantly, the growing volume of contemporary urban studies has a fairly slender base in history. The kind of issues with which social scientists deal are relatively ahistorical; they focus on problems which are of fairly recent origin. Not many researchers feel the need of the historical dimension, for which in any case they are either not or inadequately trained. Secondly, not many historians have so far opted to work on themes of urban history. This area, thus, a rapidly growing field of studies in the west, remains relatively unexplored, underworked in India.

I do not believe, as is sometimes said, that data for such studies are sparse – possibly so, if the rich abundance of the west is taken into consideration; but not wholly correct, if it is argued as a factor for the neglect of this area. More relevant probably is the relatively recent interest in theory-based depth studies, focusing on societal and economic problems. Since urban studies demand the prior development of these interests, and in India such studies themselves grew in volume only recently, it is no surprise that we have not yet advanced to exploit this field in full measure.

By now I believe the stage has been reached when urban studies can be taken in hand in real earnest. Our studies of rural economy and rural society have reached a point where they require urban studies as a complement; our studies of society have progressed to allow the urban angle to be utilised as a factor in analysis. We are now deeply aware of problems which need to be attacked from several angles, one of which is spatial and demographic.

Primarily, studies in urban history may have to take urbanisation in general and urban centres in particular as their matrix. Such studies would illumine first, the nature of the towns in a region, their institutions and the socio-psychological make-up and ethos of the urban classes. Secondly, the quality and volume of urbanisation which is fostered should help us to gauge the nature of economy in that region, the societal and economic stage at which it is.

It may thus be seen that depth studies of urbanisation would significantly improve our understanding of medieval Indian economy,society and culture. The medieval civilisation was pre-eminently an urban civilisation in the sense that its cities were the expression, the chrysalis of its heritage. We have an idea of the society, the upper class culture which came into being. But how much do we know of the stage where the magnificent drama was played, of its more intimate institutions, its recesses? We have little understanding of the dynamics of a medieval town, the distinctive growth of urban centres, specialising in craft industries, in trade, in pilgrim traffic.

Our understanding of the large towns may be limited but it is there; our knowledge of the smaller towns amounts to nothing. In his account of the twelve *subahs*, Abul Fazl refers to 2,737 *qasbas*. How much do we know about these townships apart from their obvious, and sometimes not very obvious, functions? They remain mere dots on an imaginary map, these vital links between the village and the medieval metropolis.

Some of the crucial problems of Indian history require a far more detailed analysis of urban centres and their social and economic as well as physical ecology than has been attempted so far. Take for instance, the question of the economic potential of the Mughal empire in the seventeenth century and of its capacity to generate the capitalistic breakthrough. The generation of adequate resources was, of course, in the agricultural sector, in the countryside, but not so their utilisation, their conversion into either capital with reproductive ability or into non-developmental, non-productive uses. Meaningful and productive investment of the surplus could depend not only on the availability of remunerative avenues but also on the entrepreneurial perception of those with fluid resources. The parameters within which this activity took place were almost wholly urban, and this urban setting deeply influenced not only the perception of the commercial classes but also moulded their financial and trading institutions. The interlocked pattern of mores and institutions – residential, occupational, caste – and its linkages with the political order formed the framework within which the inhibitions and stimulants of the growth process have to be investigated. It is only very recently that we have, in Baroda and Ahmedabad, begun to scratch the surface of this activity in the urban centres of Gujarat, particularly Ahmedabad and Surat.

It would be impertinent even to suggest the potential of this growing field and to indicate its value in our attempt to understand the Indian past. I have tried to bring out only the tip of the iceberg and that too in the pre-modern, pre-industrial age, which I happen to know better. As we go into the nineteenth century, into the dynamics of the colonial age, the problems become even more diversified; we approach the kind of problems which contemporary studies investigate. The transformation of the Indian scene by the intrusion of the colonial economy on the one hand and the contact with the developing west on the other brings forth a host of problems.

The process of mobilisation for instance, which followed the beginning of western-style political awareness and consequent activity, is set almost in an exclusively middle class, urban setting. The response of this urban middle class, initially professional and western educated, has been of course a subject of deep interest to students. Nearly as significant is the urban matrix, not the bigger cities alone, which were the primary and radiating centres of this growing activity but also in more multitudinous, smaller ones, which were at the receiving end. The dimensions of the national movement, the forms that it took are thus intimately related to the altering patterns of urbanisation – a dynamic and varied stage on which this process took place.

Urbanisation is not an independent variable but a dependent function of the dominant mode which inheres in a certain period, and it has to be studied as such. Nevertheless, the feedback effect of urbanisation in shaping the contours of such trends has also to be recognised; so also has to be, the role of towns, large and small, in fashioning the economic system, the social framework and the intellectual climate of an age.

I should like to conclude with a brief suggestion regarding methods of work. Problems and more significant problems particularly, do not always lie in the core of a discipline; rather they are situated at the periphery where several disciplines interact. Urban history requires, more than anything else, that we purposefully and meaningfully use the insights which are being developed by other social sciences – by economics, sociology, political science, anthropology, social psychology, architecture, and for quantification, statistics. It may be necessary, as we go further back in time, to create our own theoretical base, for insights developed for probing the contemporary scene may not always be useful or rewarding to analyse the reality of bygone but by no means less complex ages. Our studies would acquire a maturity by the time we shall have begun formulating this theory base, the hypotheses adequate for exploring our problems. The task is difficult, exacting; probably, everything worth doing is. But the pleasure of exploring, and the promise of reward, is, I am sure, even greater.

URBANISM IN EARLY HISTORIC INDIA

R.S. SHARMA

I propose to say something on the problem of urbanism in early historic India. It roughly means the period from 500 B.C. to about A.D. 500 to 600, but I would also refer to the next three or four centuries. Whenever we talk of urbanism, we are faced with the difficult question of its definition. There is a view nowadays that size and population are crucial to the concept of urbanisation in the Bronze Age cultures in which crafts and commerce did not play a significant part. But it is also argued that commerce played a vital role in Harappan urban life. When we consider the question of identifying a town, it is not only the size and the population which matter, but also the nature of the population. Basically a town has to be a concentration of non-agriculturists, and unless people living in the hinterland have attained a food-producing economy of considerable scale, unless they are able to supply the towns with food provisions from their produce, it is not possible to have a large population. As far as early historic towns in India are concerned, crafts and commerce have played a considerable role and, therefore, the presence of crafts and commerce has to be looked for not only in the archaeological record but also in literary texts. Further, there is the question of the quality of material life. We have to differentiate between the type of life which is lived in the towns and that in the rural areas. Of course, there would be class differentiation in both towns and rural areas. Even so certain articles which are considered inferior are used mostly in rural areas and are basically different from those used by the affluent sections in towns. These articles would perhaps also be used in rural areas but not on the same scale. This is my rough understanding of what a town was, and how a town could be identified in the early historical context.

Having said that we need to differentiate between the type of urbanism in the Bronze Age culture of Harappa and that in the middle Ganga plains lying between Allahabad and Rajmahal where the towns started their career from around the middle of the first millennium B.C., throve till A.D. 300 and lingered up to A.D. 600 or even beyond. One important difference is geographical or ecological. The Harappan area is an arid, semi-arid zone without much rainfall. The Harappan zone may have floods, inundation and so on but not the type of alluvial soil covered with thick vegetation that characterises the middle Ganga plains. Since rainfall in that area is slight, the problem of forest clearance does not exist. The Gangetic area on the other hand had a heavy rainfall, creating an entirely different environment. Whereas bronze and even stone tools could be effective in the Harappan area, facilitating large-scale settlements, these tools could not be effective in clearing the thick forests in the alluvial soil of the middle Ganga plain. Thus, we have urbanism in the Harappan area in the Bronze Age, and in the middle Ganga plains in the Iron Age when iron tools appeared for the first time on a considerable scale and boosted agricultural production. They helped in the clearing of forests, and in the production of the surplus much over and above what was needed for the subsistence of an ordinary peasant. This enabled him to save something that could be used for supporting rulers, priests, craftsmen, specialist artisans, army men, etc. living in the town. This surplus could be in the form of taxes and tributes or even in the form of unequal trade. In other words, what we have in the alluvial plains of the middle Ganga is a new kind of phenomenon as compared to what we have in the arid, semi-arid plains of Sind and the Punjab associated with Harappan urbanism.

The other difference is the use of metal money. In the Bronze Age culture we do come across references to the pieces of silver being used in Mesopotamia though there were various other ways and means of carrying on transactions. But in that culture nothing like coined metal money, standardised, authorised, and recognised by the state was used. That feature appears in the Old World only towards the end of the seventh century B.C. And in India, so far as the actual coins are concerned, they are not earlier than 500 B.C. if we go by archaeological evidence. Coins by themselves do not mean much, but they are an indication of the type of economic activity that began; they show petty commodity production though on a small scale. With commodity production, there was a new type of distribution in which middlemen played a vital part. All this led to trade which was enormously facilitated by the use of coins. Once coins came into being, they led to many changes. The coins became a far more convenient mode for exchange than numerous other objects including cattle. Metalled money was not easily perishable. One could easily add and subtract; book-keeping became easy. It also became possible to transport coins easily from one place to another; it was not easy to transport a large number of cattle. The coins became associated with the towns of the middle Ganga plains on a considerable scale.

There is yet another difference between Harappan urbanism and that of the middle Ganga plains. This relates to duration. The Harappan urbanism lasted shorter than urbanism in the middle Ganga plains, somewhere from 2350 B.C. to about 1750 B.C. — a period of about 600 years. Intriguingly, once Harappan urbanism disappeared there was no urbanism in that part of the country for more than a thousand years. Even more intriguing, once town planning disappeared, the use of bricks also disappeared; we do not find burnt bricks in that part of the country or in other parts, on any scale till the times of the Mauryas, that is, around 300 B.C.

On the other hand, the urbanism which started in the middle Ganga plains around 500 B.C. was never completely extinguished. It lasted much longer. Certainly it existed from about 500 B.C., though some have pushed it back to 600 B.C.; the difference of a century does not cause much concern particularly to a student of ancient history. So we start with 500 B.C. and we can go up to A.D. 600 and even later. Towns did not disappear completely, they go up to A.D. 1200 and so on. Once towns came into existence in the early historic period they suffered decay and decline but they did not completely disappear unlike the Harappan towns. Archaeological evidence regarding the sudden decline of towns in the ancient period in various parts of the country is piling day by day, and its detailed study deserves attention.

We must therefore study Harappan urbanism in the perspective of Bronze Age culture extending right from Harappa through Iran and Iraq and Asia Minor to Greece and then Egypt – it is one compact geographical area of the Bronze Age culture with many similarities. There was urbanism in this whole area, yet several traits typical of Harappan urbanism are not found in any Bronze Age urbanism outside Harappa. To study Harappan urbanism in isolation from other urban cultures also does not help us much. How else to account for its total eclipse? Why are its specific, concrete traces not found later? That is a problem which needs attention.

In any case, the type of urbanism which developed in the subcontinent in the Bronze Age had a short life while that which developed in early historic times had a much longer life. Furthermore, the urbanism which started around 500 B.C. reached its peak between 200 B.C. and A.D. 300. Archaeological excavations of this period have exposed a large number of towns spread all over the country – which of course does not mean that every bit of the country had towns. But still there were a good number of towns in this period. It was also the time when Indo-Roman trade was most thriving, particularly in the first two centuries of the Christian era, and trade with central and south-east Asia was also thriving.

A large number of crafts are mentioned in this period—about seventy-five occupations are mentioned in the *Milindapanho* which is attributed to the second century B.C., and nearly one hundred occupations each in the cities of Rajagriha and Kapilavastu are mentioned in the *Mahavastu*, a text of around the first century A.D. Description of these two capital towns is invariably accompanied by a long list of specialised occupations. In bow-making, there would be a person who just made bowstrings, another was engaged in arrow fletching, and a third made only the bow. Similarly, in dyeing industry were persons engaged in weaving, others in dyeing, and still others in the manufacture of dyes. All these are specifically mentioned in the texts. It was the period when the largest number of crafts are mentioned in literary texts and are attested by the type of excavated artefacts and coins. Thus, on the basis of excavations, we can say there were various types of potters, ivory workers, dyers (because dyeing vats have been discovered), textile workers, glass workers and various types of iron workers (because various furnaces and ovens have been discovered). There were also various types of brick layers and tilemakers. All this activity obviously was in towns.

One great difference between Harappan urbanism and the urbanism in the middle Ganga plains is that the former is characterised by monumental structures – and, as Gordon Childe rightly points out, these monuments are symbols of consumption of surplus – but where do we look for such symbols in our excavations in the middle Ganga plains? No such monument has been discovered and still we have towns. The structures seem to have been mainly mud structures in the beginning and came to be made of brick from 300 B.C. onwards. Bricks became more common from 200 B.C. onwards in north India, but even then mostly mud houses seem to have been used. In the towns there would have been cattle-sheds and doghouses too, but somehow these cattle-sheds and doghouses, thanks to our archaeologists, have not been discovered in any excavation, as far as I know, in the middle Ganga plains. It does require some archaeological skill or some special method to find out signs of such houses also.

At any rate, the main point is that early historic urbanism reached its peak in this country between 200 B.C. and about 300 A.D. Whether in north India, the Deccan, parts of south India, or in western India, we have the same phenomenon. Rajagriha, Vaishali, Chirand, Majhi, Khairadih, Banaras, Shravasti, Kaushambi and Atranjikhera are some of these towns. Not far from Dharwad is Vadgaon-Madhavapur, a Satavahana site which was excavated by the Karnataka University. There is also Kaveripattinam in Tamil Nadu. In fact, there are any number of sites in this period. I have taken note of 130 excavated sites belonging to the period between 200 B.C. and A.D. 300. These sites were prosperous in terms of artefacts, coins, structures and other types of antiquities, including semiprecious stones, ivory, ivory objects, glass articles, bones and so on.

This peak in urbanism could be associated with the growing trade and commerce in this period; and this growing trade and commerce is linked with the use of money, because money is a good and convenient medium of exchange. The numismatic evidence suggests that as many as thirty-five places issued their coins in this period. The name of the place is mentioned on the coin whether it is Kaushambi or Banaras or any other place. Each place was a mint town. In addition, many dynasties such as the Kushanas and the Satavahanas had their coins. There were fourteen tribes which are called oligarchical states and each tribe had its own coins. Recently, in a talk in Calcutta I calculated through some formula, which nobody will accept, that there were more than four million coins in circulation during this period. The number of coins actually available to us is very small. Ways and means have to be found to have an idea of the total number of coins current in a period. This has to be further related to the number of people in urban and rural settlements. I added up the coin numbers of ten museums and they came to about 1,25,000. There are as many as 50,000 Satavahana coins alone in the State Museum of Hyderabad which reflect on the overall picture of trade, commerce and crafts during this period. This is significant, for it is argued that large prosperous towns or prosperous trade can exist only if large states exist. There is some sense in that, because a state collects taxes and tributes, brings them to the towns and disburses salaries to its officials, army men etc. Thus, there is a lot of exchange activity and distribution at several levels.

On the basis of trade, coins, artefacts and structures, we can confidently say that urbanism reached its peak in ancient India in the post-Maurya period. After A.D. 300 it declined. There were two phases of decline, one around A.D. 300 and the other around A.D. 600. But before we briefly take up the question of decline, a few things about the wider relevance of this urbanism may be noted. What does this urbanism mean to society as a whole? What does it mean to the socio-economic set-up? There are all types of views. Some will argue that these towns were just parasitical entities as their inhabitants did not do any useful work; they were not engaged in production. Besides this old view, there is also the view of some eminent Bronze Age archaeologists that arts and crafts were not so important; rather they were peripheral to the existence of towns and towns did not pave the way for arts and crafts.

It would however appear that while there would have been a good many rulers, soldiers, priests and numerous state officials, who may be regarded as having been parasitical in some sense, a large number of others were engaged in production as a result of which towns could become centres of exchange, manufactures and technology. Thus the towns had their generative dimension. Moreover, they contributed to polity by facilitating large-scale payment in cash to the state employees who were paid from 48,000 *panas* to even ten *panas*. Unless taxes were collected and brought to the towns which were centres of tax collection, how would people receive that money in cash?

The *Arthashastra* of Kautilya, which incidentally was discovered in the state of Karnataka, mentions sources of income to the state, and divides them under two headings; one is from the countryside (*rashtra*) and the other from the fortified capital (*durga*). As many as twenty sources of income from the *durga* to the state are enumerated by Kautilya. The term *durga* may have included towns in general. Some of those who have worked on Roman history argue that so far as the income of the state from trade was concerned the state got only five per cent. We do not as yet have the means to calculate such income in ancient India. How much income was derived from the countryside? How much from the town? How much income did the state derive from trade and how much from agriculture?

Meanwhile, we cannot ignore the role of urbanism in ancient Indian economy. Important segments of people were involved in urban activity, even when a large section of population was left out of it. Urbanism did mean something in terms of economy and something of polity and society inasmuch as soldiers, Brahmans, artisans and merchants who lived in towns were supported by means of what was gathered by way of taxes and exchange. The towns were equally relevant to the countryside. It appears that foodgrains were supplied to the towns by the peasants living in the hinterland, while the artisans supplied the tools to the peasants. For example, we hear in a *Jataka* story how somebody deposited 500 ploughshares in a city. The obvious purpose would be to sell them to the peasants.

As to the pattern of settlements in earlier times, it appears that the town was surrounded by a cluster of villages. Because of the obvious difficulty of transportation in ancient times, towns could not receive their day-to-day requirements from distant places. There were intervening forests between one and the other clusters of villages. The Pali texts speak of forests in the vicinity of several towns. But all these are matters which have to be examined further by archaeologists. Settlement archaeology has not made sufficient progress. The spread of settlements and their relative populations need to be studied. The archaeologists have not done any work whatsoever, as far as I know, on the linkage between the hinterland and the towns. Towns did, however, play an important role; they were relevant to ancient economy and also to ancient polity. Since these towns declined after A.D. 300 and again after A.D. 600 we shall have to explain this phenomenon and also think of the people who lived in towns.

Why did the towns decline? One obvious factor was that the Indo-Roman trade stopped from the third century A.D. onwards. The Satavahana empire, which brought a lot of gold from outside, also ended; the central Asian trade also tapered off. I may venture a speculation here. There was a kind of social crisis, but not like the *jagirdari* crisis. It is reflected in the passages of the *Vishnu Purana, Bhagvata Purana* and some other Puranas which are attributed by a great Puranic scholar, Rajendra Chandra of Hazara from Calcutta, to the end of the third century A.D. and the beginning of the fourth. These Puranas vividly describe what is known as the Kali Age (*Kaliyuga*), which unfortunately seems to be unending in this country.

In ancient India, as elsewhere, social progress was accompanied by social inequality. Certain functions were assigned to certain people. Some people were meant for praying, some for writing books, some for teaching, some for doing theological work, for fighting, for administering, for collecting taxes and for maintaining law and order. Others were the principal taxpayers. P.V. Kane, the great Indologist, is of the view — which is also my view – that the Vaishyas were the principal taxpayers. They were primarily agriculturists; it was only in later times that they became primarily traders. Agriculture remained their principal occupation in ancient times when the Sudras supplied the labour power. A careful reading of the Kali passages gives the impression that the whole social order was upset – the Brahmans behaved like Sudras and the Sudras like Brahmans. There was an intermixing of functions. Whenever the Puranas use the term *varna-sankara* (on which Vivekanand Jha has done a detailed piece), it means not merely transcending caste restrictions in marriage, it also means giving up one's prescribed functions. Manu asserts that if members of various *varnas* do not perform their assigned functions the whole world will fall into chaos. That would be calamitous, to forestall which the king must exercise *danda* or coercive authority.

Also symptomatic of the social crisis were the land grants which began to be made at this time. These had been known earlier too, but now they were being made on a substantial scale. The Puranas of course do not state that *Kaliyuga* or social disorder should be put down by making land grants, but the point is that if it became difficult to collect taxes, to bring these to towns and then to disburse salaries to officials and soldiers and to give gifts to the Brahmans in terms of money or cattle, the state felt obliged to have recourse to land grants which became common from the third-fourth century A.D. onwards. In the new situation the understanding seems to have been that the state gave a village to a select person; that person fended for himself, collected taxes, maintained law and order in the village and took care of it. The state would not use its regular officers for these functions. In every state there would be a core domain (with occasional land grants) where the state officials could function and a large peripheral area in which land grants were made extensively. With the practice of land grants becoming common, there also began the practice of granting shops; even whole towns were granted, as recorded in inscriptions and also by Hiuen Tsang. The grant of shops, towns and villages meant restrictions on trade and commerce, on the free operation of traders, thus restraining the autonomy earlier enjoyed by them. It was a process of feudalization of towns.

Between the fifth and seventh century A.D. and may be even later, there were nearly fifty states in India. Rather than being political fragmentation, it was a positive development, because the state system arose in those areas which did not witness the formation of the state in earlier times. Every state had its own army, administrative machinery, judicial officers, and exercised its sovereign authority through a regular state apparatus. How could this apparatus in the core domain be maintained unless there were more villages and more productivity to provide the necessary surplus for its wherewithal?

So it appears that if towns declined, their technology was diffused. Artisans migrated from the urban to rural areas. There is no archaeological evidence to substantiate this, perhaps because the archaeology of rural sites in early medieval times has not been initiated so far. When the towns declined, the Brahmans too migrated to the countryside and thus contributed towards the spread of technology. Ramendra Nath Nandi, from Patna College, prepared a list of the original homes of the Brahmans who were granted land in the first phase of early medieval times; most of these original homes were towns. Sneh Lata Anand, from Khalsa College, Delhi, also prepared a list of such Brahmans in Gujarat who migrated from towns during the same period to enjoy land grants. This kind of examination, which takes note of the original home of the Brahmans in the grants between the fifth and eighth centuries A. D., has to be pursued further. It may be argued that the original homes given in grants were just old memory, genealogical memory. But even if this memory is a century old or still older, it would mean that their ancestors lived in towns. Diffusion of agricultural knowledge through the Brahmans who were knowledgeable about the calendar helped agrarian expansion. At the same time, it seems that technology was now thinly spread just as coins also were thinly spread. I counted dynastic coins of the period A.D. 500-1000 on the basis of ten collections in various museums, and the number was less than 25,000. On the other hand, as already mentioned, the Satavahana coins alone number more than 1,00,000. It is not only difficult in this period to find coins issued by towns but also to come by coin moulds in excavation. Similarly, evidence on guilds in this period is scarce. Seals and sealings of artisanal and mercantile guilds, so common in ancient times, almost disappear in the early medieval period. The seals and sealings available are mainly of Buddhist monasteries, and that too primarily in eastern India.

Thus, a different type of socio-economic pattern existed in early medieval India in which a class of landlords collected rent from the peasants as a result of grants and other reasons. Probably most administrative officers also were being remunerated through land assignments. While the towns existed goods and services were evaluated and obtained in terms of money; but when the towns disappeared, goods and services may have been evaluated in terms of money but they were obtained through land grants. It is most likely that the elements of the *jajmani* system, which may have existed in earlier times as indicated in Panini, were greatly strengthened when the towns declined in early medieval times. The *jajmani* system means that if I am a peasant or if I am a landlord and if I require the services of priests or various types of artisans, including a barber or a potter, I do not pay him in money but I pay him twice in a year at the time of the harvest and he is attached to me. This arrangement is now called patron-client relationship. Besides the strengthening of the *jajmani* system one could also find a few elements of what is called Asiatic mode of production in this period. The early medieval period did not exactly have a self-sufficient economy, but most local needs were locally met. This could be due to what we call an ideal blending of agricultural and artisanal activities. This situation may have lasted roughly up to about A.D. 1000 when there was a mild revival of urbanism which became prominent by the fourteenth century. But this problem needs to be discussed separately.

SOCIAL STRUCTURE AND ECONOMY OF SETTLEMENTS IN THE CENTRAL DECCAN (200 B.C.-A.D. 200)

ALOKA PARASHER

In writing about the history of urban centres one is confronted by a sea of definitions and plagued by a myriad generalisations about the role of the town in society. In certain quarters a city is understood as a socio-economic structure distinct from its rural surroundings and as presupposing an agrarian base of surplus production which in turn was revolutionised from an earlier simple state because of the use of a metal technology. Further, it is postulated that the change from self-sufficing food production to an economy based also on specialised manufacture and external trade would constitute the essential prerequisites for urban growth.[1] Other features that emerge as the outward manifestations of city life are listed as an increase in population, emergence of political and social system, the evidence of writing, monumental art, an increase in the knowledge of exact and predictive sciences and so on.[2] Childe propounded these views largely on the basis of the empirical context of West Asia and highlighted dramatically the technological variable. Though earlier he had equated the processes of becoming civilised with the process of becoming urbanised, he subsequently realised that it need not be so.[3] In the West Asian context itself, however, new empirical research has made James Mellaart raise the fundamental question whether we can

[1]Gordon Childe, *Man Makes Himself*, Mentor Books (2nd ed), 1955, 114-42.

[2]Gordon Childe, *What Happened in History*, Penguin, Harmondsworth, 1978 (rep), 97-120.

[3]Gordon Childe, 'The Urban Revolution', *Town Planning Review*, Vol. 21, 1950, 3-17.

determine urbanism only after the dispersal of a metal technology in defining Catal Huyuk as a Neolithic town.[4]

In certain other quarters it is felt that cities ultimately emerge as complex, socially stratified units and therefore, details of not only economic structures but also of the political and social systems that control and maneuovre these, need to be emphasised.[5] The clear articulation of 'a functionally interrelated set of social institutions' would mean that much of the socio-cultural development in the city would proceed largely on its own terms.[6] The other papers in the 'Symposium Collection' entitled *City Invincible* too prefer to identify the institutions through which the economy is organised and thereby link social relations to the process that brought the city into being.[7] Gideon Sjoberg in his now classic descriptions of the 'pre-industrial city' also emphasises social and especially political power, as variables on which the city was dependent.[8] The emphasis in his earlier writings on technology as an independent variable cannot however be missed.[9] He ultimately opines that cities have in them 'contradictory structures' and these in fact 'appear to be intrinsic to the system'.[10] Obviously, the 'requirements' he has in mind are of those engaged in the function of usurping power. It could perhaps be suggested that the above views converge on the characterisation that 'both internally and externally the town is an institutional expression of power'.[11]

A study of 'urban centres' located in the central Deccan would indeed emphasise the interacting elements of the techno-economic variations which determined the nature of their growth but, it is further to be emphasised that this must necessarily be viewed in the perspective of the antecedent cultures available at these places. These cultures persist as 'non-urban' forms into the early historical phase which is when urbanisation is supposed to have reached its high water-mark in the Deccan as a

[4]James Mellaart, *The Earliest Civilisations of the Near East*, Norwich 1978 (rep), 77-78.

[5]Robert McAdams, *Evolution of Urban Society: Early Mesopotamia and Pre-Hispanic Mexico*, Rochester 1965, 9-17.

[6]Robert McAdams (ed), *City Invincible*, Background papers, Chicago 1960, 270 and 291-92.

[7]Ibid.

[8]G. Sjoberg, 'The Rise and Fall of Cities', *International Journal of Comparative Sociology*, IV, 1963, 107.

[9]G. Sjoberg, *The Pre-Industrial City*, Past and Present, Glencoe, Illinois 1957, 15-17.

[10]Ibid., 13 and 140.

[11]P. Abrams, 'Towns and Economic Growth', *Towns in Societies*, Essays in Economic History and Historical Sociology (eds Philip Abrams and E. A. Wrigley), Cambridge 1978, 25.

whole. We would refrain from fitting these towns and settlements into constructed typologies of towns as has been done by scholars for studies on urbanisation in ancient India.[12] Typologies often become sterile applications of constructs known in some region and imposed on others.

Rather, we would like to analyse the *involvement of particular towns in particular processes of economic growth;* subsequently, they may or may not conform to given typologies. It has been interestingly pointed out, and this seems pertinent to our emphasis as well, that though Braudel's typology of towns breaks down, it is still useful because it is based on 'variations in the relations of social power with and between urban and non-urban social groups'.[13] It is these variations that come to prominent light in the specificity of the central Deccan(map I).

I

Though several sites in different parts of the Deccan have been excavated, no integrated picture of the stages in the evolution of the second urbanisation in these parts, or the character of individual settlements located here, has been brought forth. The so-called second urbanisation had its epicentre in the Ganges valley during the sixth century B.C.[14] It has further been stated by Champakalakshmi that the early centuries A.D. 'witnessed the most clearly visible manifestations of this urbanism'.[15] To suggest, however, that urbanisation in the Deccan should be studied in qualitative or quantitative comparison with the former, just because it was chronologically a later development, would be simplistic, and would above all, generate unsatisfactory explanations.[16] Here, a regional perspective gains importance. Though many general writings on urbanisation recognise the urban character of the settlements in the Deccan, it is accepted, implicitly if not explicitly, that these were the result of some influence of or contact with towns well-

[12]For example, V.K. Thakur, *Urbanisation in Ancient India*, New Delhi 1981, 20-21.

[13]P. Abrams, 'Town and Economic Growth', 24.

[14]D.K. Chakrabarti, 'Concept of Urban Revolution and the Indian Context', *Purattatva*, No. 6, 1972-73, 29-31; 'Some Theoretical Aspects of Early Indian Urban Growth', *Purattatva*, No. 7, 1974, 89; R. Champakalakshmi, 'Urbanisation in South India: The Role of Ideology and Polity', *IHC* (reprint), 47th Session, Srinagar 1986, 2-3.

[15]R. Champakalakshmi, 'Urbanisation in South India', 2-3.

[16]N.R. Banerjee, *The Iron Age in India*, Delhi 1965, 214; A. Ghosh, *The City in Early Historical India*, Indian Institute of Advanced Study, Shimla 1973, 12-13; D.K. Chakrabarti, 'Early Indian Urban Growth', 89.

All these works tend to compare qualitatively and quantitatively the process of urbanisation in the Deccan and south India with that of north India.

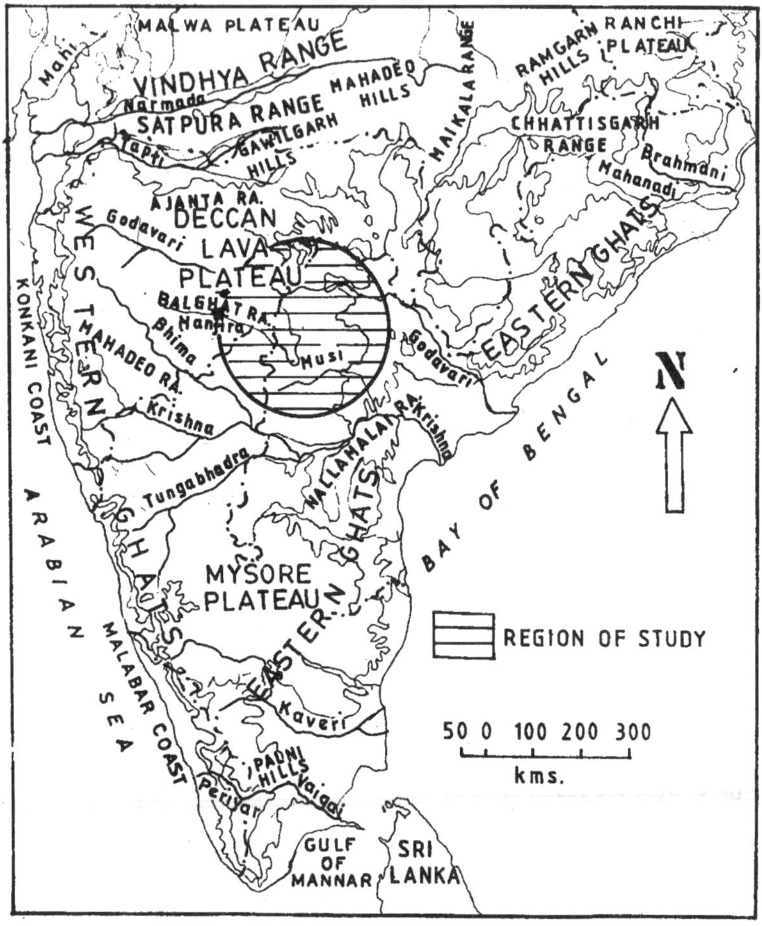

Map I Region of Study

established in north and central India. We would, on the contrary, wish to highlight the hitherto neglected aspect of the relatively autonomous and different process of urban growth in many parts of the Deccan.[17]

It is well established that the transition from Neolithic to Chalcolithic, and in many cases its overlaps, occurred independently in the Deccan and evolved gradually under a different local environment.[18] It is equally recognised, based on empirical case studies, that there was a significant coexistence of the nomadic food-procuring subsistence patterns with the sedentary food-procuring patterns over substantial parts of the Deccan.[19] It is true that the uniformity of the Megalithic or iron using cultures in the whole of south India is striking.[20] They are, however, imposed in many cases on different levels of development of the preceding phase of settlement. This aspect of individual variation becomes extremely important when we clarify the relationship or link between the proto-historic and early historic phases at the excavated sites under purview.

The question of urbanisation is intrinsically related to this transition. C^{14} dates for iron for south India are known here almost as early as for north India. At Hallur in Karnataka, however, where the earliest dates of 955 + 100 B.C. and 1105 + 105 B.C., are suggested, the occupation at the historical levels is very poor.[21] In the Vidarbha region of Maharashtra the antiquity of the Megalithic phases where iron is first known, is pushed back to 672 + 115 B.C. and 655 + 100 B.C. according to the C^{14} dates suggested by Deo for the site of Naikund.[22] More than Hallur, the Vidarbha sites of Takalghat, Khapa and Naikund, all situated near Nagpur, are important for us. First, because these dates come from habitation areas and secondly, as indicated by Krishnasastry, the burial

[17]Ruth Tringham has very adroitly questioned the theoretical basis of the diffusionist model for a study of urban centres in temperate Europe and their unfair comparison with the Mediterranean ones: 'The Concept of "Civilisation" in European Archaeology', *The Rise and Fall of Civilisation* (eds J.S. Sabloff and C.C. Lamberg-Karlovsky), California 1980, 470-84.

[18]M.K. Dhavalikar, 'Development and Decline of the Deccan Chalcolithic', *Radio Carbon and Indian Archaeology* (eds D.P. Agarwal and A. Ghosh), Bombay 1973, 138-47.

[19]M.L.K. Murthy, 'Ekistic and Subsistence Patterns in Prehistoric Archaeology of Andhra Pradesh', *The Andhra Pradesh Journal of Archaeology*, I, No. 1, 1979, 13-19.

[20]N.R. Banerjee, *Iron Age in India*, 55; Clarence Maloney, 'Archaeology in South India: Accomplishments and Prospects', *Essays on South India* (ed Burton Stein), New Delhi 1976, 1-40.

[21]M.S. Nagaraja, *The Proto-Historic Culture of the Tungabhadra Valley*, Delhi 1971, 15.

[22]S.B. Deo, 'Megalithic Problems of the Deccan', *South Asian Archaeology* (ed B. Allchin), Cambridge 1984, 222.

furniture at Megalithic phases in the mid-Godavari valley is similar to the one found in the Vidarbha region.[23] At many sites in the Deccan the early historical sites gain considerable importance due to the Mauryan presence but this is archaeologically difficult to substantiate. It is therefore not unusual to find an overlap between Megalith layers of habitation with 'Andhra' or 'Satavahana' habitational evidence.[24] Further, considerable evidence for contact with Roman trade can be mustered and this external trade as an important variable for the stimulation and growth of the Deccan urban centres cannot be denied.[25] Nevertheless, the question of stimulus from both the Mauryan intrusion and Roman contact at the micro level needs re-examination. Ultimately, the fundamental question remains; that is, of the impact of the use and distribution of iron technology over the well-established Neolithic-Chalcolithic agrarian communities. In the central Deccan the Chalcolithic phases are bleak but the use and production of iron artefacts is quite prominent beginning with the Megalithic phase.[26] Thus, some of these marked variations need to be highlighted and analysed more closely.

On a general scale it has been observed that Andhra Pradesh is the 'richest area so far as early historical sites are concerned' which are said to range from the third century B.C. to early medieval times and further, that many of these are invariably noteworthy because of Buddhist affiliation like *stupa* complexes and *viharas*.[27] Whereas for sites such as Nagarjunakonda, Yelleshwaram, Amaravati/Dharanikota, to a certain extent, the data have been organised, discussed and analysed to highlight the individual character of these settlements,[28] for others such as Dhulikatta, Chandavaram, Kotalingala Satanikota, Keesaragutta and Peddabankur, which have yielded enormous data, now piled up, coordina-

[23]V.V. Krishnasastry, *The Proto and Early Historical Cultures of Andhra Pradesh*, Hyderabad 1983, 115.

[24]Vimla Begley, 'From Iron Age to Early Historical in South Indian Archaeology', *Studies in the Archaeology of India and Pakistan* (ed J. Jacobson), AIIS, Oxford and IBH, Delhi 1981, 299-301.

[25]Discussed for the western Deccan by H.P. Ray, *Monastery and Guild: Commerce under the Satavahanas*, Oxford University Press, Delhi 1986, 112ff. and for South India in general, by R. Champakalakshmi, 'Urbanisation in South India', 2-6.

[26]The Neolithic phase is directly followed by the Megalithic phase at most of the central Deccan sites described in detail for the first time by Krishnasastry in his *Proto and Early Historical Cultures* cited above.

[27]S.B. Deo, 'Historical Archaeology: Review and Perspective', *Archaeological Perspective in India since Independence* (ed K.N. Dikshit), Delhi 1985.

[28]H.Sarkar, 'Growth of Cities in Andhradesa', Presidential Address, *Proceedings of the Andhra Pradesh History Congress* Session, Guntur 1986, 1-11.

tion is still awaited. This may partly be explained by the fact that many of these sites underwent extensive excavations only in the seventies. Of these, Dhulikatta, Kotalingala and Peddabankur will be taken up for closer scrutiny in the discussion that follows. To these may also be added the discussion on Kondapur which, though not located in the immediate vicinity of the above three, has interesting similar economic variables that enable us to understand the nature of its growth. Literary references to settlements and towns are available to us from Indian and classical writings. Inscriptions too generally help us in identifying and labelling the relative importance of urban centres. For the sites under consideration, however, no direct written accounts are available. The maximum number of inscriptions datable to the early centuries A.D. are found in the western Deccan, an area to which the mid-Godavari valley is contiguous and therefore, these do throw some light on the broader issues of inter-regional trade, its organisation and so on. The same could be said of information gleaned from the fragmentary label inscriptions found at Amravati, Bhattiprolu, Nagarjunakonda, etc.

Given these circumstances of almost non-existence of direct written source material for the central Deccan, it is but obvious that we have to give primacy to the revelations from the archaeological sources in this context. But, needless to add, one begins with a handicap in that one has to depend on the archaeological data collected by others in their own way. Methods of excavation so far adopted have tapped the sites only vertically and not horizontally, and as a result no complete plan of any ancient site has yet been exposed. Reports of excavation still being under preparation, and would be for some time to come, what is available to us at the moment is a maze of unrelated evidence emphasising the individuality of each site only. Scientific methods of dating like C^{14} have only been intermittently applied and the stratigraphy of almost all the sites under consideration is not clearly known. These being some of the limitations of our data it is intended to classify at the outset our methodological parameters of analysis in the hope that this may help overcome a segmented presentation of data and further, enable us to present a meaningful account of the possible social structure and economy of settlements/sites in the central Deccan.

II

For some time now new archaeologists have been trying to understand the prehistoric and early historic situations with particular reference to the demographic environment through a concept called 'settlement pattern'.[29] Its use became popular after the sixties and the concept has undergone considerable refinement ever since. It is often misunderstood, or rather, has been conventional to argue that this simply implies a geographical distribution of archaeological sites. In fact, in Willey's articulation of its essence, it is the study of archaeological data in terms of the effect of 'the natural environment, the level of technology on which the builders operated, and various institutions of social interaction and control which the cultures maintained'.[30] To put it simply, as is done by Trigger, it is the 'study of social relationships using archaeological data'.[31] A 'settlement' in this sense is neither a substitute for the archaeological term 'site' meaning 'locality' nor is it synonymous with the sociological term 'community'. The latter is particularly difficult to substantiate because data are rarely able to identify tangibly if a single community inhabited a permanent settlement or not. One cannot obviously go into the details of the debate among new archaeologists on the use of many of these terms.[32] It may therefore suffice to say that in any study of urban centres it is most probable that 'there may be several communities in one settlement'.[33]

We begin thus with the presumption that the tangible remains of one or several communities can be found in an archaeological settlement. What needs to be emphasised, however, is that factors such as the ecological, the economic, the technological, the socio-cultural that cause variations in settlements are to a great extent interdependent and interrelated. The three settlements of Kotalingala, Dhulikatta and Peddabankur are located in very close proximity of each other. As we shall see below, each of these has important pre-urban stages, the first two being fortified settlements of the early historical period, situated amidst several unfortified ones. Therefore, it is Trigger's analysis of settlement patterns which stresses the aspect of the interrelatedness in the composition and activities of the settlements that has been taken into account by us. He has suggested three levels of analysis: (a) the individual building or structure, (b) the settlement layout which is equated with community layout, and (c) settlement distribution on a zonal scale and thereby spatial relation-

[29]G. Willey systematically uses this concept for the first time: *Settlement Patterns in the Viru Valley*, 1980, 155.

[30]Ibid., 1.

[31]Bruce Trigger, 'The Determinants of Settlement Patterns', *Time and Tradition*, Essays in Archaeological Interpretation (ed Bruce Trigger), Edinburgh 1978, 153.

[32]Ruth Tringham (ed), *Man, Settlement and Urbanism*, Duckworth, 1972,xx-xxii.

[33]Ibid., xxi.

ship between different communities.[34] Of these three, the third level of analysis, which could be either within one ecological zone (in this case the central Deccan) or a larger geographical region (in this case Deccan as a whole), is the easiest to substantiate. The distribution of settlements is largely determined by the availability of natural resources like good soil and water, but such factors as subsistence technology, warfare, religion, trade, political organisation also play a role in determining the location of a particular settlement.[35]

The Deccan as a whole comprises several ecological zones. The nuclear area of attraction for agrarian expansion here was the Krishna-Godavari delta. During the same period one finds, however, a proliferation of urban/trade centres in all the ecological zones. This is particularly on account of the twin forces of the participation of the whole region in some form of external trade and the spread of Buddhism.[36] But the nature of the settlements varied tremendously from zone to zone. For identifying this variance one needs to turn to the second and first levels of Trigger's analysis. By his second level of analysis is meant the arrangement of buildings at a particular site which may reflect social stratification and the nature of economic activities, the particular subsistence technology which would account for the stability and size of the community and such other analytical components. Finally, in defining the first level of analysis Trigger points to the determinants which reflect on the individual structure or building, namely, materials used for construction, the technological skills employed and so on.[37] A total and free application of Trigger's first two levels of analysis is hindered mainly because there has been no uniform method of excavation adopted at the sites under study and in the Indian context in general, scientific methods of excavation are rare. Despite this we maintain the differential criteria in the three levels of Trigger's settlement pattern of analysis as an essential backdrop because of his emphasis on the interrelatedness of settlements, this being the key element in the settlement pattern of sites in the central Deccan both at the zonal as well as local levels.

III

The settlements under consideration lie in the eco-zone which is defined roughly between longitude 77°-80° east and latitude 19°-17°

[34]Bruce Trigger, 'Determinants of Settlement Patterns', 170-88.

[35]Ibid., 184-88.

[36]For a relationship of these two factors, H.P. Ray, *Monastery and Guild*, cited above.

[37]Bruce Trigger, 'Determinants of Settlement Patterns', 176-80.

north,[38] identifiable in the Telengana part of the state of Andhra Pradesh (map II). In ancient literary texts this region has been described as Asmaka or Assaka, located on the river Godavari, with its own marked geo-cultural identity. This was supposed to be contiguous to the regions of Mulaka, identified as the present-day districts of Nasik-Poona, Aurangabad, Osmanabad and Ahmednagar, and Asika, that is, the region between the rivers Godavari and Krishna.[39] Kotalingala and Peddabankur are both in the Peddapalli taluk of Karimnagar district; Dhulikatta is about ten kilometres from Peddabankur, but Kondapur, in Medak district, is about seventy kilometres from Hyderabad. Excavators have clearly pointed out that historical sites with Satavahana remains have been found in almost every alternate village in the taluks of Warangal and Karimnagar.[40] Even more significantly, the region is rich in the antecedent Neolithic and Megalithic cultures. Polakonda in Warangal district and Kadambapur in Karimnagar district, located very near the first three sites, have impressive Neolithic and Megalithic evidence. Pochampad on the river Godavari, on the border of the Nizamabad and Adilabad districts, lies to the west of these sites and is a substantial Megalithic site. The most striking feature is that Peddabankur, besides having Megalithic burials, gives indications of being a Neolithic site of considerable dimension.[41]

We begin the descriptions of the material remains from the settlements at Kotalingala, Dhulikatta, Peddabankur and Kondapur with a detailed look at the structures excavated here. This not only enables us to define the areas of activity prominent at each of these places, but also helps us delineate the physical structure of the mound/mounds thus excavated. The structural remains at each of these sites are far from uniform. They could, however, be divided into three broad categories: (a) those of a political nature in the form of remnants of fortification walls, ramparts, moats and palace-like buildings, (b) structures of clearly religious character like *stupa* and *vihara* complexes, and (c) heterogeneous structures such as dwellings, shops, storage areas, industrial working area, irrigation-related structures, burial areas and so on. In the context of the whole of north-western, western and central India and the Deccan, Margabandhu has adopted a broad chronological scheme for 'the settle-

[38] R.L. Singh, *Regional Geography of India*, Varanasi 1971, 82 1ff.

[39] H.C. Raychaudhuri, 'The Geography of the Deccan', *The Early History of the Deccan* (ed G. Yazdani), I-VI, New Delhi (rep) 1982, 3ff.

[40] V.V. Krishnasastry, 'Recent Archaeological Discoveries of the Satavahana Period in Andhra Pradesh', *Satavahana Seminar Souvenir* (ed P. Sitapati), Hyderabad 1981,1.

[41] V.V. Krishnasastry, *Proto and Early Historical Cultures*, 22, 24 and 35.

Map II Details of Early Historical Sites in Central Deccan

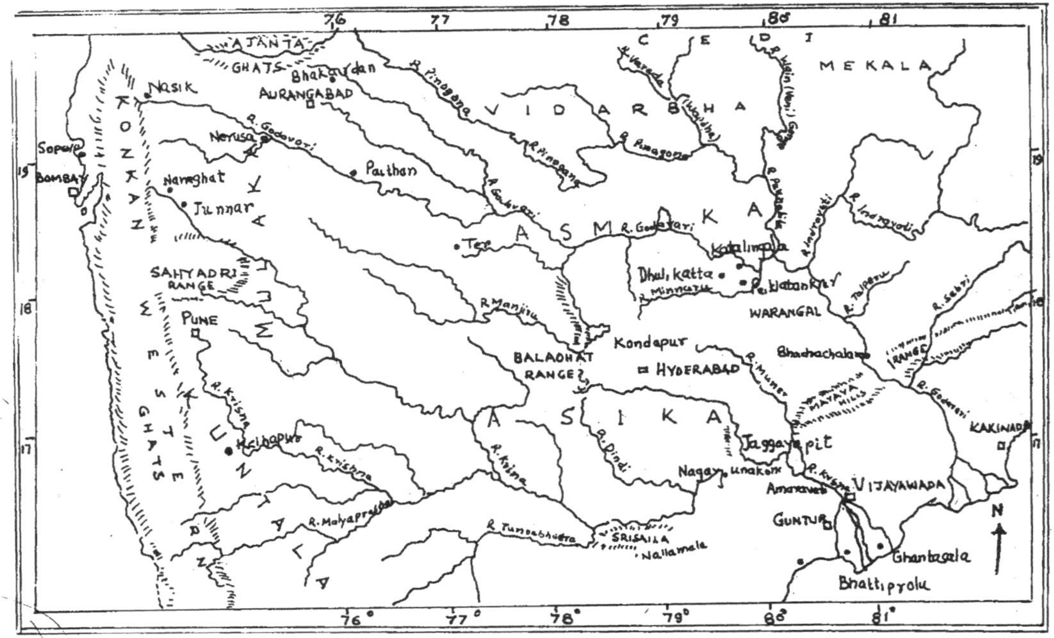

ment patterns of Early Historical times'.[42] These are period I *c.* 600-300 B.C., period II *c.*300 B.C.-A.D.200, and period III*c.* A.D. 200-400 and after. This scheme is based on the stratigraphy of the datable finds like coins and pottery and therefore, is in no way absolute. The settlements under consideration fall into period II when generally the architectural features of well-developed townships emerge in the use of standard burnt bricks and tiles, construction of roads, use of limestone plastering and so on.

At Kotalingala, situated on the confluence of the Paddavagu and Godavari rivers, was excavated the largest mound of about fifty hectares in extent, six to nine metres above the plains, and encompassed by a mudfort. The mudfort was enclosed by the river Godavari on the north and by the Kapparaopetvagu *nullah* on the east which takes a turn to the south, and thus fortifies the town at this end also. It is postulated that at all the corners of the fortification there were bastions which now appear as mounds. There is evidence of several gates opening towards the cardinal points; the main gate to the fort is noticed towards the south connecting a highway. Towards the riverside on the north and west the fort wall runs to a distance of more than three hundred metres and the bricks used were fifty to fifty-five centimetres long. The brick structure adjacent to the water course, it is said, indicates the presence of a wharf.[43] Cultural data were found on the mound in several habitational floors going to a depth of between two and two and a half metres. Four such floor levels were dug, divided into two phases. Phase I, representing floors three and four, was clearly pre-Satavahana as the fourth floor showed only the use of mud-mortared walls and rubble and no brick. Layer three does indicate the use of terracotta tiles for roofing but it is only from Phase II, that is, floor levels one and two, that brick comes into vogue and this is identified as representing Satavahana times. No radiocarbon dates are available for this site, but a very significant discovery of pre-Satavahana and early Satavahana coins was made here, some of them in a stratigraphic context, which we shall discuss below.[44]

Though Kotalingala is the largest mound so far discovered, it is at Dhulikatta that the details of a fortified town emerge more clearly.

[42]C. Margabandhu, *Archaeology of the Satavahana Kshatrapa Times*, New Delhi 1985, 18.

[43]V.V. Krishnasastry, *Proto and Early Historical Cultures*, 125 and 132.

[44]Thakur Raja Ram Singh, 'The Pre-Satavahana Andhra Kings of Central Godavari Valley. The Andhra Kings of Asmaka, Mulaka', Presented at the UGC Seminar on *Recent Archaeological Studies in Andhra Pradesh*, Kakatiya University, Warangal, March 1987 (cyclostyled), 6-8.

Dhulikatta is situated amidst fertile black soil on the right bank of the Hussainivagu. The historical mound was about eighteen hectares in extent, about six metres above the plains and enclosed by mud ramparts with a present height of three to five metres. This rampart was constructed with earth dug from trenches outside the fort and this area must have served as a moat.[45] The rampart consisted of hard yellowish morrum overlayered with black soil. Traces of a rubble foundation are found which must have been the base of a brick fort wall of which no evidence remains. Four gateways have, however, been traced at the cardinal points. At the southern gateway, it is suggested that the plans of what were possibly guardrooms appear, but these are difficult to describe as only the foundations have survived. These comprised two rectangular halls, the flooring of which was paved with bricks measuring 56 × 27 × 7 centimetres. In front of these was a gatehouse. According to Krishnasastry, this evidence of the fortification structures followed the specifications given in literary texts.[46] The mud fortifications are traced to pre-Satavahana times, while the brick-built gateway and the rows of guardrooms and pathways of *c*. 100 B.C-200 A.D. are datable as the Satavahna period. [47] The dating is done on the basis of the coins found here. Radiocarbon dates for Dhulikatta are however available as '(a) 2210 ± 100 years Before Present, (b) 1965 ± 90 years B.P.',[48] and these are used to date constructional activity at the fortified mound to as early as 320 B.C. or so.[49]

At the centre of the fortified mound at Dhulikatta was exposed a palace complex, residential quarters and granaries which are in inverted pyramidal form. As at Kotalingala, here too several phases of construction are available as occupational levels. In the first two phases a huge enclosure of 26 × 30.50 metres is identified with a single coarse rubble foundation. The buildings here are not clear because of successive phases of occupation. In the second phase a little evidence of lime concrete flooring is available. In the third phase however one finds 'spacious halls with floors paved with brick, granaries, wells, and multistoreyed buildings provided with sewage, signifying a period of prosperity'. [50] The main structure in this phase is what has been called a *chatussala* with four rectangular halls on four sides and a central courtyard. At the south-west

[45] *Indian Archaeology—A Review*, 1974-75, 3; 1975-76, 2-3; 1976-77, 4-5.
[46] V.V. Krishnasastry, *Proto and Early Historical Cultures*, 124-25 and 130-33.
[47] C. Margabandhu, *Archaeology of Satavahana Times*, 34.
[48] V.V. Krishnasastry, *Proto and Early Historical Cultures*, 232-33.
[49] Raja Ram Singh, 'Pre-Satavahana Andhra Kings', 7.
[50] V.V. Krishnasastry, *Proto and Early Historical Cultures*, 136-37.

corner inside the enclosure wall was found a brick well almost square in plan. To its north two granaries, partitioned into compartments, were located. During the fourth phase of construction all the buildings were plastered with lime and burnished to a smooth surface and lime concrete was used for paving the floors. Construction of granaries is said to have continued in this phase and along with it a soakage pit, with a partition in the middle, was noticed at the north-east corner. There is also a fifth phase which was probably raised on the ruins of the earlier. Finally, during the last and sixth phase the complexion of the habitation is supposed to have completely changed. Brick ceases to be used and small hutment-like structures appear on the ruins of the palace, probably, as Krishnasastry concludes, the habitat of artisans.[51] Thus, much of the main constructional activity during the climactic period at Dhulikatta was done with bricks of 55 × 27 centimetres or 50 × 25 centimetres, though wood and tiles may also have been used for pillars and roofing. The most outstanding structural monument discovered near the historical mound of Dhulikatta is a Buddhist *stupa* details of which we shall describe below.

Peddabankur is just ten kilometres east of Dhulikatta but can be contrasted with it in that it has no signs of fortifications. This historical site has an extent of about 30 hectares which is bounded in the south and west by a *nullah* called the Hussainivagu. The site lies amidst alluvial black soil and the surrounding hills were supposed to be good suppliers of secondary minerals such as carnelian, jasper, crystal and quartz. Krishnasastry has characterised this site as a 'village' and discussed it under the sub-heading 'Folk Architecture'.[52] What has been excavated here in terms of the many residential buildings constructed of brick and mud over rubble foundations, cisterns, wells, soakage pits, drainage systems and so on, in quantum and in variety, far exceeds what we have for the fortified townships of Kotalingala and Dhulikatta. There have been many seasons of excavation conducted at Peddabankur as evident from the early reports.[53] Following these reports Margabandhu has noted that there were two phases of structural development at this site: the early period dated to *c.* 250-100 B.C. and that which continues into the Satavahana period *c.* 50 B.C.-A.D. 200.[54] The three main enclosures

[51]Ibid., 136-38.

[52]Ibid., 138-39.

[53]*Indian Archaeology*, 1967-68, 2; 1968-69, 1-2; 1970-71, 2; 1971-72, 2-3; 1972-73, 2; and 1974-75,5.

[54]C. Margabandhu, *Archaeology of Satavahana Times*, 25.

identified and described by Krishnasastry as I, II (called a mint) and III were constructed of well-burnt bricks, squarish in plan without any adjuncts, and with walls of a breadth of nearly two metres. Enclosure I (measuring 16.80 × 15.80 metres) had a small entrance in the middle of its southern wall and outside; on its south-western corner, a brick well with terracotta rings connected to a soakage pit was located. Enclosure II (measuring 30 × 40 metres) has been identified by Krishnasastry as a mint because several thousand Satavahana coins came from here.[55] This had an entrance on the northeastern corner. Enclosure III (measuring 30.89 × 30.80 metres) was situated to the south of the first one. The bricks here were not so well burnt as they had broken to bits. The first enclosure, being the smallest, had a well outside, but the other two had two or three brick wells inside them. In Enclosure III two elliptical houses of mud walls were also found, one earlier and the other later to the date of the enclosure itself. Outside these enclosures and contemporary with them, are houses of mostly mud walls which had probably been covered with thatch or tiles. It is suggested that these may have been the habitation dwellings of common people. The purpose of the enclosures is not very clear though it is suggested that single families or groups of families may have lived here. [56]

There is no doubt that Peddabankur was a substantial and well-inhabited site. Being situated away from the river course, water must have been an absolute necessity for the people and we find that during the course of excavation nearly twenty-two wells of varying sizes and shapes were exposed. A brick drain has also been brought to light of about twelve centimetres, its floor also being paved with bricks. By far the most significant structures excavated at Peddabankur are the cisterns. These too were constructed with well-burnt bricks and some had brick-laid floors to avoid percolation. One cistern was found in the middle of Enclosure III and measured 80 × 75 centimetres. Adjoining it was a sort of unpaved washing floor bordered with bricks. In the south-west direction of Enclosure II three brick cisterns at varying distances were noticed. Of the several such cisterns found, one was discovered with fragments of iron slag which has been identified as a blacksmith's workshop.[57]

[55]In his earlier article Krishnasastry refers to Enclosure I as having been a mint: 'Archaeological Discoveries in Andhra Pradesh', *A Decade of Archaeological Studies in South India* (ed B.K. Gururaja Rao), Dharwar 1978, 60.

[56]V.V. Krishnasastry, *Proto and Early Historical Cultures*, 139-40.

[57]C. Margabandhu, *Archaeology of Satavahana Times*, 25.

Such structures as cisterns have been characterised as 'industrial buildings' and have also been discovered at Kondapur in the form of '(i) furnaces (ii) floors and pavements for workmen and (iii) depositories for storing their valuable objects'.[58] In this context Yazadani, who was the excavator of this site, emphasises the implications of these structures when he states: 'In the course of excavation remains of furnaces and of large earthen water-basins for cooling metal have been found in large numbers and it appears that smithy work flourished on an extensive scale'.[59] Kondapur is situated on a streamlet which in ancient times must have been a tributary of the Manjira, amidst largely red soil.[60] Like Peddabankur, here too, no striking fortification walls have been found. On the other hand, considerable evidence of plain houses built of either brick or rubble has been excavated. The plan of these houses is not clearly discernible but in all probability these were the residences of the inhabitants of Kondapur. Here, there are some indications to show that they housed people from different social strata. Generally, the size of the rooms unearthed was small to moderate measuring 10 × 12 feet or 10 × 8 feet. Some floors were laid with brick concrete to be made waterproof, while others were not. In the former case the roofs were probably tile-covered as large quantities of them have been found strewn all over the area. There were also structures, shops and houses, which had rubble walls. Yazadani postulates that these constructions were probably covered with straw.[61] Another indication of the economic disparity of the people of the town was that certain houses, which Yazadani calls shops, had underground chambers. Of six such chambers, three were with double rooms divided by a partition wall in the centre. Their depth varied from anything between five and twenty five feet. They were built of neat courses of brick laid in mud and their floors were either laid with bricks or small stones. These interesting constructions invariably contained such valuables as coins with their moulds, seals, beads, ornaments of gold, and terracottas, and thereby imply that they belonged either to rich households or were storage spaces for shopkeepers and merchants.[62]

The overall pattern of the style of architecture at Kondapur, it has been

[58]'Kondapur Excavations', *Annual Report*, Archaeology Department of H.E. the Nizam's Dominions, Hyderabad 1940-41, 17.

[59]G. Yazadani, 'Excavations of Kondapur, An Andhra Town *c*. 200 B.C.- 200 A.D.', *Annals of the Bhandarkar Oriental Research Institute*, XII, Pt. iii-iv, 1941, 181.

[60]Ibid., 175.

[61]Ibid., 181-82.

[62]Ibid., 183.

pointed out, was rather plain and simple but 'quite efficient and skilful'.[63] This is true of even the religious, mainly Buddhist buildings found here which quantifiably, are the maximum number of all excavated structures at this site. They are ascribable to the Hinayana sect and are located substantially in the south-western and western parts of the mound.[64] The cells of the *vihara* complex can be delineated with some certainty and in the middle of this complex traces of a *stupa* measuring nineteen feet across at foundation with a rubble core and a brick encasing was found. Two *chaityas* in perfect shape, though small, have been located towards the south. A description of these Buddhist monuments entails the most obvious conclusion that these housed a body of monks who in all probability were financially, and otherwise, supported by an infrastructure and population who were followers of the faith.

The best representative of the beginnings of Buddhism in the mid-Godavari valley is undoubtedly the *stupa* at Dhulikatta, which is said to be pre-Satavahana in its origins because no anthropomorphic representation of the Buddha was found here. [65] Its construction is thus dated to the last quarter of the third century B.C. and its further development with embellished carved *ayaka* slabs, to the first quarter of the second century B.C. Its discovery was very significant because except for the Kondapur Buddhist complex, there was earlier no structural indication of what the institutional basis of religion was in these parts. No evidence at all of any Brahmanical temple or sculptures has been found, though several terracotta figurines of Mother Goddess and Yakshas have been discovered in large numbers.[66] Other evidence such as the worship of serpent (Naga cult)[67] hardly proves that elements of Brahmanical cults were prevalent here, as Krishnasastry tends to indicate. These perhaps indicate rather, the indigenous tribal forms of belief. It is also interesting that the Dhulikatta *stupa* is located one kilometre away from the historical mound here, at a place called Venkatapur, and further, that Buddhist iconography and other elements of worship are not found integrated with the structural remains of the fort at Dhulikatta or even at Kotalingala, or at the habitation site at Peddabankur. No doubt, the *stupa* drew lay followers of Buddhism from these towns but its separateness from the main site, where perhaps only the recluses and monks formed a distinct

[63]Sreenivasachar's 'Introduction' in M.G. Dikshit, *Beads from Kondapur*, Hyderabad Archaeological Series, No. 16, Hyderabad 1952, 1.

[64]G. Yazadani, 'Excavations at Kondapur', 182.

[65]V.V. Krishnasastry, *Proto and Early Historical Cultures*, 125 and 144-45.

[66]Ibid., 186-88.

[67]Ibid., 224.

social group, is to be noted. Evidence of a monastery is found to the 'north-west of the *stupa*. In the Karimnagar region the Dhulikatta *stupa* gets easily linked with such others located at Phanigiri, Gujulabanda and Thirmalagiri and these of course are all part of the larger network of Buddhism in Andhra Pradesh.[68] Another interesting feature of the Dhulikatta *stupa* is that though it is quite large with a solid drum of bricks capped by an *anda*, fragments of limestone carvings are fairly simple in theme and include only such engravings as reliefs of *stupas*, Muchilinda *naga*, the Dharmachakra, Buddhapada and the like. There also are a few label inscriptions indicating the donations of *gahapatis*,[69] but on the whole, the simplicity of the Dhulikatta *stupa* is striking.One is not sure however, whether it was simply supported and patronised by the itinerant traders/merchants/monks who travelled through this area on their way from the western Deccan cave shrines or north India to the delta region where some of the most important Buddhist centres like Amravati were located. Or, was there a substantial local Buddhist population? Not far from Dhulikatta, in the Warangal district of Phanigiri, the ruins of more than thirty *stupas*[70] have been found which obviously means that this was a bigger and more significant centre for Buddhism in central Deccan. Further, despite considerable excavation work, neither Peddabankur nor Kotalingala have distinctly yielded any evidence of religious structures; the latter at least is thought to have been an important political centre, and this absence in its case becomes conspicuous. Monumental remains, either of religious or political/secular nature, are in any event hard to come by. What we have in the central Deccan are structures, efficiently and skilfully made, utilitarian in character, but not those that can be described as magnificent, beautiful or richly endowed.

IV

Details of individual buildings and even of the layout pattern of buildings at each of the places discussed above are far from sufficient to enable us to reconstruct a complete residential pattern of the community/communities that inhabited these settlements. Therefore, the areas of social activity that we can at present delineate are only skeletal. One can definitively state that the settlement patterns at what Trigger describes as the first and second levels of analysis, (the individual buildings and community layout respectively) at each of these sites reveals an overall

[68]H. Sarkar, 'Growth of Cities in Andhradesa', 5.
[69]V.V.Krishnasastry, *Proto and Early Historical Cultures*, 226.
[70]Ibid., 242.

pattern distinct from each other and that therefore, one cannot suggest that they were under a common administrative authority that could enforce uniform or identical layout plans or architectural forms. Thus, though they were in the proximity of each other, it is important to emphasise the separate features of architecture and construction work at Peddabankur, and that available at the other two towns of Kotalingala and Dhulikatta. Both the latter fit into the typology of the town created in the near contemporary literary texts like the *Manusmrti* and the *Milindapanho* that give us descriptions of fortified towns. Manu particularly specifies that a king should 'build a town, making for his safety a fortress, . . . well-supplied with weapons, money, grain and beasts of burden, with Brahmans, with artisans, . . . in the centre of it a spacious palace, (well) protected, habitable in every season, . . . '.[71] The *Milindapanho* further elaborates that in course of time the city becomes prosperous and diversified and, therefore, the number of social groups that inhabit it also increases. Apart from noblemen, Brahmans, merchants, soldiers, it lists at least seventy to eighty occupational groups that are supposed to inhabit the city.[72] Among these, the majority are artisan castes like metal and textile workers, carvers, rope and basket makers, small merchants and traders along with such groups as flower and fruit sellers, fishmongers, butchers, dealers in strong drink, wood-workers and different kind of entertainers.[73] More than Kotalingala and Dhulikatta, the quantity and variety of artefacts and antiquities discovered at Peddabankur and Kondapur indicate that they could be categorised as primarily manufacturing and trading centres which probably housed a variety of craftsmen, rather than take the view that a lack of fortification walls at these two sites makes them totally non-urban in character.

Against this background one would like to suggest that in the context of the development of urbanisation in the central Deccan, there emerged an essential interdependence between the fortified and so-called non-fortified towns. From the remnants of structures that have survived in the fort areas at Dhulikatta and Kotalingala, such as residential quarters, some kind of palace complex, and the granaries, one can deduce that a sort of ruling class or dominant group inhabited this area. At Dhulikatta particularly, the innumerable granary structures must have been under their control. This, in all probability, meant that they asserted some form of authority to appropriate the surplus produce of the adjoining country-

[71]*Manusmrti*, VII, 70 and 75-76.
[72]*Milindapanho*, V, 4, 231-32.
[73]Ibid., 232.

side. At both these towns their entrances on the riverside indicate the presence of wharf-like structures as transportation along the river must have been cheaper and easier. The exact nature of this ruling elite is difficult to discern. We have a solitary inscriptional find dated palaeographically to the second century A.D., from the *chatussala* area at Dhulikatta in an ivory sealing shaped as a cup on the pedestal with the words *Ajani Siriya Game Kumariya*. This has been interpreted in one case as the mother goddess Kumari from Grama Ajani Siriya which is identified as Dhulikatta itself.[74] Elsewhere, it has been interpreted as a 'royal lady' from the village of Ajani Siriya. [75] At Kotalingala the evidence of royalty is clearer and significant in the discovery of several pre-Satavahana and Satavahana coins, some of which have been found in a stratified context.[76] Unlike the numismatic evidence from Dhulikatta and other places, the Kotalingala finds are outstanding because a number of coins of a certain Chimukha (25), 'founder of the Satavahana dynasty' have been collected.[77] Several coins of such early rulers of this dynasty like Satavahana (234) and Satakarni (47) have also been found. [78] Apart from these, those of Samagopa (68), Mahatalavara (13), Gobadha (17) and Narana (9), open up a new vista of the history of the region. [79] These have been identified and analysed by scholars in a variety of ways. Parabrahma Sastry identifies the Gobhadra and Samagopa coins with the Sunga dynasty of Vidisha that ruled over these parts.[80] Thakur Raja Ram Singh in a recent analysis identifies them with the descendants of the Andhakarattas referred to by Budhagosha who ruled from Kotalingala as pre-Satavahana Andhra kings.[81] On a broader plane, Ajayamitra Sastry points to the fact that coins of these two kings along with some others, were also found in the Vidarbha region and attributes them to some 'ruling chiefs' whose 'family affiliations and exact date' one cannot be sure of.[82]

A diversion into an elaboration of these coin finds was made to highlight specifically the control of politically powerful groups that had

[74]V.V. Krishnasastry, *Proto and Early Historical Cultures*, 183.

[75]V.V. Krishnasastry, 'Archaeological Discoveries in Andhra Pradesh', 65.

[76]Raja Ram Singh, 'Pre-Satavahana Andhra Kings', 8.

[77]V.V. Krishnasastry, *Proto and Early Historical Cultures*, 126 and 132.

[78]Raja Ram Singh, 'Pre-Satavahana Andhra Kings', 8.

[79]Ibid.

[80]P.V. Parabrahma Sastry, 'Coins of Simuka Satavahana Discovered', *The Andhra Pradesh Journal of Archaeology*, I, No. 1, 1979, 136-37.

[81]Raja Ram Singh, 'Pre-Satavahana Andhra Kings', 14.

[82]Ajayamitra Sastri, 'Pre-Satavahana and Satavahana Coinage of the Deccan', *Journal of the Numismatic Society of India*, XLIV, 1982, 4.

become a force continuously from pre-Satavahana times. One may not agree with Singh's view that there existed in the central Deccan a 'confederation of Petty and Tribal rulers and other kingdoms controlled by Andhra Kings'.[83] These Andhra kings, according to him, were located at Kotalingala, which he thinks is an older site than Dhulikatta.[84] But what emerges is that power relations here were rooted in old kin ties. The prefix 'go' in the names of chiefs like Gobadhra and Samagopa, who are said to have ruled from Kotalingala, may indicate their origin in pastoral communities. A stone pillar, now lying in a paddy field one kilometre away from the Kotalingala fortress, bears a label inscription *Naga gopi nikaya*,[85] meaning 'assemblage' or 'group' of Naga gopi which may have also referred to a kin group living in a settlement outside the fortified township. The location of Dhulikatta amidst fertile black soil and the considerable number of granaries in the fort area may indicate that the ruling clans probably were from powerful land-owning agricultural communities. It is impossible to establish a connection, political or otherwise, between the various ruling families who were in control of these fortified towns and the surrounding populations, but that there was a concerted need felt by them to defend themselves is evident in the apparently massive fortification walls built by them. It is pertinent to point out at this juncture that both Kotalingala and Dhulikatta are surrounded by early historical sites.[86] Kotalingala is surrounded by two such small sites on both the right and left banks of the Godavari. On the right bank is Vemnurru, a site of three to four hectares and here 'the presence of iron slag and iron ore may indicate the existence of an indigenous iron industry'.[87] On the other bank is Karnamamidi which has yielded typical early historical pottery and bricks.[88] Similarly, Peddabankur is just ten kilometres away from Dhulikatta and another early historical mound of Chinnabankur is about four kilometres north of Peddabankur.[89]

Of all these, it may be suggested that Peddabankur probably had an independent political and economic existence. Both here, as well as at Kondapur, a large number of coins, punchamarked ones and also early Satavahana types, have been found. I.K. Sarma suggests that Ped-

[83]Raja Ram Singh, 'Pre-Satavahana Andhra Kings', 3.
[84]Ibid., 8.
[85]V.V. Krishnasastry, *Proto and Early Historical Cultures*, 148.
[86]Ibid., 125-30.
[87]Ibid., 125.
[88]Ibid., 128.
[89]Ibid., 125.

dabankur was a mint centre;[90] Krishnasastry locates this mint in Enclosure II where scores of coins were found during excavation.[91] Sarma deduces this particularly on the basis of a large number of terracotta moulds found in stratified deposits and the existence of hundreds of small die-struck pieces in pots. Two hoards of punch-marked coins have also been found here.[92] A variety of coins of different types were reported also from Kondapur and this had led Yazadani to designate it as 'an important Andhra town where coins were minted'.[93] Here too, thousands of punch-marked and early type of Satavahana coins were found along with a discovery of coin moulds to which the punch-marked coins fitted.[94] Roman coins, though not very substantial in number, as well as their imitations in clay bullae or lead with gold plating were recovered from all these settlements in the central Deccan. The coexistence of a variety of coin types at these centres converges on one obvious conclusion, namely, that the regional economy was dependent on trade and commercial transactions of a certain magnitude.

V

An even more fundamental question is that if the urban economy was so developed, what were the mechanisms through which local groups participated in spheres of economic activity like trade and commodity production? For instance, especially in pre-Satavahana times, which were the social groups that minted the coins and what gave them the authority to do so? It is interesting that both Peddabankur and Kondapur that have been designated as 'mint centres' were not fortified towns and, therefore, probably not seats of royal power. It has been suggested that the Peddabankur Enclosures, one of which has been named a mint, 'appear like small castles and have only a single gateway either in the north-east or north-west. These were evidently occupied by the wealthy individual families'.[95] As indicated above, such groups also inhabited Kondapur, particularly in dwellings with the underground chambers. From the fragmentary label inscriptions found on the Dhulikatta *stupa* we get references to *gahapatis* who made donations to the Buddhist order – *gahapatino pathalasa mathuya danam.*[96] It is difficult to postulate the

[90]I.K. Sarma, *Coinage of the Satavahana Empire*, New Delhi 1980, 35.
[91]V.V. Krishnasastry, *Proto and Early Historical Cultures*, 139.
[92]Ibid., 200.
[93]G. Yazadani, 'Excavations at Kondapur', 180.
[94]'Kondapur Excavations', *Annual Report*, 1940-41,20.
[95]V.V. Krishnasastry, *Proto and Early Historical Cultures*, 241.
[96]Ibid., 226.

exact relationship this group/groups had with the institutional bearers of the Buddhist monastery. At Kondapur, particularly, the recluses must have lived on alms from the inhabitants of the town and the popularity of Buddhism is evident from a considerable amount of ritual pottery that has been found here.[97] Undoubtedly, the monks here formed a substantial part of the population. It would, however, be simplistic to conclude that these centres were inhabited by only rich merchants and artisans.

So far, we have concentrated on a reconstruction of the possible social structure in these settlements based on the partial details of some of the structures unearthed and some of the prominent archaeological finds, and therefore, have only described what Rouse calls the 'Professional Co-People'.[98] But as pertinently observed by him 'the professional and sustaining co-peoples (both) share civilisation' though both act as independent variables. Further, they 'may both be urban, both rural, or one may be urban and the other rural'.[99] We thus, next turn to examine the 'sustaining co-peoples' who, in the ecological zone of the central Deccan had to be crucially integrated into the urban economy.

Subsistence strategies and basic elements of craft production are best known to us from the tool types the communities used. That a surplus had been generated by the well-settled communities of the central Deccan during the early centuries A.D. is evident enough from the structures they built to store it, as also the other manifestations of urban life. The economy of the whole region was indeed transformed by the extensive use of iron for both weaponry and agricultural implements, a process which began well before Satavahana or early historical times, during what is popularly called the Megalithic phase of habitation. Habitation in the Karimnagar region can generally be traced back to Palaeolithic and Mesolithic times. These, it has been pointed out, were particularly spread around the river Godavari and its tributaries. [100] At Dhulikatta, below a sterile layer which underlay Satavahana deposits were found a few microlith-like cores, blades and flakes. [101] Kondapur is considered to

[97]G. Yazadani, 'Excavations at Kondapur', 176.

[98]Irving Rouse, 'Settlement Patterns in Archaeology' in Ruth Tringham (ed), *Man, Settlement and Urbanism*, 103; also, 100-4. Rouse's analysis is particularly pertinent as through his concept of 'remnant settlement archaeology' he differentiates between 'sustaining' or original community, essentially rural, and the later or 'professional' one which is urban in character, as both constitute a different settlement pattern which he terms as 'co-pattern' or 'co-people' leading ultimately to the formation of a distinct 'co-culture'.

[99]Ibid., 105.

[100]Raja Ram Singh, 'Prehistoric sites in Karimnagar Region, Andhra Pradesh', *Andhra Pradesh Journal of Archaeology*, I, No. 2, 1979,1-10.

[101]*Indian Archaeology*, 1974-75, 25.

have been a factory site for blades and flakes of the Middle Stone Age.[102]

The above data taken as a whole are indicative of a very substantial food-gathering economy in these parts. It is of some importance to note that sites like Polakonda and Kadambapur, which best exemplify the Neolithic economy, are also important Megalithic sites. Kadambapur is situated amidst the early historical sites of Dhulikatta, Kotalingala and Peddabankur and though it has no early historical remains, it is a very rich Megalithic site situated in the proximity of irrigation tanks.[103] More than at any of these antecedent settlements the continuity and overlap of cultures at Peddabankur is most striking. It was a Neolithic site of considerable scale because of the scores of ground stone tools found here;[104] Neolithic axes and microliths find their way at early historical levels as well.[105] Besides, it has yielded considerable amount of Megalith-related artefacts like horse remains, tools and implements of iron, cattle remains and so on.[106] In a region which even today borders the tribal area, it is not unusual to postulate that there was an interdependence of different kinds of subsistence patterns, and this may perhaps have been one of the reasons that led the excavator of Peddabankur to style it as a 'Satavahana village'.[107] We would like to highlight that at Peddabankur as well as at other Megalithic sites like Pochampad and Kadambapur, the use and production of iron weapons, tools and implements is substantial. The ability of the Megalithic economy to generate iron objects on a large scale is undoubtedly related to the development of iron technology and its availability in the region.[108] It must however be mentioned that this large-scale use of iron did not transform the Megalithic economy totally into an agrarian one and, in fact, at Pochampad and Peddabankur in particular, we find a considerable amount of bone remains of such domesticated animals as cattle, sheep, goat and swine.[109] These are found along with agricultural implements such as flat-axes, sickles and hoes.

The expansion of the agrarian base is, however, linked with the proliferation of early historical sites in the region. It is in this phase that it can be postulated that there was an increase in population. In the sites under discussion the maximum number of iron implements have been

[102]Br. R. Allchin, *The Birth of Indian Civilisation*, Penguin, Harmondsworth, 1968, 76.
[103]V.V. Krishnasastry, *Proto and Early Historical Cultures*, 92-95, 105-6 and 239.
[104]Ibid., 22.
[105]Ibid., 24 and 35.
[106]Ibid., 95-97.
[107]Ibid., 124.
[108]Ibid., 107; Raja Ram Singh, 'Pre-Satavahana Andhra Kings', 4-5.
[109]V.V. Krishnasastry, *Proto and Early Historical Cultures*, 106.

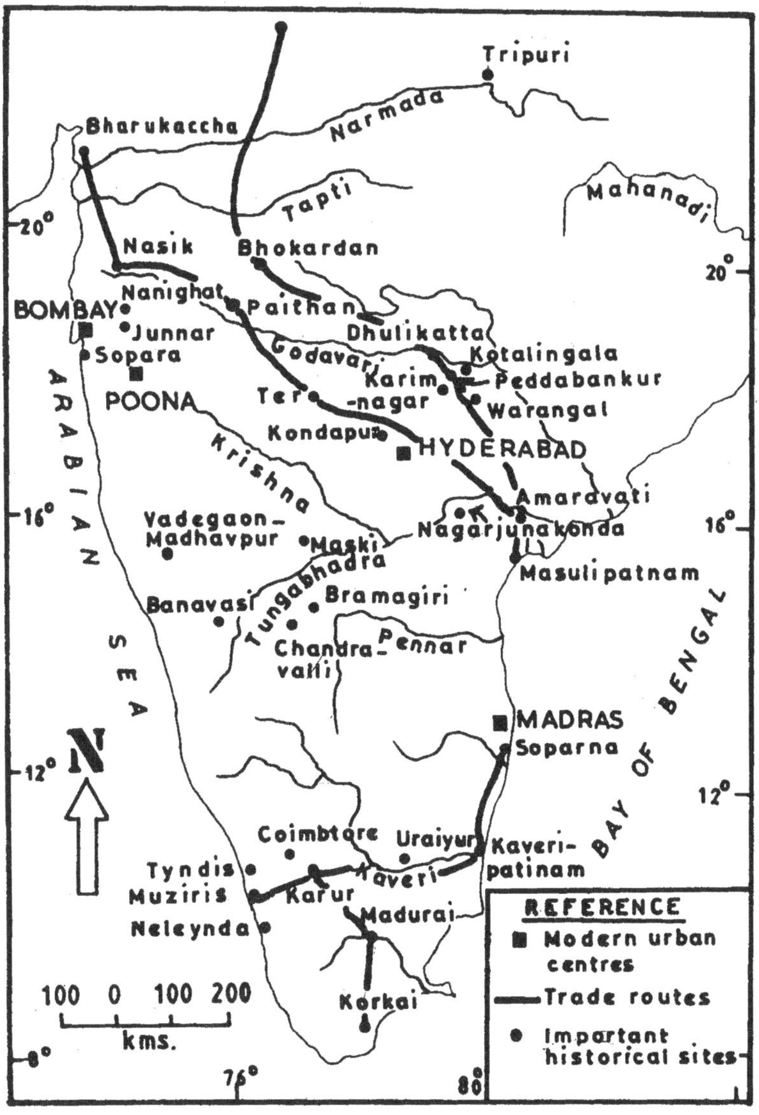

Map III Trade Routes in Early Historic Deccan

recovered from Peddabankur and Kondapur. The impact and use of the iron technology must, none the less, be understood in the context of a limited ecological base, where because of the non-availability of fertile tracts, other than those along the river, large-scale agricultural operations were not possible. Village settlements thus continued to be dependent on other modes of production such as pastoralism, gathering and fishing. But, what is particularly striking is that even small settlements in the mid-Godavari valley give evidence for the production of iron objects. It has been pointed out that a 'number of ancient iron working spots were located in Karimnagar region at Regonda, Tellakunta etc.' and at the latter site, enormous deposits of iron slag and nodules of calcium carbonate indicate this. Indeed, here 'the entire hill range is scattered with iron ore'.[110] At one site of Bommareddy Palli an iron slag mound of considerable extent and height was noticed.[111] This has made Krishnasastry conclude that during early historical times the iron industry reached a high water-mark in this region.[112] For instance, at Dhulikatta was found a crucible of iron fifteen centimetres in diameter with 'considerable amount of charred wood, leafy material and mud, besides big well-burnt terracotta cakes were found adhered to the concave crucible'. This, it has been suggested, 'may go to prove that iron and steel metallurgy was practised as a home industry'.[113] Further, at Peddabankur, the evidence of a terracotta forge measuring twenty centimetres in diameter, gives interesting indication of how the forging of iron was done and the fact that 'the working floor of the forge was thickly embedded with fragments of iron slag', along with associated finished products such as iron nails, a sickle, a knife and a ring, all giving graphic description of the work place of a blacksmith.[114]

VI

In the light of the above one would like to suggest the possibilities of the existence of social groups, organised most probably on kinship lines, involved in the craft production of smelting and forging iron. Thus, trade in these parts was stimulated not so much by the export of an agricultural surplus, but rather, by the supply of iron objects and other related

[110]Ibid., 107.

[111]Raja Ram Singh, 'Pre-Satavahana Andhra Kings', 4.

[112]V.V. Krishnasastry, *Proto and Early Historical Cultures*, 151-52;154-65; 'Archaeological Discoveries of the Satavahana Period', 1-4.

[113]V.V. Krishnasastry, *Proto and Early Historical Cultures*, 153.

[114]Ibid., 153-54.

commodities for which places like Peddabankur and Kondapur were centres of production. This explains the existence of such large number of coins of various types at both these places. In addition, Peddabankur and Dhulikatta were famous for the terracottas that were produced here.[115] Kondapur, on the other hand, besides being rich in terracottas, is a site, 'unequalled by any other single site in India' where the largest amount of bead materials have been found in excavation.[116] These industries as well as others such as working in precious metals like gold and semiprecious stones and pottery-making flourished on a large scale. A large chunk of the 'sustaining co-people' in the mid-Godavari complex were thus artisanal groups with perhaps strong ties of kinship persisting in the organisation of their work. Their prosperity was fundamentally linked to the larger networks of trade in the western Deccan and the Krishna-Godavari delta. One of the arterial routes that connected these two regions passed through Kondapur on its way to Ter and beyond, and the other touched Dhulikatta on its way to Vidisha and Ujjain. [117] This undoubtedly activated inland trade and stimulated the growth of new areas of economic activity in a region that was not supported by a large and extensive agrarian base. This would also explain the existence of so many historical sites clustered together in the mid-Godavari valley though all of them cannot be characterised as urban (map III).

It must be reiterated that interdependence among the sites was a characteristic of settlement patterns in these parts. The widespread existence of microliths even at historical layers of habitation, and Peddabankur is one such classic example, indicates that the tribal/nomadic populations were also integrated into the new economic system. The heterogeneity in the social structure of the sites in the mid-Godavari valley thus cannot be missed. Their economic structures were strengthened in the concomitant increase in internal and external trade during the early centuries of the Christian era, and in their ability to meet the demands of the commodities they specialised in. It would not be an exaggeration to state that it was the capacity of the dominant social groups in the region to maintain the networks of trade and production that resulted in the growing strength of certain local elite. Even from pre-Satavahana times, their practice of striking the coin with their names inscribed on it, is evidence enough that they recognised the importance of commerce for the sustenance of their settlements. Political power in pre-Satavahana times was necessarily

[115] Ibid., 179-85.
[116] M.G. Dikshit, *Beads from Kondapur*, cited above.
[117] H. Sarkar, 'Growth of Cities in Andhradesa', 5.

segmented, but under the new forces of social change begun as a consequence of expanding agriculture and mercantile activities which enabled the well-settled tribal communities to interact with each other efficiently, it became possible for the early Satavahanas to establish a larger network of political and economic control with the mid-Godavari valley as their original nucleus. Thus, though Ghosh doubts if peoples in the south were able to 'shed their tribal character',[118] they were indeed able to concentrate and organise themselves in settlements which, due to the geo-cultural and techno-economic, as well as institutional constraints and possibilities developed an individual character, different in content and style from similar contemporaneous centres in the western Deccan or coastal Andhra, as also from other parts of India.

[118]A. Ghosh, *City in Early Historical India*, 13.

URBAN PROCESSES IN EARLY MEDIEVAL TAMIL NADU

R. CHAMPAKALAKSHMI

In recent years much of the historical research on early and medieval south India has concerned itself with agrarian structures, peasant settlements and the general pattern of socio-economic changes. Problems of interpretation of epigraphic records and the inadequacy of statistical data have deterred scholars from reconstructing the history of urban development, despite their interest in trade patterns, merchant and craft organisations and state participation in such activities. With the dependable framework of agrarian development now provided by recent studies, however, it is possible and necessary to venture into urban history.

Two major periods of urbanisation can be seen in Tamil Nadu, the first coinciding with the early centuries of the Christian era, called the Sangam period, and the second with the period of the Cholas from the ninth to thirteenth century. The intervening period from the fourth to the eighth century provided a fairly large-scale agrarian expansion and institutional organisation to serve as the basis for the growth of urban centres in the Chola period.

I

It would be useful to survey, however briefly, the nature of urban development in the first period in order to highlight the underlying differences in the processes of urban growth in the second. The most crucial factor in the urbanisation of the early period appears to have been maritime trade, in which the early tribal kingdoms of the Cholas, Cheras and Pandyas actively participated. Emerging in the main rice-producing regions of the Kaveri (delta), Vaigai and Tamraparni and the Periyar, the Cholas, Pandyas and Cheras controlled vast tracts of agricultural land in these river valleys. Evidence of irrigation works in these areas is provided by Sangam literature although archaeological corroboration is at the moment non-existent.

The establishment of these incipient states was preceded by centuries of expansion of what is called the Megalithic culture, the earliest extant archaeological evidence of a uniform culture in south India, the distinguishing traits of which were use of iron implements and the Black and Redware pottery. In fact, the Sangam period seems to represent the end phases of this culture and the emergence of Tamil civilisation, which may be attributed to urbanisation stimulated by maritime trade. Socio-political dominance of this early Tamil society was shared by the three 'crowned kings' – *vendar* of the Chola, Chera and Pandya lines and the minor chieftains called *velirs*. Strife among the crowned kings was a common feature for control over the other river valleys and minor chiefdoms, each of which had an administrative or political centre.[1] More important was their attempt to control the coastal region adjacent to their kingdoms through which they could regulate the trade that was carried on with distant lands. The Sangam rulers tried to control this trade actively by levying tolls and customs, apart from being consumers of luxury goods. Hence, we see the emergence of dual centres of political and commercial activity in each of the kingdoms of Uraiyur and Kaverippattinam for the Cholas,[2] Madurai and Korkai for the Pandyas and Karuvur and Muchiri for the Cheras. Some of the *velir* chieftains also appear to have controlled this trade as seen in the literary description of Virai as a *velir* stronghold, which may be identified with Virampattinam, close to which emerged the Roman trading station of Arikamedu, the Produca of the Greek classical sources.

This extensive trade, as described in the *Maduraikkanci* and *Pattinappalai*,[3] included import of luxury items and Roman wine brought by Yavana ships, much desired by the ruling elite as articles probably of

[1] Was this strife more for plunder and loot than for control over these areas?

[2] Kaveripattinam is described as a Chola port built up by Karikala, the Sangam Chola.

[3] These two works are the major sources on the two cities of Madurai and Kaveripattinam respectively, while other works of the *Ettuttogai* and *Pattuppattu* collections also refer to these centres.

'socio-technic' or 'ideo-technic' value.[4] Among the exports was the highly priced south Indian cloth resembling the slough of a snake. South India was also the entrepot for the trade in spices and perhaps also camphor, which the south Indian traders as middlemen passed on from south Asia to the Roman west for Yavana gold. While direct sailing from south-east Asia brought several items and Yavana ships unloaded their goods at the Coromandel ports, coastal shipping must have helped in the relay of goods to many other coastal towns for exchange in the neighbouring regions. The Coromandel coast is marked by coastal settlements of considerable antiquity, some of which developed into big emporia of trade, while others, dotted along the coast, were perhaps used as halting centres for coastal shipping, a few surviving well into the medieval and modern times. Kaverippattinam was perhaps the largest trading mart for all such goods, as seen from the reference to merchant colonies at the Chola port housing people speaking different languages. Another port, called Perimula or Perimuda and described as 'the greatest emporium of trade in India', has been tentatively located at the mouth of the Vaigai near Ramesvaram on the Gulf of Mannar noted for its pearls. Objects like gold and gems have not been unearthed in excavations, although evidence in the form of Roman pottery – the arretine and rouletted ware – its imitations, Roman amphorae and Roman coins, apart from a few local dynastic issues, has been found.

Literary references to ports, towns and cities are numerous,the Greek sources alone giving the names of about a hundred, including emporia of trade on the coast, metropolises, marts, cities and inland towns as political and trade centres. The literary descriptions of fortified cities and coastal towns with several quarters for merchants and other social groups would suggest a sophistication in urban development far beyond the meagre archaeological remains unearthed so far at places like Kaverippattinam, Kanci and Uraiyur. Continuous occupation in centres like Kanci and Madurai has rendered meaningful horizontal excavations nearly impossible. Even in places like Kaverippattinam, the decline of the port due to the rise of new ones in medieval times has made no significant difference to excavations, for much of the old port city has so far eluded the most systematic search and perhaps still lies under water or under the surrounding rice fields.[5] The few structures unearthed in

[4] For the importance of primitive valuables in tribal societies, see S.Ratnagar, *Encounters: The Westerly Trade of the Harappa Civilisation*, Delhi 1981, 242.

[5] Investigations with the help of a Proton magnetometer in this area have not been able to tap underground remains of structures. Some efforts are now afloat to explore the possibilities of underwater archaeology.

Kaverippattinam, such as the reservoir and wharf and the later fifth century Buddhist *vihara*, are no indications of monumental architectural efforts.

Some of the more interesting discoveries are the remains of dyeing vats excavated both at Arikamedu and Uraiyur, establishing beyond doubt the importance of textile manufacture, although Kanci and Madurai, two major textile-producing centres, have not come up with such evidence. Much more significant is the distribution of Roman coin hoards and punch-marked coin hoards, marking major lines of transport and communication from the western coast, from Cochin area through the Palghat gap via Coimbatore, the region of the Cheras, Tiruchirappalli of the Cholas, Pudukkottai, a buffer region (*velir* area) to Madurai and Tirunelveli, the region of the Pandyas. The Coimbatore region, known for its beryl mines, has a concentration of coin hoards. While many of the punch-marked coins were issued by merchant guilds, the use of the fish symbol on the Bodinay-akkanur hoard shows that some at least were dynastic issues, or the issuer had the sanction of the ruling family.

Guild organisation was evidently as important as in the Deccan for it seems to have regulated the movement of goods to different places. In this context, reference to the *nigma* of Tiruvelarai in an early Tamil Brahmi inscription from Mankulam and the *Silappadikaram* reference to Kovalan's father as a Masattuvan or Great Sarthavaha or carvan leader are of great significance. Tamil traders are mentioned in the early Brahmi inscriptions of Sri Lanka, and those of Sri Lanka figure as donors in the Tamil Brahmi records.

The social groups involved in this trade included Buddhists and Jains, apart from those of other faiths. Diversity of occupation is corroborated by Brahmi inscriptions referring to lapidaries, merchants dealing in gold, cloth, iron and salt. Archaeological evidence of social complexity is not recognisable from excavations. Thus, while the urban centres of the Deccan and Andhra region show a marked predominance of the Buddhist faith over others, only one of the coastal towns of Tamil Nadu shows evidence of a sizeable Buddhist following. Interior towns like Kacci, Karuvur and Madurai are known to have had Jain population as well. But neither was the dominant religion in such urban centres. Tamil Brahmi inscriptions provide references to Buddhist and Jain ascetics who were patronised by merchants and rulers. The occurrence of such inscriptions on the major route from Karnataka and Kerala into Tamil Nadu—a route followed down to the medieval times by itinerant merchants – is significant.

The decline of maritime trade around the third century A.D. led to the decline of most ports and with them perhaps the decline of the three ruling families who seem to disappear quite suddenly from the political scene after the second century. In fact, a political vacuum sets in from the third century onwards with no clear evidence of any political authority till about the middle of the sixth century. The Pallavas are heard of as rulers of Kanci in the fourth century but their early activity is confined to the Andhra region and their political presence in the Tamil region is felt only from the sixth century A.D. onwards.

Pallava dominance over the Tamil region north of the Kaveri and revival of Pandya power in Madurai marked a major shift in agrarian organisation through the introduction of new elements as integrative forces – the *brahmadeya* and the temple. As suggested earlier, the period from the fourth to eighth centuries provided the institutional framework for agrarian expansion and the basis for urban growth in the succeeding centuries.

Medieval south India, and Tamil Nadu in particular, would provide a conspicuous example of a rural-urban continuum without a clear-cut demarcation of the rural-urban boundaries. In this context, it would be relevant to raise certain crucial questions relating to pre-industrial societies. What are the links between agricultural production and urban growth? Are agricultural growth and availability of surplus a necessary pre-condition to urban development? Does the increase in commerce and overseas trade and the consequent emergence of centres of commodity exchange or entrepot markets stimulate agricultural production? To what extent did towns develop as centres of commodity production or as distribution centres, in response to internal factors as opposed to growth of towns in response to demands of overseas trade?

II

In order to find answers to the above questions in the south Indian context, the first point to be highlighted is that in the period between the ninth and twelfth centuries, urban growth in south India refers to the expansion of existing rural settlements. These settlements are the *brahmadeyas* or Brahman settlements originating from land grants to Brahmans as learned men in charge of education and as temple priests. Clusters of such settlements emerge in the core areas or delta regions in the river valleys forming the nuclei of medieval kingdoms. They are pluralistic settlements with several temples as centres of different socio-religious groups pursuing various economic activities centring round the temple.

Land grants to Brahmans and temples by ruling classes and socially important groups like *velala* land-owners were a common feature from the seventh century onwards in Tamil Nadu and earlier in the Deccan and Andhra Pradesh, marking the beginning of agrarian expansion and integration after the decline of the overseas trade of the earlier period. Temples as the institutional base for socio-economic and political integration assume great significance from the time of the Bhakti movement in south India, from the seventh century. Some of these Bhakti centres became leading political centres and religious and pilgrimage centres and evolved into huge urban complexes either around a single large temple or with multiple temples together forming parts of an urban complex. Such temples were built by the major ruling dynasties either to legitimise their sovereignty, or as Bhakti centres. Temples became landed magnates with tenants and temple servants remunerated through lands. They also received gold and money endowments from the ninth and tenth centuries and, in all probability, invested such grants again in land or occasionally in trade. The growth in the activities of such temples led to urban development. There was also a corresponding expansion in the architectural structure of the temple from a small nuclear shrine to huge horizontal temple complexes with several enclosures and towering gateways encompassing many shrines, halls of educational activities, hospitals attached to temples, monastic establishments with lineages of religious heads controlling temple administration. Thus one could look for urban growth initially in the core regions where clusters of *brahmadeyas* and *devadanas* emerged.[6]

Rural-urban continuum is best illustrated in centres which had a dependable hinterland where agricultural output was assuredly above subsistence level. The trade in agricultural commodities and local goods as well as in luxuries and exotic items from distant lands that was attracted by such centres must be seen as a complementary factor in this development. The demand generated by the local elite and the temple for locally unavailable goods brought itinerant trade to the market of such areas and encouraged large-scale settlement of craftsmen and artisans who were eventually accommodated in the temple centre. One of the leading examples of such urban growth is Kudamukku – Palaiyarai,

[6] While *brahmadeya* represents land granted to Brahmans, *devadana* was land made over to the temple. Sometimes whole villages were granted as *devadanas*.

the residential capital and twin city of the Cholas.[7]

This twin city came up on the banks of the Arisitary and Mudikondan – the distributaries of the Kaveri in the delta region which was the resource base of the Cholas both in the early period, and later, when they re-emerged into power as the most powerful south Indian dynasty. The river system here was probably carefully built up into an irrigation network from about the ninth century by the Cholas and thus came to represent a rich source of revenue for them, with a large surplus to support a large concentration of population. Archaeologically, the region shows evidence of colonisation perhaps even before the Cholas became an important ruling family in the period of the spread of Black and Redware pottery and iron of the Megalithic culture.

After a brief period of political vacuum this region became the bone of contention between the Pallavas and Pandyas during the seventh to ninth centuries, before the re-emergence of the Cholas from this area as their nucleus. The foundation of Tanjavur and Gangaikondacholapuram as their capitals was perhaps determined by their anxiety to protect this rich resource base.

The resource potential of this region is indicated both by numerous peasant settlements from the beginning of the Christian era and also by the tendency of early *brahmadeyas* to cluster together and proliferate rapidly in this area. Statistical data show that the *brahmadeyas* were densest around Kumbakonam. An early township called Tiraimur also emerged here from the late ninth century; Kudamukku represents the religious complex of the twin city and Paliyarai, the palace complex. In both the areas temples came up at different points of time from the ninth to the thirteenth centuries and every one of them had a settlement around it, somewhat akin to a modern colony in a large city. The temples were dedicated to the two major deities of Hinduism Shiva and Vishnu, particularly from the time of the Bhakti movement. Every one of the Chola kings built a temple both as an act of religious merit and as a process of legitimising his authority. The Jains, who had a major settlement in this region, were displaced by the Shaivas after the spread of the Bhakti ideology and the spread of the Puranic religions of Shaivism and Vaishnavism. Thus the expansion of both the complexes was through the emergence of a series of temple settlements and their architectural elaboration. With such elaboration each of these temples came to play an

[7] The discussion on this city is based on the more elaborate version in a previous paper. See R. Champakalakshmi, 'Growth of Urban Centres in South India: Kudamukku-Palaiyarai, the twin city of the Colas', *Studies in History*, No. 1, January-June, 1979.

increasing role in the socio-economic and political activities of this centre. The Bhakti ideology and the temple as the main institutional force were in fact the means through which the Cholas brought about socio-political and economic integration.[8]

The major economic activities centring round these temples are reflected through endowments in the form of land, cows, sheep, gold and money for a variety of purposes like religious festivals, feeding of Brahmans and other ascetics, burning of lamps, reconstruction and renovation of temple structures, ornaments to the deities, religious discourses and educational institutions. The temples had their treasuries, archives and administrative machinery, usually controlled by the landed groups, particularly Brahmans and high caste non-Brahmans or *velalas*.

The social groups involved in these activities were members of the royal family, Chola officials of high rank, palace servants, personal retinue of the royal family, members of elephant corps, leading land-owners from other parts of the Chola kingdom, local merchants, horse traders from the distant Kerala region and merchants from other districts of Tamil Nadu and the itinerant merchant guilds. In order to look after the temples' movable property, like cows and sheep, there was a special class of shepherds called *manradis*. The *kaikkolas* were another important community who were part-time soldiers and weavers. Weaving became their major occupation after the decline of the Cholas.

Land gifts came mainly from the land-owning groups while gold and monetary gifts came more often from merchants, local and itinerant. Coined money as an exchange medium became regular from the tenth century onwards. The Chola mint was located in Kudamukku.

Due to the incessant architectural and sculptural activity going on between the ninth and the thirteenth centuries regular colonies of architects and sculptors must have existed throughout the Chola period and after. Two of the major industries of the Chola period, metal ware and textiles, were located in this complex. Apart from making of copper and brass vessels, the ritual needs of the temples led to the evolution of a big centre of the art of casting bronze images for the temples, a craft in which the Chola artists achieved unparalleled skill and excellence. To this day the Kumbakonam region remains a major centre of bronze casting and vessel making. Weaving was the second major industry, so renowned that in the sixteenth and seventeenth centuries weavers from Saurashtra in western India migrated and settled down in Kumbakonam.

[8] While this idea is found vaguely hinted at in various recent works, a systematic analysis of the process of this integration is attempted in a forthcoming paper by this author on 'The Bhakti ideology and socio-political integration in Tamil Nadu'.

With the decline of the Cholas the administrative and political importance of this city as the nerve centre of Chola administration also declined and Palaiyarai or the palace or residential complex disintegrated into small villages and hamlets which are at present suburbs of modern Kumbakonam, which is a taluk headquarters.

III

Apart from the core region of the Cholas situations of a similar nature led to urban growth in other areas, although the pace and quantum of growth differed in various degrees.

Madurantaka Chahuvedimangalam in the Chingleput district (a *taniyur* in Kalattur-kottam in Jayankonda Cholamandalam) became the nucleus of an urban centre from the time of Parantaka I, its various quarters developing around Vaishnava and Shaiva temples built by the imperial Cholas in the tenth and eleventh centuries.[9] It acquired several hamlets through endowments,[10] and a market place called Viracholapperangadi.[11] In comparison with the huge urban complexes in the core region of the Cholas and Pandyas of the twelfth and thirteenth centuries, this centre may be categorised as a small town. Uttiamerur, an early *brahmadeya*, also attained the status of a *taniyur* in Kaliyur-kottam by the tenth century. Ennayiram and Tribhuvani in the south Arcot district belonged to the same category. The former with a huge Vedic college and a hostel attached to the temple attracted Valanjiyar merchants who traded in articles required by the hostel in return for money deposited with them. Triukkalukkunram, a *taniyur* in Kalattur-kottam, with three temples, one of which dated from Pallava times, had its own *nagaram* or marketing centre by the eleventh century.

Two major *brahmadeyas* of the Tirunelveli district became the nuclei of a huge urban complex with the occupation of the Pandya country by the imperial Cholas in the eleventh century. Rajaraja Chaturvedimangalam, the present Mannarkoyil, which grew around a Vishnu temple built by the Chera subordinate of the Cholas, developed into an urban centre by the twelfth century. Vindanur was its nearest *nagaram*. The present

[9] Kulottunga I acquired the epithet of 'Sungam tavirtta Chola'(the Chola who abolished tolls) repeatedly mentioned in his inscriptions.

[10] M.M. Abraham, 'Religion and Trade: Some Aspects of the Relationship between India, Burma and Sri Lanka A.D. 1070-1300', unpublished research paper.

[11] Nos. 23, 24 and 28 of 1919. Here a royal officer under Rajaraja I made enquiries regarding taxes on salt pans and organised fresh scale of expenses in the local temple in the eleventh century.

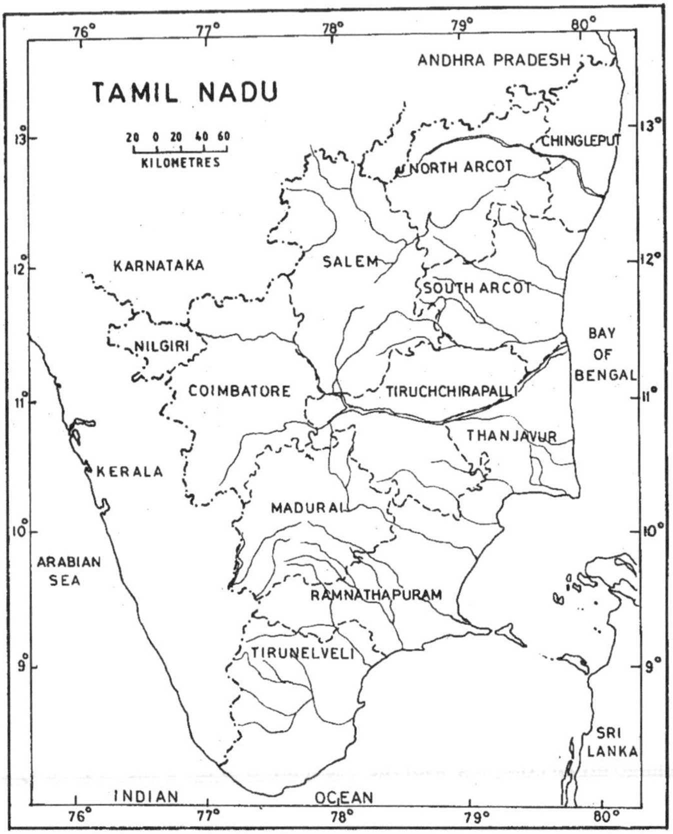

Map of Champaklakshmi

Tiruvalisyaram and Ambasamudram, north and south of Mannarkoyil, were parts of this *brahmadeya*. In Brahmadesam, east of Mannarkoyil one may recognise its origins as a *brahmadeya*.

The *Nanadesi Tisai Ayirattu Ainnurruvar* frequented this centre in the twelfth and thirteenth centuries and merchants from distant towns like Kumaramarttandapuram near Kumbakonam are mentioned in local records from the tenth century. The Chola-Pandya viceroys of the imperial Cholas had their residential quarters in the city. The Chola army, called *munrukai mahasenai*, was in charge of the temple at Tiruvalisvaram. It is also significant that Tiruvalisvaram became an *erivirapattanam* called Rajaraja Erivirapattanam, a merchant town protected by armed troops.

In the urban development of this region the Golaki-matha of Tiruvalisvaram contributed no less in the thirteenth century. Lying between the Tamraparni and Gatana rivers, called Mudikonda Cholapperaru Rajarajappararu respectively in Chola inscriptions, this centre is located in the picturesque amphitheatre that descends from the Podiyil hills commanding the entry into the Pandya country from the Chera land. The whole area between the two rivers forms a rich agricultural tract, which the Cholas selected as their base in the Pandya region, creating new *brahmadeyas*. The size of this urban complex was about thirty square kilometres, comparable to the Kudamukkil complex in the Chola heartland.

Further east was Seravanmadevichaturvedimangalam on the south bank of the Tamraparni, dating back to the period of Rajaraja I, with a cluster of small settlements linked to the main *brahmadeya*. Among the more important hamlets were Karisulndamangalam or Kailasamangalam or Ten-Tiruvengadam and Pattalmadai with huge Vishnu temples in addition to the major Vishnu and Shiva temples of the main centre. The *nagaram* of Rajendrasolapuram with its palace served as the major market centre of this region from the eleventh century.

The merchant corporations of the Five Hundred patronised the Vishnu temple of Nigarilisola Vinnagarattar in this centre. Kailkkola and Saliya weavers and Terinda-Kaikkola army men, sculptors and merchants, both local and from other towns, were among the many socio-economic groups involved in the commercial activities of this centre. Shaiva and Vaishnava *mathas* and a Sarasvati *bhandara* or library attached to one of the Vishnu temples were the other institutional forces which contributed to the urban growth of this centre in the twelfth and thirteenth centuries. The location of the Chola palace in this region and the concerted efforts of the Cholas towards the development of this region in the eleventh century seem to have been greatly influenced by their trade policy as also by their interest in the northern parts of Sri Lanka which are visibly heightened in this period.

A major consequence of the earlier agrarian expansion of the seventh to ninth centuries was an increase in commercial activity from the ninth century onwards. In the pre-Chola period large-scale commercial activity was confined to certain areas. Kacci of the Sangam period assumed the role of the premier city in south India from Pallava times both as a seat of political power and as the largest commercial centre, apart from its character as a Ghatikasthana or seat of learning. It became a sacred centre by acquiring under the Pallavas and Cholas a large number of Shaiva and Vaishnava temples. Kacci was Sanskritised into Kanchipura and Kanchimanagara, the latter indicative of its commercial growth into a great or more prestigious market.

Kanchi was the centre of one of the two major cotton producing regions of Tamil Nadu, the other being Madurai. The demand, both inland and foreign, for the cotton cloth of south India encouraged new centres of production and Kanchi developed into a premier weaving centre in south India. Although Pallava inscriptions hardly provide detailed evidence of this process of growth, the early Chola records, particularly of the period of Uttama Chola, make special provisions for the weaver communities, indicating that by the tenth century this city had become the most prestigious textile production centre, with weavers specially chosen for producing royal garments. With the emergence of numerous weaving centres around Kanchipuram, this city came to represent the venue of the *mahanadu* or corporate organisation of the weavers, which controlled production of cloth, its marketing and trade with the outside world.

Such a *managaram* more often owed its creation to state sponsorship than did a mere *nagaram* or market centre. The other *managaram* of the Pallavas was the port of Mamallapuram on the coast. Both acted as the centres of a large network of maritime commerce which connected Tondaimandalam with the outside world. While Mamallapuram is on the coast, Kanchipuram's location on the banks of the Palar provided easy access to the port of Mamallapuram as also to Vayalur, another important Pallava centre on the coast at the mouth of the Palar.

IV

Using the networks and centres model in his study of market centres in south India in the Pallava-Chola period, Kenneth R. Hall has argued that Kanchi's economic growth was also linked to the development of inland commerce in which it played a dominant role. There is no clear evidence, however, of such a link in the Pallava period, for the earliest datable reference to a *nagaram*, which served as the nuclear marketing centre of the agrarian unit called the *nadu*, which was its local marketing territory, is of the early Chola period. In the Pallava inscriptions very few *nagarams* are met with and their relation to the agrarian unit called *kurram* or *kottam* of the Pallava period cannot be ascertained. In all there are four *nagarams* known from Pallava inscriptions. These are, Virincipuram in the north Arcot district on the south bank of the Palar (Seruvalaimanglam) of the eighth century; Tiruvadigai, near Cuddalore on the coast, in the south Arcot district, of the late ninth century; Kilur in the south Arcot district, an inland market centre on the banks of the Ponniar; and Tirunagesvaram (Kumaramarttandapuram) in the Tanjavur district on the banks of the Arisil, a distributary in the Kaveri delta. Twenty-four *kottams* or *kurrams* are traditionally assigned to the Tondaimandalam region, of which only a few are known from Pallava records. Such a network-centre model is hence not useful in the context of the Pallava period. Hall's study of the *nagaram* of the Chola period is, however, more consistent with this marketing system into which the itinerant merchant guilds were drawn from the eleventh century onwards. Itinerant merchant guilds trading with South-east Asia and Ceylon are visible in the Pallava records only from the ninth century. The *manigramam* is the only such guild known to Pallava inscriptions from Takua Pa on the Isthmus of Kra in south-east Asia.

Kanchipuram became a secondary political centre under the Cholas, but its commercial character continued as before. Even when it lost its importance as a political centre at the end of the Chola period, its sacred character helped to retain its vitality as a commercial centre down to modern times. Mamallapuram was superseded by Nagappattinam as the chief port of the Cholas, but continued to be a part of the huge commercial network till about the thirteenth century.

The *nagarams* of Tiruvadi, Tirukkovalur (Kilur) and Virincipuram continued as market centres under the Cholas, but their sustained importance as religious centres helped in their continuance as urban centres in the Vijayanagar and post-Vijayanagar periods. Evidence of monetary transactions in the Pallava period is absent and no recognisable

Pallava coinage has survived. The use of gold in religious gifts shows that gold deposits were made with the temple for various purposes, including rituals and payments in paddy for services.

The increasing commercial activity in the Chola period, together with the use of money, is reflected in the emergence of *nagarams* from the ninth century as marketing centres. The proliferation of *nagarams* and the pattern of their distribution have led Hall to treat them as marketing centres for the respective *nadus* in which they were located, each *nadu* serving as the local marketing territory for the *nagaram*. Eventually the *nagarams* became points of intersection for the exchange of local goods for exotic and locally unavailable goods in which the itinerant merchant corporations traded. Thus, the *nagarams* were brought into a wider network of international trade from the eleventh century onwards with a heightened activity in the twelfth and thirteenth centuries. Hall has built up the interesting theory of networks-centres, the villages of the *nadu* connected to the *nagarams* (one per *nadu*), the *nagarams* in turn linked with higher marketing centres or trade centres called *erivirapattanas* and *managarams* where the guilds controlled a major part of the trade and commercial activities. This proved to be a major factor in the urbanisation of the twelfth and thirteenth centuries, what Burten Stein calls 'temple urbanisation', for the temples, particularly larger ones, were the largest consumers, apart from the ruling elite, of goods both from inland and abroad.

The simultaneous appearance of a large number of diverse non-agricultural occupational groups in such centres resulted in an elaboration of the temple centres with separate quarters for merchants, artisans and weavers in particular, most of whom were accommodated in the *tirumadaivilagam* of the temple as seen in Manimangalam and Chidambaram in the twelfth and thirteenth centuries. The highly complex social stratification of the twelfth and thirteenth centuries, with the dual division of the Right and Left Hand castes, apart from the Brahman and high caste non-Brahman *(velala)* groups seems to be another notable feature of this urbanisation. The Right and Left Hand divisions have baffled all attempts at a clear definition of caste groupings but their connection with the emergence of specialised crafts and artisan groups is undeniable.

Nagarams, undoubtedly, represented potential centres of urban growth, but not all *nagarams* became huge urban centres. Most of them were no more than a common market for the *nadu* villages and helped in the exchange of local goods including paddy. In places where the demand for goods from distant regions created a market for the itinerant merchant groups traversing all parts of south India, irrespective of political boundaries, the urban growth was rapid, and at times, phenomenal.

The route character of some regions like Pudukkottai-Ramanathapuram and Salem-Coimbatore also acted as a stimulant to the growth of urban centres. The Pudukkottai region, which was a buffer between the Chola and Pandya heartlands, assumed great significance from the tenth century when the imperial Cholas struck up a close alliance through matrimonial ties with the Irukkuvel chiefs of Kodumbalur in order to extend their control over Madurai and surrounding regions and over the trade that passed through it to Sri Lanka.

As a buffer zone between the Cholas and Pandyas, the major battles between these two powers were fought in or on the outskirts of the region. Its commercial importance in the Sangam Age is recognised through such numismatic and epigraphic evidence as the hoard of Roman coins probably deposited there in the late first or early second century A.D. and the early Tamil Brahmi inscriptions in Sittannavasal in the Pudukkottai region. Sittannavasal was a major centre of the Jains and looking at the distribution of early Jain centres (Tamil-Brahmi inscriptions in natural caverns on hills) it seems that they tended to appear along old trade routes.

In this region commerce was not linked with a concentration of population or local demand as in the rich Kaveri valley. The *manigramam* of Kaverippattinam migrated and settled in this region around the tenth or eleventh century. The nearby post of Tondi received in the early period products such as aloeswood, silk and sandal, which are known from the same region even as late as in the thirteenth century under the Pandyas.

The marked increase in commerce from the tenth to the thirteenth centuries is reflected also in the activity of the *ayyavole* or *ainnurruvar* guild and the *manigramam* which appear here around the tenth century and become extremely active in both Pudukkottai and Ramanathapuram areas, the latter being known as Chettinad in modern times.

Kodumbalur was a *nagaram* of considerable size where the *manigramam* was active, apart from being the political or administrative centre of the *irukkuvels* of Konadu. Narttamalai (Nagarattarmalai) on the way to Kodumbalur was a *nagaram* with which the *Tisai Ayirattu Ainnurruvar* or the merchant corporation of the Five Hundred had active links in the eleventh century.

South of Pudukkottai in the Ramanathapuram district two major centres of merchant activity were Kamudi and Piranmalai, where in the tenth and thirteenth centuries members of several merchant organisations met and recorded their endowments to the local deities in a joint donation. In both the records reference is made to eighteen *pattinams*, thirty-two *valarpurams* and sixty-four *kadigaittavalams* from which members hailed. While a few of these places can be identified with well-known towns, quite a large number of them cannot be located. *Tavalam* would seem to represent a fair, while *pattinam* was undoubtedly a town of considerable commercial importance, and more often a port. *Valarpuram* would perhaps have been a growing trade centre.

In the twelfth and thirteenth centuries the merchant corporations of the Five Hundred and the *valanjiyar* of Sri Lanka are seen making endowments at the temples of Shivapuri, Tirunelveli and Aruppukkottai, also in the Ramanathapuram district, during the period of the Pandyas who recovered this region slowly by the end of the twelfth century.

Several *nagarams* of this region are known to have interacted with the itinenant guilds. They are Vanavanmadevipuram (Sattur), Kulasekkarapuram (Devadanam), Rajanarayanapuram (Pillaiyarpatti) and Velangudi (Veniya-nagaram). A late thirteenth century inscription from Tittandatanapuram records an agreement made by several merchant groups like the Anjuvnnam, Manigramam and the Samanta Pandasalis on the levy of certain taxes on commodities sold and purchased for the rebuilding expenses of the local Shiva temple. An *erivirappattinam* was located at Idaivali (Tirumalagandarkottai, Pudukkottai taluk, Ramnad district), probably one of several such warehouses protected by the merchant guilds with their own troops.

Erivirapattanas have been described as 'inland ports' by Hall and as having come up only in remote and inhospitable areas. This view is based on the fact that the Ramanathapuram region has been classified as a tribal area, where the martial tribe of Maravars was predominant even from the Sangam Age. It would, however, be more correct to look at these as centres on trade routes used as warehouses by itinerant merchants, who often got such centres converted into specially protected warehouses with royal sanction or sometimes on their own in the absence of a recognisable political overlord and defended them with their own troops. *Erivira*, which Hall interprets as heroes of the road, had been earlier translated as mercenary soldiers armed with spears and hence associated with armed protection. The militant character of these merchant guilds, whose caravans moved with armed protection, is well attested by epigraphic references to their use of force in some centres. *Erivirapattanas* on such trade routes were Basinikonda (Siravalli) in Chittur district, Tirumalagandarkottai (Ramnad district), Vikramacholapuram (eleventh century Vembatti, Coimbatore district) and Ayyapolil Kattur (Ponneri taluk, Chingleput district). The reference to an *erivirapattana* called Rajaraja *Erivirapattana* in the Tirunelveli district is particularly significant as it was part of a large urban settlement where the temple, its treasury and temple servants had been placed under the protection of the army called *munrukai mahasenai,* taken to be the Chola army stationed there after the Pandya country was conquered and placed under Chola-Pandya viceroys.

V

In south India, the revival of long-distance trade in the tenth century as a part of the increase in South Asian trade involved not only the merchant guilds but considerably influenced the external policy of the Cholas. The Chola wars in south Karnataka may be described as an attempt to establish trade links and to control the major trade route between Karnataka and Tamil Nadu, facilitating the easy movement of the *ayyavole* or *nanadesis.* Their attacks on northern Sri Lanka and their occupation of it for nearly eight decades in the eleventh century were not mere pillaging or plundering attacks as held by G.W. Spencer, but a deliberate policy of encouraging new trade ventures by enabling already existing pockets of Tamil culture dominated by merchants to engage in lucrative commercial ventures. Presumably, mutual benefit rather than attempts at tight political control over trade and trading communities was the motivating force behind such ventures. The same motive led to the two major maritime expeditions of Rajendra I and Kulottunga I in South-east Asia ending up in Srivijaya, obviously to establish trading rights in these regions and over the much coveted Isthmus of Kra to reach China. Chola missions to China in the eleventh century and Kulottunga's physical presence in Cambodia, his coins, exchange of gifts, including the 'tribute missions' mentioned in the Smaller Leiden Grant, grants of lands and villages to the Buddhist *vihara* at Nagappattinam and abolition of tolls are all part of a trade policy of this early medieval dynasty. It is significant that in the wake of these military expeditions, the south Indian trade guilds begin to appear in Sri Lanka, Burma, Malaysia and Java. The recent excavations in Takua Pa indicate a great deal of Tamil influence between the ninth and twelfth centuries. Recent work on the dynamics of South Asian trade shows that trade overtures or agreements acquired some legitimacy through religious donations to temples and *viharas*. This is clearly illustrated in the elaboration of the port of Nagappattinam where a Buddhist *vihara* of considerable size and importance was erected by the Sailendra king to which the Chola rulers made liberal endowments. Earlier Nagappattinam is known through literary references as a *bhakti* centre of Shaiva and Vaishnava creeds. It was drawn into the huge network of overseas trade with the active trade policy of Rajaraja I and Rajendra and later Kulottunga I in the eleventh century.

The persistence of Buddhist influence in Nagappattinam, particularly Theravada influence, in the eleventh and twelfth centuries may be attributed to the trade relationships of South–east Asian countries with the south Coromandel coast. Through Srivijaya, at first China, and later, Burma and Sri Lanka were involved in this activity. Reference has been made to the tribute missions from South-east Asian islands. Chinese gold came into the port in the eleventh century. Chola missions to China during the period of Rajaraja I and Kulottunga I are recorded in Chinese annals.

With Kulottunga's accession to the Chola throne much of the trade in the Andhra region was also regulated by the Chola kings through the itinerant guilds Visakhapattinam, also called Kulottungasolan-pattinam, became a leading port where the *ayyavole* acted jointly with the *anjuvannam* or Arab merchant organisation known to have traded even in the ninth century on the Kerala coast.

State patronage of the *ayyavole* and other major guilds is increasingly attested by several inscriptions of the Cholas and Pandyas, and oral tradition refers to a specific invitation by the Pandyas to a Vaishya community which was part of the guild to settle in their kingdom. In consolidating their conquests, the Cholas, particularly Rajaraja I and Rajendra I, seem to have used the *nagaram* as much as the *brahmadeya* as interdependent agents of political synthesis in Karnataka and elsewhere in south India. A major example of this policy is seen in the conquest of Pandya country and the appearance of *brahmadeya* and *nagaram*, together with the itinerant merchant guild, in Rajaraja *chaturvedimangalam* and Servanmadevi *chaturvedimangalam*.

A recent study of the *ayyavole* guild has shown that such guilds were controlled not by one religious community, but various groups including the *agrahara* Brahmans who were either collectively or individually land owners. One can perceive a changing pattern of land ownership in the twelfth century when non-agricultural groups figure more prominently in control of land and at the same time exercising commercial influence.

The *citrameli periyanadu* of Tamil Nadu, evidently an organisation of land owners drawn from various social groups, wielded great economic and political influence from the twelfth century onwards. Consisting of many non-Brahman landlords *(velalas)*, this body joined with merchant guilds in control of trade in certain areas, particularly urban centres. In addition to textiles, fragrant woods, spices and incense, in which the merchant guilds traded, a number of agricultural commodities are also found mentioned in inscriptions referring to both these organisations. There is some indication that agricultural surplus was mobilised and brought from rural areas to urban settlements through *nagaram* members. Thus agricultural surplus made possible the expansion of urban settlements as seen from the marked development of such centres from the twelfth century onwards. The rise in the power of these land-owning groups, *velalas*, the *kaikkolas* or the weavers and merchants also indicates a greater sharing of authority between the Brahman and non-Brahman caste groups and increasing social mobility, whereas in the earlier period, the power structure was mainly controlled by a small ruling class and high Brahman castes, both as priests and land owners.

Areas of economic importance in medieval Tamil Nadu have not been clearly defined. Much of the commercial importance of Pudukkottai region and the Tamraparni valley may be due to the nature of commodities traded in. Inscriptional data on this are tantalisingly meagre, although one could expect to get some details by a close examination of the unpublished texts.

Production and craft centres are equally difficult to locate, as inscriptions present a great many problems of interpretation. It has been possible, however, to locate centres of textile industry, the earliest known industry of south India, in Kanchipuram, Madurai, Kumbakonam and Coimbatore. One of the promising areas for a study of craft production is the region of Coimbatore and Salem usually called Kongunadu, where thirteenth century inscriptions indicate large-scale artisan activity contributing to 'temple urbanisation', and their participation in important civic duties for which they were conferred special privileges. *Idangai, valangai* divisions are more prominently mentioned in the records coming from such areas. In such places the merchants assumed control and management of temples and even acted as protectors of the craftsmen and artisans, obviously due to the interdependence of these two sections of the commercial world. Erode and Mudikondan were specially noted for merchant domination over local temples, particularly in the latter (Desi Uyyakkondapattana) where merchants of the eighteen towns north and south of the river Kaveri made several grants to the local Vishnu temple. Mudikondan was not only a commercial town of great importance on the route from Tamil Nadu to Karnataka founded by Rajendra I, but it also later became a military station of the Hoysala Ballala II in the twelfth century.

VI

The presence of *paraga-nagarattar*, seafaring merchants, in the Salem region as early as the tenth century is perhaps indicative of the potential of this region for long-distance trade.

The revival of south India's active participation in Asian trade from the ninth century once again saw the emergence of coastal towns with a significant shift in the location of major ports now oriented to serve new hinterlands, as for example, Nagappattinam at the mouth of the Kaveri serving the core region of the Cholas. Nagappattinam superseded Mamallapuram, the latter still the outlet for the Kanhcipuram hinterland but subordinate to other Chola ports. None of the Sangam Age ports, with the exception of Korkai on the Pandya coast and perhaps also Marakkanam-Sopatma, are heard of on the Chola coast. A series of secondary towns, however, once more dot the coastal line starting from Tiruppalaivanam (Ponneri taluk, Chingleput district), the northernmost in the Tamil region, down south to the coast of Tiruneveli district where Korkai and Kayal are located.

Tiruppalaivanam, which later gave place to Pulicat north of Madras, Kattur an Erivirappattana and Mayilarppil (now in Madras) together served the region north of Kanchipuram from the eleventh to thirteenth centuries.

Kovlam, Tiruvadandia and Taiyur close to Tiruvadandai north of Mamallapuram Sadurangappattinam and Puduppattinam south of Mamallapuram show the increase in the coastal towns towards the end of the thirteenth century, where the constant presence of the merchant groups of the Five Hundred suggests that most of them served as halting places for the itinerant traders on a coastal road or even perhaps coastal shipping right through.

Marakkanam, called Rajarajapperalam, Tiruvadi with salt manufacturing villages around it and modern Cuddalore known in medieval times as Nissankamallan-pattana, Tirumanikuli, and Tiruttinainagar (Tirthanagari), all on the coast in the Cuddalore taluk of the south Arcot district, represent a series of salt manufacturing centres and trade centres between the eleventh and the thirteenth centuries. Kaverippattinam and modern Porto Novo, both in the delta region at the mouth of the Kaveri, served the core areas of the Cholas. Korkai and Kayalpattinam of the Pandyan coast served the extreme southern areas under Pandya control.

BIBLIOGRAPHY

Abraham, M.M., *The Ayyavole Guild of Early Medieval South India*, unpublished M.Phil. Dissertation, Jawaharlal Nehru University, New Delhi 1978.

Appadorai, Arjun, 'Right and Left Hand Castes in South India', *Indian Economic and Social History Review*, Vol. II, Nos. 2 and 3, 1974.

Aravamuthan, T.G., 'A Pandyan Issue of Punch Marked Coins', *Journal of Numismatic Society of India*, Vol. VI, 1944.

Champakalakshmi, R., 'Archaeology and Tamil Literary Tradition', *Puratattva*, No. 8, 1975-76.

-------'Growth of Urban Centres in South India: Kudamukku-Palaiyarai, the twin city of the Colas', *Studies in History*, Vol I, No. 1, January-June 1979.

-------'South India', *Jain Art and Architecture*, Vol. I, Bharatiya Jnanpith, New Delhi 1974.

------'Urbanization in South India: The Role of Ideology and Polity, Presidential Address: Ancient Indian Section, *Proceedings Indian History Congress*, Srinagar 1986.

Govindasamy, M.S., *The Role of Feudatories in Later Chola History*, Annamalai University, Annamalainagar, 1979.

Hall, Kenneth R., *Trade and Statecraft in the Age of the Colas*, New Delhi 1980.

Mahadevan, I., 'Corpus of Tamil Brahmi Inscriptions', *Seminar on Inscriptions* (ed R. Nagaswamy), Madras 1968.

-------'The Ancient Name of Arikamedus', *Suryanarayana Sastri Centenary Volume* (ed N. Subrahmaniam), Madurai 1970.

-------Tamil Brahmi Inscription', Department of Archaeology, Tamil Nadu 1970.

Mahalingam, T.V., *Kancipuram in Early South Indian History*, Madras 1969.

Maloney, Clarence, 'Archaeology in South India: Accomplishments and Prospects', *Essays on South India* (ed B. Stein), New Delhi 1976.

-------'The Beginnings of Civilization in South India', *Journal of Asian Studies*, Vol. XXIX, No. 3, 1970.

Minakshi, C., *Administration and Social Life under the Pallavas*, Madras 1977 (rev ed).

Narayanan, M.G.S., *Cultural Symbiosis in Kerala*, Trivandrum 1972.

Nayar, Balakrishnan T., *The Dowlaishe Varam Hoard of Eastern Chalukyan and Chola Coins*, Bulletin of the Madras Government Museum, Vol IX, No. 2, 1966.

Ramasamy, Vijaya, *The Weaver Communities of the Kanchipuram Region, circa A.D. 700-1700*, unpublished M.Phil Dissertation, Jawaharlal Nehru University, New Delhi.

Ratnagar, S., *Encounters: The Westerly Trade of the Harappa Civilization*, Delhi 1981.

Sastri, K.A. Nilakantha, *The Colas*, Madras 1975 (reprint).

Spencer, G.W., 'The Politics of Plunder: The Cholas in Eleventh Century Ceylon', *Journal of Asian Studies*, Vol. XXV, May 1976.

Stein, B., 'Integration of the Agrarian System of South India', *Land Control and Social Structure in Indian History* (ed R.E. Frykenberg), Wisconsin University Press, Madison 1969.

------*Peasant State and Society in Medieval South India*, Oxford University Press, New Delhi 1980.

-------'The State and the Agrarian Order in South India: A Historiographical Critique, *Essays on South India* (ed B. Stein), New Delhi 1976.

Subbarayalu, Y., *Political Geography of the Chola Country*, Tamil Nadu Department of Archaeology, Madras 1973.

Vanaja, R., *The Madras Museum Collection of Punch Marked Coins – A Study*, unpublished M.Litt. Dissertation, Madras University, Madras 1955.

Wheeler, R.E.M. 'Arikamedu: An Indo-Roman Trading Station on the East Coast of India', *Ancient India*, No.2, July 1946.

HISTORICAL WRITING ON URBANISATION IN MEDIEVAL INDIA

J.S. GREWAL

Insistence on the paucity of urban studies may be taken as a sure sign of growing interest in the study of urbanisation in India. Dr K.N. Chaudhuri observes, for instance, that few aspects of Indian studies are more neglected than historical geography and within this area of neglect urban history occupies a special place.[1] Dr Howard Spodek underlines this neglect in a bibliographical analysis of urban studies in India.[2] In the first 'occasional paper' published by the Urban History Association of India, Prof. S.C. Misra refers to urban history as an area which has remained relatively unexplored in India. He goes on to explain that since urban studies demand the prior development of interest in theory-based depth studies focusing on social and economic problems, and in India such studies themselves grew in volume only recently, it is no surprise that we have not yet advanced to exploit this field in full measure.[3]

I

Interest in urbanisation has surely increased recently, but the pioneers of social and economic history in India did not neglect this aspect of socio-

[1] 'Some Reflections on the Town and Country in Mughal India', *Modern Asian Studies*, 12, Part 1 (1978), 77.

[2] 'Urbanization in India', *Journal of Urban History* (May 1980), 250-52.

[3] 'Urban History in India: Possibilities and Perspectives', Occasional Papers Series: 1, UHAI, Amritsar 1982, 6 and 7.

economic history altogether. Dr K.M. Ashraf, for instance, was aware of the role played by towns and cities in the growth of industries in northern India: 'the producers of a commodity in small towns arranged with dealers of those goods in a big city to supply them with finished goods for distribution inland or for export outside'.[4] While discussing the major industries like textiles, metalwork, stone and brick work, paper, sugar and leather-work, Dr Ashraf refers to specific urban centres: for instance, Deogir, famous for exceptionally fine and beautiful cloth; Cambay, famous for costly silks; Delhi, known as much for its masons and stonecutters as for its metalwork and markets.[5]

With their network of markets, the towns and cities played a vital role in trade and commerce.The surplus corn was usually carried to the neighbouring towns for distribution over the country. 'Industrial goods were usually made or manufactured expressly for sale in a suitable market'. A number of roads and pathways all over the country, kept in good condition by the state for administrative purposes, were used by traders as well. Administrative centres like Multan and Lahore, or capital cities like Delhi, served as big clearing-houses for whole provinces. Just as there were hereditary caste guilds for manufacture, there were special classes or particular communities for large-scale business. The petty business of the town was also in the hands of professional merchants. The Multanis in the north and the Gujarati Banias on the western coast were the most important business communities; the foreign merchants were important in foreign trade; the *banjaras* were famous as carriers of commodities; the Bhats of Rajasthan were well known as guides of caravans; there was an organised class of brokers in all large towns and cities; legal agents or *vakils* were regularly employed by principals to conduct business on their behalf; a system of banking was prevalent all over the country, making use of *hundis;* and a whole class of moneylenders, called *sahukars* or *mahajans*, advanced loans *inter alia* to support commercial undertakings.[6]

Dr Ashraf makes brief comments on the changing appearance of the cities. Spacious mosques, domes, gateways and arches were added to temples, tanks and massive buildings of the pre-Turkish town. The site of a town was carefully chosen for reasons of security, defence and the supply of water. Intersecting roads were connected with the main gates

Life and Conditions of the People of Hindustan, Munshiram Manoharlal, New Delhi 1970 (2nd ed), 124-25.

[5]Ibid., 127, 128, 130 and 134.

[6]Ibid., 136, 137, 138, 139 and 140.

of the city wall, providing the main bazars or shopping centres of the city. Different wings of the bazars were occupied by special classes of tradesmen and guilds of craftsmen. The city as a whole was divided into separate quarters for various social groups on the basis of race, creed, caste or occupation. The scavengers, leather-dressers, beggars and the like were made to live on the outskirts of towns and cities. Social differentiation was reflected also in the size and structure of houses. The large cities, according to Dr Ashraf, had a population of 200,000 or more.[7] These observations leave no doubt that towns and cities figure prominently in the *Life and Conditions of the People of Hindustan*. It is also evident, however, that Dr Ashraf was not interested in urbanisation as such.

Over fifteen years later, in the early 1950s, Prof. Muhammad Habib put forth a general hypothesis of 'urban revolution' in northern India during the thirteenth and fourteenth centuries. According to him, in pre-Turkish India, 'the higher classes appropriated the cities and towns exclusively to themselves while the workers lived in unprotected villages and in settlements outside the city wall'.[8] With the coming of the Turks in the thirteenth century all discrimination against the city workers was removed. 'When the Turks entered the cities, the Hindu low-caste workers entered along with them. And they came to stay.' They were needed by the new rulers for industrial as well as administrative purposes. 'The cities, under the new regime, were developing into thriving centres of industry and commerce'.[9] This 'revolution' was made possible by the emancipation and multiplication of labouring classes in spite of 'the unchanging instruments of production'.[10] The Turkish ruling class helped the 'revolution' by their preference for fortified towns and cities rather than the countryside.[11]

According to Prof. Muhammad Habib, the rapid growth of the city of Delhi under the Turkish Sultans reflected the 'great changes' that were coming over the country as a whole. The rulers with their palaces and huge establishments, imitated by the members of the Turkish governing class with their large mansions and enormous retinues, spent much of the surplus collected from the provinces in the markets of the city of Delhi. 'There were general markets for things of common use and specialised

[7]Ibid., 198, 199, 200, 205, 275 and 283-84.

[8]'Introduction', Elliot and Dowson's *History of India As Told by Its Own Historians*, II, Cosmopolitan, Aligarh 1952, 43.

[9]Ibid., 55.

[10]Ibid., 61 and 62.

[11]Ibid., 69 and 70.

markets for grain, cloth, horses, and slaves of all nationalities'. Industries grew up along with commerce, supported by the activity of merchants and brokers and *sahukars*, besides the artisans and craftsmen. The city developed its own culture, with its colleges as well as its courtesans, its taverns and brothels as well as its dancing girls. 'Delhi by the end of the thirteenth century had come to occupy a unique position in the Asian world'.[12]

The hypothesis of urban revolution has been examined critically by Prof. Irfan Habib in the light of more empirical evidence and better understanding of the social and economic history of the period.[13] He supports the view that there was expansion in the urban economy during the thirteenth and fourteenth centuries; the size, and possibly the number, of cities increased; and there was increase in craft production and commerce. The replacement of Rajput rural nobility by the Turkish urban ruling class, together with a new system of appropriating surplus produce from land, resulted in the consumption of a large part of that surplus in cities and towns. Prof. Irfan Habib does not, however, subscribe to the view that the city workers, or the peasants in the countryside, came to enjoy a larger degree of emancipation under the Turks. Nor does he subscribe to the view that there was no change in the instruments of production. He argues in fact that important changes and improvement in technology came about during this period, leading to larger production.[14] The view that the pace of urbanisation increased in northern India after the establishment of Turkish rule appears now to be correct.[15]

It is significant to note, however, that virtually no single town or city of the pre-Mughal period has been studied so far. The generalisations on urbanisation during the period are based on scattered references in contemporary sources to matters having a bearing on urban centres, crafts, commerce, morphological features and elements of population. The only attempt to concentrate on the history of an urban centre has a symbolic value. The circumstances of the foundation of Batala in the Upper Bari Doab during the late fifteenth century and its rapid growth in the first fifty years of its history in relation to extension of cultivation

[12]Ibid., 62-68.

[13]'Economic History of the Delhi Sultanate — An Essay in Interpretation', *The Indian Historical Review*, IV, No. 2 (January 1978), 287-303.

[14]Irfan Habib, 'Technological Changes and Society: 13th and 14th Centuries', *Proceedings Indian History Congress*, Varanasi 1969.

[15]For example, S. Nurul Hasan, 'Inaugural Address', *Studies in Urban History* (eds J. S. Grewal and Indu Banga), Guru Nanak Dev University, Amritsar 1981, 4-5.

providing a suitable hinterland, and a network of trade providing links with the outside world and attracting business communities and craftsmen to the town, come out clearly from bits and pieces of evidence put together and interpreted in the political context of the times.[16] We also know that batala was not the only town to be newly founded in the Punjab during the late fifteenth century.[17]

II

The work done on urbanisation during the Mughal period is relatively large.[18] The pioneer for the urban history of Mughal India, W.H. Moreland, wrote in the twenties, a decade before Ashraf. According to Moreland, the contemporary Europeans noticed the 'abundance of towns' in the Mughal empire; they were also impressed by the size of Indian cities. His own estimate, from a quarter to half a million of persons, for the largest cities of India during the sixteenth century is worth serious consideration.[19] We do not know the proportion of urban population in the ten million estimated for the whole of India by Moreland. That the large majority of population lived in the countryside is pretty evident from the evidence we have.

In *India at the Death of Akbar*, Moreland makes many other observations which are relevant for urbanisation in Mughal India. He notices, for example, that the administration of the principal cities and seaports in the Mughal empire was in the hands of 'separate officers'.[20] The position of the men of business depended upon the personality of the *kotwal*, or the officer in charge of local administration where there was no *kotwal*; on the whole, 'the cities appear to have been reasonably comfortable places for residence and business'.[21] The personality of the local administrator affected also the custom duties, the scales for which as a matter of policy were 'distinctly moderate'.[22] For inland transit dues, however, the position of merchants was less favourable.[23] The cost of bribes, presents, taxes and even thefts had in the long run to be borne by the consumer. Therefore, these conditions did not seriously interfere with trade and

[16]J.S. Grewal, *In the By-Lanes of History*, Indian Institute of Advanced Study, Shimla 1975, 'Introduction'.

[17]J.S. Grewal, *Guru Nanak in History*, Panjab University, Chandigarh 1979 (2nd ed), 10-11.

[18]S. Nurul Hasan, 'Inaugural Address', *Studies in Urban History*, 5.

[19]*India at the Death of Akbar*, Atma Ram & Sons, Delhi 1962 (reprint), 7, 8, 9, 12, 14 and 21.

[20]Ibid., 31. [21]Ibid., 35. [22]Ibid., 43. [23]Ibid., 45.

commerce. Nevertheless, these conditions were not favourable to the establishment of industry 'on a capitalist basis'.[24]

Moreland assumed that towns and cities were the centres of crafts production. The urban ruling class constituted the chief consumers of the most noticed crafts: jewellery, ivory work, perfumes and drugs.[25] Silk-weaving industry was localised in Cambay, Ahmedabad and Pattan in the province of Gujarat; and in the capital cities in Kashmir, Lahore and Multan, while Agra and Fatehpur had royal *karkhanas*. Manufacture of woollens was localised in Kashmir, Lahore and Agra; and these centres were also known for carpet weaving.[26] Similarly, many cities were known as the centres of cotton textiles: Agra, Lahore, Multan, Sukkar, Thatta, Ahmedabad, Pattan, Baroda, Broach, Surat, Cambay, Burhanpur and Golconda. The cotton industry was by far the most important handicraft in India during the Mughal period.[27]

The manner in which industry was organised in cities and towns is defined by Moreland as 'the artisan system of production'. The management of business was not separated from the work of manufacture, and production was carried on by artisans without superior capitalist direction. It did not imply, however, that it was not possible to undertake great enterprises. Such enterprises were made possible by the system of contracts in a large number of small units of work. The royal *karkhanas* represented another kind of industrial organisation. Moreland visualises the possibility of 'private workshops of similar type' in the case of some handicrafts. Generally, however, the artisans worked for the benefit of merchants and middlemen depending upon them for benefit of depending upon them for current expenses. Patronage by persons in power could protect individuals, but the great majority of the workers had not much to hope beyond subsistence.[28] Moreland refers to the flow of the rural population to urban centres in search of employment, and briefly discusses urban wages.[29]

In connection with trade and commerce, Moreland takes into account the principal Indian seaports as distinct from the establishment of European ports in the Indian Ocean. Similarly, he takes notice of the

[24]Ibid., 47. [25]Ibid., 150. [26]Ibid., 163-66. [27]Ibid., 170-71.
[28]Ibid., 172-76.

According to S. Nurul Hasan, the various categories of *zamindars* and *ashraf* had something to do with the growth and expansion of handicrafts and trade and, consequently, the growth of towns: *Studies in Urban History*, 4-5.

[29]*India at the Death of Akbar*, 177-80.

trade routes in the subcontinent before commenting on the organisation of trade. Commerce in India was carried on by a small number of castes: the *Banias* of Gujarat and the *Chettis* of the Coromandel coast, besides the Muslim merchants of the seaboard. Though he had no information on the trading communities of northern India, Moreland surmised that they were largely the same as in the early twentieth century. The distribution of a few communities over a large area was favourable to the development of business organisation, particularly the system of credit as it obtained in India during the sixteenth and seventeenth centuries.[30] Moreland underlines the important role played by the merchant-princes, like Virji Vohra of Surat and Malaya of Pulicat, who dominated the commercial outlook of the period. An Indian commercial centre contained an indefinite number of men of business graded in accordance with their ability and command over capital, all eager to participate in commercial ventures not conflicting with the interests of the topmost merchants.[31]

During the seventeenth century, on the whole, new markets became available to Indian producers of indigo, calico, saltpetre and raw silk, but there was only a limited market for import trade. The mass of the people were too poor to be interested in available foreign goods; the middle classes were few in number; and the market offered by the rulers and the nobility was governed by fashion or caprice. The general effect of administrative activities was to leave very little to producers, and to offer the surplus in rewards to energy or ingenuity exerted in unproductive ways. Thus, a relatively large number of producers contributed half their gross income to the support of a relatively small number of economic parasites. 'The unproductive population was to be found mainly in towns or camps, while production was carried on chiefly in the villages'; therefore the economic system of the period might be regarded as operating 'to provide the urban population with subsistence below cost'.[32] This system was collapsing towards the end of the seventeenth century. 'Weavers naked themselves, toiled to clothe others. Peasants, themselves hungry, toiled to feed the towns and cities.' Increase in production was the only way out of the impasse and that was virtually

[30]Ibid., 190-99, 204-7, 230, 231, 232-33.

[31]*From Akbar to Aurangzeb*, Oriental Books Reprint Corporation, New Delhi 1972, 152-58.

[32]Ibid., 297-304. Cf. *India at the Death of Akbar*, 87-88.

barred by the administrative methods in vogue.[33]

Moreland's interest in urban centres and urban activity is carried forward by Dr H.K. Naqvi. The *Urban Centres and Industries in Upper India*, as the title of the work suggests, is divided neatly into two parts, one dealing with industries and the other with urban centres, though it is assumed all along that industries by and large were an urban phenomenon. The cities chosen for study are the capital cities of Delhi, Agra and Lahore and the 'commercial towns' of Patna and Banaras. The evidence collected by Dr Naqvi on these cities relates to their location, hinterland, industry, commerce, morphology, population and functional role. But this information remains disproportionate and disjointed, though she tells us much more about these urban centres and industries in general than all of Moreland's work put together. What is clearly demonstrated by Dr Naqvi in her work is that industry and trade played a crucial role in the rise and decline of cities.[34]

Dr Naqvi has produced another monograph, *Urbanisation and Urban Centres under the Great Mughals*, in which the approach is slightly different, and a few more relevant aspects of the subject are brought out. In this volume Dr Naqvi is more explicit about the multiple role of towns, their dependence upon the hinterland and the importance of their links with one another. Differences in the degree of urbanisation in the various regions of the empire were due to the differences of economic development. Dr Naqvi is inclined to attribute urban development in medieval India to the conscious policy of the 'Muslim' rulers, an insistence which is a legacy of a particular brand of political history and which is quite out of place in a socio-economic study. This concern does, however, underline the importance of state action and state policies for urbanisation. In this volume too Dr Naqvi makes a substantial advance upon Moreland in terms of information on the natural resources of the empire, the means of communication and transportation and the chief trading centres of the Mughal empire: Kabul, Lahiri Bandar, Thatta, Ahmedabad, Cambay, Surat, Burhanpur, Anjeli, Jalesar, Satgaon and Hooghly.[35] The attempt here is to complement the information provided in the earlier volume.

[33] *From Akbar to Aurangzeb*, 304-5. The possibility of capitalistic formations in Mughal India has been the subject of study and speculation in the past two decades and nearly all eminent medievalists like S. Nurul Hasan, Satish Chandra and Irfan Habib have expressed their views on this issue.

[34] *Urban Centres and Industries in Upper India 1556-1803*, Asia, Bombay 1968.

[35] *Urbanisation and Urban Centres under the Great Mughals 1556-1707*, Indian Institute of Advanced Study, Shimla 1972.

More work is being done on urban centres and urbanisation in Mughal India than on the earlier period, notably on medieval Gujarat and the medieval Punjab.[36] With one exception, no single city of Mughal India has been given a monographic treatment.[37] Nevertheless we know something about the large cities, but very little about the average or small towns. The only exception is Batala: its growth in the sixteenth and seventeenth centuries, its morphology and townscape, its demographic history, the manufactures and business of the town, its intimate connection with the hinterland and its links with the towns and cities in the region, and indirectly with cities outside the region, and something of its social and cultural life.[38] This brief study of Batala demonstrates the possibilities of writing about many other towns of the Mughal empire. It should be remembered, however, that 'biographies' of towns and cities do not necessarily constitute urban history. [39]

III

A good deal of theoretical 'speculation' on urbanisation has been made possible by empirical research by the social and economic historians of medieval India as well as the general theories of urbanisation. We are able to define the town in terms of the density of population and the non-agricultural occupations of the majority of its inhabitants. The dependence of the town on the surplus produce of the countryside gets underlined in the process, and so does the industrial and commercial activity of the town. Given the interdependence of the country and the town, the role of urban centres in the evolution of society and civilisation can be clearly seen.Consequently, the study of urban history becomes the study of the expansion and contraction of urban centres in dialectical relationship with the economic system, the political apparatus and the societal network.[40] Discarding all Eurocentric definitions of the city, we may grasp the role of cities in our civilisation by concentrating on the

[36]Apart from research projects on urban history of Gujarat and the Punjab by the History Departments of the M.S. University at Baroda and Guru Nanak Dev University at Amritsar, seminars have been organised by these Departments and doctoral research has been encouraged. At Delhi University, Dr S.P. Gupta has completed doctoral research on the urban centres of Mughal Gujarat.

[37]Stephen P. Blake, *Dar-ul-Khilafat-i-Shahjahanabad :The Padshahi Shahar in Mughal India, 1556-1739*, Ph.D. Thesis, University of Chicago, 1974.

[38]J.S. Grewal, *In the By-Lanes of History*,'Introduction'.

[39]S.C. Misra, 'Urban History in India', 5.

[40]Ibid., 7-10.

functions of urban centres as products of the prevailing forms of technology and social institutions.[41]

The empirical work done on Mughal India as well as the readily available evidence makes it obvious that towns and cities were never merely the centres of administration. Quite distinct from their political and military role, they performed economic and cultural functions. There were cities indeed, like the seaport of Surat, which had little political significance.[42] Even when general polity remained relevant for the foundation or initial growth of a town it generally assumed an economic role independent of that polity. The survival of towns despite political changes was invariably due to their economic significance.[43]

The towns were linked not only with the immediate hinterland but also with one another. Prof. Ravinder Kumar's hypothesis of vertical and horizontal linkages appears to find support in known evidence.[44] The *qasba*, or the township of the smallest size, was administratively and economically connected with a score or two of the villages around. There was a market for the surplus produce of the villages, and there were some shopkeepers selling articles not produced in the villages. A few *sahukars* provided credit to cultivators. There were some artisans and craftsmen who manufactured goods for local consumption, including the villages around. Obviously, the *qasba* occupied a crucial position as a link between the rural and urban population.

Almost all *qasbas* were linked to medium-size towns or small cities. As the size of the township increased there came a point when further increase in size brought about qualitative changes so that the medium-size town did not remain merely a large version of the *qasba*. The medium-size towns in turn were linked with a large apical city in the region, completing the vertical network of linkages. The distinctive features of apical cities varied from region to region, and their character depended upon the economic texture and social configuration of the region. The vertical linkages were rather enduring in character.

Horizontal linkages, or linkages between the apical cities of different regions, were meant to facilitate the exchange of material goods and cultural values. The rate of exchange was relatively high under large

[41]K.N. Chaudhuri, 'Some Reflections on the Town and Country in Mughal India', 95.

[42]Ibid., 88-89.

[43]Indu Banga, 'Polity, Economy and Urbanisation in the Upper Bari Doab (1700-1947)', *Studies in Urban History*, 192-205.

[44]Ravinder Kumar, 'The Changing Structure of Urban Society in Colonial India', *The Indian Historical Review*, Vol V, No. 1-2 (July 1978- January 1979), 200-15.

states or empires, as in the sixteenth and seventeenth centuries; it tended to be lower in a polity characterised by regional states, as in the late eighteenth century; but the relation of exchange between different urban constellations did not altogether break down in the absence of a subcontinental empire. On the whole, thus, as the centres of political power and economic and cultural exchange, cities performed a vital role in social life.

IV

In the absence of substantial empirical research, general reflection on urbanisation may not be entirely satisfactory. Equally unsatisfactory, however, would be an empirical study which does not take into account the ideas springing from general reflection. It is possible to concentrate on a single urban centre for grasping the changing contours of urban reality in the concrete. But for a regional study it should be more fruitful to study urban centres in terms of their vertical linkages. For covering more than one region it is necessary to take up all aspects of horizontal linkages too. For a meaningful study of urbanisation, attention may be paid to morphology, social structure, economic functions and ideas in the broad context of polity and economy involving the study of political changes, administrative organisation and state action in relation to physical and social environment, and the study of production and its distribution and exchange. A good number of issues raised about urbanisation in Mughal India can be resolved only by empirical research and theory interacting in dialectical relationship.

SOME ASPECTS OF URBANISATION IN MEDIEVAL INDIA

SATISH CHANDRA

The study of urban centres and urbanisation in India is a part and parcel of the growing recent interest in economic and social history of India. In the fifties, when I was at Aligarh, a Ph.D. thesis had been prepared under the supervision of Prof. Sheikh Abdul Rashid. I was indirectly associated, because the researcher had been my former student at Allahabad and frequently consulted me. An interesting point which emerged from that study was that the concept of Bernier that Indian cities were merely military camps was not supported by the evidence at our disposal. Another interesting conclusion which emerged was that the extent of urbanisation in India during the seventeenth century was much higher than what it was in British India at the beginning of the century. The thesis unfortunately has not been published till now, but I recall that the percentage of the urban population in northern India worked out to over 15 per cent. Prof. Irfan Habib has worked out a figure of about 12.5 to 15 per cent for the urban centres in Mughal India.

Not only Bernier's statement, but unfortunately, the repetition of the idea by Marx in his letters that the cities in India were mere military camps has for long become a barrier in the growth of urban studies in India. Even now perhaps, we have not been able to cross it completely. Some of our notions rest on the models of economic and urban growth put forward in Europe in the forties. I have in mind the model of the development of medieval Europe put forward by Henry Pirenne in which he postulated that towns grow with the growth of trade, particularly long-distance trade, and secondly, that the entire development of society, the growth of a new social order, the capitalist order, is predicated on a kind of a division of labour between the cities and the towns, industry or handicrafts being concentrated largely in the towns and the countryside merely supplying the raw materials and the foodstuffs. In other words, it postulated what might be called a kind of internal colonial structure where the dynamic developmental factors were concentrated in the towns, and the peasants merely were, as Leon Trotsky once observed, 'the pack mules of history'.

The role of agricultural production was largely ignored in this model. In fact, it was virtually assumed that agricultural productivity remained static during the medieval age. Also, demographic factors were not taken into account. With much greater information on medieval times, both the agricultural and the demographic factors have been woven into the new studies. Writers such as Guy Bois have shown that demography and prices had a direct effect on expansion of land under cultivation, with productivity declining on account of cultivation of marginal lands. When population outstripped production, famines reduced population, land fell out of cultivation and productivity rose. This cyclic movement had a direct impact on urban population and urban industry. In some of the early western writings on India, the fact that the towns were not the foci of industry has been emphasised. That in India the towns did not have a separate juridical entity, like the towns in Europe, was used as another argument to prove that the towns in India were merely exploiters, and thus to underline that the totally stagnant oriental society as a whole was incapable of developing. When we look at the processes of development of our society, we have first to discard these ideas and models which have been discarded in the West but unfortunately continue to influence thinking in our country.

We are now moving away from excessive dependence on long-distance trade as a vehicle of social and economic change. This point has been brought out well by Dr Nandi in his Presidential Address to the Ancient Indian History Section of the Indian History Congress in 1984. Dr Nandi has pointed out that the towns in India started reviving in the eleventh century and that feudalisation in the early period did mean a considerable growth of agriculture. This has implications which need careful thinking. Those who do not like the word feudalism are welcome to use some other term as long as we are clear about the basic concept. What I imply by feudalism is a society in which the cultivator is exploited by extra-economic means, by a class which does not work on the land itself. Whether or not this exploitation has a tendency to increase production is an arguable point. Quite obviously, exploitation cannot increase without production growing simultaneously. So, when we try to understand the process of the growth of towns, or the lack of such a process, the growth of agricultural production, the manner in which agricultural surplus is distributed, the structure of the village society, the development as well as the inhibiting factors, all become important. What precise role the growth or decline of long-distance trade plays in the process needs detailed examination.

Prof. R.S. Sharma has argued in his extremely valuable thesis about growth of feudalism in India, that growth of localism was linked on the one hand with the process of giving grants of land to the Brahmans and political decentralisation, and on the other with the decline of long-distance trade. He has further traced the absence of gold coins in north India between the seventh and tenth centuries to decline of long-distance north-south trade in India. Perhaps this thesis could have been fully accepted if there had been a decline of town life all over India during the period. While some of the bigger towns declined, the extent of the decline of town life all over India is still a moot question.

In his address, Dr Nandi has emphasised the decline of coins of small value. Quite obviously, coins of small value had much greater importance for the smaller towns, for local trade and local transactions rather than for long-distance trade. When did the process of urban revival begin? With the arrival of the Turks in the thirteenth century, or earlier, in the eleventh? The arrival of the Turks helped in the process of political integration by breaking down localism, and they helped in opening overland commerce between India, Central Asia and West Asia. These were important factors in the process of the growth of towns in India in the thirteenth and fourteenth centuries. If, however, the process of the revival of towns starts not in the thirteenth century but in the eleventh century, the entire matter would have to be reconsidered. The question is important, because it is possible to argue that historians have a tendency to link political developments too closely with processes such as the growth of towns. The argument that the period before the arrival of the Turks in India was a period of political disintegration, and therefore one during which the growth of towns was not possible, can be equally applied to the period after the decline of the Tughlaq empire, that is, the fifteenth century. It is, in general, a period of political disintegration, especially in north India. But I am somewhat doubtful of its also being a period of the decline of towns. The Sultanate of Delhi shrank to half its former size under Firoz Tughlaq. Yet there is no shrinkage of towns; the period witnessed in fact the establishment of many new towns. It is clear that the entire growth of towns during the period of Firoz Tughlaq is closely linked with agricultural expansion, with the canal network, the improvement of horticulture and the establishment of large numbers of gardens all around the towns. I suppose that the development of gardens and horticulture in the neighbourhood of Delhi would not have been possible without assured supply of water. Even today, if anybody has anything to do with the development of orchards in areas near Delhi, assured supply of water is essential. So, attention to supply of water for irrigation, either through canals or through wells, was a very important development. This applied not only to the Sultanate which helped to popularise a more efficient type of water-wheel (*arhatta*) but also the provincial kingdom which laid considerable emphasis on agriculture. The role of the Afghans in the agricultural expansion also needs to be rethought. We have tended to dismiss the Afghans as merely warriors, as people who were mercenaries of one category of warlords or the other. But the very fact that the Afghans, as distinct from the Turks, settled in the countryside suggests that they must have had something more to do with agriculture, not merely as people who in one way or an other extracted surplus. So, if we are to broaden our earlier understanding, and to link the growth of towns not only with the growth of trade and industry, but also with the growth of agriculture, the so-called period of decline and disintegration would perhaps emerge in a new light.

This would be equally applicable to the eighteenth century. Just as the fifteenth century is projected as a period of disintegration and decline, because of the downfall of the Delhi Sultanate, the eighteenth century has traditionally been presented as a period of disintegration, in which urban life registered a precipitate decline. I have argued elsewhere that even in the context of large towns, such as Agra and Delhi, perhaps we have been too much influenced by the literary outpourings of Urdu poets such as Sauda. The *Shahr Ashob*, in which Sauda lamented the decline of Delhi, is not as much a reflection of reality as we have been inclined to believe. The entire tradition of *Shahr Ashob* was a literary device, and as early as in the middle of the seventeenth century, we find the practice of writing *Shahr Ashob* where the poet wrote of the decline of handicrafts, rise of unworthy competent people, and the low castes. This tradition continued. A stray remark of the author of the *Ma'asir-ul-Umara* in 1772 shows that Delhi was a very flourishing city and that all kinds of arts and crafts were practised there. What do we do when we are faced with diametrically opposite evidence? We try to strike a balance. There certainly was a decline of Delhi. But what type of decline, is a point which needs to be studied because there is no one-to-one relationship. It does not mean that as soon as a city ceases to be an administrative capital, it declines. A great deal depends upon the basis upon which a city was first selected or emerged as an administrative centre, whether it had an agricultural hinterland, the advantage of communications, and so on and so forth.

Another point relates to small towns and their study on a regional basis. Quite obviously, the pattern of small towns would differ from region to region and also from area to area. The growth of *qasbas* in the sixteenth and seventeenth centuries is emphasised. Moreover, whereas in the Sultanate period a *qasba* was a village with a fort, in the sixteenth, and seventeenth centuries, a *qasba* was a village with a market. So the entire concept of the *qasba* changed during the period. How and why, we do not know. Regarding the distribution of the *qasbas* distance-wise, the study of the communication network is very very useful in this process. But we also know that the distribution of towns in their spatial dimensions varied considerably from area to area. We know that throughout the medieval period, there was a maximum distance which the travellers who used horses or oxen normally travelled. Within a distance from ten to twelve miles, there had to be a place where they could stay. This meant a *sarai* or a substantial village, or a *qasba* or some such place. In many cases, the *sarais* were either located in the *qasba* or subsequently *qasbas* developed around them. But quite obviously this does not apply equally to every area. For instance, I do not think that the distribution of *qasbas* in Rajasthan could match the distribution of *qasbas* in the Ganga-Yamuna Doab.

The third point which needs to be studied is the cultural role of the towns. I think we should not consider the cultural aspect to be unimportant. For instance, we always talk of a Delhi culture or of a Lucknow culture. The manner in which these cultures developed is a matter which needs detailed study. I have pointed out elsewhere that even an orthodox ruler like Aurangzeb was not able to suppress the liberal integrationist aspects of Delhi culture. When Aurangzeb went to the south, he sent his daughter Roshanara to Delhi. Roshanara soon set up a centre *(Bait-ul-Ulum)* at Delhi for poets and others who continued the old tradition of liberal integrationist studies. More important, the type of people who were involved in the centre were not merely the nobles, but people drawn from a much broader stratum, the middle class. The economic role of the middle classes has been studied by some scholars, including Dr Iqtidar Alam Khan. To what extent was the middle class able to provide a cultural ethos also? Perhaps this might be linked with the fact that many of the nobles built *mandis* and had their own orchards. Thus, they and their descendants no longer depended upon the patronage of the government. They could live even if they were denied a *jagir* or a *mansab* or if the yield of one had dried up. It was this class which kept life in the city going and provided backing and support to cultural life.

The last point relates to the neglected role of the Marathas. I do not think any careful study has so far been done about the role of the Marathas in relation to the process of urbanisation. The development of Pune alone does not signify a growing process of urbanisation. Even though the hoarded wealth of nobles, *sahukars* etc. all over the Mughal empire was flowing into the Maratha coffers through the process of plunder, we do not see any outburst of manufacturing industries or the arts. The armaments of the Maratha army remained primitive. The Maratha cavalrymen were supposed to be armed only with a spear. Even later, they did not acquire the type of musket which had been developed and was being used by the Afghans. In fact, it was the musket-firing Afghan infantry which was able to repel the Maratha onslaught at Shukar-tal (1752). Contemporary British writers have pointed to the rather primitive nature of the Maratha artillery. Does it mean that the Marathas did not have a strong base of metallurgy, since a strong tradition of metallurgy could only have been provided by the towns? In other words, a low level of urbanisation, or poorly developed artisanal base, particularly in metallurgy, had a much more significant long-range effect on the Marathas than has been postulated so far. To an extent, this was closely linked to the position of the small towns because the small towns not only acted as markets and centres of sale of agricultural produce but also developed as centres of handicrafts. The metallurgical base of the small towns in the upper Ganga valley enabled the Afghan soldiers to be equipped with muskets and all their other requirements.

These are some of the points which need deeper study. Such a study can be made only if we use the records in various regions of the country. We are all extremely eager to develop regional studies. But if all we do in the name of regional study is merely to try and project local heroes to the national level, we neither do any service to the cause of national integration nor arrive at a better understanding of the process of the development of our society. Since we are meeting in south India, in one of its cultural centres located in an extremely rich agricultural hinterland and one which has always had extensive overland and overseas trade links, I hope that some young scholars of the region would undertake an intensive study of the process of urbanisation in the region and answer some of the questions I have broached here.

THE MORPHOLOGY OF A MEDIEVAL INDIAN CITY: A CASE STUDY OF SHAHJAHANABAD

S. NURUL HASAN

It is a welcome sign that Indian historians have turned their serious attention to urban history, at a time when the fast changing landscape of cities has left many of the old recognisable features still intact. Sooner rather than later, many of these would also disappear, leaving behind a few important monuments. It would be difficult then to appreciate fully the meaning of the written record or to fill the gaps on the basis of surviving features.

As is well known, Delhi was populated several times; each time a new part was populated, the earlier parts lost their glory, though they were never depopulated. The ancient Indraprastha (Inderpat) was repopulated when Humayun rebuilt its old fort and the township. The cities of the Tomars survived as three suburban villages; the fort of Prithviraj Chauhan was never fully depopulated as it retained a part of its importance due to Qutb Minar, Quwwat-ul-Islam mosque and the Alai Darwaza. Hauz Khas and the tomb of Shaikh Qutb-ud-din Bakhtiyar Kaki in Mehrauli, Ghiyaspur (which acquired fame due to the tomb of Shaikh Nizam-ud-din Auliya), Kilokheri, Siri, Mubarakpur, Tughlaqabad, Firozabad, Khizrabad, Sher Mandal and Salimgarh have all survived through the centuries in one form or another. The last Mughal capital was, of course, Shahjahanabad, whose foundation stone was laid by Shah Jahan on 9 Muharram 1049H/12 May 1639. The construction of the main Shah Jahan buildings of the fort was completed in nine years. Where the city of Shahjahanabad now stands, some monuments of the Sultanate period have survived, such as the *dargah* of Shah Turkman Biyabani (632H/

1234-35) or the Kalan Masjid, now called Kali Masjid, built by Khan-i-Jahan Maqbul in 789H/1387 . Another important landmark is the Khari Bawri or Baoli (stepwell) as it is called today, which bears two inscriptions of Islam Shah's reign, 952 H/1545 and another 958 H/1551 (being the date of the completion of the Baoli).

This paper, however, deals only with Shahjahanabad. Apart from the still existing old names, and some early eighteenth and nineteenth century works, extensive use has been made of two early Persian works, both of which are published but not used in the present context.

One is *Muraqqa-i-Dehli* by Dargah Quli Khan, who wrote the work as a travelogue when he visited Delhi in 1151 H/1738-39 along with Nizam-ul Mulk Asaf Jah.[1] This work deals with shrines, monuments, important men and women in the arts, especially music. Its principal value is for the study of social life in Delhi and of the monuments of the city and its suburbs, but it has also been found to be valuable for the study of the layout of the city and the functional features of the different landmarks.

The other work which has been used is the *Sair-ul-Manazil* of Sangin Beg, son of Ali Akbar Beg, which was written at the instance of Charles Metcalf, Resident at Delhi (1811-19 and again during 1825-27) and completed around the year 1827.[2] The name of William Frazer, deputy superintendent, was also added to that of Metcalf, though perhaps later. This work seeks to describe the various localities, districts, layout, streets and some of the monuments. Written about twenty years before Sir Syed Ahmed Khan's famous work, *Asar-us-Sanadid,* it has attracted much less attention of scholars.

It is beyond the scope of this brief paper to give a description of the city of Shahjahanabad during the period under study. Certain broad functional features may, however, be pointed out.

The number of streets and *mohallas* which have continued to exist under the same name is remarkably large. Some of these have retained their traditional features, while in many other cases though the names have survived, the type of activity and the character of the population has undergone a complete change. For example, in Paiwalan near Jami Masjid, one can still buy fireworks; similarly, in Chawri Bazar, shops selling copper or brass utensils are still found.[3]

[1]The printed version in the library of Anjuman Taraqqi-i-Urdu (Hind), New Delhi, has been used.

[2]The text has been edited by Dr Sharif Husain Qasimi of Delhi University and published by Ghalib Institute, New Delhi in 1982 has been used. There is another work of the same title by Dr Naeem Ahmad.

[3]*Sair-ul-Manazil,* Editor's 'Introduction'.

One of the most significant features of Shahjahanabad is that there is no segregation of the houses of the rich and the poor, or of residential parts and the commercial parts—a feature that developed under the British. While many localities were predominantly inhabited by a single community, the localities where people of the other communities were not interspersed, lived in close proximity. This was as true of religious communities as of caste or professional groups. For example the following description may be seen:[4]

> From the south of Hauz-i-Qazi till Turkman Gate, along with streets on both sides are:
>
> On one side, the shop of a *halwai* (sweetmeat seller), Kucha Bazar Imli, Mohalla and Kucha of Pati Ram, Bangla of Hafiz Fida, Kucha Murghian (birds and fowl), residence of ryots *(makan-i-riaya)*, houses of Kashmiri Pandits, *haveli* of Dudhadhari, house of Lala Gulab Rai Pandit, the Tahsildar of Palam proper, Kucha of Mai Das, Than of Panj Piran, Kucha of Shidi Qasim, which leads to Kucha of Pati Ram. In the Kucha of Shidi Qasim there is the residence of Govardhan Kashmiri and of Mir Khan Tunda, who is unsurpassable in singing and dancing, the house of Mirza Fathullah Beg Chela, *haveli* of Maulavi Fath Ali Sahib the *jagirdar*, houses of other ryots (*riaya*), the well of Naurang Rai, *havelis* of Banias (*baqqalan*). And in the Kucha going towards the city wall, there is the property (*riyasat*) of *khatiks* who work with leather (*chirm sazan*), the small garden of Tansukh Rai Kaghazi, the *hauz*(tank) of Nawab Muzaffar Khan and the residences of ryots (*riaya*).
>
> From the Than of Panj Piran, may be found *havelis* of Lal Basanti Ram and Sadasukh Pandit, and Bazar Sita Ram, the Katra of Jani Khan and the *riyasat* (properties) of the ryots. On the opposite side there is a Kucha going towards the Chhatta of Shah Haji. Before that there is a *doraha* (bifurcated road): One goes towards the *mohalla* of *churigaran* (bangle-makers) and the other towards the *hammam* (public bath) of Sital Das, who lived at the time of Shah Alam. Further down is the *haveli* of Rai Shambhu Nath, the stables (*tawela*) of Murtaza Khan, *haveli* of Raja Kedar Nath and the *katra* of *gari-banan* (cart drivers). One road is adjacent to the above mentioned well with saline water, and the other is towards the *bangla* of Shidi Faulad Khan, the *kucha* of Imam and the houses of the ryots.

[4] *Muraqqa-i-Dehli*, 7-8.

It has been mentioned above that though sometimes the localities where Hindus and Muslims lived were separated, there was nevertheless a great deal of intermixture between the two communities. Only some examples of joint celebrations of festivals and the absence of distinction between Shias and Sunnis in the observance of Muharram may be quoted here :[5]

'Although the tomb of Shaikh Nasir-ud-Din Chiragh-i-Delhi was situated at a distance of three *krohs* from Shahjahanabad, it was considered sacred by both Hindus and Muslims (presumably of the city as well) who celebrated in large number the festival of 'light' every year at the tomb during the month of Diwali. Muhammad Shah had built a *pucca* enclosure, and musical performances were of great importance. The other example is that of a person who was held in great veneration by Hindus and Muslims alike, namely, Majnun Nanak Shahi.[6] Similarly, the celebration of Basant (*Basant Panchmi*) was started from the shrine of the footprint of the Prophet and joined by musicians and public of both the communities'.[7]

About the celebration of Muharram, similarly, there is no indication that its observance was confined only to one sect. For example, the followers of the same Manjnun Nanak Shahi observed in their own way the tenth of Muharram where everyone participated.[8] In the *ashur khana* managed by Jawed Khan, the famous *marsia khwan* (reciter of elegies of Imam Husain), everyone assembled.[9] The popularity of the *marsias*, written in *rekhta* (early Urdu) by three brothers, Miskin, Hazin and Ghamgin was considerable. *Tazia* keeping was fairly common and people from all walks of life came to the *tazia khana* of Imam Husain.[10] Although the word *Imambara* is not used in *Muraqqa-i-Dehli*, it is used in *Sair-ul-Manazil*, for example, *Imambara* of Mir Askari.[11]

The city of Shahjahanabad centred basically round the fort (which was the Imperial Palace) and the Jami Masjid. It was surrounded by the city walls, many parts of which still survive along with the city gates, for example, Dehli Darwaza, Ajmeri Darwaza, Turkman Darwaza, Kashmiri Darwaza, Lahori Darwaza, Mori Darwaza. The famous Chandni Chowk, going from west to east (starting by the side of Jami Masjid

[5]Ibid., 23.
[6]Ibid., 30.
[7]*Sair-ul-Manazil*, 23.
[8]*Muraqqa-i-Dehli*, 25.
[9]Ibid., 50.
[10]Ibid., 51-52.
[11]*Sair-ul-Manazil*, 35.

towards the west and going towards the fort in the east), was for all purposes what a 'down-town' or city 'Centrum' would be called in the west.

A chowk is a 'square', though in many cases it would be a rectangle. It is a central market-place with many streets joining it. It also serves as a meeting place, as well as a centre of professional entertainment. The most important such place in Shahjahanabad was Chandni Chowk, still retaining its importance, but much changed during the last fifty years. A description given by Dargah Quli Khan in 1738 is not without interest:[12]

'Chandni Chowk is more pleasant and entertaining than the other *chowks*, and compared to other streets and roads much more decorated. It is a place where important people come for entertainment and pleasure, and sight-seeing for beauty and elegance. Articles of every description are found in its adjoining streets, and goods from every locality are available here in plenty. In the middle of it is a beautiful canal. On one street are jewellers where rubies and pearls and all the gems are available in plenty. On another side are the perfumeries, oils and apothecaries. On yet another side are arms and daggers. China-ware is also readily available along with glass-ware of different shapes and sizes, whose decoration defies all description. They have arranged such attractive (wine) glasses that an austere and pious man, hundred years old, would feel tempted to drink wine. Several other articles of common use are sold here which would probably never be available even in the *karkhanas* of the nobles'.

'Apart from the merchandise, it is a place which is extremely pleasant for an evening stroll. It is attractive to the eye and its fragrance provides great freshness, so much so that going through a pleasure garden would not be so enjoyable. In its many *qahwa khanas* (coffee houses), literary personalities gather every day and recite their pieces to each other. It is such a pleasure resort that the great *amirs*, in spite of their elevated status, enjoy the sight of this *chowk*, and if they wish to purchase its novelties, even the great wealth of Qarun would disappear. If the son of an *amir* wishes to visit this chowk for enjoying life, his mother would secretly give him a lakh of rupees out of the moneys left by his father, even though she would offer the excuse that she did not have enough money, hoping that the son would buy novelties from the *chowk*, but the pleasure loving young man would blow up the money in things that attract his fancy'.

The largest number of sacred places was naturally that of mosques, of which, apart from Jami Masjid and Kalan Masjid (Kali Masjid) there

[12]*Muraqqa-i-Dehli*, 17-19.

were many. The next in number was that of tombs, variously referred to as just *qabr*, or if the superstructure was imposing, as *maqbara*, or *rauza* (as of Shah Turkman Biyabani). Other names for tombs were *turbat kada*, *dargah* (as of Qadam Sharif), *astana*, *takiya*, and *mazar*. *Kashana* could be used for a place where *qawwali* was recited, while for places connected with the observance of Muharram, the names used were *chauki khana*, *aza khana*, *tazia khana*, *ashur khana*, and presumably later, *Imambara* and *Panja*.[13] *Karbala* was naturally not mentioned within the city walls of Shahjahanabad, though it existed outside. *Majlis khanas* are mentioned.

Among the charitable places were *madrasas*, of which quite a few have been mentioned in Shahjahanabad. There is only one hospital mentioned, the *darush-shafa*, founded by Shah Jahan.

No temples are recorded in either of the two works within the city walls of Shahjahanabad, though there are references to Rajghat, Nigambodh Ghat and Ghat Kela, as well as to *mandirs* of Paras Nath, Jogmayaji, Kalkaji, Hanumanji and Makan Shitla.[14] In the Chhatta of Nigambodh Ghat there were houses of Gosains, Thakurdwaras, *chhatris* and places held sacred by the Hindus.

The most common word for streets was *kucha*, which quite frequently is used along with the word *bazaar*. It could be named after a person, or of the dominant community residing there, or a profession. Examples would be Kucha-i-Bulaqi Begum or Kucha-i-Pati Ram, Kucha-i-Balli Maran and Kucha-i-Jogiwara. *Sarak* is not mentioned in any of the two works. In common parlance, some of the *kuchas* are now called *gali*, such as *kucha samosa*[15] is called *Samose wali gali*, or *kucha batasha wala* is popularly called *batashe wali gali*. *Gandhi gali*, for perfumes, is mentioned by that name.[16] Where a road bifurcates it is called *siraha* such as *siraha* Bairam Khan.[17]

As in the case of streets, the most commonly used term for a locality is *mohalla*. It could be named after an individual, such as Mohalla Hakim Muhsin Khan or Mohalla Muhammad Ali Khan, but the commonest are those named after artisans, such as *mohalla churigaran* (mentioned above), *mohalla dhobiwala* (quarters of washermen) or *mohalla kashti-*

[13]Both *Muraqqa-i-Dehli* and *Sair-ul-Manazil* mention all the places, except Imambara and Panja which are mentioned by the latter only.

[14]*Sair-ul-Manazil*, 43.

[15]Ibid., 21.

[16]Ibid., 36.

[17]Ibid., 28 and 30.

banan (boatmen). Some of the *mohallas* bear the name of some characteristic feature of the place, such as *mohalla imli* (tamarind) or *mohalla chah-i-rahat* (well with a Persian wheel). In the case of Matia Mahal, *mohalla* changes its form.

In the same way, the markets were generally known as *bazaar*,though the largest ones, as mentioned before, were *chowks*, such as Chandni Chowk or Chowk Saadullah Khan. *Bazaar* is hardly ever used in the context of Shahjahanabad as a covered market, but there are shops on both sides of a street and behind the shops are residential houses. Most derive their names from persons, such as Bazar Sita Ram or Bazar Nawab Mir (Amir?) Khan Chaghta, or Faiz Bazar, or after craftsmen, such as Jauhari (jewellers) Bazar, or Bazar Mazid Parcha.

Market-places which were specially built for retail or wholesale shops were referred to as Ganj, but their names were not necessarily associated with any particular feature, such as Daryaganj, Paharganj, Jahangirganj, Rakabganj.

Shops were sometimes collectively referred to as *dakakin* such as *dakakin-bisatiyan* (general merchants), *dakakin-chirimaran* (bird catchers), *dakakin halwaiyan* (sweetmeat sellers); or where an individual shop *(dukan)* gave its name to many adjoining shops, as in the case of Dukan Thande Baqqal or Dukan Tek Chand or Dukan Kishan Chand Sarraf.

Yet another name for a market would be *mandi* or *mandvi*, usually wholesale market of a commodity, as in the case of *sabzimandi* (vegetable market) or *mandvi pan* (betel leaf) or *mandvi gulfaroshan* (market for flower-sellers).

Two interesting names are *chhatta* and *katra*. *Chhatta* literally means a covered lane or *bazaar*, but it frequently refers to the locality where artisans practising a particular craft lived and/or worked, such as *chhatta mimaran* (masons), or *chhatta momgaran* (wax-makers). In many cases, a *chhatta* would be named after the person who built it, or with a place with which it may otherwise have been associated, such as Chhatta Lala Tansukh Rai or Chhatta Jan Nisar Khan, or Chhatta Nigambodh Ghat or Chhatta Lahori Darwaza.

Katra literally means a small square *bazaar*, but quite often it refers to wholesale market or where stocks were kept. There is a *nishan* of Nur Jahan Begum ordering officers not to interfere with the merchants stocking their merchandise in a *katra*.[18] Some of these were named after merchants of a particular commodity, such as *katra bazzazan* (cloth

[18]S.A.I. Tirmizi, ed, *Edicts from the Mughal Harem*, 29.

merchants), *katra roghan zard* or *ghi* (clarified butter) *ka katra, katra nil* (indigo); but quite often it was named after the builder or the owner, such as Katra Adina Beg Khan, or Katra Munshi Kanwal Nain.

Tirpolia (literally three gates) was also used as a term denoting a locality. In Tirpolia were the *makan* of Shagunchand Sahu, *mandvi gul faroshan*, a *sharab-khana* (wine-house), Mumtazganj, the habitation of *gari-banan* (cart owners or drivers) later the royal artillery, going up to Kauriapul (bridge over Faiz canal).

Unfortunately, not much is known about the institution of the Nagar Seth in Shahjahanabad, but that the institution existed here may be deduced from the reference to Haveli Nagar Seth in *Sair-ul-Manazil*.[19] Presumably his duties and privileges were the same as those of the famous Nagar Seth of Ahmedabad. We may also assume that what has been described in *ain-i-kotwal*,[20] as the appointment of a notable of each community of artisans and a headman of each *mohalla* must have existed in Shahjahanabad, though its form may have changed. An indication may be had from the fact that even now there is supposed to be only one entrance to a *mohalla* or *katra* or *bazaar*.

It seems that the residences were generally named according to plan, size and the status of the person who built or owned it. First would come the *haveli*, such as Haveli Ibrahim Ali Khan, or Haveli Azam Khan or Haveli Bakhshi Bhavani Shanker. But there are certain obvious exceptions which the present writer is unable to explain, like *Haveli* Puran *khaiyat* (tailor) or *haveli* Zeenat *tawaif* (dancing girl and/or prostitute), or *haveli mimaran* (masons) or *haveliyat baqqalan* (Banias).

A *haveli* was a house complex with its *deorhi* (entrance), *sahn* (courtyard), *mahal saras* (living quarters), *bala-khana* (the upper storey), *jilaw-khana* (upper storey with a projecting balcony and external access) and *diwan khana* (office rooms). Bala-khana Shaikh Badrul-Din Muhr-kun or Bala-Khana Nawab Fathulla Beg Khan are mentioned. Similarly, Diwan-khana Hakim Qudrat-ullah Khan and Diwan-khana Nawab Faiz-ullah Khan are also mentioned, while a *jilaw-khana* in Chowk Sadullah Khan is mentioned in *Muraqqa-i-Dehli*.[21] A *burj* (engaged quoin or tower with rooms) was also an important feature of many *havelis* but for various reasons it occasionally acquired an independent position.[22]

[19] *Sair-ul-Manazil*, 29.

[20] Abul Fazl, *Ain-i-Akbari* (tr H.S. Jarrett), Atlantic Publishers and Distributors, New Delhi 1989 (rep), Vol. II, 44.

[21] *Muraqqa-i-Dehli*, 14.

[22] Loc. cit.

Other names, lower in the hierarchy were just *makan* as those of Bajna *tawaif*, or of Bag Singh. As in the case of *haveli*, *makan* would also be sometimes used for important people, as in the case of Makan Raja Jai Singh, or Makan Nawab Fathullah Beg Khan. *Makanat* (pl. of *makan*) was a collection of houses, used either for a social entity or for houses owned by an individual. Makanat-i-Panditan-i-Kashmiri, Makanat Qaum Khatri or Makanat-i-Murshidzadaha (princes) would be examples of the former, while Makanat-i-Muhammad Amin Khan, Makanat-i-Nawab Faiz Muhammad Khan, Makanat-i-Nawab Qamar-ud-Din, would be examples of the latter.

Manzil, so common among Urdu-speaking people today, was rarely used; the only example we have is in the plural – Manazil Nawab Jahan Ara Begum. *Kothi*, which literally is a diminutive of fort, and was commonly used in the sense of 'factories' owned by the European companies, or *kothars*[23] used in the same period as godowns, for example, *kothar* of Hathras or of Marehra,[24] has not been used in either of the two works, nor is it used today in the walled city except in its diminutive form *kothri* (for a very small room or even a cell). *Kothi*, however, is frequently used as denoting an upper-class residence, whether of Indians or Europeans. Examples would be Kothi Nawab Ahmed Bakhsh Khan, Kothi Nawab Faiz Muhammad Khan Bahadur, Kothi Lala Saudagar Mal, Kothi Lala Mangat Rai. In the case of the Europeans, though most of these residences were outside the city walls, they were a part of the city, such as Kothi Daktar Ludlow Saheb (Ludlow Castle) and Kothi Col. James Skinner.

The term *bangla* (bungalow) seems to have come from Bengal. Its use in *Muraqqa-i-Dehli* wherein it is stated that there were *banglas* in every locality,[24] suggests that it had been used for long, though the term and the type of the houses it denoted appear to have been popularised by the British. Among the many names mentioned in *Sair-ul-Manazil*, Bangla Hafiz Fida, Bangla Saiyid Firoz, Bangla Shidi Faulad Khan and Bangla Sukunat-i-Angrez (residences of Englishmen) may be mentioned here. In contrast to a *haveli*, a *bangla* was essentially a detached house.

Gardens were presumably laid by individuals, as pleasure resorts, but in course of time became public gardens, such as Bagh Begum Saheba. Bagh of Begum Sumroo was just outside the city walls. Smaller gardens or parks were Baghicha Tansukh Rai Kaghazi (paper manufacturer or

[23]'Du Jardin Papers', *Indian Historical Review*, Vol.V. No. 1-2 (July 1978-January 1979), 196.

[24]*Muraqqa-i-Delhi*, 12 and 13.

dealer). Baghicha Guruji Pandit, Baghicha Muhammad Karora and Baghicha Zeenat Bari, etc.

Water-bodies were mainly *hauz* or *talab* (tanks), *nahr* (canal), *chah* (wells), *bawri* or *baoli* (stepwells) in Shahjahanabad, for these provided water to the city. Some of these were fitted with Persian wheels *(rahat)*.

When we look at the earlier part of the eighteenth century, we find Shahjahanabad as a vibrant city with artisans, trade and commerce, with residences of wealthy *jagirdars* and merchants, a city of pleasure and sin, as well as of sacred edifices and monuments. Then came the catastrophes: Nadir Shah's invasion, Ahmad Shah Durrani's invasions, the domination of the Marathas and the Afghans, virtual independence of the governors and, finally the establishment of the British domination in 1803. This was the time of which the poets expressed their grief, such as Sauda, who wrote his *Shahr Ashob*, on the migration of Mir Taqi Mir to Lucknow, and his famous lines, rendered in English:*

> Delhi, which was a city Select of the World where the elite of the Times lived;
> It has been robbed and destroyed by circumstances;
> I belong to that very desolate city.

The evidence of decline cannot be overlooked; the loss of source of power and wealth of the landed aristocracy and the impoverishment of the king, took their toll in terms of the city's prosperity. And yet it remained a well-populated city marked by its graces and culture.

**Dilli jo ek shahr tha, Alam men intikhab*
Rehte the muntakhab hi jahan rozgar ke
Usko falak ne loot ke barbad kar diya
Ham rehne wale hain usi ujre diyar ke

BIBLIOGRAPHY

Ahmad Ali, *Twilight in Delhi*, London 1966.

Bashirud-Din Ahmad, *Waqiat-i-Darul Hukumat-i-Dehli* (Urdu) Vol. II, Agra 1919.

Beadon, H.C., *Gazetteer of Delhi District*, 1912.

Carr, Stephen, *The Archaeological and Monumental Remains of Delhi*, Calcutta 1876.

Delhi Gazetteer, Delhi, 1976.

Fanshawe, H.C., *Shah Jahan's Delhi—Past and Present*, Delhi 1979(rep).

List of Muhammadan and Hindu Monuments, Vol. I, Shahjahanabad, Archaeological Survey of India, Calcutta 1916.

Nurul-Hasan Ansari, *Muraqqa-i-Dehli*, Delhi 1982. This is another edition with Urdu translation of the same title cited on page 2.

S. Nurul-Hasan, 'Du Jardin Papers', *Indian Historical Review*, Vol. V, Nos. 1-2 (July 1978-January 1979).

Sayyad Abdul Hai, *Dehli aur uske Atraf* (Urdu), Delhi 1958.

Sayyad Ahmad, *Asarus-Sanadid* (Urdu) 1st edn, Delhi 1847.

URBAN ECONOMY IN WESTERN INDIA IN LATE EIGHTEENTH CENTURY

G.D. SHARMA

By the middle of the eighteenth century, the Mughal empire in many parts of the Indian subcontinent was replaced by regional states. The absence of central political control did not, however, necessarily imply any serious disruption in regional economies. The financial policies of the Marathas and the Rajputs were dictated by their immediate requirements, and their methods resulted in a process of commercialisation in which merchant capital played a vital role. Consequently, not only the cities but also the *pargana* towns became centres of trade and commerce which in turn strengthened merchant capital.

The study of urban economy in western India during the second half of the eighteenth century has been made possible by the discovery of new evidence in recent years.[1] This consists of family records of merchants and bankers, statements of income and expenditure of the revenue of

[1]G.D. Sharma, *Rajput Polity*, New Delhi 1977; 'Rajasthani Sources on the Economic History of Rajasthan during the Mughal Period', *The Sources on the Social and Economic History of Rajasthan*, Centre of Rajasthan Studies, University of Rajasthan, Jaipur; 'The Marwaris: Foundations of the Modern Capitalist Class of India', *Business Communities of India* (ed Dwijendra Tripathi), New Delhi 1984; 'Economy and Society of Rural Gujarat in the Second Half of the 18th Century', *Proceedings Indian History Congress* (1984), 367-74; 'Business and Accounting in Western India during the 18th Century', ibid. (1985), G.D. Sharma and Jaspal Kaur Dhot, 'Marathi Records on the State Revenue in Gujarat during the Second Half of the 18th Century', *Proceedings Indian Historical Records Commission* (1985), 83-98; S.P. Gupta, *The Agrarian System in Eastern Rajasthan*, New Delhi 1987; Jaspal Kaur Dhot, 'Jama Documents Pertaining to Cambay', *The Indian Archives* (1983).

parganas, known as *jamabandis*, maintained by states like Marwar and Bikaner, and other state records like the income and expenditure of the city of Jodhpur for 1784, the *hundis* received against the revenue of Tappah Sadari for 1782, the statement of income and expenditure of Pali for 1770 and the income and expenditure of Kotwali Chautra of Jodhpur for 1775. Records of the family of Mirzamal have been published recently and archival sources in Modi script have been brought to light for the study of economy in Gujarat. They relate to revenue accounts, directives for the collection of revenue and the management of *parganas*, and include documents like *sanads* and *chitthis*. Records of the merchant bankers of Gujarat have also been brought to light like the records of the firm of Haribhakti, a leading banking house of Baroda.

On the basis of information available in archival sources and records selected from private collections, it has become possible to study the structure of urban economy in western India, the working of the market and role of the *arhtias* and *marfatias* and *dalals*, the role of the bankers and the nature of merchant capital. It is clear from this evidence that the state played an important role in the economy of western India during the second half of the eighteenth century.

I

The Gaekwads of Baroda maintained irregular horse and foot, including mercenaries known as *sibandis*.[2] They were employed as guards in towns and the fortresses and, later on, in state administration as well. By the end of the eighteenth century, their numbers had increased considerably.[3] Their presence in the state opened a new opportunity for the bankers, who paid the salaries of soldiers and their commanders on behalf of the state. A regular system was evolved for this purpose and the bankers became virtually *bakhshis*. They were repaid either through pay-orders (*barats*) issued to the *pargana* administrators (*kamavisdars*) or were assigned revenues of parganas directly.[4] Most bankers of the state have entries on every page of their account books relating to payments made to soldiers. Also old accounts were carried forward and fresh advances made in the current year were added to them.[5]

[2]The mercenaries consisted mainly of Arabs and Sindhis. Some of the latter were meant for the collection of revenue and paid by the *kamavisadars;* the others meant for defence purposes were paid by the government: Walker to Grant, 22 August 1803, *The Gaekwads of Baroda* (ed Gense and Banaji), VI, 186.

[3]Wellesley to Duncan, 2 August 1803, *The Gaekwads of Baroda*, VI, 158.

[4]Ibid., V, 102; VII, 148.

[5]Walker to Warden, 29 July 1805, ibid., VI, 137.

According to Grant Duff, the Haribhakti family was one of the two most important bankers in Baroda that gained great wealth by advances made at exorbitant interest to the Arab and other mercenaries of the Gaekwads.[6] The accounts of this house confirm that it played an extremely important role in the payment of salaries to *siledars* and *sibandis* and in advancing loans to the Maratha army commanders.[7] Mairal Narain was another prominent banker who became the chief manager of the *siledars* and their horses in the camp.[8] Rattanji Kahandas, a banker of Kathiawad, enjoyed influence at the Gaekwad's court and worked for the financial management of his territories in Kathiawad, sometimes actively participating in his campaigns of conquest *(mulkgiri)*.[9] Sanal Bechar and Mangal Sakhidas, two other bankers are known to have acted as army paymasters. They acquired great prominence and influence as leaders of the *sibandis* and exercised considerable influence in matters of state.

The second important feature of the revenue administration was the system of farming (*ijara*). The system had become increasingly important in the various provinces of Mughal empire during the early eighteenth century, particularly in the reign of Bahadur Shah. The Rajput rulers continued the practice and let out the revenues of whole *parganas* on *ijara*. The farmer (*ijaradar*) was obliged to furnish the surety (*zamini*) of a *jagirdar* or an accredited banker.[10] With the expansion of *ijara* system more bankers and larger sums became involved. The system of *ijara* was also adopted in spheres other than land revenue and the merchants' involvement became more significant, though their main focus still remained their ancestral business.[11]

In the territories of Gaekwads the *ijara* system was closely allied with the revenue administration of the Marathas in which the administrators of *parganas* (*kamavisdar*) themselves were allowed to act as revenue farmers. On obtaining the *ijara*, a *kamavisdar* had to pay about half of the assessed revenue in advance. In addition, he had to provide *rasad* to the

[6]Grant Duff, *History of the Marathas*, 1971 (reprint), III, 215.

[7]*Badadyantil Sardar, Siledar, Jamadar, Dwarkhdar va Parakh Yanchya Gharanchya Nannukhinchya Vagaire Haqiqat*, Baroda 1987, XII, 133; *The Gaekwads of Baroda*, X, 237.

[8]*Selections from the Baroda State Records*, II, 573.

[9]Account Books in the Baroda Records Office: Haribhakti Collection.

[10]G.D. Sharma (ed), *Vakil Reports Maharajgon*, New Delhi 1987, 'Introduction'; S.P. Gupta, *The Agrarian System in Eastern Rajasthan*, 16-17.

[11]G.D.Sharma, 'The Marwaris', *Business Communities of India*; 'Vyaparis and Mahajans in Western Rajasthan During the Eighteenth Century', *Proceedings Indian History Congress* (1980), 377-85.

state, for which the bankers and the merchants (*pareekhs* and *shahs*) provided the mandatory surety, known as *manoti* (synonymous with the *zamini* of Rajasthan). The rate of interest charged on *manoti* and on other advances by the bankers and merchants varied from year to year and from *pargana* to *pargana*. In this process they came to assume a three-fold role. They acted as sureties for the payment of *rasad*; they lent money on interest to the *kamavisdars* and enabled them to pay *rasad* and they acquired rights over the collection of land revenue and other taxes. Since they conducted their principle business in cities and towns, they became an important link between the country and the town and between the towns and the cities. [12]

The third important feature of state administration was related to levies other than land revenue, generally known as *sair* or *sair-jihat* or as *sairat*. These levies appear to have assumed much greater importance under the Rajputs and Marathas than under the Mughals. In the first place, Rajput and Maratha rulers adopted a systematic policy for attracting traders and merchants to their cities and towns,[13] giving them concessions in cesses such as, *rahdari*, *mapa-dan* and *varas* and sometimes even exempting them totally, and offering some of them monetary help to open shops in the markets (*mandis*) and in the periodic fairs. During the second half of the eighteenth century, the bankers and merchants were allowed to take over the *sairat* in *ijara*. Consequently, an administrative machinery for the realisation of *sairat* came into existence. The official concerned came to be known as collector of *sairat* (*sair ra odhedar*).[14] *Naqas* (check-posts) were established in towns and cities for realisation of octroi, and *thanas* were established in the countryside generally at the junctions of the trade routes.

Annual accounts of *sairat* were kept for every *pargana*. Given below are entries of the account book (*sair-bahi*) for *pargana* Jaitaran for the years 1746 and 1747.[15] The table shows that a number of cesses were levied in *sairat*, the most important source here being the *thana*. *Amadni*, next in importance, consisted mainly of the *chungi* and the *mandi* taxes.

[12]In charge of a *pargana*, the *kamavisdar* performed revenue and magisterial functions. The Marathas generally gave revenues in *ijara* to their *kamavisdars*. In due course the office came to be auctioned to the highest bidder who paid a stipulated sum to the government and collected *jamabandis*, *nazrana*, *ghasdana* and other cesses. This information comes from the agreements signed by some of the *kamavisdars* lying in the Baroda Records Office.

[13]G.D. Sharma, 'Vyaparis and Mahajans'.

[14]*Jama-Kharach Bahi of Sayer Kacheri* pertaining to the Jodhpur State in Rajasthan State Archives, Bikaner.

[15]From 1760 onwards, *jamabandis* of *sair* are available in the Archives: Appendix I.

Head	A.D. 1746 *Jama* in Rupee-Anna-Paisa	A.D. 1747 *Jama* in Rupee-Anna-Paisa
Amadni	1432-08-03	1296-13-03
Thana	2323-08-02	2920-05-03
Bija Pag	35-08-01	8-01-03
Farohi	10-15-02	22-13-01
Kasaratra	00-01-03	00-08-02
Ijarara		23-00-00
Battara		09-02-03
Hundawana		01-01-02
	3848-06-03	4281-15-01
	Kharach	*Kharach*
Mahinadar	906-08-00	250-10-01
Extra		
Shenai Thana	6-12-00	6-05-00

A general review of the available evidence however makes it clear that the two most important heads under the *sairat* were *mapa-dan* and *rahdari*.[16] *Mapadan* denoted primarily the levies imposed on the sale of goods and their entry in the markets (*mandis*), its rate being computed on the basis of either the price of an article or its quantity. In *Pargana* Nagore, for instance, the rate of *dan* was 35.5 *dams* per rupee for grain, while in *pargana* Sanchor it ranged between 1.8 and 2.8 rupees per *kalsi* (unit of weight).[17] The rates varied also from *pargana* to *pargana* and also depended on the status of a merchant. In *pargana* Sanchor, for example, the *mahajans* known as Pichhayati were paying almost double the rate for cattle of what mahajans known as Talpadu paid.[18] Remissions ranged between 25 and 50 per cent of the *mapa*, and sometimes 100 per cent.[19]

Rahdari, known as *bathwan* in Rajasthan, was an old tax but its pattern appears to have changed under the Rajput rulers. Computed with reference to the value of an article, it was levied on goods imported for

[16]*Pargana Jaitaran ri Sayer ri Jama*, V.S. 1843/A.D. 1786, Rajasthan State Archives, Bikaner.

[17]It was a metal pot used for weighing *ghee* as well as grain.

[18]*Sanad-Bahi*, No.228, V.S. 1827/A.D. 1770; *Sayer Jama-Kharach Bahi* (Parbastar), No.25, V.S. 1834/A.D. 1777; *Sanad-Bahi*, No 287, V.S. 1824/A.D. 1767.

[19]G.D. Sharma, 'Vyaparis and Mahajans'.

sale into a *pargana* or taken out from it,[20] reckoning also by camel-load or cart-load. The rates were more or less uniform all over the state, with only a few local variations. The rate was lower for traders.[21] For traders travelling over long distances there was provision for single point payment in order to facilitate movement.[22] The state could also remit the cess in part or entirely.[23] Remissions were common for traders participating in the periodic fairs (*melas*). Concessions were also extended to some specified goods carried for certain specific purposes, such as seed and grain during a famine.

Among other cesses were *vatwal* (literally, 'an observer'),*tulavat-vazandari* (a cess on weighing), and *dalali* (a cess on brokers). For the collection of taxes in towns and *thanas* there was a well organised hierarchy of officials with the *daroga* at the top, and under him other officials known as *mushrifs, potedars, thanayets, navisandas, dani vatwals, kayals* and *naqayats*.[24] They were directly appointed by the state and their duties and remunerations were specified. The location and size of the place, the volume of trade, and the amount of work involved accounted for variations in remunerations in different units.[25]

The amount and percentage of *sair* varied from *pargana* to *pargana* and from year to year. In *pargana* Nagore, for example, in 1751 the total amount of *sair* was a little more than 73,850 rupees and it constituted more than 23 per cent of the total *jama*. For later years, the figures were, nearly 26 per cent and less than 33,500 rupees in 1756; over 38 per cent and less than 56,200 rupees in 1771; more than 53 per cent and more than 76,500 rupees in 1776; and more than 34 per cent and more than 55,500 rupees in 1784. In *pargana* Merta the lowest percentage was in 1765, less than 9, and the total collection was about 22,225 rupees; the percentage in 1771 was the highest, 30 per cent, and the total collection was more than 39,300 rupees. In *pargana* Sojat the lowest percentage, less than 7, was in 1795, and the total collection was a little less than 2,800 rupees; when, in 1772, the percentage was the highest, more than 30, the total

[20]*Sayer Jama-Kharach* (Parbastar), No.24, V.S. 1833/A.D. 1777; (Jalore), No. 147, V.S. 1829/A.D. 1772; (Pali), V.S. 1831/A.D. 1774.

[21]*Bahis* for *parganas* Pali, Sanchore and Bhinmal are available, respectively, for 1770, 1772 and 1790. The rate of *rahdari* in *pargana* Sanchore was 12.5 *dams* per rupee.

[22]*Sanad-Bahi*, No.286, V.S. 1818-20/A.D. 1761-63.

[23]*Khas Rukka-Parwana Bahi*, No. 1, V.S. 1822/A.D.1765 and V.S. 1828/A.D.1771; *Sanad-Bahi*, No.285, V.S. 1811-14/A.D. 1754-57.

[24]*Pargana Pali Taleqa Jama-Kharach va Goswal*, V.S. 1827/A.D. 1770; *Pali Takhtgarh Jodhpur ka Kotwali-Chotra ra Jama-Kharach*, V.S. 1832/A.D. 1775.

[25]*Sanad Parwana Naqal-Bahi*, No.2, V.S. 1822/A.D. 1765 and No.8, V.S. 1825/A.D. 1768; *Sanad-Bahi*, No.288, V.S. 1827/A.D. 1770.

collection was a little less than 8,000 rupees.[26] Notwithstanding these variations, it is possible to argue, on the basis of the figures available for these three *parganas* during the second half of the eighteenth century, that *sair* taxes went on increasing with the passage of time. State policy appears to have encouraged trade and commerce, resulting in the growth of merchant capital. The decrease in the total *jama* during the late eighteenth century can be attributed to decrease in land revenue due to the increasing claims of the *bhomis* and to the establishment of *thikanas.*[27]

Some interesting information is available on the revenues in general and the revenues from the non-agrarian sources in particular. The detail of the receipt and debit for 1770 in the *pargana* Pali, given below, illustrates this. We notice that the revenue realised from *mapa* was larger than from *rahdari* and the latter was far higher than the receipts from *sair* for fairs. The total collection from the fairs *(sair-mela)* was more than 7,000 rupees. The inclusion of receipt on account of *hundis* makes it clear that the state was involved with the system of *hundis*.

Receipt in Rupee-Anna-Paisa	Items
16,661-12-3	*Mal Hasil*
67,213-02-3	*Mapa, Rahadari* and *Sayer Mela*
	35511-14-1 receipt from *Mapa*
	19741-06-1 receipt from *Rahadari*
	930-06-3 receipt from *Sayer Mela*
7306-11-3	*Hasil Sayer Mela*
332-00-3	Receipt on account of recovery of credit
71-07-0	Receipt on account of *Hundawan*

The Peshwa and the Gaekwad used to divide the revenues of the city of Ahmedabad equally.[28] *Sair* consisted of the standard revenue *(ain-jama)* and the additional revenue *(sawai-jama)*. For 1761 the former amounted to about 24,250 rupees and the latter to a little more than 34,000 rupees. *Sair* constituted about 30 per cent of the total revenues of *pargana* Ahmedabad and bout 45 per cent of the total revenues of the

[26] *Jamabandi-Bahis*, Jodhpur Branch, Rajasthan State Archives, Bikaner: Appendix II.
[27] G.D. Sharma, *Rajput Polity*, 'Conclusion'.
[28] *Gujarat-Jamav*, Rumal No.40, Pune Records Office, Pune; ibid., *Kalambandi*, V.S. 1817/A.D. 1760; ibid., *Taleband*, A.D. 1870; *Viaj-Vahi* and *Nodh-Bahi*, Jharti, A.D. 1761. Also, Appendix III.

smaller unit called Haveli Ahmedabad. Important among the *sair* taxes were the taxes levied in the markets *(mandis)*, such as taxes for loading the goods *(bharai)*, taxes for packing the goods *(vajankosi)*, tax levied on the shops *(mahajani)*, toll tax *(chungi)*, taxes called *balai* and *sawai-balai* and *izafa*. Babapur, Hajipur, Behrampur, Raghunathpur, Rajpur, Saraspur, Shahganj, Methakhali and Bakarabad were some of the markets in which most of these taxes were levied.

Sawai-jama constituted a major portion of *sair*. In 1761, for instance, it amounted to more than 58 per cent. Under *sawai-jama,* the most important head was *mahajani* (43 per cent of the total *sawai-jama)*, followed by *tolai* (more than 15 per cent), *balai* (about 11 per cent) and *izafa* (a little more than 9 per cent). One inference that can be safely drawn from this information is that the number of shops in the city of Ahmedabad was quite large. The most important market in the city was that of Shahganj followed by Behrampur, Raghunathpura and Rajpura.

The city of Ahmedabad continued to be an emporium of trade and commerce during the rule of the Gaekwads. The revenues of the fort area *(kot)* were equally divided between the Peshwa and the Gaekwad, each of whom had his local representative in the city in 1761. Interestingly. Muslims were assessed much more leniently than the Hindus. An important source of *sair* was grocery *(kirana)*, for there were about 486 *kirana* shops in the city. Similarly, there was a large number of retail dealers and the total revenue collected from them was more than 10,500 rupees. There were other taxes, like the entry tax *(dakhlai)*, which was levied on silk as well as grocery in 1770. The taxes on the former amounted to about 1,300 rupees at the rate of five rupees and five annas per maund. The rate on *kirana* was eleven annas per hundred rupees worth of groceries and the total amount collected under this head was about five hundred rupees. In other words, grocery worth about 72,000 rupees entered the city in 1770. *Naqadari* was collected at several points of entry to the city and amounted to 1,940 rupees. The taxes from the city markets made a considerable contribution to the state exchequer. The city was divided into a number of *chaklas* for the collection of *nazrana*. There is interesting information in our records on the collection of *nazrana*. For example, an oil presser *(teli)* used to pay two rupees as *nazarana*, and there were twelve oil pressers in the city.

The evolution of *sair* as an independent unit of revenue in state finances indicates that the state was exploring new sources of revenue. Marwad was not alone in adopting the policy of organising revenue resources from trade and commerce. A similar policy had been adopted in the early eighteenth century in the state of Amber (Jaipur). There is enough evidence also to suggest that the rulers of Amber evolved a systematic policy and mechanism for exploiting *sair* resources. It is also clear that the system of *ijara* was introduced and institutionalised in the sphere of *sair* taxes.[29] On the whole, it seems that the tax policies followed by the Rajput rulers during the eighteenth century had a close bearing on the growth of merchant capital. There is clear evidence also for the patronage extended to traders and merchants in Gujarat. Major Walker, for instance, observed that Gujarat had been the resort of many firms of India. Among others, he referred to Balkisan Seth, Kushalchand Ambaidas and Trivedi Arjunji. Indeed there was a well-established network of bankers and traders in the state of Baroda.[30] There is clear evidence also of the prevalence of *ijara* for taxes other than land revenue.[31]

II

The state played a vital role in the economy not merely by extending patronage to bankers and traders but also by direct participation in their enterprises, becoming a co-sharer in the benefits accruing from the merchant capital. A study of the *jamabandis* of the state of Jodhpur during the second half of the eighteenth century makes this abundantly clear. In 1770, for instance, the total money given on credit by the state in *pargana* Pali was more than 15,750 rupees. A little more than 15,440 rupees had been received out of this and about 332 rupees remained as balance. The number of banker-traders involved in the transactions was 45. Although the individual credit ranging from less than a rupee to 2,800 rupees was not large, the involvement of such a large number of bankers in a single *pargana* demonstrates the general trend in commercial enterprise.

Financial transactions involving huge sums were done not in cash but through various forms of money-orders, the *hundi* being the most common. The *hundi* covered almost all the areas of money transmission and payment by both government and private business. In western Rajasthan, the major portion of land revenue was apparently transmitted

[29]This information comes from the *chittis* of the years 1710 and 1711.

[30]*Sadari Pargana-ri Hundia*, V.S. 1839/A.D. 1782, Jodhpur Branch, Rajasthan State Archives, Bikaner.

[31]*Viaj-Bahi*, No.45, V.S. 1843/A.D. 1787 and *Nodh-Bahi*, No.48, give information on the revenues derived from the *naqas* and *mandis* of Baroda, Ahmedabad and other towns: Haribhakti Collection.

to the government treasury through *hundis*. The small town of Tappa Sadari contributed 27,777 rupees to the state treasury through *hundis* in 1782. The *hundis* were drawn in the names of Vimal Tarachand (425 rupees), Gopichand Maha Singh (275 rupees), Khasi Kushal Singh (1706 rupees), Shah Deep Singh and Maha Singh (10,001 rupees) and Hathi Singh (76 rupees), all of them bankers of Pali. The state had to pay *hundawan* or *batta* on *hundis* at rates respectively ranging from 0.94 to 3 per cent and 1.5 to 4 per cent. The practice of getting payment through *hundis* drawn on a place other than the receiver's own was quite common in the commercial enterprises and was managed systematically. *Barats* and *chitthis* were also used as instruments of credit by the state. The amount transferred through *barats* was very high, as the state used to defray through them the salaries, loans and money taken on credit. The whole business of credit and money transaction was looked after by the *potedars* who became the back-bone of the state economy.[32]

The entire system of money transaction, credit and accountancy acquired a prominent place in financial dealings. The traditional system of Indian banking proved expedient for the financial requirements of the contemporary society and polity. The multiplicity of money transactions and expansion of credit network promoted a sophisticated form of accountancy which enabled the business firms to adopt or evolve the system of double entry, and the use of different types of books *(bahis)* for cross reference.[33] The entries made in the *bahis* preserved in the Haribhakti Collection, which varied according to the subject of transaction make it clear that the Indian banking system had attained necessary qualification to meet the demand of the developed commercial economy of the eighteenth century. For example, Bahi No. 13 of V.S. 1835/A.D. 1778, named *Sarviaya-Nodh*, or the balance sheet of the firm, contains the accounts of all the bankers, the *sarkar* or the ruler and other prominent persons who had financial dealings with the Haribhakti firm. Prominent among them were Ratanji Kahanji, Samal Bechar, Mairal Narain and Sakhidas Pareekh.

The accounts of credit and debit of some of the bankers are cited below:

[32]The *potedar* or *fotedar* at the *pargana* level was responsible for keeping records of income and expenditure, the safe custody of cash, and exchange of coins. With the introduction of the *ijara* system his office became more important and it began to be given generally to *Mahajans*.

[33]G.D. Sharma, 'Business and Accountancy in Western India'.

KHATU RAJSHREE MAIRAL NARAIN, Margh sudi 1 to Asoj vadi 15 (1835 V.S.)

Credit		Debit	
Rs.16,23,039-14-3		Rs.6,95,955-13-3	
9,27,084-00-00	*baqi deno*	9,27,084-00-00	*baqi deno*
		16,23,039-13-03	
KHATU KAMAVISDAR SAMALDAS BHAKTIDAS			
Rs.11,28,728-08-03	II.III	Rs.14,99,187-08-15	
3,10,459-00-04	II *baqi leno*	3,10,459-00-04	II *baqi leno*
14,99,187-00-15			
KHATU PAREEKH SAMALDAS BACHERDAS			
Rs.7,17,708-00-04	III	Rs.8,47,487-00-02	
1,29,779-00-22	I *baqi leno*	1,29,779-00-22	I *baqi leno*
KHATU MANGAL SAKHIDAS PAREEKH			
2,827-08-03	I	2,82,103-04-22	II
1,29,779-00-22	I *baqi leno*	305-12-19	II *baqi deno*
2,82,103-04-22	II		

There are similar entries of credit and debit in this *bahi* for sixty-six bankers, all of whom had money transactions with the Haribhakti firm. Besides the bankers, entries are also made of many prominent persons of the Gaekwad nobility as well as the ruler. The firm maintained a separate account of the credit and debit of the *sarkar* of Shrimant Anandrao Gaekwad. The summary is cited below:

Credit	Debit	
Rs.28,06,576-12-02	Rs.48,30,696-04-01	
Rs.20,24,119-06-03	20,24,119-06-03	*baqi leno*
	24,27,356-06-03	*leno*
	3,227-00-00	*deno*

There are similar other *bahis* for the years following. There are other *bahis* furnishing detail and monthly financial transactions of the firm and all its branches. Among these the *hundi-vahis* need special mention. These *bahis* contain year-wise abstracts of all the *hundis* credited and debited.[34] The *hundi-vahi* of V.S. 1855/A.D. 1798 records a series of *hundis* operated by the firm, carrying the entry of the flow of capital (on account) in transaction, the names of the bankers and clients, and the places of issue and payment. A study of this *bahi* reveals that, besides *hundis*, a large part of the money on credit and in transaction was carried on by *chitthis* as the instrument of credit. The *chitthis* were used both for transmission of money and its payment to the party concerned as well as to confirm financial transactions carried through *hundis*.[35]

The state of currency and exchange that prevailed in the Baroda state is revealed by a *bahi* of V.S. 1857/A.D. 1800. The rate of conversion of *Panchantari* coins to the current currency is shown as Rs.0-12-0. An examination of the *bahis* pertaining to the period of our study indicates the existence of different kinds of coins. References are made to the Baroda, Broach, Shikai, British and Spanish coins. The prevalence of different kinds of coins necessitated the mediation of the *shroffs* (bankers) who changed the currency from one kind to another after charging *vatav (batta)* or discount. In the Baroda state the rate of exchange was constantly fluctuating in accordance with the market demand. At the time of brisk import trade, goods were bought with British money, while during the cotton season (March to May) cotton was purchased with Baroda rupees. The rate of exchange for the former period was 100 British rupees against 120 Baroda rupees. The *bahis* however, record that the intrinsic value of 114 ½ Baroda rupees *(babasahi)* and 102 ½ *shikai* were equal to 95 British rupees. In Rajasthan too, the business of exchange was quite lucrative due to the prevalence of different kinds of coins.[36] The state kept its own *shroff* to test the coins and to determine their exchange value.[37]

The intensification of commercial activities in the urban centres stratified the class of commercial intermediaries known as *arhtias* and *dalals* and *marfatias*. The prevalence of taxes like *dalali* and *arhat* indicates the importance of these two classes in the urban centres of Rajasthan and Gujarat. *Dalali* was charged from the professional brokers *(dalals)* by the state. The *dalal* worked as a middleman to the traders and

[34]Several *chitthis* in Haribhakti Collection, in Gujarati and Modi scripts, show the rate of interest on the capital and *manoti*. The rate of *hundawan* appears to have been one per cent.

[35]*Chittis* having bearing on financial transactions are long and detailed and, hence, extremely useful. Also, Appendix IV.

[36]*Chitthi* from Diwan Ramchandra to Purohit Syamram (A.D. 1710), *Diwan Huzuri*.

[37]*Pali Jama-Kharach Bahi*, V.S. 1827/A.D. 1770.

bankers in the purchase and sale of commodities and payment of *hundis*. The commission he received from the sellers and the buyers too was known as *dalali*.[38] The tax called *arhat* was collected on the commodities belonging to other traders and sold by, or collected at, the shop of an *arhatia* or commission agent. *Arhat* brought a good amount of revenue to the state treasury, and the *arhat* of the *mandi* was sometimes given on *ijara* to merchants and bankers of the town.[39] Merchants had to sell or purchase their commodities with the consent or in consultation with the authorised *arhatia*.[40]

A sample study of the Haribhakti firm shows a significant increase in the number of its agents *(marfatias)* at the various urban centres.[41] Like the Mirzamal Collection, the references cited in the documents of Haribhakti Collection make it clear that the *marfatias* and *gumastas* occupied an important position in the trade and banking establishment of that firm.[42] They were an integral part of the machinery evolved by the Haribhakti house for the realisation of land revenue and commercial taxes and formed the backbone of the trading operations conducted at the urban centres of Gujarat.[43] Among the prominent *marfatias* were Karamchand Phoolchand, Mithachand Karamchand, Bacher Kastur, Anupchand Jangir and Devchand Purshottam who worked in different markets of the towns and cities. The *marfatias* and *arhatias* assisted the firm in the collection of *sair* and *rahdari* in the urban centres like Ahmedabad, Nadiad, Baroda, Dhaboi and Jambhusar. They worked in cooperation with the Pareekhs, the Shahs and Vanotaras, with whom the firm had dealings. There are known instances of *marfatias* at Chakla Limda, Sarkhej, Raipur Mandi and Khanpur appointed by the firm in order to collect their dues. The principal *marfatias* operating at these places were Chaturbhuj, Pitamber Jivan and Atmaram. Even the *mahajans* trading in raw sugar, tobacco and other goods were unable to evade the payment of *sukhdi* and other taxes to the *marfatias*.[44] Significantly, the shares of both

[38] *Sanad-Bahi*, No. 287, V.S. 1824/A.D. 1767.

[39] *Sanad-Bahi*, No. 286, V.S.1818, 1820/A.D. 1761, 1763; No. 190, V.S. 1827/A.D. 1770; Jama-bandi (Nawâ), No.1352, V.S. 1830/A.D. 1773.

[40] For the rates of *arhat* in Rajasthan, G.D. Sharma, 'State and Business in Rajasthan During the Eighteenth Century', paper presented at the seminar on *Rajasthan History and Culture* at the University of Rajasthan, Jaipur in December 1987.

[41] The *chitthis* and *bahis* indicate the increase in numbers by the end of the century.

[42] Govind Agrawal, *Vanijay-Vyapar mein Munim Gumasto ki Bhumika*, Churu 1983.

[43] G.D. Sharma, 'Economy and Society in Rural Gujarat'.

[44] Shirin Mehta, 'The Mahajans and the Business Communities of Ahmedabad', *Business Communities of India; Revenue Department Volumes*, Maharashtra State Archives, Bombay 1830; no.9/290, 223-81.

the Peshwa and the Gaekwad were managed by the same *marfatias*.

Some of the *marfatias* were commissioned agents. A tobacco owner, shipping his goods from Cambay, employed a *marfatia* or a *dalal* of that place who had a running account with the *phoorza* or the Customs House at Cambay; he was not called upon to pay down the cash for duties on a consignment until he had received advice that the sale had been effected at the place to which the consignment was sent. A transaction between Cambay and Bombay was managed through *hundis* remitted to the Bombay *dalals* who deducted all their charges and forwarded the balance to the owners in the same way.[45] A similar pattern was observed in relation to trade transactions between Cambay, Surat, Konkan and the Gulf countries.

The introduction of *kamavisdari* and *ijaradari* and the involvement of the business class in the agrarian system for financial gain made the town market the focal point of economy in western India during the late eighteenth century. The Maratha financial policy intensified the economic activities of town markets. A study of town markets like Nadiad, Dhabhoi, Kapatvang, Aumreth and Mahmudabad in Gujarat, and Pali, Sanchor, Jalore and Jaitaran in western Rajasthan reveals that there were towns with geographical location which served as centres of distribution and collection of goods but not as *pargana* headquarters. The presence of the Company's *dalals* or *marfatias* in the different units of production and the involvement of local traders in collection and distribution of goods generated competition at the smallest unit of the trade.[46]

Considering the flow of capital, the volume of trade and the participation of traders, urban markets could be classified into three categories:

1. The central vein of the urban economy was, perhaps, the town markets that canalised the movement of commodities between the countryside and the town on the one hand and the town and the city market on the other. These markets were the primary sector of the credit and capital investment controlled by the *dalals* and *marfatias* representing the firms of the *pargana* towns and the city.
2. The markets which had grown and developed at the *pargana* headquarters catered to all commercial activities of the town as well as the *pargana*. In some of these markets money transactions had become highly commercialised and had developed links with the external regional markets. Baroda, Khera and Godhara in Gujarat and Pali,

[45]Ibid., 1842, 9/1342, 216.

[46]Jaspal Kaur Dhot, *Society and Economy of North Gujarat* (with special reference to Khera), Ph.D. Thesis, M.S. University of Baroda, 1987.

Phalodi and Pokharan in western Rajasthan could be placed in this category. Each of these towns had highly developed banking and commercial network and therefore formed a part of the larger framework of trade and money market.

3. In the third category fell those markets which were operating at the top, canalising the demand and supply of the regional and foreign markets. Their commercial activities were predominantly governed by the geographical and economic considerations, as in the case of Ahmedabad and Surat which continued to flourish in spite of the political upheavals.

The towns which had become centres of trade and commerce during the seventeenth century appear to have continued their dominance in the century following. Though the pattern of the markets, thus, remained the same, the business capital advanced significantly and intensified the capital investment in the market. A study of the money markets of Baroda and Surat, operated by the Haribhakti firm as reflected in the *hundis* issued from Surat to Baroda, Ujjain and the Deccan, makes it clear that Surat was contributing the maximum amount of cash to these places through *hundis*. The total flow of the money through *hundis* was 4,80,361 rupees in 1786 for Surat, Ahmedabad, Jambusar, Patlad, Ujjain and the Deccan. A study of the money transactions made through *barats* and *chitthis* suggests that Surat continued to maintain its prime position in the commercial and money market throughout the eighteenth century notwithstanding the emergence of Bombay as the main centre of India's trade with Europe. Though Surat catered to foreign trade and maintained the character of a port city, it had equally flourishing trading links with the internal markets of the country.

III

We can see in retrospect that the regional powers which replaced the Mughal empire in the eighteenth century did their best to develop the credit and banking network in the towns and cities of their dominions. Traders and bankers continued to enjoy freedom in their enterprises and enhanced their commercial capital by availing themselves of new opportunities. The trade in commodities was accompanied by a corresponding trade in liquid money capital.

Credit dealings with the government in the case of almost all the leading bankers of northern India became a regular feature of the period and an important branch of business from the beginning of the century.

The increasing penetration of the European companies in inland trade and the restrictions imposed on the local traders' participation in foreign trade obliged the Indian traders to concentrate on local and interregional trade.

The system of payment through bills was helpful not only to the merchants but also for transactions in general. Since the state itself had become a party to the system of credit, the bills of exchange became more and more the instrument of commercial credit, and usury became an accepted phenomenon in the market economy.

From one point of view the political change during the eighteenth century provided greater impetus for economic growth. The first impulse to the money market did not come from the side of supply or from capital seeking investment but from the demand from the princes due to their pressing need for money. The supply of commercial capital in the market significantly increased as a result of the money employment in the *ijara* of land revenue and other taxes on a considerable scale. Many Gujarati and Marwari merchants settled in the major cities and towns of western and central India where they helped in promoting trade and commerce as much as capital investment.

A major distinction, perhaps between the Indian bankers and their counterparts in Europe was that the former did not resort to mobilisation of savings from small household savers. This not only deprived them of the opportunities of augmenting their working capital and getting profit by acquiring it at lower rate of interest and lending it at higher, but also prevented them from developing a modern banking system. But the Indian merchants did not have any restrictions on their trading activities imposed by political boundaries, a situation they faced in the first half of the nineteenth century. It was this tendency which was prevalent during the Mughal period and was intensified during the eighteenth century. This freedom enjoyed by the traders and bankers was the most powerful incentive for shifting their centres of enterprise and establishments to new locales depending upon their convenience and patronage. It was this feature which made the business of commission possible and so enormously extended the number of those who could share in the advantages of the growing money market.

The merchant associations were local assemblies aiming at dealing in bills of exchange and loans of capital for commerce. The transaction of this business was a common object which brought together merchants of diverse backgrounds who otherwise had nothing in common. The associations were able to deal with one another directly in buying and selling bills and loans of common capital. Although dominated by Gujaratis and Marwaris, these assemblies included merchants of all regions and religions.

APPENDIX I
PARGANA JAITARAN RI SAIR RI JAMA
(in Rupees -Annas- paisas)

JAMA V.S.1843/A.D.1786		JAMA V.S.1844/A.D.1787		JAMA V.S.1845/A.D.1788	
12 months		**13 months**		**12 months**	
1432-02-3	Amadni	1296-13-3	Amadni	2299-04-1	Amadni
2332-10-0	Thana	2920-05-3	Thana	2148-01-2	Thana
18-11-3	Ijara	23-00-0	Ijara		Ijara
	Villages		Villages	24-00-0	Villages
35-08-1	Other par.	8-04-3	Other par.	22-11-2	Other par.
13-05-0	Batta	9-11-0	Batta	——	
10-15-2	Farohi	22-13-1	Farohi	30-06-3	Farohi
00-01-3	Kasarayat	00-08-2	Kasarayat	00-02-2	Kasarayat
		1-01-2	Hundawan	——	
				2-12-0	Talbana
				3-08-3	Badhtira
3843-06-3		4281-15-1		4530-15-1	
Kharch		**Kharch**		**Kharch**	
906-08-0	Mahinadar	950-10-1	Mahinadar	950-10-1	Mahinadar
283-00-0	Sayer	283-00-0	Sayar	293-00-0	
	Kacheri		Talaqe 3		Sayer 4
110-00-0	Daroga		Men		Men
	11 Months	667-10-1	Thana 9	667-10-1	
	@ 10/-		Men 18		Thana 9
77-00-0	Mushrif		Months 12		Men 18
	@ 7/-		Rs. 648/-		Months 12
66-00-0	Navisanda		13 months		Rs. 648/-
	at the office		Rs. 667-06-1		Months 13
	of Daroga				Rs. 667-11-1
253-00-0	Received	950-10-1		857-10-1	
	from Kacheri	7-05-0	senai ra	Baqi Rs. 3324	
30-00-0	Vatwal one		Thana 9		
	@2½	957-15-1			
			Baqi 3324/-		
283-00-0					
623-08-0	Thana9,Men				
	18 @ Rs. 3 P.M.				
906-08-0					
6-12-0	paid later to				
	Sahnas of Thana 9				
	@ 12 per Thana P.A.				
913-04-0					
	Baqi 2930-02-3				
	of 12 months				

APPENDIX II

YEAR	PARGANA NAGOR			PARGANA MERTA			PARGANA SOJAT		
V. S. / A. D.	Total Jama	Sair Jama	Percentage	Total Jama	Sair Jama	Percentage	Total Jama	Sair Jama	Percentage
	Rs.-Annas-Ps.	Rs.-Annas-Ps.		Rs.-Annas-Ps.	Rs.-Annas-Ps.		Rs.-Annas-Ps.	Rs.-Annas-Ps.	
1808-1751	316552-1-2	73855-14-2	23.33	-	-	-	-	-	-
1813/1756	130050-7-1	33283-14-2	25.59	-	-	-	66191-2-0	7825-13-1	11.82
1817/1760	190229-8-2	44111-15-2	23.19	-	-	-	-	-	-
1818/1761	-	-	-	-	-	-	58576-12-0	6520-12-0	11.13
1819/1762	-	-	-	-	-	-	65990-0-0	6510-12-1	9.87
1821/1764	-	-	-	156498-11-3	23700-14-2	15.14	-	-	-
1822/1765	149136-7-2	44753-10-3	30.01	260038-8-2	22224-1-3	8.55	55257-4-0	7488-3-1	13.55
1823/1766	-	-	-	-	-	-	41710-14-1	7000-6-3	16.78
1824/1767	-	-	-	147088-2-3	27069-12-2	18.40	38078-6-3	10886-13-3	28.59
1825/1768	133320-10-3	44821-9-1	33.62	129686-4-1	25173-9-1	19.41	61034-11-2	7548-10-3	12.37
1826/1769	1159960-7-0	60538-14-3	37.85	167859-6-0	35881-13-1	21.39	32034-12-2	6045-7-2	18.88
1827/1770	-	-	-	-	-	-	38549-1-3	7057-0-1	18.31
1828/1771	147179-11-2	56108-00-3	38.12	129683-14-0	39325-8-1	30.32	43663-8-2	10380-3-2	23.77
1829/1772	160038-10-2	51638-2-3	32.27	-	-	-	50699-11-2	10444-2-1	20.60
1830/1773	214138-12-1	55864-12-0	26.08	-	-	-	56813-8-2	11836-3-1	20.19
1832/1775	1126811-3-2	57586-8-3	45.41	-	-	-	-	-	-
1833/1776	131744-10-1	70690-4-3	53.66	86856-12-2	12277-7-3	14.13	-	-	-
1834/1777	131677-7-1	58329-15-3	30.43	-	-	-	-	-	-
1835/1778	-	-	-	110156-9-3	12146-14-3	11.20	-	-	-
1836/1779	188217-6-1	35811-11-0	19.03	-	-	-	-	-	-
1837/1780	183764-2-2	63416-5-3	34.51	-	-	-	-	-	-
1838/1781	241862-6-1	74384-6-3	30.75	160585-0-0	32799-3-3	20.42	-	-	-
1839/1782	-	-	-	135776-2-0	20346-9-2	14.99	25831-10-0	7952-8-0	30.78
1841/1784	162435-12-3	55543-8-1	-	-	-	-	-	-	-
1850-1793	-	-	-	-	-	-	41341-1-1	2772-13-0	6.71

Note : The table is based on the Jama-bandi Bahis available at the Jodhpur branch of the Rajasthan State Archives, Bikaner.

APPENDIX III

REVENUE FROM SIWAI-JAMA OF SAIR

Mandi	Bharai	Vajankasi	Chungi	Mahajani	Balai	Siwai Balai	Ijafa	Total
Batipur	39-3-1	140-11-1	45-5-0	1315-12-0	192-3-3	240-0-0	408-13-1	2383-0-0
Hajipur	26-6-2	50-1-0	37-13-2	1825-1-0	72-5-2	115-11-1	156-9-3	2284-9-2
Behrampur	86-1-0	139-6-3	105-14-0	2912-14-0	253-11-2	342-14-2	1485-9-1	5326-7-0
Raghunathpur	14-1-3	43-4-3	62-11-3	4378-8-0	91-9-1	57-4-0	312-12-0	4960-3-2
Rajpur	14-14-3	106-3-3	67-12-0	3612-5-1	50-4-0	63-13-1	592-14-3	4568-3-3
Saraspur	18-5-0	54-4-0	19-1-0	525-11-2	304-1-2	50-8-1	111-10-0	1083-9-0
Shahganj	150-15-0	0-6-3	355-1-0	62-9-2	76-8-2	696-11-1	24-6-0	1367-0-2
Meetha Khali	14-1-3	25-2-0	25-2-0	-	561-5-0	-	-	625-10-3
Bakarabad	1-3-2	-	56-1-2	-	-	-	-	57-5-0
				Misc.	1602-00			
Total	471-6-1	559-8-3	723-2-0	14632-14-0	3771-15-3	1566-14-2	3092-11-0	22656-5-0

APPENDIX IV
FLOW OF CAPITAL THROUGH HUNDIS
(in rupees)

Cities and Towns	1786 A.D.	1809A.D.
Ahmedabad to Baroda	--	193000
Ahmedabad to Deccan	12101	—
Ahmedabad to Poona	—	2500
Amerethi to Petlad	—	861
Baroda to Ahmedabad	19012	—
Baroda to Deccan	75000	5000
Baroda to Navnagar	—	85000
Baroda to Petlad	4600	—
Baroda to Jambusar	300	—
Baroda to Bombay	—	9700
Baroda to Surat	36895	—
Baroda to Ujjain	26000	—
Bombay to Baroda	38000	—
Bombay to Deccan	--	7000
Barsad to Petlad	—	6350
Broach to Baroda	—	2000
Cambay to Baroda	—	2406
Cambay to Petlad	—	3600
Deccan to Baroda	1751	—
Deccan to Surat	—	6600
Jambusar to Petlad	—	5529
Kadi to Baroda	—	1800
Kheda to Petlad	--	102
Mahmudabad to Baroda	—	725
Nadiad to Baroda	6000	—
Nadiad to Petlad	—	102
Nadiad to Surat	6000	—
Navsari to Broach	--	305
Petlad to Baroda	—	6785
Petlad to Cambay	--	87
Petlad to Surat	—	8075
Ratlam to Baroda	—	2500
Ratlam to Surat	1700	—
Surat to Petlad	—	1100
Songarh to Surat	—	4500

Cities and Towns	1786 A.D.	1809 A.D.
Surat to Baroda	—	2500
Surat to Deccan	89457	77000
Surat to Ujjain	1500	2500
Songarh to Baroda	—	35
Sojetra to Petlad	—	—
Ujjain to Deccan	190000	2001
Vaso to Petlad	--	2000
	508296	443663

URBANISM IN SOUTH INDIA : EIGHTEENTH–NINETEENTH CENTURIES

NARAYANI GUPTA*

The cobbled path of Indian urban history has all too often been steam-rollered by generalisations. Stereotypes of oriental/western towns, pre-industrial/modern towns, medieval/modern towns should be put aside, and more attention given to regional patterns and to indigenous perceptions. For the recent centuries, the concept of the 'colonial town' is undergoing constant modification – as can be seen in the work of one of the pioneers in this field – Professor Rhoads Murphey.[1] The colonial towns have been most intensively studied in South America and South–east Asia.[2] Much less research has been done on South Asia and on Africa.[3] There is often a tendency to transfer concepts valid for Latin America and South-east Asia to other colonial regimes. This is to ignore the time factor, and fail to give sufficient weightage to pre-colonial

*The author would like to thank the Homi Bhabha Fellowships Council for the award of a Fellowship in 1981-83 which made it possible to do research on this fascinating subject.

[1]Compare his *Shanghai: Key to Modern China*, Harvard 1953, with 'Traditionalism and Colonialism: Changing Urban Roles in Asia', *Journal of Asian Studies*, Vol. XXIX, November 1969, and again with *The Outsiders: The Western Experience in India and China*, Ann Arbor 1977.

[2]For South America, compare the works of T.Caplow, R.M. Morse, C.T. Smith and R.C. Smith, for South–east Asia, the works of N.S. Ginsburg, C. Geertz, T.G. McGee and R.R. Reed.

[3]There are some empirical studies of aspects of Indian urbanism, but archaeologists, architects, historians, sociologists and geographers still tend to work in isolation from each other. For Africa, only two areas have received attention – the West and the North (the latter relatively more because of the affinities of its towns with those of the Middle East).

urbanism. A distinction has to be initially made between towns created by the colonial regime and others that existed in the colonial empire but were antecedent to it. It is only comparatively recently that urban systems and characteristics of the pre-colonial or non-colonised non-western world (Russia, China, Japan) have been studied.[4] These will have some bearing for the Indian situation. Indians have yet to produce a corpus of writings on their own urban history comparable at least to the volume of output on agrarian history, which has been so far a convenient field for research because of the excellent series of revenue data. For urban history, the lack of systematic data makes it difficult to answer many questions.

In India, colonial policy and economy were superimposed on a pre-existing pattern. The rationale and content of Indian urbanism have to be studied, and comparisons made in terms of location, morphology, range of economic and civic activity, of communities, between these towns and a colonial enclave like Madras. Such comparison has to some extent been done for Calcutta and Bombay, but not for Madras.[5] The justification for studying the south Indian case is that it was here that British military rule was first established, though it was not till the 1820s that the administrative settlement of Madras Presidency was completed. From 1698 (when the Mughals conquered Jinji) to 1806 (when the last stage of the south Indian revolt was suppressed), India south of the Krishna was the arena for a 'struggle for supremacy'. In such a situation of prolonged instability, the urban areas played an important part, and their fortunes were tied up with the changing economic and political map.

I

Writers in south India have for centuries been quite clear that town and country were distinct; the suggestion that the town is merely a large village has begun only with sociologists recently.[6] There is a basic common element of planning in both rural and urban settlements with the

[4]Gilbert Rozman, *Urban Networks in Russia 1750-1809 and Premodern Periodisation*, Princeton 1974; P. Wheatley, *Pivot of the Four Quarters*, Edinburgh 1971. See, P. Wheatley and Thomas, *From Court to Capital: A Tentative Interpretation of the Origins of the Japanese Urban Tradition*, Chicago 1978.

[5]For Calcutta, Atiya Habeeb, *Characteristics of Colonial Urbanisation –A Case Study of Calcutta and its Hinterland, 1872-1921*, Ph.D. Thesis, Jawaharlal Nehru University, Delhi 1979. For Bombay, Lakshmi Subramanian, 'Bombay and the West Coast in the 1740s', *Indian Economic and Social History Review*, XVIII, No. 2, April-June 1981.

[6]D.F. Pocock, 'Sociologies: Urban and Rural', *Contributions to Indian Sociology*, IV, Leiden 1960.

division into the Brahman area *(agraharam)* and the non-Brahman area *(cheri)*, a buffer zone, and a grid pattern dictated empirically by the climate and by the central position accorded to the temple and the *ratha* (temple chariot), and theoretically by the *Silpa Sastras*. Classical Tamil rejoices in the city, in its design, its architecture, its culture. As for medieval European towns, each was seen as possessed of distinctive attributes – strength, beauty, wealth. At the same time, the sense of the unity of mankind was conveyed in lines of incomparable beauty: 'Every town our home town, every man a kinsman'.[7]

One of the earliest instances of ecotype classification are the five types of landscape in the Puram (exterior) poems of the Cankan (Sangam) period, with details of their inhabitants, vegetation, and settlement patterns. These are *kurinci* (forest) where the settlement pattern was of small hamlets, *palai* (wasteland) with villages or forts, *mullai* (forest) with small settlements (*pati* or *cheri*), *neytal* (seashore) with large ports, *marutam* (cultivated fields) with large towns.[8] Here is a very workable set of typologies – towns along river valleys and the coast, fortifications in rugged territory, small communities of gatherers in the forests which cannot accommodate larger urban clusters and which are by their impenetrability their own defence. David Ludden in his excellent work on the Tirunelveli district has shown how 'ecological zones are selective and adaptive arenas in the processes of cultural diffusion' and how they 'select' their populations, since only certain types of people will live in particular zones.[9]

Another case of perception from within is the traditional division of south India into *mandalas* (regional units) which have often in the past coincided with political units.[10] These are not only the major linguistic areas but further subdivisions, essentially geographical. Topography dictated routes for the passage of goods and of armies and, later, the political frontiers of those 'in control of the means of destruction, protection and extraction'. This seemingly obvious point has to be made because of the barrier that has persisted between geographers and historians, with the link of cultural geography having been forged only recently, and that too only for an earlier period of south Indian history.

[7]A.K. Ramanujan, *Poems of Love and War*, Delhi 1985, 162.

[8]K. Zvelebil, *The Smile of Murugan*, Leiden 1973, 94; Xaviers S. Thani Nayagam, *Landscape and Poetry*, Bombay 1966.

[9]D. Ludden, 'Ecological Zones and the Cultural Economy of Irrigation in Southern Tamilnadu', *South Asia*, I, No. 1, 1978.

[10]C. Mackenzie, MSS British Museum (cited hereafter as BM), Addl. 13660, f. 46 ff 'History'.

The irrationality of the boundaries of the Madras Presidency has not been adequately appreciated and the political history of the last two centuries has treated it as a unit. Therefore, the geographical and historical and cultural unity of Kerala, cutting across political frontiers, and the *mandala* divisions of the Tamil areas, subdividing a political unit and the unique position of the Mysore region, have been passed by. The *Mandalas* of the Tamil macro-region were Tondaimandalam, Naduvil-nadu, Cholamandalam, Kongunad and Pandyamandalam. Mysore was Gangavadi, Kerala a separate unit. Kongunad was an area which came under the control of Karnataka rulers occasionally. The Pandyamandalam itself could be divided into the northern and southern, divided by the Vaigai-Tambraparni Doab. The first was in the direct line of influence from the Tamil country, the second had links with Kerala and overseas. These differences were appreciated in the eighteenth century, but the levelling effect of British administration after 1800 obscured them.

An urban pattern with a few large towns and many small ones (as in the Ganga plain) is characteristic of a well-coordinated transport network by road/river,[11] or of a powerful regime, where the rulers live in garrison towns.[12] In the latter situation, large numbers of people are commandeered or attracted to live in and near the town. South India in the eighteenth century did not have either of these features. This, together with its variegated geography, made it then and since, a region of many middle-size towns. It is worth pondering that older towns continued to be populous, but that Gangai-Kondacholapuram and Vijayanagar – artificially founded capitals – lasted only as long as their empires.

The geography of south India made the establishment of a stable large empire there difficult. The Chola and the Vijayanagar empires must be regarded as exceptions. For this reason, great interest attaches to the urban situation during these regimes, because a well-developed urban network is a condition of a stable large empire in the pre-railway age. The basic issue of the degree of central control in the Chola empire is a subject of controversy.[13] Tied up with this is a rather fundamental question: were urban places under the Cholas simply areas where a high density of population had occurred around a temple, or were the *nagarams* autono-

[11] J. Deloche, *La Circulation en Inde avant la Revolution des Transports* (cited hereafter as *La Circulation en Inde*)I, Paris 1980, 103.

[12] K.N. Chaudhuri, 'Reflections on Town and Country in Mughal India', *Modern Asian Studies*, 12, No. 1, February 1978.

[13] Burton Stein, *Peasant State and Society in Medieval South India*, Delhi 1980, and the two reviews of it in *The Indian Economic and Social History Review*, XVIII, Nos. 3 & 4, July-December 1981.

mous units where the inhabitants were economically independent enough to support or oppose the superior regime as it suited them?[14] If the latter be true, it assumes that the towns were vital in holding the empire together, by reason of their control of trade and manufacture, even when the latter was not necessarily carried on inside the town boundaries. This would appear to have been the case, since the geography of the macro-region made it difficult for the imperial government to control the many 'knot-towns' (that is, towns at intersection points, in gaps in the mountains or in the area between highland and plain, or at crossings of arterial roads).

Another feature affecting urbanism was the large volume of trade along the coasts, spanning the countries from Africa to China. This meant that while there were many urban dwellers engaged in trade, few towns were closely connected commercially with their immediate hinterlands. Likewise, the merchant communities, whether Chettis or Labbais, had strong regional links but weak local ones.

The great volume of coastal and overseas trade necessitated warehousing, and quarters for merchants, local and foreign, which accounted for the towns on the Kerala coast. This is in contrast to the absence of urban concentrations in the interior of Kerala, whose people had a marked antipathy to living in towns. The Mysore plateau favoured one central emporium (Bangalore/Mysore/Srirangapattanam) and garrison towns on its frontiers. The agricultural abundance of the Kaveri valley encouraged many large urban settlements. There were sub-regions of rocky terrain and dense forests where roads did not penetrate, but the peninsula was criss-crossed with arterial roads. Density of population varied greatly. The major towns in the eighteenth century were Nagar, Hosur, Salem Erode, Dindigul, Madurai, Tirupattur, Tiruchirapalli, Tanjavur, Kanchi, Bangalore, Srirangapattanam, and the ports.[15] The rural areas were serviced by middle-size towns (known as *qasbas*, as in north India) and by small towns.

Certain patterns of trade in south India were constant over a long period- the sale of sea salt from the coast and grain from the river valleys to the interior by *banjaras* (itinerant traders), the large number of harbours on the Kerala coast and the relatively few on the inhospitable east, the trade link between Coromandel and Ceylon, the trade between the Kaveri valley and the Mysore plateau by way of the

[14] Kenneth R. Hall, *Trade and Statecraft in the Age of the Cholas*, Delhi 1980.

[15] The route maps prepared for the eighteenth century campaigns, and those compiled by Orme, help us to identify significant towns and *choultries* in the 1750s and 1760s.

Kongunad area, and of Kerala with Mysore and with the Kaveri valley by way of Palghat. The great difference between the price of grain in Madras and in Tiruchirapalli in the 1780s indicates that communications, while steady, were slow. Time and again it was commented that there were commodities of long-distance trade necessary for the needs of the common man. It was also often noticed that urban areas bred their own demands of items of conspicuous consumption. These multiplied as political power became fragmented.[16]

The most permanent of the urban settlements in south India were the pilgrim sites, which can be regarded as culturally generative. To speak of 'temple towns' is a tautology, for every town had one or more temples with more or less of a catchment area in terms of worshippers. Some had attracted large numbers of pilgrims from all over the subcontinent through the centuries, despite various political changes. Hinduism was unique in having a regional aspect to its pilgrimage pattern.[17] In south India, six Shaivite shrines and six Murugan temples were listed[18] – the original tourist industry complete with package tours. The twenty-two major shrines (especially Kumbakonam, Tiruchirapalli, Kanchi and Madurai), had been economic nodal points at the time of their inception. But over the centuries their piety itself became their rationale, and the reason for their being linked by trunk roads. The mental geography of a Tamilian's mind is illustrated by a palanquin bearer's offer to a traveller, to take him as far as Kashi. When the Raja of Tanjavur went on a pilgrimage in the 1820s, it was to Kashi.[19] The Baramahal Records of the 1780s noticed the shrines of Tiruvannamalai and Tirupati (the northern frontier of the Tamil cultural region) as the venues of the most important festivals.[20]

Urban places with major temples became pilgrimage sites, or halting points on pilgrim routes. From Sangam times there are references to the grand road from Kanchi to the Kaveri delta, which formed a section of the trunk road from Kalahasti to Kanya Kumari via Madurai, and the major one from Tirupati to Kanchi, Tiruvannamalai, Chidambaram, Madurai

[16] Research on the eighteenth century has concentrated on overseas trade, and Mysore-Malabar trade. There is no work on trade within the Tamil Nadu area for this period except Brian Murton's work on the Coimbatore region.

[17] S.M. Bhardwaj, *Hindu Places of Pilgrimage in India, California* 1973; J Deloche, *La Circulation en Inde*, I, 93-94.

[18] F.W. Clothey, *The Many Faces of Murugan*, The Hague 1978.

[19] King Sarfoji, *Tristhalli Yatrechya Lavanya* (text and translation), Tanjore 1951.

[20] *Baramanal Records*, Section III, *Inhabitants*, Madras 1907.

and to Rameswaram.[21] A state of warfare was not a deterrent to the pious, and in the 1760s there are descriptions of the great crowds which gathered at Tirupati every August, and of a convoy of 4,000 Jain pilgrims.[22] Bowland in the 1790s was surprised to note that 'the spirit of erecting these buildings (that is *choultries*) is not yet extinguished'.[23] Since building roads and *choultries* were acts of piety, these routes were well maintained. Bartolomeo noted that to destroy a *choultry* was reckoned a crime. Corneille in the mid- eighteenth century stated that there were *choultries* at distances of one hour's travel, and the 'the fashionable crime of highway robbery' was totally absent.[24] (More daunting were the 200 strong herds of elephants that moved at night in the stretch between Kaveripak and Venkatagiri!). The political capitals were dramatic but unstable rivals of the major shrines. Those which were not involved in military skirmishes, as was Srirangam because of its proximity to Tiruchirapalli, were not affected demographically. A place of pilgrimage for Muslims has been described in the ballad of the *nawab* of Arcot's ceremonial pilgrimage to Nagore.[25]

The functional classification of towns raises serious inadequacies. Were Bhavani and Tirunelveli important becacuse of their sanctity as *sangams* (confluence of two rivers) or because they were situated at key points on east - west routes? Was Coimbatore's significance religious or strategic? Were Madurai and Karur important as shrines or because they were located at conveniently fordable points of the river? Were Arcot and Vellore commercial centres or defensive points?[26] The answer is that sites at convenient geographic points became commercial centres and therefore had to be defended, and that the main arteries of pilgrim traffic led to central places becoming large towns.

The successor states to the Vijayanagar empire were not based in new towns (as were the successor states of the Mughal empire) but reverted to established central places – Tanjavur/Kumbakonam, Madurai, Vellore/Gingee, Mysore/ Srirangapattanam. In the eighteenth century, the changes that occurred were: (a) the shift of the Deccan political centre from Bijapur, Golconda and the Raichur Doab to Hyderabad; (b) the

[21] Deloche, *La Circulation Inde*, I, 77.

[22] Col. Cosby 'My Indian Campaigns, 1767-78', MS British Library, Addl. 29898, f. 278.

[23] Walker of Bowland Papers, National Library of Scotland, Edinburgh, MS. 13626, f. 58.

[24] J. Corneille, *Journal of My Service in India*, Folio Society, London 1966, 60.

[25] *Bahar-i-Azam Jahi* (trans. by Nainar), Madras 1950.

[26] A. Ramesh, 'Some Aspects of the Functional Morphology of the Towns in Tamilnadu and Deccan', *Urban Geography in Developing Countries*, Proceedings of IUG Symposium, No. 15, Varanasi.

establishment of a state in Mysore; (c) the swift increase in economic activity linked to ports with bad harbours on the Coromandel coast – Madras and Pondichery. In the 1730s and 1740s there was a large volume of trade controlled by the British merchants of Madras which was to decline in relative terms after the conquest of Bengal. The 1760s-1790s saw a major increase in Mysore-Malabar trade. Trade and deviance are more important imperatives to the maintenance of roads than is revenue collection. The myth of the eighteenth century as a century of chaos breaks down when we note the excellent condition of the roads. The detailed lists of places and *choultries* compiled and mapped by Robert Orme indicate that traffic on the roads was chiefly of pedestrians, merchants, coolies and (some) pilgrims, with halting places spaced eight miles apart.[27] Coolies and the poorer inhabitants of towns were prepared to carry goods only to the nearest town, but palanquin-bearers could cover distance of thirty-five miles a night.[28]

In a century of changing political frontiers, geography ruled supreme in deciding urban concentrations. The number of fortified places multiplied in direct proportion to the degrees of insecurity. Colin Mackenzie distinguished places with the suffix '*kotta*' from those named '*durgam*', seeing the first as earlier, fortified to protect all inhabitants, while the latter came into being in the last days of Vijayanagar and were meant solely to protect the viceroy's family and retainers.[29] During the Vijayanagar period Gingee, Dindigul, Madurai, Tanjavur, Tiruchirapalli, Vellore, Bangalore, and Chandragiri were fortified defensive points. They acted as a catalyst in bringing large numbers of people together in confined places. It also made these towns very broad-based in linguistic and religious composition, with no indication of tension between different groups. Stein's statement that these were 'intended to support Telugu migrants as well as provide a command presence over the Tamil plain'[30] implies a divide between rulers and ruled that has yet to be substantiated by empirical evidence. What is striking from early population tabulations is the cosmopolitanism of all the larger towns.

The groping fashion in which, in the days of its decline, the capital of the Vijayanagar empire was moved successively eastward to Penukonda to Chandragiri and then Vellore, indicated a sense of insecurity in face of

[27] Orme MSS, India Office Library (cited hereafter as IOL), Vol.50.

[28] R.R. Bowyer, 'Journal 1781-4', IOL MSS n.f.

[29] C. Mackenzie, 'Journal of Remarks and Observations made on the march from Hyderabad to Seringapatam and the Mysore Campaign of 1798-99', BM Addl. 13663.

[30] B. Stein, *Peasant State and Society in Medieval South India*, 394.

the defiance of the eastern kingdoms of Tanjavur, Gingee and Madurai (Tirumala Nayak himself shifted the capital from Tiruchirapalli to Madurai because the latter was more central), and also a quest for an impregnable capital. It may be stated as an axiom that as regimes become more insecure, they retreat to places of greater and greater height. The balkanisation that followed Talikota did not create a stable situation, because the separatist kingdoms were based on only very rough geographical divisions. Therefore the need to have many forts to defend the frontiers of each against each. The *nayakaships* were divided into *palayams* (cantonments) manned by local inhabitants. Pudukottai, Kalaijarkoil and Tirupattur were the forts of the Madurai *nayakas*. The headquarters of each cantonment *(palayam)* became an urban place. The map of places with the suffix '*palayam*' would indicate areas of greatest vulnerability – Tanjavur area had no town with this suffix, whereas the Comibatore area, vital in the power struggle between Mysore and the Coromandel coast had ninety-four.[31] Ringing the cities of Mysore and Bangalore were the forts of Kotagiri, Venkatagiri, Mulbagal, Kolar and Arakal. In 1716 the local deputy of the Nizam, located in the triangular area of Vellore-Gingee-Tiruchirapalli, felt secure enough to move the capital to the more open Arcot. Later *nawabs* of Arcot had a ring of forts round their territory.

There is a comment in the critical years of the 1780s about busy activity at a rock-fort belonging to Hyder Ali near Bangalore. The most inaccessible areas of the mountains and forests were the headquarters- '*les petites villes*-[32]of the *palaiyagars* ('poligars'-military commanders). By virtue of their locale they were able to hold out longest against British engulfment. The axes of the coordinated rising of 1801 were Belgaum, Anagundi, Dharwar, Soonda, Harappanahalli, Shikarpur, Bellum, Pazhassy, Wynaad, Deli, Tiruchirapalli, Virupakshi, Sivaganga, Sivagiri, Ramnad, and Panjalam Kurichi. The rebel leagues were those of Ramnad, Tirunelveli, Dindigul, Malabar (Marudu Pandya was a link between the Tirunelvli and Dindigul Leagues, Tipu and the Gounders of Coimbatore between Dindigul and Malabar, the Kallars between the Coimbatore groups and the Tamil groups).[33] As in the case of the Marathas, while geography enabled these areas to withstand conquest it also made for their mutual isolation.

[31] S. Natesan, 'Some-Place-Names of the Coimbatore Region', *Journal of the Madras Geographical Association*, 2 and 3, 1930, and S. Natesan, 'A Study of the Place-Names of the Tanjore District': ibid, XII, No. 2, July 1937.

[32] Lettres *Edifiantes et Curieuses*, Paris 1865, 269.

[33] K. Rajayyan, *South Indian Rebellion*, Madras 1971.

The demilitarisation of the *palaiyagars'* forts created a large degree of dislocation for the erstwhile military personnel, the 'peons'. These either joined the British army or turned to trade (in the case of Muslim retainers recruited from elsewhere) or agriculture (in the case of local recruits). This was the first large scale de-urbanisation that occurred as a result of the change of regime in the 1790s.[34] The majority of these places, however, retained their economic function as distributing centres, even after their forts were destroyed. Towns in the Kongunad – Erode, Coimbatore and Salem, are the best examples of this.[35]

The late eighteenth century in north and eastern India has a large number of poems on the 'ruined city'. Early Tamil literature has magnificent descriptions of towns, but there is no such strain in the eighteenth century ballads. The inference is that the towns affected by the wars suffered less devastation than did those of the north, and that the spoliation of a town was not an occasion for total grief, because the inhabitants could make a new beginning in the countryside.[36]

Srirangapattanam before its fall had a population of more than 150,000, and Tanjavur 100,000. A fort like Sivagiri had 10,000 houses in the 1760s.[37] There is no remark by Europeans from Paris or London that south Indian towns were crowded or the lanes narrow; in fact, their comments were usually complimentary.[38] It is significant that Rennell should have stated that Indian towns accommodated fewer people in the same area than did a European city.[39] Much land was reserved for gardens and reservoirs. Tiruchirapalli and Bangalore had numerous gardens, and in Tiruvattur, at least, there was a ban on the cutting of trees in the fort.[40] Thoroughfares were very wide – the *rath* streets around the Coimbatore, Pudukottai and Tanjavur palaces, and the Madurai temple, and that

[34] It would be worthwhile comparing the rising of 1801 in south India with that of 1857 in north and central India in terms of the participation by dispossessed retainers and small rulers.

[35] Brian Murton, 'Evolution of Settlement Structure in North Kongu till 1966', B.E.F. Beck (ed), *Perspectives in a Regional Culture*, Delhi 1979; and 'Towns and Markets in Salem in the 18th Century'(MSS).

[36] A.K. Ramanujam, 'Towards an Anthology of City Images', R.G. Fox (ed), *Urban India*, Duke 1970.

[37] Madras Board of Revenue Consultations, 1798, Walker of Bowland MSS, Vol 13615 B: Orme MSS, IOL (India Office Library), Vol. 4-5, ff. 308-9.

[38] Narayani Gupta, 'The Hunt for that Elusive Hero: The Indian Craftsman-Builder', *Design*, October/December 1982, 24.

[39] J. Rennel, *Memoir of a Map of Hindoostan*, London 1793, 58 (Information supplied by Prof. S. Bhattacharya).

[40] British Library Addl. MSS 29898. f. 259.

between the palace and the Ekambareswara temple in Kanchi are typical. This was a feature of all predominantly Hindu towns.[41] Processions – royal, religious, and to celebrate weddings – were an integral part of town life.

Buchanan's statement that in large towns, Brahmans occupied a special quarter, generally the best fortified one, has to be read to mean that they occupied the fort, in their capacity as officials.[42] Triponathera in Cochin was typical of Kerala towns; it had a very small *petta* (inhabited chiefly by local Christians) next to the fort.[43] The pattern of trade in Kerala was such as to make a large commercial *petta* unnecessary. The Nairs lived in their *tharwads* (family estates), away from urban areas. Merchants – Hindus, Europeans or Muslims – tended to cluster together. Rulers, when leasing out towns to Europeans, specified that the houses of Brahmans should not be occupied by people of other castes, but there does not seem to have been a spatial division between neighbourhoods of different castes.[44] The Europeans made a fetish of respecting caste divisions, and the difference between Right-hand and Left-hand castes. (This curious *vertical* division cutting through the *varna* differences, prevailed in Tamil Nadu, Karnataka and Andhra).[45] When Black Town in Madras was being rebuilt, it was specified 'that different quarters should be assigned to the several castes'.[46] In Pondichery and Madras, separate streets were allocated to each.[47] In Nagapattanam, the Dutch at one point decided that mixed marriages were the only means to 'maintain their power in India'.[48] But from the middle of the eighteenth century there was little open mingling of the races.

[41] Julian S. Smith, 'Madurai, India: The Architecture of a City', M. Arch., M.I.T., 1976. There are many descriptions of these in contemporary visitors' accounts.

[42] F. Buchanan, *A Journey from Madras through the Countries of Mysore, Canara, Malabar*, Vol. I, London 1807, 55.

[43] *Geographical and Statistical Memoir of the Survey of Travancore and Cochin, 1810-21*, Vol. 4. Madras 1893, 1.

[44] This conclusion is based on contemporary descriptions of towns, in particular the detailed census of the town of Tanjavur in 1788: Walker of Bowland MSS, Edinburgh, Vol. 13615B.

[45] Arjun Appadurai, 'Right and Left Hand Castes in South India', *Indian Economic and Social History Review*, II, Nos. 2 and 3, 1974.

[46] H. Dodwell, *Calendar of the Madras Despatches, 1744-55*, Madras 1920, 194: also P.A. Roche, 'Caste and the British Merchant Government in Madras 1639-1749', *Indian Economic and Social History Review*, XII, No. 4, 1975.

[47] C. Anthony (ed), Gazetteer of Pondicherry (MSS), f. 350.

[48] T. Ray Chaudhuri, *Jan Company in Coromandel, 1605-1690*, S. Gravenhage, 1962, 202.

Towns grew by accretion. Most towns had strong stone forts which enclosed a well-planned urban area, some had concentric walls indicating the growth of population (Srirangam had seven, Chidambaram three). Exceptions were Arcot and Kanchi, which were open cities. In most cases, there were one or more *pettas* outside the walls. Certain occupational groups always lived beyond the fort, such as weavers, who needed wide straight roads shaded by trees (compare Carre's remark in 1673 of 'a large suburb of fine, large and wide streets').[49] The ballad of Condavidu described the ruler dismantling the buildings of the old city, with which he 'built a citadel -in the lower *mamlah* on the west side of the fort...and built a town there' and, later, that 'Aminullah established a *petta* on the south of the city and another *petta* on the north'.[50] Kanchi was not one city, but two, each centred on a different cult temple, and linked by a long bazaar. Some urban complexes broke up after the British conquest and demilitarisation. Such was the Gingee-Padaividu urban complex, sixteen miles in circumference, which split up later into fort, village and market area.[51] The Madras complex, on the other hand, was a federation of villages (at its maximum numbering 26)[52] adjoining Fort St. George (for example, Chintadripetta was a 'weaving village', all the revenues of which were controlled by one family). This pattern of growth by accretion instead of by extension is explained by the preference of Indians for settling in villages near the town (only the Europeans had the curious habit of building sprawling houses in open country) and also by the needs of drainage, which made channels between different clusters of habitation necessary.[53] Predominantly commercial towns like Vellore had ribbon development. Vellore fort at the turn of the century had two *pettas* near it, one old and full of buildings, another comparatively new. Apart from the fort proper, the *petta* was also often fortified. The forts of the Mysore area, like those of the Marathas in similar terrain, were often at a distance from the urban complex (ten to fifteen miles' distance). In the case of towns in the plains, by contrast, the fort and *petta* were close together. The Europeans found this proximity inconvenient, since their method of warfare was by assault and not by siege. When they occupied towns they cleared houses to create a buffer, paying the owners compensation. Relations between town and rural hinterland were not

[49] *Travels of Abbe Carre in India and the Near East 1672-74*, London 1947, 70.
[50] F.W. Ellis, Blackburne and T. Munro, Three Treatises on Mirasi Right, Madras 1852.
[51] C.S. Srinivasachari, *A History of Gingee and its Rulers*, Annamalainagar, 1943, 32-33.
[52] J. Dupuis, *Madras et le nord du Coromandel*, Paris 1960, 403-29.
[53] Ibid., 402-10.

strained – as is best illustrated in the question of sanctuary. There were cases in the mid-eighteenth century of villagers fleeing with their livestock to towns for refuge from attack, as well as of townsmen melting into the countryside, when their town was besieged. This process was described by the Telugu/Kannada word, *wulsa*. [54]

Drainage and water were provided in the major towns and even in fort towns built at an elevation for example, Tanjavur, Gingee and Vellore. Towns were scrupulously clean. The simplicity (as distinct from penury) that characterised dwellings in rural areas contrasted with the quality of houses and palaces and temples in the towns. Dubois contrasted the very wealthy one-eighth and the comfortably off one-fourth with the rest of the population.[55] Stone, wood, or brick surfaced with *chunam* was used to create permanence and thermal control. Bartolomeo was surprised to find houses four centuries old in Kerala.[56] Bowland, and many others, spoke of the remarkable workmanship of buildings in Madurai and Tiruchirapalli and of Tipu's palace in Coimbatore.[57] Others commented on the palaces of Ramnad, Bangalore and Bednur.[58] There was the occasional flight of fantasy like the Madurai *nayaka's* plan for an observatory from which he could see the sea.[59] Descriptions of Indian methods of building indicate that this was a continuous activity in the eighteenth and early nineteenth centuries.[60] There was a rule that no building should exceed the height of the temple *gopuram*. Ram Raz of Tanjanvur, at the behest of the British, in 1834 translated the *Silpa Sastras*, which indicated the sophistication of Indian town planning.[61] The Tanjavur ruler Sarfoji's specifications for an elaborate *chattram*-complex planned in the 1820s indicate the holistic nature of Indian planning where areas were demarcated at the outset for houses, places of worship, schools and tanks.[62]

[54] M. Wilks, *Historical Sketches of the South of India*, Vol. I, London 1810, 344; R. Orme MSS, IOL, Vols. 308 and 309, ff. 19-24. [Shevagerry] fort and pettah contain over 10,000 of which inhabitants have fled to the hills... but the multitude cannot go there'.

[55] Abb Dubois, *Hindu Manners, Customs and Ceremonies*, I (Eng. ed), Oxford 1897, 83.

[56] Fra Bartolomeo, *A Voyage to the East Indies*, London 1800, 2.

[57] Walker of Bowland MSS, National Library, Edinburgh, Vol. 13626, f. 57, H. Pearson, *Memoirs of the Life and Correspondence of Rev. C.F. Swarts*, London 1834, 148.

[58] 'Statistical and Geographical Memoir of Ramnad', IOL Map, MSS No. 6; M. Wilks, *Historical Sketches of the South of India*, I, London 1810, 502; British Library Addl, MS 26552, f. 36.

[59] Walker of Bowland MSS, Vol. 13626, f. 63.

[60] The most distinctive examples of architectural exuberance in merchants' houses were the houses of the Natukottai Chettiars who adopted a florid style much admired and copied by individuals of other communities.

[61] Ram Raz, *Essays on the Architecture of the Hindus*, London 1834.

[62] Madras Deptt. of Revenue, Consultations 1805, Vol. 145, f. 2519.

Land within the fort areas belonged to the ruler, and that of adjoining *pettas* to the entrepreneurs. Merchants were always mentally prepared to move base, if necessary, and till the 1820s there is no evidence of their investing in urban property or building sumptuously. Contemporary observers were struck by the unostentatious lifestyles of very rich merchants, and in assessing the house tax the appearance of houses was found to bear no relation to the wealth of the owner. 'The frequency of emigration and the danger to which the building of a good house exposed the owner of being fined on account of his supposed wealth...have prevented the erection of comfortable habitations'.[63] Their mobility is well illustrated during the mid-eighteenth century crises in Madras and Pondichery, and the later flight of merchants from Indian capital cities.[64] They were a cosmopolitan community, tied to their fraternities rather than to a specific area or town. Large towns had many shops catering to luxury needs, and all of them had an amazingly large number of neighbourhood stores, partially green grocers.[65] Even a small town like Gubbi in Mysore which had only 360 houses, had 154 shops.[66]

II

The changes when British rule was established at the end of the eighteenth century were initially minimal, as with earlier political changes, being essentially only a change of nomenclature, as remarked by Dubois in the 1790s.[67] The rule of the *nayakas* had been superimposed on the *mahanattar sabhas* (regional assemblies) which continued to function till the end of the eighteenth century in Travancore. Munro said that 'Hindus of all descriptions are very desirous of having every kind of business discussed in public assemblies'. This democratic institution atrophied under British rule, though Munro suggested its revival in 1824.[68] The bureaucratic monopoly of Brahmans had been retained under Hyder and Tipu and continued subsequently.[69] Discharged soldiers of conquered rulers were often enlisted into the British army. One unfortunate policy was the British refusal to allow the wardens of the military

[63]Munro, IOL MSS G.73.

[64] H. Dodwell, *Calendar of the Madras Despatches 1744-55*, Madras 1920, 53.

[65] Walker of Bowland MSS. Vol. 13615B, 'Statistical Report on Tanjore, 1788'.

[66] F. Buchanan, *A Journey from Madras through the Countries of Mysore, Canara and Malabar*, II (cited hereafter as *A Journey from Madras*), London 1807.

[67] Dubois, *Hindu Manners, Customs and Ceremonies*, I,6.

[68] F.W. Ellis, Blackburne and Munro, *Three Treatises on Mirasi Right*, Madras 1852, 145; Minute by T. Munro 31 December 1824.

[69] F. Buchanan, *A Journey from Madras*, I,45.

outposts (the *palaiyagars*) to retain their office, particularly in the Maravar and Kallar country of Madurai and Tirunelveli.[70] The institutional cohesion given to these inhabitants by the law-and-order institution of *nattar* and *ambalakkarar* was shattered by the repressive British policy, begun in 1755 and later whitewashed by terming these ethnic groups as 'criminal tribes'. This led to the prolonged warfare of the 1790s, and to the wanton destruction of the *kavil* system, thus necessitating a substitute police force.[71] Within towns, caste associations and the temple's role in maintaining vital statistics, continued, but the police *kotwals*, after 1808, were retained only in major towns and garrison points.[72]

In the early nineteenth century, many towns were described as being 'ruined', and in 1855 a guidebook pointed out as one of the charms of south India that it was 'a land of ruined cities'.[73] Taking a cue from this, a recent historian has written that 'the valleys of Tamilnadu were strewn with the remains of political headquarters and temple centres- Kanchi, Arcot, Trichy, Madurai, Ramnad, Tenkasi and Palamcottah'.[74] 'Ruined' can mean one of three things-political demotion, the bypassing or paralysis of trade, or demographic decline by compulsion or choice. Cornwallis could take much of the credit for the last. Madurai's 400 houses had 'sunk to 250 by the expeditions of Cornwallis' and 'been reduced to 100 by Tipu's oppression' (note the semantic nuances).[75] Many buildings and part of the suburbs of Tanjavur were destroyed in 1776.[76] As late as the 1830s, Coimbatore and Chingleput are noticed as erstwhile centres of large populations.[77] In 1796 the Board of Revenue noticed the flight of inhabitants in the *jagir* (that is, Madras-Chingleput) to the Madras settlement. This was obviously for sanctuary during war, but was optimistically explained as being because 'men of talent must always resort to the great capitals'.[78] In 1803 it was repeated that 'all the non-cultivating people in the jagir were flocking to Madras'. It was added, and this was the significant point, that the only other major towns

[70] S.H. Blackburne 'The Kallars: A Tamil Criminal Tribe Reconsidered, *South Asia*, I, No. 1, 1978.

[71] D. Kadhirvel, *History of the Maravas 1700-1802*, Madurai 1977,17.

[72] Madras Board of Revenue Consultations 1808, Vol. f. 2093.

[73] J. Murray, *A Handbook for India-Part I -Madras*, London 1859.

[74] C.J. Baker, *An Indian Rural Economy 1880-1955: The Tamilnad Countryside*, Oxford 1984, 334.

[75] F. Buchanan, *A Journey from Madras*, I, 139.

[76] *Tanjore Papers*, I: The Orders of the Court of Directors, London 1777, 116.

[77] *Statistics of Madras Collectorates*, Madras 1838.

[78] Madras Board of Revenue Consultations, 1796, Vol. 157, f. 5395.

were Kanchi and Tiruvallur 'which are supported by the importance of their temples'.[79] As the multi nodal economy gave place to the political and commercial monopoly of Madras, its mercantile, artisan and service population was bound to grow, just as had those of Vijayanagar and Srirangapattanam. It is easy to derive from this the corollary that 'the British established a new pattern of urban growth – Madras city was the capital, and the lesser towns were subordinate ports and administrative headquarters'.[80] An examination of the 'lesser towns' will show that they were not all that new.

As the towns were recycled, so was the building stock. But this was in limited supply, since the British had destroyed to conquer. When a house tax was imposed in 1802, those of the building profession were exempted.[81] There was a building boom in the collectorate towns that year, where buildings were needed for courts of justice and collectorates. Like all such activity, this was characterised by shoddy workmanship, in contrast to the excellent buildings of the 1760s.[82] A lot had to be done, for the British troops had been thorough in their work of 'reducing' people and places. Cities like Arcot had to be built up quickly, from the ruins into which it had fallen, because it was important in the trade netowrk. Many buildings were renovated – like the Madurai palace (which was being used by weavers) and the Coimbatore palace (described as 'an ornament to the town').[83] The rebuilding in Mysore led to this being described by Valentia as 'the new town of Mysore';[84] amnesia blotted out the picture of the burning of the Mysore Raja's palace in 1798. As *nayakas* and *nawabs* and *palaiyagars* in the past had done, order was being restored after about fifty years of intermittent warfare, by building up the old urban centres. To describe this as the beginning of urbanisation under *Pax Britannica* is as hagiographical as Indian chroniclers glossing over a ruler's sanguinary beginning and emphasising his (literally) constructive role in building tanks, *choultries* and *pettas*.

If the British were heirs to a well-developed urban pattern, they had also inherited a well-developed road network. By the 1780s, their homework for the acquisition of the peninsula had been so thorough in

[79] Madras Board of Revenue Consultations, 1803, Vol. 363, f. 12908.

[80] C.J. Baker, *An Indian Rural Economy 1880-1955: The Tamilnad Countryside*, 334.

[81] Madras Board of Revenue Consultations, 1802, Vol. 335, f. 14791.

[82] Madras Council Reforms MSS IOL Eur. G 63/1, para 24.

[83] Skelly Papers MSS, IOL, Book 2, f. 26.

[84] George Viscount Valentia, *Voyages and Travels to India, Ceylon, the Red Sea, in the Years 1802–6*, Vol. I, London 1809 (cited hereafter as *Voyages*) ,425.

terms of mapping, that the Coromandel was better known to them than were parts of Europe. The Malabar coast was already familiar, but its interior remained blank on the map for some decades subsequently. Pilgrim feet, the speedy carriage of merchandise, and the movement of gun-carriages had made the arterial roads what they were: phrases like 'the great road to Sivaganga' (Valentia in 1802)[85] and Buchanan's description of Tipu's 'Gun Roads' between Malabar and Mysore as 'the best in India'.[86] Bertrand's description of the Tiruchirapalli-Madurai road as '*la route royale, tracees par les anciens rajas, et ombragee par des arbres magnifiques*' [87] and the good condition of *choultries*, all indicate that the wars did not lead to these highways deteriorating. In the first half of the nineteenth century, the British contribution was minimal, being limited to repair and renovation. The rulers of Mysore had a stringent rule that all damage should be instantly repaired. The British lacked any such regulation, and had to cope with the problems of tanks run dry and roads falling into decay in a big way. In 1798 Colin Mackenzie had noted that in the wars 'many avenues planted by Hindu rulers have been destroyed' and suggested, that 'it would be noble if we were to plant some'.[88] The 'Pioneers' cut roads through the Sivaganga forests during the massive military activity against the *palaiyagars* and later in Malabar.[89]

In the 1840s and 1850s it was recommended that, to cope with the increased produce resulting from the major irrigation works in the Presidency, new markets should be opened up 'so that the local market is not overcharged'.[90] Roads were planned to the large towns, particularly east-west routes (Madras-Vikravandy, Agumbe Ghat-Mangalore, Mercara-Virajendrapet. This called attention to the existing roads. The need to maintain the excellent old roads near Salem and Tiruchirapalli, and to build roads through Malabar, was urgent. Dykes in 1853 admitted that people tended to say about the roads that 'there are not works like these done nowadays. The country is going fast to ruin'.[91] The neglect of the Chittoor – Vellore road led to the disappearance of an important line of trade.[92] The Tanjavur roads were excellent – due chiefly to the

[85] Valentia, *Voyages*, 353.

[86] F. Buchanan, *A Journey from Madras*, II, 435.

[87] C. Mackenzie, 'Journal', Addl. 13663. This can be translated as: The royal road, built by the rulers of old, and shaded by magnificent trees.

[88] C. Mackenzie, MSS, Addl. 13663, f. 68.

[89] Madras Board of Revenue Consultations, 16 Feb. 1801, f.1876.

[90] House of Commons, *Report on Public Works at Madras, 1854*, P.P. XLVIII,115.

[91] J.W.B. Dykes, *Salem*, London, 1853, 494.

[92] *Selections from the Old Records of Madurai Collectorate*, Madras 1932, No. 238.

interest and investments by the Raja.[93]

It is excessive to claim that 'the geography of south India changed under the British', and that jungles became plains as a result.[94] To a limited extent this happened when forests were cleared for the railways in the 1850s. (But even in the 1850s there were those in the interior who thought they were ruled by the Pandyas, and had not heard of Good Queen Victoria!).[95] The American Civil War led to the building of the great Cotton Roads from Madras to Tuticorin (financed by temple funds), from Ettiyapuram (financed by the local *zamindar)* to Ramnad and Palayamcotta and from Tirunelveli to Trivandrum.[96] These were not all new. The Tiruchirapalli – Ramnad road had in 1814 been described as 'a grand carriage road' but had been since allowed to decay.[97]

The British monopolies – of salt, tobacco and timber – did not create a necessity for new roads. There was also no basic change in local consumption patterns among the inhabitants, except that of the switch-over to British cloth. The commodities and the carriers of goods, human and animal, and the venues of commodity exchange did not change qualitatively in the fist half of the nineteenth century. What did change was the cut that the imperial regime derived from trade. Two other factors making for possible change were that: first, in place of the massive production of many varieties of cloth, there was now the import of British cloth, and secondly, in place of the numerous points of exit, external trade was now routed chiefly through Madras, Calicut and Cochin.

III

The first three quarters of the eighteenth century had seen a major boom in textile production. Orme's vivid description of south Indians as a nation of weavers illustrates this.[98] Churches in Quilon were being used as warehouses for textiles, and the Madurai palace for weaving cloth. The *qasba* towns housed large communities of weavers, and the bigger towns

[93] House of Commons *Papers Relating to Public Works, Madras*, 149.

[94] R.L. Hardgrave, *Nadars of Tamilnadu*, California 1969.

[95] F.E. Penny, *On the Coromandel Coast*, London, 1908, 168. The reference is to a conversation between Bishop Caldwell and the inhabitants of a village near Courtallam. When asked about the Europeans, they replied: 'They live on the coast. They only come here to shoot'.

[96] V. Tyagarajan, 'Tuticorin, a Town Study', *Indian Geographical Journal*, April-June 1941, XVI, 2.

[97] Statistical and Geographical Memoir of Rlamnad, IOL, Map, MSS No. 6, 141.

[98] Orme MSS, IOL, India, Vol. I, Ch. 7, 'Of the Manufactures'.

had busy redistributing functions – Bednur in Canara (brought into the mainstream of trade as a result of Hyder's territorial expansion), and Soonda and Siva as Mysore's frontier towns.[99] Buchanan described many towns in the Mysore area (Sirjapur, Lacor, Kolar) as 'manufacturing towns'.[100] Weavers equally with merchants contributed to temple festivals. The economy was a cash one, and even in small towns, transactions were in cash, not by barter.

Their troubles started with the wars of attrition, from the 1780s till 1800. In 1792 the Board of Revenue started to levy taxes – Company fees, *pagoda* (temple) fees, customs fees and *kanakapillai* fees. The *mohturpha* tax on goods and professions was a complicated one, which varied from one district of south India to another. It was abolished by the Bengal government in 1793, by Bombay in 1844, but in Madras only in 1861. In the southern districts, the weavers paid a loom tax to the temples or to their landlords. When the Company assumed control over the temples, they not only collected the loom tax, but also charged the weavers rent for the land they occupied. A second burden was imposed in 1802, when the *chowky* system was introduced in all towns. This led to the weavers deserting the *chowky* towns for villages.[101] Trevelyan in 1825 criticised the double taxation of the weaver. 'It is surprising that Manufacture, commerce and industry can be carried out at all in Madras Presidency'.[102] When to this was added the forcible substitution of British textiles, the cotton weavers were in a more desperate situation. (In 1812 Munro had explained the lack of interest among Indians in European goods by the following reasons – 'climate, religious and civil habits, and more than anything the excellence of their own manufactures').[103]

The weavers' plight was not a specifically urban one, since they lived in both villages and towns, but it led to the weavers' *pettas* and quarters in *qasba* towns decaying, and the weavers turning to agriculture. All the towns mentioned above declined to the status of villages by 1810.[104] In

[99] F. Buchanan, *A Journey from Madras* I, passim.

[100] Ibid.

[101] Munro, MSS (IOL), MSS. Eur. G. 73, n.f., dated 28 January 1805: 'The emigration of weavers is much greater than that of any other tradesmen from *chouky* towns. In another year or two, few will be found in towns excepting those who are employed by contractors'.

[102] Charles Trevelyan MSS (Newcastle on Tyne University), bundle 1823-59, CET. 19, handwritten note of 1825.

[103] Munro's evidence, cited in W.K. Firminger (ed), *The Fifth Report from the Select Committee of the House of Commons on the Affairs of the East India Company*, 28 July 1812 (cited hencefoth as *The Fifth Report*), 15.

[104] Madras Board of Revenue Consultations 1803, Vol. 363, f. 12734: 'Those which were (large towns) under the Bidnur government are now only small villages'.

terms of occupational change, that of the weavers was later in time but greater in magnitude than that of the soldiers of the southern Tamil and the Mysore regions. The census returns after 1871 show how the large numbers of weavers turned to agriculture. In the 1840s, groups of weavers repeatedly petitioned to the officials for redress of grievances, hinting that if they did not heed their appeal, 'the world will be darkened' and that 'Madras and all its dependencies will be rebelled' *(sic)*. [105] The powers-that-were did not take action, nor was there any popular rising.

The uncertainties of the decades of warfare, coupled with the subsequent fumbling policy of taxation, had also affected the mercantile groups. The town of Hosapetta, the market of which was destroyed by General Mathews, was an example of what could happen in war.[106] Hyder's reign had seen an increase in the volume of trade, and Tipu's its decline, because of his ban on trade with the Coromandel coast and with Hyderabad.[107] British rule also brought its monopolies and trade restrictions. Merchants' protest through *hartals* had been reported by Carre in 1673;[108] these occurred again in the 1780s.[109] The paper manufacturers of Kumbakonam, and the betel-sellers of Tanjavur, were to protest effectively against taxes in 1809, by strike action.[110] The end of the eighteenth century also saw the spectacular rise of the *dubashes*, who became *rentiers* and landowners in Madras when property was sold in distress sales. (Their power was noticed in the *Fifth Report* of 1812).[111] Their authority created discord among the merchants, who had hitherto had a strong voice in deciding prices of goods in different markets.[112] As the war laid waste large areas, it became necessary to 'establish' bazaars by hoisting a flag which would attract merchants.[113] During the debate on taxes, they made it clear that they would not stand for anything that was not '*Mamool*'.[114] When the proposed imposition of town duties was announced, the merchants abandoned the towns for the villages, as Munro and Buchanan noticed.[115]

[105] Government of India, Home (Revenue) Consultations, 19 April 1850, ff. 14-39.
[106] F. Buchanan, *A Journey from Madras*, II, 130.
[107] C. Mackenzie MSS, British Library, Addl. 13663, f. 19.
[108] *Travels of Abbe Carre in India and the Near East 1672-4*, London 1947, 356.
[109] R.R. Bowyer, 'Journal 1781-4, n.p.
[110] Records of the Tanjore Collectorate, Vol. 3264, ff. 18-19, and ff. 126-8.
[111] *The Fifth Report*.
[112] Jodrell Papers, Photo Eur. 136 IOL, n.f.
[113] *Baramahal Records*, Madras 1933, Section XXII, 'Review'.
[114] Cf. Madras Board of Revenue Consultations for the 1790s, passim.
[115] Munro MSS, IOL,MSS, Eur. G. 73, n.f., memo, dated 28 January 1805.

There were instances like those of the Vaniambady Chettiar merchants who left that *qasba* and set up 'a new village', and laid the foundation stone of the first shop.[116] On the other hand, till the 1830s, the British army encouraged the establishment of markets at the military bazaar stations of Vellore, Masulipattanam, Bellary, Cannanore, Tiruchirapalli and Oothacamund.

The increasing power of the Chettiars is seen in their keeping the Janrawar traders out of Tiruvallur in 1801, and in the Right-hand and Left-hand contests for local authority and control over temples. [117] The interconnection between mercantile activity, temple control and *choultry* construction was noticed by many. In 1803, at the time the town duties were settled, there was faction fighting in different towns between groups of merchants; the British authorities decided to ignore this. [118] (In the north, some decades later, similar conflict occurred between established Hindu merchants and newly arrived Marwaris). Stein's analysis that 'the stress of progressive urbanisation of south Indian society from the twelfth century on was manifested in the relationships between Right and Left caste groupings...and especially in the continuously improving terms of advantage of the mobile craftsmen and traders who were the core of the *idangai* (Left hand) groups'[119] sees as a *longue duree* phenomenon what probably had more specific contexts. Until more empirical research is done, it may not be wise to generalise about Right and Left hand conflicts for the whole Presidency.

In the early years of the nineteenth century, in repairing the fabric so badly torn by the wars, the merchants took advantage of the government's offers to tax-farmers and to individuals prepared to accept wasteland on condition of erecting *choultries.* [120] Deserted parts of existing towns were also acquired for *pettas.* [121] In 1819 a group of Chettiars cheated the collector of Vriddhachalam by getting loans from him for building a new *petta,* providing (unknown to him) mutual security, building substandard houses and disappearing without repaying the interest.[122] Apart from the Chettiars, the Shanars also expanded their area of activity and bought land in towns. Nonetheless, Hardrave's descrip-

[116] *Baramahal Records*, Section XXII, Review, 10.

[117] Madras Board of Revenue Consultations, 1801, Vol. 292A, f. 8938.

[118] Munro, MSS, IOL, MSS, Eur. G. 73.

[119] B. Stein, *Peasant State and Society in Medieval South India*,479.

[120] There is copious evidence for this in the proceedings of the Madras Department of Revenue from the 1790s to the 1830s.

[121] R. Caldwell, *The Tinnevelly Shanars,* London 1850.

[122] Madras Board of Revenue Consultations, 1819, Vol. 841, f. 10851.

tion of their revolutionary move from their traditional occupation of toddy-tapping to trade in the early ninteenth century as a direct result of British rule [123] is hard to sustain in view of the fact that they were described as 'big traders' as early as the early 1800s. Munro in 1812 believed that European traders could be active only on the coast, for trade in the interior was something best left to the Indians (who, he added wryly, are 'as much a nation of shopkeepers as we are').[124]

The effect of the heavy *mohturpha* duties and the edging out of the cotton weavers was to reduce many middle-size towns to the status of villagers.(A place was described as a *grama* in one case in the 1830s, and it was earlier identified as a *qasba*). A curious statement that education in the towns had declined because of the fall-off in cloth manufacture and of grain sales after British troops had been moved to the Presidency frontiers[125] would read to mean a decline in prosperity in urban areas caused by declining income from trade and manufacture. The rumour carried to Tanjavur by pilgrims in 1813, that in Madras there was popular discontent because of the taxes and the handkerchiefs with the emblem of the cross distributed by missionaries[126] was not to be dismissed as imaginary, as the collector of Tanjavur did. In 1812 it had been proposed that 'town consumption duties' as were in force in Madras should be extended to Tiruchirapalli, Kumbakonam. Nagore and Nagapattanam.[127] If this had been done, the population of these central places might have decreased.

In many larger towns there was depopulation, caused by the loss of employment for certain other categories – officials of Indian rulers, those employed in arsenal factories and in the manufacture of luxury items of furniture or transportation equipment. This was particularly marked in Tanjavur and Srirangapattanam. In the latter, in 1800 the population of over 150,000 had dwindled to under 30,000. In Tanjavur, the population of over 100,000 was reduced to 80,000 by the wars of the 1780s, and remained at this level till 1855, when the abolition of dynasty led to many groups losing employment. These included officials, craftsmen, merchants, palanquin-bearers and leather-workers.[128] The overseas migration from south India was largely caused by distress; the Chettiars'

[123] R.L. Hardgrave, *Nadars of Tamilnadu, California* 1969.

[124] Munro's evidence, cited in *The Fifth Report*, 150.

[125] *Asiatic Journal*, May 1828, 616-20, 'The State of Education in South India'.

[126] Tanjore Collectorate Records, Vol. 3272, f. 29.

[127] Madras Board of Revenue Consultations, 1812, Vol. 570, f. 4526.

[128] This is seen by comparing the Census of Tanjore of 1788 and that of 1871.

mercantile activities also accounted for part of it. In the distress migration, a large percentage was from the Tanjavur district, traditionally called the garden or the rice bowl of south India which had in the previous century regularly exported rice to Ceylon.[129]

By the 1850s, therefore, in demographic terms certain changes had occurred – Bangalore, of which Hyder's chronicler said, 'It is the envy of Kashmir, for on it depended many cities, pleasant and rich', was now enlarged by a cantonment, bigger and more populous than the original *petta*. It had again become 'a mart for goods from all parts of India.[130] Vellore, a military base, recovered its position as a major entrepot, especially after the railway was built.[131] Coimbatore and Mettupalayam developed to provision Oothacamund and Wynaad. Salem was thriving even though it was forced to send goods to Madras instead of Cuddalore.[132]

The main reason given for the over-urbanisation of Calcutta in contrast to the other towns in its hinterland has been the disproportionate growth of the tertiary sector in that city.[133] In the case of Madras, a comparison can be done for 1871 with Tanjavur, to see how far this is true in the south.[134]

	Madras		*Tanjavur*	
Area	23 sq.m (8,978 acres)		530 acres	
Total Population	397,552		52,175	
Total number following some occupation:	140,651		16,667	
Government service	6,318	(8.00%)	251	(2.00%)
Military service	4,761	(3.50%)	657	(2.70%)
Learned professions	1,092	(14.00%)	245	(0.83%)
Personal services	17,854	(8.00%)	2931	(5.00%)
Traders	18,579	(10.00%)	1,944	(8.00%)

*The figures in brackets refer to the percentage of working population.

This indicates that, even after the removal of the royal family and the demographic stagnation of Tanjavur, the basic occupational character of

[129] G. Slater, *Economic Studies. Vol. I, Some South Indian Villages,* Oxford 1918, 82.

[130] British Library MSS, Addl, 29898.

[131] J. Dupuis, *Madras et le Nord du Coromandel,* Paris 1960, 380-85.

[132] Minute of Charles Trevelyan on his Tour of Madras Presidency 1859-60, *Madras Govt. Progs.* (Public), March 1860.

[133] See, in the present collection, Atiya Habeeb Kidwai, 'Urban Atrophy in Colonial India: Some Demographic Indicators'.

[134] *Census of Tanjore 1871,* Madras 1873, and *Census of Madras City 1871,* Madras 1873.

the city continued. The 2 per cent of government and personal services would have been, as in Madras, 8 per cent if the census had been taken before 1855.

Apart from the large size of the total Madras urban area, there was nothing in the census of 1871 that marked a revolution in the urban pattern. Mysore and Kerala had the largest proportion of urban dwellers, mostly in small towns. Tamil Nadu had a few large and several middle-size towns. The twelve largest (excluding Madras) continued to be Tiruchirapalli, Madurai, Tanjavur, Kumbakonam, Kanchi, Bangalore, Vellore, Salem, Coimbatore, Palghat, Cuddalore, Nagapattanam and Calicut – five pilgrimage centres, four strategic sites, and three ports, all twelve important central places over the centuries. The British had not created any new pattern of urbanism, apart from setting up the enclave of Madras. The fifty years of upheaval, political and military, had been followed by a century of peace but not necessarily of accelerated urbanisation. Similarly, the stability of the trunk roads has to be attributed to the permanence of the major towns. Baker's belief that in 1871-91 the biggest single influence on town growth was that of the government needs to be modified in this light.[135]

IV

'The colonial government featured in South Indian Society more by its failure to carry out traditonal functions than by its pursuit of modernity'.[136] Ignoring the provocative second part of this statement, we can agree that the imposition of British rule led not only to a dislocation of a long-established commercial pattern, but to the atrophying of a long-established pattern of urban regulations. An important feature in this was the temple. All towns in south India were temple towns, some mosque-towns and others church towns. Worship was an integral part of people's lives, and the officials of religious institutions had an immunity which was respected by rulers of all faiths, and the violation of which was rare (like the episode of the desecration of Srirangam by the French troops in the 1780s). Strict purity-fetishes ensured that temple precincts with their reserves of wealth were inviolate, and this was buttressed by strong fortifications. To the Anglican British, the temples posed a strange set of problems, since they were employers and landlords, in addition to

[135] C.J. Baker, *An Indian Rural Economy, 1880-1955*, 385.

[136] S. Kaufman, *Popular Christianity, Caste and Hindu Society in South India, 1800-1915*, Ph. D. Thesis, Cambridge 1980, 8 (since published).

exercising a charisma they had not encountered in Europe.

Initially, seeing the temples as rival claimants on loyalty, they used Kanchi as a test case. They suspended the warden of the temple in 1790, and two years later banned the temple festival. The popular opposition they encountered led them to be more cautious. [137] Also, as the pilgrim traffic, after its sharp decline in the 1780s and 1790s, picked up again, the Board of Revenue realised that it was 'the means of creating an influx of wealth into the jagir and switched to a policy of supporting them much as the former rulers had done.[138] They soon found themselves in another web of confusion which they would have understood if they recalled their own pre-Reformation Church. Temples earned a variety of incomes – in the form of *maniams*, rents, donations and taxes. In order to enjoy some of these, the temples were brought under official control, and funds disbursed to them according to their needs. In 1802, at the time the war of attrition against the *palaiyagars* was ending, the temples were restored to their committees of management, and given their former allowances.[139] During festivals, the government sold to tradesmen the right to erect shops outside the temple.

Acceptance of this role of patronage meant involvement in judicial aspects of the temple authority. By tradition, Right and Left hand caste disputes could be settled only by the Brahmans of Kanchi; group leaders often took advantage of British ignorance to get themselves vital positions of power as temple governors. Tradition, real or fabricated, was an argument which the British courts were powerless against. [140] Common law courts would have been the answer, but who was to define that law? The *dubashes* became unnecessary as the Fort William principle of Englishmen learning Indian languages was explored, but the need for the dependable intermediary remained. It was these individuals who entrenched themselves in positions of power in the temple as well as in the bureaucracy and as landowners.[141]

From the 1820s, the Christian missionaries (whose institutions enjoyed none of the privileges, like rent-free land, of mosques and temples) mounted an attack on the official indulgence of 'idolatry', conveniently forgetting how Hinduised in ritual their own worship had become. Their

[137] Madras Board of Revenue Consultations 1792, Vol. 60, f. 2841.

[138] Ibid, 1796, Vol. 157, f. 5395.

[139] Madras Board of Revenue Consultations 1802, Vol. 311, f. 2094.

[140] For a detailed micro-study of this problem, see Arjun Appadurai, *Worship and Conflict under Colonial Rule*, Cambridge 1981.

[141] R. Suntharalingam, *Politics and Nationalist Awakening in South India*, 1852-91, Arizona 1974, 29.

pressure led to the decision to restore the temples to a position of independence from official control, in 1841.[142] Either way, the role of the temple in the lives of people remained crucial. When Satyanatha lyer in the 1930s, writing narrative history, said that Madurai was 'the centre of civilisation and the heart of the kingdom in every respect'[143] he was uttering an unconsciously telling phrase.

When the connection with the temples was severed the financial implication was overwhelming. The commutation of temple dues had led to a large surplus over and above the running costs of the temples. This amounted to 4,26,000 rupees of which 80,000 rupees came from Tanjavur.[144] In 1846, these 'surplus pagoda funds' were set aside for town improvements.[145] In the British 'pursuit of modernity' urban amenities took a very low priority, because of the costs involved. In the northern provinces, this had been sought to be met by an octroi at the town frontiers. In the Madras Presidency, already burdened with monopolies on essential commodities and by the *mohturpha,* this was difficult.

In 1836 an enquiry by the collectors had shown that a town duty for 'improvements' would be unpopular.[146] Twenty years later, the people of Kanchi were still hostile.[147] In contrast, the citizens of Madurai and Nagapattanam demanded municipalities and civil improvement.[148] Blackburne, collector of Madurai, said that no south Indian town was as rich as those of Bengal. At the same time, he believed the inhabitants should be made to contribute for the benefits of the broad roads, drainage and the police force that British rule had given them.[149] Here we see the beginnings of the-no doubt honest-belief that British rule had made Indian towns civilised places. That the broad streets were made for the temple festivals, that drainage and water supply were worked out to a fine art and had fallen into decay because of the dismantling of forts and the wanton neglect of the water-courses and tanks (just as wanton neglect kept empty the splendid granaries that existed in big towns, in the interests of free trade in grain), that caste riots like those in Tirunelveli in 1858 occurred because the *kaval* system had been replaced by a police

[142]Government of India, Home (Revenue) Consultations, 10 August 1840, 2/9.

[143]R. Sathyanatha Aiyer, *History of the Nayaks of Madurai,* Oxford 1924, 114.

[144]Government of India, Home (Revenue) Consultations, 2 September 1843, 4/11.

[145] Ibid.

[146] *Selections from the Old Records of Madura Collectorate,* Madras 1932, No. 92.

[147]*Report on the Administration of Public Affairs in Madras Presidency 1856-7,* 12.

[148] Minute of Charles Trevelyan on his Tour of Madras Presidency, 1859-60, *Madras Govt. Progs. (Public),* March 1860.

[149] Proceedings of the Board of Revenue, Madras, 1860, III, Progs. No. 1270.

force, that Tipu had collected a house tax for keeping the towns clean[150] –all this was forgotten. British perception was exemplified by the remark of the intrepid lady who ventured into the *petta* of Bangalore. She found the Indian women 'painting their doorstep instead of sweeping it'.[151] She failed to understand the wonderful sense of renewed hope symbolised by the *kolam* decoration. A positive British perception had to wait, like elsewhere in India, for Patrick Geddes. In 1919 he pointed out the values of south India's urbanism, and the need to limit civic action to 'conservative surgery'.[152]

The tradition of south India urbanism was one where a society with a clearly demarcated code of conduct lived in a limited area, and accommodated people from other areas and traditions. Tanjavur, with its population of Marathis, Telugus and Tamilians, and the various port towns with large numbers of foreigners, was as cosmopolitan as Madras. Madras, on a sprawling spatial plane (26 villages within the municipal limits) was a federation rather than an Indian city writ large. To draw a dichotomy between it and Madurai is to create a distinction based on theory, not fact.[153] Peter Marshall's remark that the Indians living in Calcutta showed little interest in things European, and looked to Nadia, Puri, Varanasi, and Brindavan, holds true for Madras too.[154] The Europeans frequently comment on the polished urbanity of the Indian, his tenacious insistence on maintaining a distance, an apartheid sought more by him than by the Europeans, this courtesy in providing the frivolous details of an English lifestyle not for himself but to enable the English visitor to relax. Two telling episodes indicate how the Indians regarded the Englishmen. In one, an English officer who ventured into 'Black/Town' (the Indian section of Madras) happened upon a scene which made him aghast – a party of *dubashes*, absorbed in mimicking their masters with total and devastating accuracy.[155] In the other, an Indian asks a missionary how, if the British were sincere Christians (and believed, with Christ, that it was easier for a camel to pass through the eye of a needle than for a rich man to enter the kingdom of heaven), their chief concern in India seemed to be to amass wealth![156]

[150] Madras Board of Revenue Consultations, 1801, Vol. 292 B, f. 914B.

[151] *Letters from Madras 1836-9*, By A Lady, London 1846, 139.

[152] P. Geddes, *Report on Tours in Madras Presidency*, Coimbatore 1915.

[153] Susan J. Lewandowski, 'Changing Form and Function in the Ceremonial and the Colonial Port City in India: An Historical Analysis of Madurai and Madras', *Economy and Society* (ed K.N. Chaudhuri and C.J. Dewey), Delhi 1979.

[154] P.J. Marshall, '18th Century Calcutta' (MS).

[155] Innes Munro, *A Narrative of the Military Operations on the Coromandel Coast*, London 1789.

[156] E. Hoole, *Madras, Mysore and South India*, London 1844, 235.

URBAN ATROPHY IN COLONIAL INDIA: SOME DEMOGRAPHIC INDICATORS

ATIYA HABEEB KIDWAI

Our concern in this paper is with the identification of some demographic indicators of urban atrophy which characterised the process of urbanisation during the last phase of colonial rule in India.[1] This period is of significance for urban studies in the country because the processes which have historically patterned the contemporary urban structure either emerged or became pronounced during this phase of colonialism. After the establishment of the British Imperial Government and the advent of the railways in the 1850s, the spatial organisation of the Indian economy was considerably restructured in response to the imperial policies, as a result of which the colonial processes of urbanisation became strongly entrenched in the country.

This paper analyses the pattern and trends of colonial urbanisation as a process which led to urban atrophy in terms of diminution in the population size and stagnation in productive economic activities in urban areas manifested through the interrelated sub-processes of de-urbanisation, urban de-industrialisation and spurious tertiarisation of the urban

[1] It is necessary to distinguish between two components of the general concept of urbanism, namely, urbanisation and urban process. Whereas the former can be interpreted as denoting the rate of change in the proportion of urban dwellers to total population, the urban process is to be understood as a complex nexus of functionally interrelated, parallel-trending changes by means of which increasing numbers of people in society at large become involved in some way in the affairs of the city. In this study our concern is with both these components. For elaboration of distinction between the two concepts see Paul Wheatley and Thomas See, *From Court to Capital*, University of Chicago, 1978, 3.

economy. De-urbanisation is thus seen as a demographic process marking the reversal of the indices of urbanisation to a point on the growth scale which they had already crossed; de-industrialisation is the lessening of the importance of the industrial or secondary sector in the urban economy both in an absolute and relative sense; and spurious tertiarisation signifies proliferation of urban services not linked or conducive to economic development.

The paper has been divided into three sections. In section I, a general analytical framework within which the process of colonial urbanisation can be analysed is outlined and factors which were crucial in shaping the qualitative and quantitative attributes of the colonial structure in India are highlighted. In section II, which forms the main body of the paper, an empirical analysis of the process of urban atrophy is attempted. In this section the process of urban atrophy has been statistically analysed through selected demographic indicators for the census decades between 1872 and 1921. The emphasis throughout this analysis has been on demonstrating the salient processes through widely accepted techniques rather than on determining the relative efficiency of the statistical methods available. The universe of analysis has been restricted to the hinterland of only one of the four major ports of nineteenth-century India, that is, of the port of Calcutta. This is done on the assumption that although the analysis draws on the experience of a limited region it will have wider relevance because the port hinterlands in India were subject to more or less similar forces of colonial exploitation and went through almost identical phases of spatial organisation. The conclusions are presented in section III.

I

The analytical framework proposed in this paper is based on the premise that towns of a specific period can be viewed as 'moments' in the process of the development (or underdevelopment) of societies.[2] Further, that within each historical period the processes leading to urbanisation, that is, the concentration of population and activities in urban areas are triggered off by different sets of factors and are articulated in different patterns. These sets of factors in all epochs are, however, linked to the modes of production and economic integration prevalent in the economy and to the ways in which economic surplus is generated, appropriated and

[2] Philip Abrams, 'Towns and Economic Growth' in P. Abrams and E.A. Wrigley (eds), *Towns in Societies*, Cambridge University Press, 1978, 31. Abrams reiterates the expression used by David Harvey in *Social Justice and the City*, Arnold, 250.

utilised. Hence, by implication, urbanisation as a process of reorganisation of the size of the population, and of urban activities and urban space, becomes linked to the processes whereby economic surplus gets geographically concentrated in patterns directed by the circulation of goods and services; by a movement of people; and, in a money economy, by the circulation of investment, money and credit.

From this point of view the qualitative and quantitative attributes of urbanisation are determined by two factors: (a) the total quantity of surplus appropriated and in circulation, and (b) the degree to which this surplus is available in a concentratable form. These two factors govern both the pace and degree of urbanisation as well as the fate of individual urban centres.[3]

We begin with the premise that colonial urbanisation in India cannot be understood as a separate structure with its own laws of transformation and construction but should be analysed as an expression of a set of relationships of domination and dependence which evolved *vis-a-vis* a metropolitan economy.[4] Two types of interrelated domination coexisted in nineteenth-century India which affected the structure of urbanisation during this period: (a) Colonial domination with the essential objectives of direct administration and intensive exploitation of resources; and (b) Capitalist-commercial domination effected through the terms of exchange by which raw material was procured below its value and manufactured goods were sold (in deliberately created markets) at prices higher than their value.

These systems of domination resulted in a relationship which was essentially asymmetrical. This asymmetry altered the qualitative and quantitative attributes of urbanisation by introducing the following changes in the economy: (a) the surplus appropriated was largely funnelled out of the system and thus reduced its total quantity available

[3] For a detailed discussion of this analytical framework see Atiya Habeeb, 'Urban Growth: A Historical Perspective' in *Problems de Croissance Urbaine dans le Monde Tropical*, Travaux et ocuments de Geographic Tropicale, CECET, Bordeaux 1981, No. 45. This discussion has drawn heavily on David Harvey, *Social Justice and the City*, 246-48.

[4] Represented by the work of some neo-Marxist writers like Frank and Amin, this approach focuses upon the crucial role of Third World cities as institutional structures that assist the accummulation of capital in Third World countries and its siphoning off to the metropolitan centres of the developed countries: Andre Gunder Frank, *Capitalism and Underdevelopment in Latin America*, Monthly Review Press, New York 1967; A. Amin, *Accumulation on a World Scale: A Critique of the Theory of Underdevelopment*, Monthly Review Press, New York 1974. Cf.B. Warren, 'Imperialism and Capitalist Industrialization', *New Left Review*, 81, (September-October) 1973; B. Roberts, *Cities of Peasants: The Political Economy of Urbanization in the Third World*, Arnold, London 1928.

within the system; and (b) the channels of circulation of this surplus were changed both in terms of spatial and social linkages. This naturally reduced the degree and pace of urbanisation in colonial India and produced a new geographical configuration, which was superimposed over the pre-colonial structure.[5]

II

Historical evidence suggests that in Akbar's empire there were 120 cities (*shahar*) and 3,200 townships (*qasbas*).[6] Furthermore, the level of urbanisation (in terms of the proportion of urban to total population) in India was higher at the end of the seventeenth century than at the end of the nineteenth.[7] Even as late as 1770, north India is said to have had about sixty 'larger cities' and about 180 'substantial places'.[8] In 1800 the number of cities does not appear to have changed very much in the size group of 10,000 to about 1,00,000. Smaller centres did not decline in number either.[9] The percentage of population inhabiting places with distinct urban characteristics was larger at the end of the eighteenth century than at the beginning, though there had been displacement of population from the largest into medium-size and small places.[10] Thus, in the first half of the nineteenth century as a whole, there appears to have been a clear-cut but not startling growth of the total population living in towns of over 5,000, and the rate of growth of urban population exceeded, though only marginally, the rate of growth of the population as a whole.[11]

[5]See Atiya Habeeb, *Characteristics and Processes of Urbanization in Colonial India-A Case Study of Calcutta and its Hinterland (1872-1921)*, Ph.D. Thesis, Jawaharlal Nehru University, New Delhi 1979.

[6]*Tabaquat-i-Akbari*, III, 545-46 cited in Irfan Habib, *Agrarian System of Mughal India*, Asia, Bombay 1963, 75.

[7]Irfan Habib, *Agrarian System*, 76. Habib notes that the 'few data that we have suggest a very high ratio of urban to the total population of the country; and from what we know of the great depopulation of the towns in the nineteenth century, it is unlikely that this ratio was exceeded till very recent times'.

[8]C.A. Bayly, *Rulers, Townsmen and Bazaars*, Cambridge University Press, 1983, 111-12. These larger centres consisted of retail centres and bulking points, besides transit centres in long-distance trade or headquarters of regional rulers.

[9]Ibid., 112.

[10]Ibid., 113. Bayly estimates that towards the end of the eighteenth century, about 15 per cent of the population of north India was urban out of which 7 per cent lived in towns with a population of over 5,000 and 3 per cent in cities of over 10,000.

[11]Ibid., 304-5. Bayly's view is that this represents not so much the stagnation of a stable urban population but a sharp contention between forces pushing urbanisation forward and equally powerful ones tending to its decline.

We may safely assume therefore that the process of urbanisation in the latter half of the nineteenth century was yoked to an urban structure which was not very weak, at least in terms of the size of its base. New political and economic factors had however started exerting their limiting effects on the growth of towns.[12]

The British colonial policy had undergone a shift during this period. During the first half of the nineteenth century this policy was focused primarily on increasing the resources of the Company through land revenue.[13] There also was a maximisation of mercantile profits during this phase.[14] Nevertheless, with the stabilisation of industrial development in Britain and the consequent accumulation of large amounts of industrial capital, new areas and avenues of investment had to be found. India offered favourable grounds. British capital investment increased from 365 million pound sterling in 1901-10 to 500 million pound sterling in 1914-15.[15] Most of this capital was invested in government, railways, plantations and finance, that is, in purposes auxiliary to the commercial penetration of the country.[16] The principal and returns on account of this capital flowing back into Britain in time came to rival the size of the Indian tribute.[17] It was estimated to be 3.5 million pound sterling a year in 1848,[18] which increased to 146.5 million pound sterling in 1921.[19] This reflected change in the quality and methods of exploitation developing

[12]Bayly calls the period during 1800-57 as one of 'conflict and change' in the cities of north India. The decline of the military and royal establishments led to a decline of both service and artisan communities, specially in the smaller towns. More 'basic features of the economy and society also tended to limit the growth of town and to increase their instability'. The development of the commercial economy contributed to the growth of only those towns which acquired entrepot functions in the new milieu: ibid., 305-6.

[13]The land revenue increased from 3.9 million in 1792-93 to 12.67 million in 1837-38, i.e., fourfold within fifty years: R.C. Dutt, *The Economic History of India*, Publications Division, Government of India, New Delhi 1901, Vol I, 277-82.

[14]Between 1814 and 1835 British cotton manufactures exported to India rose from less than one million yards to over fifty-one million yards. In the same period Indian cotton piecegoods imported into Britain fell from 1.4 million pieces to 306,000 pieces and by 1844 to 63,000 pieces. By 1850, India which had for centuries exported cotton goods to the whole world, was importing one-fourth of all British cotton exports: R.P. Dutt, *India Today*, Manisha, Calcutta 1970 (2nd Indian ed) 119.

[15]Ibid., 137. The figure for 1909-10 excludes private capital other than that of the companies, i.e., capital for which no documentary evidence was readily available.

[16]Ibid., 139.

[17]Ranjit Sau, *Unequal Exchange, Imperialism and Under-development*, Oxford University Press, New Delhi 1978, 39.

[18]R.P. Dutt, *India Today*, 131,n 14.

[19]Ibid., 143.

out of the conditions of industrial and free trade capitalism and its transformation into finance capitalism.

The urban structure and the process of urbanisation were affected by the drain of the appropriated surplus, the increase in foreign trade consisting of imports of cheap machine-made goods and exports of industrial raw material, and the changes in the channels of trade, both spatial and social. The railways disturbed the traditional trade routes. The centripetal inter-settlement linkages which had evolved over time based on a by and large introverted road system, were replaced by the centrifugal pulls generated by the metropolitan economy through the establishment of new port towns and orientation of the railway network and internal commodity flows towards them. A process of urban atrophy was thus set in motion in the old towns and cities, affecting their population, size, industries and economic activities in general.

We shall first investigate the process of de-urbanisation. This process can be measured in several ways, but statistically, the process of de-urbanisation is marked by the following: (a) a decline or stagnation in the level, pace and concentration of urbanisation; (b) a decline or stagnation in the rates of growth of towns in each size class; (c) the presence of a significant proportion of urban centres with negative rates of growth; (d) a high degree of variability in the ranks of the higher order urban centres accompanied by an absolute decrease in their population; (e) a general movement of towns to lower classes; and (f) accentuation of urban primacy.

Each of these measures have been calculated for the region under investigation, that is, the hinterland of Calcutta which is taken to include the British provinces of Bengal, Bihar and Orissa, Awadh, Central Provinces and Berar.[20] Our study is based on a time series analysis of 151 administrative units consisting of ninety-eight British districts and fifty-three feudatory states for five decades between 1872 (when the first

[20]The economic regions which had evolved within this hinterland comprised, first the fertile agricultural tracts of Bengal Delta, the middle Ganga plains and the Utkal plains, and secondly, of the rich mineral and forest belts of the Chhotanagpur plateau. The hinterland of Calcutta contained about one-fourth of the area of the subcontinent and about half of its population which was reported to be more closely packed than the most crowded manufacturing countries in England. This hinterland has been delineated on the basis of migration streams, expansion of the railway network and the pattern of freight movement: M. Raza and A. Habeeb, 'Characteristics and Processes of Colonial Urbanization' in M. Alam (ed), *Urbanization in Developing Countries*, Osmania, India 1976; S. Munsi, 'Expansion of the Railway Network Growth in Eastern India, 1854-1910', Occasional Paper No.3, Centre for Studies in Social Sciences, Calcutta; and M. Ghosh, A.K. Dutta and B. Ray, *Calcutta, A Study in Urban Growth Dynamics*, Firma K.L. Mukhopadhyay, Calcutta 1972.

census of India was taken) and 1921. The data for the seventeen districts of East Bengal, now in Bangladesh, are given separately in most of the tables so that a comparative picture of the eastern and western hinterland of the port city can be obtained and figures for districts now falling in the two countries are made distinguishable. For convenience all these administrative units included in the analysis will be referred to as districts throughout the paper.

Level, Concentration and Pace of Urbanisation

The level of urbanisation has been calculated here in terms of the expected value of the city size in a given region called the mean city size (MCS), using the index formulated by Arriaga.[21] The MCS indicated the average size of the city where the urban population of the region resides. The MCS values for the districts in the hinterland of Calcutta are given in Table 1. The distribution of the districts in the different size ranges clearly shows that during all the decades under investigation the level of urbanisation in the region was very low as the MCS range for a majority of the districts was only between 0 and 1,000. It was in very few districts that the MCS rose above 25,000.

By calculating the degree of urbanisation for this region by the conventional method, that is, in terms of the percentage of total population in urban places and through rural-urban ratios, the low urban base of the region may be further demonstrated. In the majority of the western districts the level of urbanisation was between 5 and 10 per cent.[22] In the districts of East Bengal it was less than 2.5 per cent.[23]

[21]Arriaga measures the degree of urbanisation by obtaining the average of the size of cities where the population resides in a given region. The statistical concept of this index is the expected value of the size of the cities. According to the statistical concept of expected value, the index is expressed as,

$$U = \frac{\sum_{i=1}^{N} Ci^2}{P}$$

Where, C = the population of the ith city N = the total number of cities
P = total population of the region whose U is being calculated. This index reflects the average city size in a region as well as the disparity in their distribution and is a more appropriate measure of the level of urbanisation when change in this level has to be measured.: E.E. Arriaga, 'Selected Measures of Urbanization' in S. Goldestein and D.F. Sly (eds), *The Measurement of Urbanization and Projection of Urban Population*, Working Paper 2, International Union for Scientific Study of Population, Liege, Belgium 1976, 29-31.

[22]See Satwant Ghosal, 'Some Indices of Urbanization in Eastern India', Centre for the Study of Regional Development, Jawaharlal Nehru Univerisity, New Delhi 1974 (Mimeo).

[23]R.A. Rumi, *Some Aspects of the Regional Structure of Bangladesh (1850-1970)*, Unpublished M.Phil Dissertation, Centre for the Study of Regional Development, Jawaharlal Nehru University, New Delhi 1981.

Table 1: Level of Urbanisation in the Hinterland of Calcutta

	Number of Districts and Feudatory States											
	1872		1881		1891		1901		1911		1921	
	W	E	W	E	W	E	W	E.	W	E	W	E
Above 25,000	3	-	2	-	3	-	4	-	3	-	6	-
10,001 -25,000	4	-	2	-	2	-	6	-	6	-	4	-
5,001 -10,000	4	-	5	-	6	-	8	-	6	-	10	-
2,001 -5,000	12	-	14	-	18	-	16	-	16	-	14	-
1,001 -2,000	23	1	26	1	23	1	25	1	26	1	28	1
0 -1,000	89	15	86	15	83	15	76	15	78	15	73	15
Total	135	16	135	16	135	16	135	16	135	16	135	16

Source : Based on Census of India (1872-1921) Part II, Imperial Tables for Population in Towns.

Note : W = Districts in the western hinterland;
E = Districts now in Bangladesh.

It may be interesting to note the comments and observations offered by the British officials to explain the absence of urbanisation in Bengal. The census commissioner of the province reported in 1901 that race possibly was an important factor in determining the level of urbanisation: 'The Mongoloid element in the population of Bengal may be less inclined to congregate in towns than the Dravidian and Aryan inhabitants of other parts. Assam which is even more markedly Mongoloid has the smallest urban population of any part of India'.[24] Not satisfied with this explanation the census commissioner in 1931 refuted the hypothesis: 'It may, however, be questioned whether race has in this case anything to do with the matter and we should be inclined to account for the phenomena not by race but by rainfall. The areas of the greatest precipitation in the peninsula are Bengal, Assam and lower Burma, and if living in cities is unpopular, as it certainly is in these regions, it is perhaps on account of the greater degree of discomfort which it involves than on account of the racial composition of the people'.[25]

The low base of urbanisation and the absence of urban spread in the region are brought out by the index of concentration [26] given in Table 2

[24]*Census of India (1901)*, Vol. I, Part I, *Report*,27-28.

[25]*Census of India (1931)*, Vol. I, Part I, *Report*, 49.

[26]The index has been calculated using the formula C=U/P
U = Index of urbanisation
P = Total population of the region whose U is being calculated.

and the location quotients (LQ) given in Table 3. When we consider the index of concentration we find that in about eighty-three (that is, 55 per cent) of the total districts the index value was very low and ranged from 0 to 0.49 on a concentration scale measuring from 0 to 1,000. Even the highest values of the index in the region obtained by Calcutta were quite low and ranged between 150 and 320.

Table 2: Index of Concentration of Urbanisation in the Hinterland of Calcutta

Index X^{-3}_{10}	Number of Districts and Feudatory States											
	1872		1881		1891		1901		1911		1921	
	W	E	W	E	W	E	W	E	W	E	W	E
Above 10	9	-	8	-	6	-	8	-	10	-	15	-
From 7 to 9.99	8	-	10	-	8	-	12	-	20	-	10	-
From 1.50 to 6.99	10	-	12	-	13	-	24	-	12	-	14	-
From 1.00 to 1.49	23	-	18	-	12	-	14	-	17	-	6	-
From. 0.50 to 0:99	17	-	20	-	26	-	12	-	8	-	22	-
From 0 to 0.49	68	16	59	16	70	16	65	16	68	16	68	16
Total	135	16	135	16	135	16	135	16	135	16	135	16

Source : Based on Census of India (1872-1921) Part II, Imperial Tables for Population in Towns.

Note : Since the index values were very small they have been indicated in units 10, i.e. the scale of concentration ranges from 0 to 1,000.

The location quotients in Table 3 likewise show that only two or three districts claimed a comparatively significant share (quotients above 5) in the total urban population of the region. In fact, the number of districts with very low LQ values (between 0 and 1.99) was not only very large but increased from 126 in 1872 to 129 in 1921. The LQs for the districts of Lucknow, Patna, Banaras and Allahabad, which were four of the most urbanised districts in the region, continuously declined. The quotients for Calcutta remained the highest throughout the period though they did not show any appreciable increase.

Table 3: Location Quotients for Urban Population in the Hinterland of Calcutta

Quotients	Number of Districts and Feudatory States											
	1872		1881		1891		1901		1911		1921	
	W	E	W	E	W	E	W	E	W	E	W	E
11.00 - 11.99	1_c	-	-	-	-	-	1_c	-	1_c	-	1_c	-
10.00 - 10.99	-	-	-	-	1_c	-	-	-	-	-	-	-
9.00 - 9.99	-	-	1_c	-	-	-	-	-	-	-	-	-
8.00 - 8.99	-	-	-	-		-		-		-		-
7.00 - 7.99	-	-		-		-		-		-		-
6.00 - 6.99	1	-		-		-		-		-		-
5.00 - 5.99	1	-		-		-		-		-		-
4.00 - 4.99	-	-	2	-	3	-	1	-	-	-	-	-
3.00 - 3.99	4	1	3	1	4	-	5	-	2	-	4	-
2.00 - 2.99	15	2	12	2	12	1	12	1	16	1	15	1
1.00 - 1.99	27	4	29	7	31	7	29	6	25	8	25	10
0.00 - 0.99	86	6	88	6	84	8	87	9	90	7	89	5
Total	135	16	135	16	135	16	135	16	135	16	135	16

Source : Based on Census of India (1872-1921) Part II, Imperial Tables for Population.
Note : In Tables 2 and 3 W refers to the western hinterland and E to districts now in Bangladesh.

When we consider the pace of urbanisation[27] in the region under investigation (Table 4), we find that in only about half of the districts, and in some decades in less than that number, the pace was positive between 1872 and 1921, thus indicating that forces of urbanisation in the region were very weak.

Growth Rates of Towns in Each Size Class

It has been usually observed in the studies on the relationship between growth and size of urban settlements pertaining to the industrialised countries that cities above a certain size do not decline.[28] Thompson likens this to an 'urban ratchet', implying that at a certain point of the urban size scale a growth mechanism similar to a ratchet comes into being which locks in the past growth and prevents contraction. The 'threshold range' is set by the degree of isolation of the urban place, the nature of its hinterland, the level of industrial development in the country and cultural factors.[29]

[27]Pace of urbanisation is taken to be the geometric mean of the annual rate of change of urbanisation as defined in footnote 26, above.

[28]Wibur R. Thompson, *A Preface to Urban Economics*, Baltimore 1965, 22.

[29]Loc. cit.

Table 4: Pace of Urbanisation in the Western Hinterland of Calcutta

	Number of Districts and Feudatory States				
	1872-81	1881-91	1891-01	1901-11	1911-21
Above 5.00	7	7	6	3	11
2.50-4.99	13	10	12	10	16
1.00-2.49	14	29	25	24	14
0-0.99	22	25	19	26	23
0.00	28	0	10	7	0
0(-0.99)	4	15	16	14	10
(-1.0)-(-4.99)	12	25	25	26	39
Below (-5.00)	35	24	22	25	22
Total	135	135	135	135	135
Districts with positive pace (A)	56	71	62	63	64
Districts with zero or negative pace (B)	79	64	73	72	71
Ratio of B/A (C)	1.41	0.90	1.18	1.14	1.14

Source: Based on Census of India, Imperial Tables for Population in Towns (1872-1921).

The growth patterns of the colonial cities, however, do not give any indication of the existence of a similar urban ratchet. A general decline characterised both the larger and the smaller cities. Table 5 gives the means and variances of growth rates for each of the size classes of towns in the hinterland of Calcutta. The table indicates that the mean growth rates (X) tended to be negative for both the smaller as well as the larger towns. The decline was all-pervasive in the smaller towns. All towns in classes II-VI experienced a negative growth in the decades under consideration. The values for standard deviations and coefficient of variations (V %) indicate that though no systematic trend was evident in the growth rate of towns, the smaller ones (classes IV-VI) declined at a slower rate than the larger ones.[30]

[30]Cf. Brian T. Robson, *Urban Growth: An Approach*, Methuen, 1973, 93-94. Robson observes that during the same period the towns of England and Wales followed a distinct pattern as far as their rate of growth was concerned. All these towns experienced an increase in their population and there was a systematic decrease in the V%.

Table 5 : Means and Dispersions of Growth Rates of Towns in Different Population Size Groups in the Hinterland of Calcutta

Period		Population Size Groups					
		VI 5,000	V 5,000-	IV 9,999-	III 19,999-	II 49,999	I 99,999-
1872-81	N	5	149	68	28	10	6
	X	64.37	-48.35	-27.55	-0.48	7.06	1.03
	S	30.57	98.87	79.46	35.86	15.15	20.46
	V%	47.49	-204.5	288.41	7318.4	214.61	1986.4
1881-91	N	104	143	76	28	12	7
	X	-46.04	-24.91	-16.203	2.09	-10.50	8.28
	S	237.04	72.77	58.11	12.49	46.92	14.02
	V%	514.80	292.13	358.61	597.6	44.86	169.32
1891-1901	N	99	152	84	31	10	8
	X	39.4	25.56	12.17	1.76	9.87	4.00
	S	153.62	67.34	53.13	22.29	15.77	17.25
	V%	389.89	263.45	436.53	1266.8	159.77	431.09
1901-11	N	110	148	92	32	8	8
	X	-00.04	-20.26	-12.48	-4.60	-23.95	-0.74
	S	144.41	58.39	42.21	22.74	29.74	12.02
	V%	240.64	288.20	338.22	494.81	124.19	1615.65
1911-21	N	109	147	78	40	6	9
	X	-16.84	-7.72	-2.48	0.435	-9.70	5.09
	S	65.69	35.04	33.11	19.30	5.62	15.89
	V%	390.09	953.94	1334.50	4436.78	57.92	312.11

Note : N = No. of towns; X=Growth rate; S= Standard deviation of growth rates; and V% = Coefficient of variation (%) of growth rates (magnitude).

Urban Areas with Negative Rates of Growth

During the nineteenth century the presence of urban areas with negative rates of growth was not the exception but the rule and this phenomenon characterised towns of all classes. Table 6 gives the total number and the percentage of towns which showed negative growth rates in each size class during 1872-1921. It becomes evident from the table that the proportion of towns with negative rates of growth was very large. It ranged from 48.49 in 1872-81 to 64.82 in 1901-11. Moreover, this proportion tended to increase with time specially in the class II and class V towns and during 1901-21. Table 6 brings out clearly that in each class the proportion of decaying towns was smaller during the initial decades and increased towards the close of this period. The smaller urban centres (classes IV, V and VI) had a larger proportion of towns with negative rates of growth (between 50 and 70 per cent), but the proportion was significant even in the class I centres (30-50 per cent). These conclusions lend ample credibility to our contention that the nineteenth century was marked by de-urbanisation.

Table 6(a): Urban Areas in the Hinterland of Calcutta with Negative Rates of Growth (NGR) during 1872-1921 (percentages are in terms of the total number of towns)

	1872-1881			1881-1891			1891-1901		
Class of towns	Total	NGR	%	Total	NGR	%	Total	NGR	%
I	6	2	33.33	7	2	28.57	8	4	50.00
II	10	4	40.00	12	2	33.33	10	7	70.00
III	28	9	32.14	28	12	42.86	31	19	61.29
IV	68	35	51.47	76	38	50.00	84	48	57.14
V	149	79	53.02	143	76	53.15	152	83	54.61
VI	5	0	00	104	68	65.38	99	62	62.62
Total	266	129	48.49	370	200	54.05	388	223	57.47

	1901-1911			1911-1921		
Class of towns	Total	NGR	%	Total	NGR	%
I	8	4	50.00	9	4	44.44
II	8	7	87.5	6	5	83.33
III	32	20	62.50	40	20	50.00
IV	92	51	55.43	78	41	52.56
V	148	99	66.89	147	99	67.35
VI	110	77	70.00	109	63	57.79
Total	398	258	64.82	389	232	59.64

Table 6 (b): Decades with Maximum and Minimum Percentage of Towns with NGR in Different Size Classes

Class	Maximum		Minimum	
	Decade	%	Decade	%
I	1891-1901	57.14	1881-91	28.57
II	1911-21	100.00	1881-91	33.33
III	1901-11	58.82	1872-81	31.03
IV	1901-11	54.84	1911-21	51.25
V	1911-21	58.87	1881-91	54.24
VI	1901-11	63.70	1872-81	0.00

Variability of the Ranks of Urban Areas

The general decline or stagnation reflected in the indices of urbanisation discussed above is also indicated by the measure of the degree of variability and the net gain or loss of population in the twenty-five largest urban centres within the western hinterland (Table 7). The measures of the degree of variability are the average rank, the average deviation of the ranks and the range. The first measure states the average position of each city during 1872-1921, and indicates their average position in the urban hierarchy. The second measure states the degree of consistency of a city's position in the system of settlements. The third gives the number of positions over which the city's rank has varied.

Some significant facts about the growth patterns of the twenty-five largest cities in the hinterland of Calcutta are revealed in Table 7 in which the cities seem to fall into three classes according to their range of variation of rank: sixteen cities show relative stability, their ranks varying less than ten positions; two show extreme variation of forty positions or more (Murshidabad and Kanpur); the remaining six show a shift of ten to forty positions. Further, of the twenty-five cities, seventeen (68 per cent) experienced a net loss in rank, four experienced no net change (Calcutta, Lucknow, Banaras and Gaya) and only four showed a net gain (Kanpur, Howrah, Jabalpur and Fyzabad). When we compare the net gain or loss of ranks of cities with the net gain or loss of their population during 1872-1921 we find that out of the four cities which showed no gain or loss, two experienced a net loss in their population (Lucknow and Patna), and out of the seventeen cities which experienced a net loss in rank fourteen also experienced a net loss in population.

It is apparent from the table that cities like Murshidabad, Mirzapur,

Table 7: Variability of Ranks of Selected Cities at each Census in the Hinterland of Calcutta

Towns	Rank in						Average rank	Average deviation	Range of rank	Net Gain or loss(-) during period	Population		Ratio
	1872	1881	1891	1901	1911	1921					1872	1921	1921/1872
1. Calcutta	1	1	1	1	1	1	1	0	0	0	447601	907851	2.02
2. Lucknow	2	2	2	2	2	2	2	0	0	0	284779	217167	0.76
3. Benaras	3	3	3	3	3	3	3	0	0	0	175188	195373	1.12
4. Patna	4	4	4	7	7	8	5.66	1.68	4	-4	158900	119976	0.76
5. Allahabad	5	6	6	5	5	6	5.05	0.50	1	-1	143692	145605	1.01
6. Kanpur	6	5	5	4	6	5	5.16	1.50	2	+1	122770	195085	1.58
7. Howrah	7	7	7	6	4	4	5.83	1.22	3	-3	97784	195301	1.99
8. Farrukhabad	8	5	13	16	13	19	12.33	3.89	14	-11	79204	48331	0.61
9. Bhagalpur	9	14	15	11	10	10	11.05	2.00	6	-1	69678	68878	0.98
10. Mirzapur	10	9	10	10	31	13	13.83	5.72	22	-3	67274	54994	0.82
11. Gaya	11	10	11	12	15	11	11.66	1.22	5	0	66843	67562	1.01
12. Monghyr	12	17	18	30	19	20	19.33	3.78	18	-8	59698	46825	0.78
13. Jabalpur	13	11	9	9	9	10	10.00	1.33	4	+4	55188	108617	1.97
14. Gorakhpur	14	16	16	15	17	18	16	1.00	4	-4	51117	50498	0.98
15. Cuttack	15	25	21	19	14	17	18.05	3.17	11	-2	50878	51007	1.02
16. Darbhanga	16	15	12	14	11	15	12.16	4.16	9	-9	47450	53700	1.13
17. Kamptee	17	19	27	29	28	60	35	16.00	43	-43	48831	20226	0.41
18. Chapra	18	18	17	21	23	21	19.66	2.00	6	-3	46287	42415	0.92
19. Murshidabad	19	27	30	57	59	61	42.16	16.83	42	-42	46182	10669	0.23
20. Sagar	20	21	24	27	20	25	22.83	2.50	7	-5	45655	39319	0.86
21. Bihar	21	20	20	23	28	28	23.33	3.10	8	-7	44295	36720	0.82
22. Arrah	22	23	22	20	25	23	19.16	3.34	5	-1	39386	40769	1.04
23. Ghazipur	23	22	23	28	45	45	31	9.33	23	-22	38853	24708	0.64
24. Muzaffarpur	24	26	19	22	32	24.16		3.22	13	-8	38223	32755	0.86
25. Fyzabad	25	13	14	13	18	16	16.05	3.33	12	+9	37804	51342	1.36

Note : The largest twenty-five cities in 1872 were selected as the starting point and their ranks in the total urban areas were noted for the subsequent decades.

Kamptee and Ghazipur which were the apex of an earlier system of spatial organisation showed a high degree of variability compared with those which had emerged to subserve the colonial rule like Kanpur, Howrah and Jabalpur. On the whole, the picture is one of decline or stagnation.

Movement of Towns in terms of Size Classes

The census statistics on the 'births and deaths' of towns are perhaps the most difficult to rely on and to interpret because these suffer both from over and under-counting and are totally intertwined with the ephemerality of census definitions. But problems of this sort are an inevitable conjunct of any work on urban growth and should not deter us from verifying our hypothesis in general terms.

Transition matrices were constructed for the five decades under consideration in which births, deaths and movements of individual towns between the six classes were noted.[31] Table 8 based on these transition matrices indicates the number of towns which remained in the same class or moved to higher or lower classes during the decades under consideration. As the data indicate, very few towns moved to higher or lower classes. The proportion of towns moving to a higher class ranged from 4.97 per cent to 15.56 per cent and of those moving to a lower class ranged from 6.44 per cent to 15.14 per cent. Moreover, the majority of the towns (between 74.78 per cent and 88.59 per cent) remained in the same class. These observations further point to the general stagnation in the processes of urbanisation in the region.

Table 8: Movement of Towns to Higher or Lower Classes in the Western Hinterland of Calcutta

	Number of towns at the end of decade									
	1872-81		1881-91		1891-1901		1901-11		1911-21	
	No.	%	No.	%	No.	%	No.	%	No.	%
1. Towns remain--ing in the same class	168	79.24	270	83.85	303	88.59	267	74.78	308	83.46
2. Moving to lower class	11	5.18	24	7.45	22	6.44	54	15.14	32	8.68
2. Moving to higher class	33	15.56	28	8.70	17	4.97	36	10.08	29	7.86
Total	212	100	322	100	342	100	357	100	369	100

[31]These matrices were constructed using the method devised by Brian T. Robson in *Urban Growth: An Approach*, 93-94.

Note: The number of towns 'dead' and 'born' in each decade have been excluded from the analysis because these towns are affected most by changes in census definitions.

Development and Accentuation of Primacy

Urbanisation in colonial India was characterised by the existence of high degree of primacy, that is, a high difference between the population sizes of the largest and the second largest city in the region. This was accompanied by an absence of formal urban systems with regional core areas of higher growth, surrounded by urban areas with lower growth. The point may be illustrated with reference to the spatial pattern in industrially developed countries like the United States and Britain during the late nineteenth century.[32]

The historical process of urban growth in the United States can be seen as a consistent sequence of westward expansion followed by subsequent in-filling as the frontier of development was pushed progressively further west. A radical alteration in the general configuration of the spatial pattern of urban growth in England and Wales took place with the advancement of the nineteenth century, from the dominance of a single core, that is, London in Lowland Britain during the period before the Industrial Revolution, to the shift of the focus of growth to the mineral-bearing and carboniferous areas of Highland Britain. The industrial nodes in the provinces formed the cores of regional sub-systems and each of the leading regional centres developed sequentially as the leading cities of the period.[33]

In sharp contrast to the trends mentioned above, the medieval urban system of India, which had comprised several sub-systems that had evolved around regional cores, was replaced during the colonial period by a pattern characterised by the emergence of only a few dominant cores

[32]See, for example, the works of Bogue, Perloff and Duncan. Bogue, in his study of metropolitan dominance has argued that the sixty-seven major metropolitan centres in the United States acted as poles around which the regional population distribution and types of economic activity were articulated: D.J Bogue, *The Structure of the Metropolitan Community*, Ann Arbor, Michigan 1950. Perloff et al. in their analysis of the spatial patterns of the post-war period in the USA also point to the presence of a single dominant national core area of the long established manufacturing belt and several regional sub-systems which were subordinate to this core: H.S. Perloff et al., *Regions, Resources and Economic Growth*, Baltimore 1960. Duncan et al. find a similar spatial pattern while analysing the structure of metropolitan centres of more than 300,000 population in the USA: O.P. Duncan et al., *Metropolis and Region*, Baltimore 1960.

[33]Brian T. Robson, *Urban Growth: An Approach*, 93-94, n.35.

and the general decline and decay of provincial cities. A primate city size distribution was strongly entrenched in the region under consideration. Let us look at the values of the degree of primacy of Calcutta as given below:

Table 9 : Degree of Primacy of Calcutta

Calcutta	1872	1881	1891	1901	1911	1921	Absolute increase in 1921 over 1872
1. Within British Indian empire (*vis-a-vis* Bombay)	0.01	1.23	1.30	1.71	1.56	1.32	1.31
2. Within the hinterland (*vis-a-vis* Lucknow)	3.17	3.87	4.14	5.38	6.19	6.93	3.76

Note: Degree of primacy here refers to the ratio of the population of the largest city to the second largest in the region under consideration.

The table indicates that Calcutta had been established as the primate city of the country by 1921 though its primacy was much more marked within its hinterland than it was within the British Indian empire. It was a regional primate, a phenomenon that did not usually occur in the other colonial countries which were in most cases characterised by the emergence of one major port which was also the national primate.

Forces which would have counteracted the enhancement of this primacy were either absent or were considerably weak in India. In the case of England and Wales, on the other hand, the domination by London of the national space economy was challenged during the nineteenth century by regional nodes with specific factor endowments.[34] The processes of region formation which formed the backdrop against which spatial patterns designed themselves in India were strongly linked to the satellitic primate which instead of encouraging regional urban centres actually undermined their growth.

[34]In England and Wales growth industries progressed through the sequence of textiles, iron, coal and the motor car. Each of the leading regional centres in each of these industries developed sequentially as the leading cities of the period with Manchester and Birmingham rising first (1840s), were followed by Leeds and Bradford (1870s), and London regaining supremacy in the 1880s or the 1890s: Asa Briggs, *The Victorian Cities*, Penguin paperback, 1963.

Spatial Pattern of Urban Growth

By plotting the standardised growth rates of towns for each decade,[35] we find that towns with high rates of growth, though the number of such towns was quite small,[36] were generally located along the newly constructed railway lines in the agricultural belt of the Ganga plains during the period 1872-91. In the subsequent decades between 1891 and 1911, the towns in the Ganga plains lost their relative importance and the towns in the southern areas of Central Provinces and Berar came up significantly on the scene. These were the areas which had been linked to the ports of Bombay and Calcutta in the preceding decades. Between 1901 and 1921, the areas in the Ganga plains which had been the earliest focus of urban growth re-emerged as areas of high urban growth. The areas in Berar, however, maintained their relative position. The spatial changes in the pattern of urban growth seem to be related to the economic history of the period.

The towns which showed high rates of growth at some time or the other during 1872-1921 were those which were linked with the colonial economic activities. They may be grouped as follows:

1. Centres of British industrial enterprise: Kanpur and Howrah;
2. Railway junctions: Bhagalpur, Khagul, Darbhanga, Bhadrasur, Bilaspur, Asansol, Jhansi, Gorakhpur, Katihar, Cuttack, Nagpur, Katol Khandwa, Burhanpur and Harda;
3. Agricultural marketing and collection centres: Gaya, Monghyr, Gaura-Barhaj and Mubarakpur;
4. Centres of sugar manufacture: Padrauna and Basti;
5. Centres of extraction in the mineral belts: Ranchi and Hazaribagh;
6. Cantonments: Dinapur, Jhansi and Sitapur;
7. Resort towns: Darjeeling.

[35]As indicated in Table 5, the deviation of growth rates is very wide for small places and relatively narrow for larger places. Some form of standardisation was, therefore, needed which would take account of these differences. Standard scores for this purpose express each town's growth rate as a deviation from the average growth rate of the size group to which it belongs in any decade. The calculation is based on the formula,

$$Zi = \frac{Gi.n - G n}{On}$$

Where *Gi.n* is the growth rate of the [th] town whose population places it within the [nth] size group of towns, *Gn* and *n* are the mean and standard deviation of the [nth] size: Brian T. Robson, *Urban Growth: An Approach*, 98.

[36]The number of towns with high rates of growth in each decade was 10 (3.75 per cent) in 1872-81, 8(2.43 per cent) in 1881-91, 9(2.31 per cent) in 1891-1901, 14 (3.51 per cent) in 1901-11 and 25 (6.42 per cent) in 1911-21. Percentages relate to the total number of towns.

It may be noted that these centres did not become cores in the true sense of the word, that is, cross with a cluster of urban areas having high rates of growth surrounding them. This latter phenomenon was one of the most important characteristics of urban growth in the industrialised countries, as pointed out above.

Diminution in the Productive Activities within Urban Centres

The penetration of international capitalism brought about certain structural changes in the traditional economy of urban areas. These changes were in response to the severance of ties between the urban productive and commercial activities on the one hand, and the rural-peasant economies on the other; they had also been caused by the greater concentration of capital and business activities in the hands of the capitalist entrepreneur (both native and foreign). Gradually, the traditional urban industrial base which had been made up by the indigenous handicraft production was destroyed by the influx of cheap manufactured goods from Europe and, consequently, economic activities in the colonial cities were reduced to the collection and handling of raw materials, channelling of manufactured goods and to the maintenance of the ancillary services to the colonial economy. The bazaar system of these cities centres around trade, transport and other service activities.[37] The industries that were developed in the region by British enterprise were either primary processing industries which did not always seek an urban location. Alternatively, these were simpler forms of engineering works, which though urban based, required a time which may be 'measured by generations'[38] to bring about a transformation of the urban economy and make a dent in the urban occupational structure.

The economic structure of the colonial cities took shape in response to the structural changes in the economy and the changed role that these cities had to play. It was characterised by a diminution on the productive functions reflected in terms of the following: (a) a stultification of the manufacturing activities in the urban areas; (b) accompanying unprofit-

[37]The concept of the bazaar economy implied here is adapted from the concept given by C. Geertz. It refers not only to the distributive activities of the urban areas but also to their manufacturing productive activities. It is characterised by fragmentation of transactions, a sliding price system and fractionalisation of risks. It is labour-intensive and is based on a highly developed division of labour: see C. Geertz, *Peddlers and Princes*, Chicago 1963, 24-28; also, Atiya Habeeb, 'Economic Structure of the Colonial Cities in India: A Review of Sectoral Trends 1872-1921' (eds J.S Grewal and Indu Banga), Guru Nanak Dev University, Amritsar 1981, 175-91.

[38]D.H. Buchanan, *The Development of Capitalist Enterprise in India*, Macmillan, New York 1939, 141.

able proliferation of tertiary activities; (c) persistence of primary (agricultural) activities; and (d) the residual nature of the tertiary sector.

To analyse these characteristics we have applied Sabolo's index of relative absorption of labour by the tertiary sector.[39] We have taken the sectoral distribution of the working population for twelve cities in the hinterland of Calcutta and for nine other cities in India for which almost complete time series data (1881-1921) are available. In order to make a cross-country comparison data for the first twelve cities (ranked) for England and Wales (1871-1921) have also been considered. From the analysis we find that almost all the cities identified in England and Wales had acquired a well-developed industrial base even before the modern phase of industrialisation (after the end of World War I) had set in.[40] On the other hand, the proportion of workers in the secondary sector of Indian cities remained very low throughout the period of investigation. The analysis of the sectoral distribution of the working population further shows that the primary activities in the cities of England and Wales had become negligible by 1871 and the tertiary sector, though substantially developed was still less significant than the secondary sector. On the other hand, in the contemporary cities in India, the secondary sector was not only insignificant (the highest proportional values of the secondary sector were comparable to the lowest recorded for the contemporary cities in England and Wales) but became further subverted with the passage of time and with the proportion of workers in the tertiary sector becoming conspicuously large. Moreover, the Indian urban centres accommodated a significant proportion of agricultural workers, the proportion being as high as 45 per cent in some cities.

When we consider the index of tertiarisation (Table 10) for the cities under consideration for 1871 and 1921, that is, the base and the final years of the period of investigation, we find that the values for the cities in England and Wales were much lower than those for their Indian counterparts. The characteristic trend observed is that these values tend to decrease in the cities of England and Wales and increase phenomenally

[39] Y. Sabolo, *The Service Industries*, International Labour Organization, Geneva 1975. Sabolo, however, used the index to make comparative analysis of countries and not cities but the index can be fruitfully applied to the analysis of urban economies. In the present analysis this index has been calculated thus,

I_T = (workers in non-secondary sectors/workers in secondary sectors)100

[40] The tables which give the sectoral distribution of the working population for these cities between 1871 and 1921 have not been reproduced here for want of space. Table 10, which gives the index of tertiarisation (I_T) for these cities is, however, indicative of the extent of the development of the secondary sector. Low I_T values denote a high development of the secondary sector.

Table 10 : The I_T (Tertiarization) Values for cities of England and Wales

Cities of England and Wales	1971	1911	Cities in Calcutta's hinterland	1881	1921
Less than 100					
Birmingham	45	44	Calcutta	575	276
Manchester	44	79	Howrah		147
Sheffield	40	56	Lucknow	142	432
Leicester	41	43	Kanpur	108	315
Sunderland	70	61	Allahabad	117	394
Huddersfield	39	55	Banaras	106	120
			Mirzapur	132	94
			Jaunpur	117	124
			Gorakhpur	84	221
			Fyzabad	156	437
More than 100			Other important cities of India		
London	113	127	Ahmedabad	514	281
Liverpool	139	150	Bombay	411	276
Portsmouth	184	123	Bangalore	304	318
Cardiff	189	138	Delhi	218	299
Swansea	160	151	Hyderabad	330	248
			Madras	223	300
			Nagpur	218	123

in the Indian cities. One may conclude from this that the tertiarisation of the urban economy had become a universal phenomenon for the cities of India under colonial rule even before their secondary sector had attained any importance.

III

In this paper we have attempted to establish a framework within which the specific phenomenon of colonial urbanisation can be analysed. Using this framework for the study of urbanisation in the hinterland of Calcutta during 1872-1921 we find that the processes of urbanisation specific to colonial India of the nineteenth century should be viewed as an expression of the set of relationships which evolved *vis-a-vis* the metropolitan economy of the colonising power. In response to this relationship (which essentially was a dominance-dependence relationship) certain changes, crucial in the determination of the qualitative and quantitative attributes of urbanisation were introduced in the space economy. The capitalist commercial domination destroyed the regional specialisation they had achieved during the medieval period. As a consequence general urban decay set in.

Colonial urbanisation was thus characterised by urban atrophy. This phenomenon as diminution in size was reflected in terms of the following:

(a) a very low and stagnant level of urbanisation in which only about 10 per cent of the districts achieved a comparatively significant level; (b) a very low and stagnant index of urban concentration; (c) an increase in the number of districts with low location quotients for urban population; (d) a large number of districts (about 50 per cent) with negative pace of urbanisation; (e) a general decline in the rates of growth of both the larger and the smaller size classes of towns; (f) a large proportion of towns (between 50 and 65 per cent) with negative rates of growth and a general increase in their proportion with the passage of time; (g) a high variability in the ranks of the higher order towns (out of the first twenty-five cities 68 per cent experienced a net loss of rank and in 83 per cent of these the population also declined in absolute terms); and, (h) a very insignificant movement of towns to higher class (in 1881-15.56 per cent and 4.97 per cent in 1891) and a subsequent decrease in the proportion of such towns.

In terms of spatial patterns, colonial urbanisation replaced the medieval urban structure which had comprised several sub-systems (evolved around regional cores) with a pattern in which there was one dominant core surrounded by smaller provincial cities. A primate city size distribution was strongly entrenched in the region under consideration. The towns which showed high rates of growth at some time or the other during 1872-1921 were usually those which were aligned along the new transport routes, and were linked with entrepot functions. These towns, however, were spatially dispersed and belonged to the lower-size classes which were not potent enough to act as strong cores triggering off urban growth in the surrounding areas.

Urban atrophy as diminution in the productive activities within urban areas was reflected in terms of the following characteristics: (a) an initially constricted secondary sector further depressed by a subsequent reduction in its size (the proportion of total workers in the secondary sector decreased in seven out of the ten cities considered); (b) an enormous expansion and proliferation of a tertiary sector which, being unrelated to city growth, was essentially residual in character; and, (c) a persistent existence and further intensification of the primary sector in all the ten cities considered.

One may conclude from this study that the deep-seated disequilibrium and asymmetrical growth that characterised the economy of India during the second half of the nineteenth and the first quarter of the twentieth century are evident in the characteristics and processes of post-independence urbanisation in the country. Hence, to understand contemporary reality properly it needs to be analysed with reference to the specificities generated by the historical developments under colonial rule.

URBAN MORPHOLOGY UNDER COLONIAL RULE

REETA GREWAL

An important aspect of urban studies is the study of the inner structure of towns, or their morphology. The physical form and structure, and the developments which influence this form, add to the understanding of the history and growth of towns and cities.[1] In fact, knowledge of the morphology of urban areas 'facilitates the understanding of the general characteristics of cities'.[2] Urban geographers have taken keen interest in the morphological aspect of urban units and have studied them essentially as forms of space utilisation. Among other things, they take up the 'function of site factors, historical vicissitudes and the impact of successive cultures and economic setting and development', and also the 'street system, plot pattern and building fabric' within the town.[3] The functional zones, route plans and housing, besides institutions and transportation system are also taken into account.[4] Urban morphology in the domain of urban history, however, is just beginning to draw some scholarly

[1]K.D. Sharma, *Urban Development in Metropolitan Shadow*, Inter-India, New Delhi 1985, 54.

[2]Gerald Breese, *Urbanization in Newly Developing Countries*, Prentice Hall of India, New Delhi 1978, 54.

[3]Awadhesh Kumar Singh Anal, 'Begusarai: A Study in Urban Morphology', *The Deccan Geographer*, X, No. 1, January-June 1972, 40-47. See also, C.S. Yadav (ed), *Morphology of Towns*, Perspectives in Urban Geography, X, Concept, New Delhi 1987.

[4]Om Prakash Singh, 'Functional Morphology of Service Centres in Uttar Pradesh: A Case Study', *The Deccan Geographer*, XII, No. 1, January-June 1974, 38-97.

interest.[5] The present discussion focuses on urban morphology in the Punjab under colonial rule.

The Punjab was annexed to the British Indian empire in 1849. The boundaries of the Punjab province remained changing till 1912. The paper relates to the plain areas between the rivers Sutlej and the Indus, excluding the Delhi territory, the north-west frontier tract and the hill region. Since it is not possible to go into detail for each individual town in the Punjab plains, an attempt is made here to study the basic morphological types of towns and cities in the region and their functional areas. A comparison of urban zones with models of form and structure of towns is also attempted to understand the nature of the physical growth of the urban centres of the region.

I

In the evolution of the physical structure of the urban centres in the Punjab two basic forms can be noticed – the walled town and the open city; the basic ground plans are irregular in the case of most walled towns, and regular, radial or grid patterned in the case of the planned towns.[6] Most towns, however, do not fully conform to either of these categories as few urban centres were planned and they usually developed by a process of accretion. A continuous process of remodelling has superimposed regular geometric patterns on an irregular system. The final version becomes a heterogeneous structure of different basic forms.

Some form of town planning has been done in India since the earliest times. In ancient India, several types of town plans have been identified.[7] These towns were generally walled, with two wide main streets dominating the otherwise irregular and narrow street system, while the palace, fort or temple formed the core areas. Class division was rigidly followed in residential areas and the internal layout of the houses was determined

[5]For example, Anthony D. King, *Colonial Urban Development: Culture, Social Power and Environment*, Routledge and Kegan Paul, London 1976.

[6]Arthur B. Gallion and Simon Eisner, *The Urban Pattern*, CBS Publishers and Distributors, New Delhi 1984 (Ist Indian edition), 11. See also Harold Carter, *The Study of Urban Geography*, Arnold Hienemann, New Delhi 1979 (1st Indian rep), 144.

[7]Among the types of town plans was *dandaka* where the male deities were in the north and the female deities outside; *saroathobhadra* in which the temple dominated the centre; *nandyavarta* for square or circular sites with the deity in the centre; *padmaka* resembled a lotus in shape; other town plans were *sivastika*, *prastara*, *karmuka* and *chaturmukha*: K.S. Rame Gowda, *Urban and Regional Planning*, University of Mysore, Mysore 1972, 3-8. See also A. Ghosh, *The City in Early Historical India*, Indian Institute of Advanced Study, Shimla 1990 (reprint), 51-52.

by regulations and specifications of buildings.[8] This pattern continued to be followed in the medieval period, with a notable contribution in the sphere of architecture.[9] A marked difference was, however, brought about by the British when they entered the scene with their principles of town planning. This meant the addition of 'western' extensions to the already existing towns in the form of civil lines or cantonments and also the founding of new towns planned with geometrical regularity.

In the Punjab under British rule three distinct types of urban centres can be identified from the viewpoint of morphology: the 'indigenous', which underwent very little visible change in its form; the 'anglicised', which had 'western' additions; and the new, planned, 'model' colony towns, which were founded by the British administrators in the western Punjab.[10]

Numerous indigenous towns dotted the entire region. Most of the small urban centres were in this category and morphologically saw very little visible change during the period. New additions to their structure did not alter their basic form.[11] The indigenous small towns were generally walled, like Phul, Nabha, Rewari, Farrukhnagar, Kaithal, Shujabad, Jind, Dadri and Sunam. All walled towns and cities had gates: the small towns had four to six gates while the cities, like Lahore and Amritsar, had twelve gates each. The town was traversed by one, or sometimes two, main roads, the latter cutting across at right angles to each other.[12] These roads were wider than others and were usually paved,

[8]The *Silpa Sastras* laid down procedures for buildings: K.S. Rame Gowda, *Urban and Regional Planning*, 8-11. For details of ancient towns in other parts of the world see Arthur Gallion and Simon Eisner, *The Urban Pattern*, 11-16.

[9]K.S. Rame Gowda, *Urban and Regional Planning*, 12. For residential pattern of a medieval town, see S.C. Misra, 'Some Aspects of the Self-Administering Institutions in Medieval Indian Towns', *Studies in Urban History* (eds J.S. Grewal and Indu Banga), Guru Nanak Dev University, Amritsar 1981, 80-90.

[10]Cf. Sudha Saxena, *Trends of Urbanisation in Uttar Pradesh*, Satish Book Enterprise, Agra 1972, 160. Three patterns are noted in Uttar Pradesh, namely, the indigenous, anglicised and modern. The indigenous and anglicised towns are also noted by A.E. Smailes, 'The Indian City: A Descriptive Model', *Geographic Zeit Schrift* (photocopy seen in the Guru Ramdas School of Planning, Guru Nanak Dev University, Amritsar), 57.

[11]Information on this aspect is gathered largely from the *District Gazetteers* (cited hereafter as *DG*), published by the British government in the Punjab in 1884, 1897, 1904 and 1912.

The morphology of the indigenous town is brought out in Diagram 1.

[12]For instance, Kamalia, Rajanpur, Muktsar, Payal, Nowshera, Kila Didar Singh and Hafizabad had one main street while Shujabad, Dadri, Jind, Dipalpur, Hodal, Zira and Kaithal had two.

THE INDIGENOUS TOWN

THEORETICAL

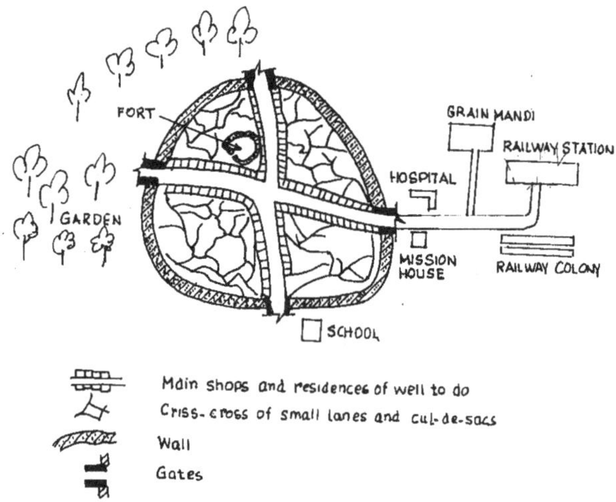

© REETA GREWAL : Diagram One.

with open drains either in the centre or on both sides. These primary roads housed the main bazaars and had the better looking buildings of the town on them. These buildings were two or three storeys high, closely built and often with good masonry fronts.

Houses were generally built of bricks or stones. There was usually an open space enclosed by rooms with windows generally on the front side only. The entrance opened into a vestibule known as *deorhi*. Latrines were generally on the roof. Town houses were generally dingy, with little light and fresh air.[13]

The streets of the urban centres, other than the main roads, were a wormlike system of narrow, tortuous lanes often ending in *cul-de-sacs*.[14] Drains ran through the centre or sides of the lanes and most of them were unpaved.[15]

These irregular streets enclosed *mohallas* or localities, which were walled at times, and were based on caste or communal groupings. The *mohallas* generally had their own shrine for worship. They were densely built and absorbed a large population. Some towns had small suburbs close to the town, as in Jullundur, Daska, Firozpur Jhirka, Mithankot, and Safidon. Gardens too were generally on the outskirts of the towns, as in Batala, Zira, Bhera, Leiah, Kunjpura, Tank, Phul, Bawal and Dhanaula. Sometimes gardens were located within the walled area of the town, as in Kunja.

II

With the extension of British rule and, later the introduction of railways, some changes occurred in the physical form of some of these towns.[16] The British in an effort to 'improve' the towns began by widening roads and cutting across through the more congested areas to allocate building sites wherever they could be most easily found.[17] They also added a wide

[13]For detail see Prakash Tandon, *Punjabi Century*, Hind Pocket Books, Delhi 1972 (first published 1961), 91-94, and A. Gauba, *Amritsar 1849-1947: A Study in Urban History*, Ph.D. Thesis, Guru Nanak Dev University, Amritsar 1980, 71-75.

[14]Apart from the *District Gazetteers*, these streets are described by Gerald Breese, *Urbanization in Newly Developing Countries*, 64; K.D. Sharma, *Urban Development in Metropolitan Shadow*, 57, 74-78.

[15]Some urban centres where the small streets were paved were Amritsar, Batala, Sohna, Pak Pattan, Gujranwala, Nakodar, Pundri, Gujrat, Sanaur, Daska, Alawalpur, Sangrur, Kila Sobha Singh, Kasur and Pasrur: Information collected from various *District Gazetteers*.

[16]This has been noted in the case of other Indian cities by Gerald Breese, *Urbanization in Newly Developing Countries*, 56. A similar development is also noted in specific cases, as in Rohtak: K.D. Sharma, *Urban Development in Metropolitan Shadow*, 61.

[17]Jacqueline Tyrwhitt, *Patrick Geddes in India*, Lund Humphries, London 1947, 19.

circular road around the town, as for instance in Amritsar, Batala, Jampur, Rohtak, Nabha, Rewari, Ferozepore and Dera Ismail Khan, thus, bringing about a minor change in the existing form of towns.[18] The coming of railway in the 1860s onwards added a new railway suburb to the towns it passed through. As it could not penetrate the old city it came as close as possible, where the railway colony was founded for the workers. The grain *mandi* came to be located close to the railway station as for instance in Jullundur, Bhatinda and Pak Pattan. These railway suburbs, however, remained small and did not alter the indigenous pattern to any considerable extent. Over time some additions like offices, schools and factories sprang up in the areas between the railway suburb and the old town forming a linear extension to the town.

The 'anglicised' or 'western' town was not superimposed on the existing one but sprang up initially as a suburb, and extended in various directions to encircle the old city or town, becoming after some time a distinct ring and yet remaining a connected part of the town as a whole (diagram 2). This kind of combined 'east-west' towns developed mainly in the district headquarters.[19]

When the British established their administrative centres in the Punjab they found the condition of towns 'unhealthy, noisy and distasteful'.[20] This prompted them to start independent colonies outside the towns. The officials and the professional people as well as the well-to-do businessmen lived in the civil lines while the army built the cantonments. The area between the old town and the new settlement was divided by maintaining a green belt of gardens between the two.

The civil lines and cantonments were planned settlements and stood in sharp contrast to the indigenous town.[21] Wide, tree-lined roads formed a gridiron parallel to the central road – the Mall. These were further divided into regular plots of land housing the bungalows of the civil and

[18]Based on the *District Gazetteers of Amritsar, Gurdaspur, Rohtak, Ferozepore, Dera Ismail Khan* and the *Gazetteer of the Phulkian States* of Patiala, Nabha and Jind brought out in 1883-84.

[19]See, for example, Kanchan Jyoti, *The City of Jullundur: A Study, in Urban History (1846 - 1947)*, Ph.D. Thesis, Guru Nanak Dev University, Amritsar 1988, 65-97. A similar development has also been noted in Uttar Pradesh. For details see Sudha Saxena, *Trends of Urbanisation in Uttar Pradesh*, 161.

[20]Jacqueline Tyrwhitt, *Patrick Geddes in India*, 19.

[21]A description of these areas is based on information in the *District Gazetteers* of the period and it conforms to Gerald Breese, *Urbanization in Newly Developing Countries*, 65-66, and K.D. Sharma, *Urban Development in Metropolitan Shadow*, 61, 95-98, 80-85.

THE ANGLICIZD TOWN

THEORETICAL

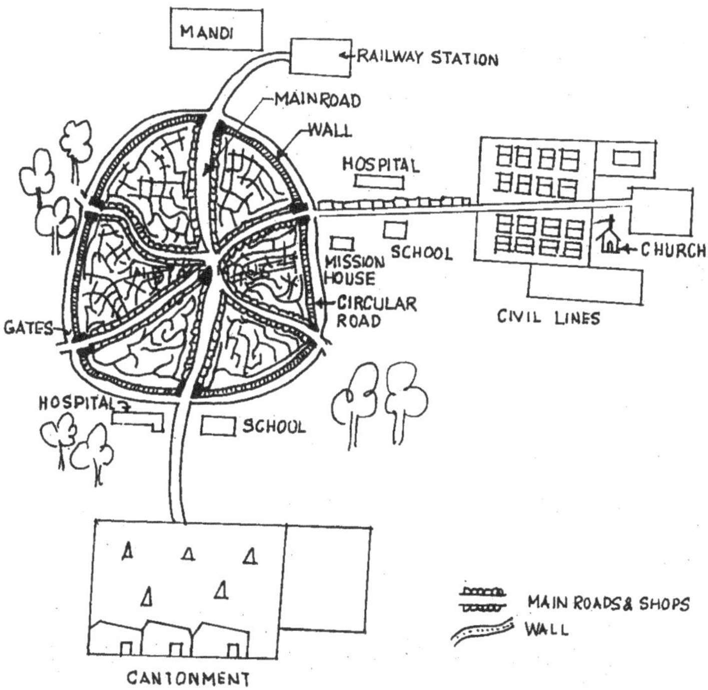

© REETA GREWAL : Diagram Two

military officers spread over several acres. A standard bungalow set in a large garden had eight rooms and separate mud huts as servants' quarters as well as sheds for the horses and ponies.[22] Sites for building houses in the civil station were sold by the government to prominent persons.[23] The offices were constructed between the residential area and the old town. Chapels, churches, schools, and the inevitable 'Sadar Bazar' as an adjunct of the cantonment, soon followed. Most stations had a cemetery as well. Recreation areas in the form of gymkhanas, clubs, games courts and racecourses were also added.[24] The civil station covered a large area yet had a low density of population and much less density of built-up area than the old city.[25]

In suburban areas the sites for commercial and industrial uses were auctioned by the government.[26] Over time schools, mission houses, institutes and hospitals were also established here, contributing to the growth of the suburb and adding to the physical form of the city. Residential suburbs, such as Model Town at Lahore, also came up and were cooperative ventures.[27] The junctions of roads leading to other urban centres became the most likely points of such additions to the town. For example, in Jullundur several extensions and suburbs sprang up on the roads leading to Nakodar, Kapurthala, Tanda and the G.T. Road.[28] The 'anglicised' accretion thus at times encircled the indigenous town and grew around it. It was physically a 'collection of period pieces' with its contrasting old and new areas.[29] In course of time, these 'anglicised' towns seemed as closely knit as a jig-saw.

The third category of towns was the colony town, founded in the canal colonies developed since 1885 by the British in the arid and sparsely populated alluvial plains of the western Punjab. These towns, such as Lyallpur, Okara, Chichawatni, Sargodha, Gojra, Toba Tek Singh, Sangla and Arifwala, were laid out as planned 'model' settlements (diagram 3). The western Punjab came to have small towns as well as those which over the period developed into large urban centres.

[22] Al Carthill, *Madampur*, William Blackwood, London 1931, 47-49.

[23] At Montgomery and Lyallpur, for example, the rate was Rs. 50 per acre: *DG Montgomery 1933*, 72.

[24] Lahore, Amritsar and Jullundur, for example, had racecourses.

[25] Gerald Breese, *Urbanization in Newly Developing Countries*, 65-66.

[26] As in the new 'model' towns of Okara, Chichawatni, Toba Tek Singh and Arifwala in the canal colony areas.

[27] This cooperative society was formed by retired government officials in 1925: Prakash Tandon, *Punjabi Century*, 239.

[28] Kanchan Jyoti, *The City of Jullundur*, 87-95.

[29] Emrys Jones, *Towns and Cities*, Oxford University Press, London 1966, 43.

THE COLONY TOWN

THEORETICAL

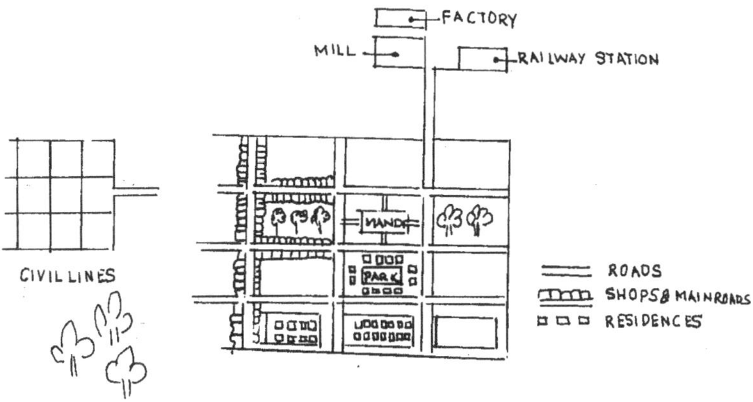

GRID TYPE ROADS

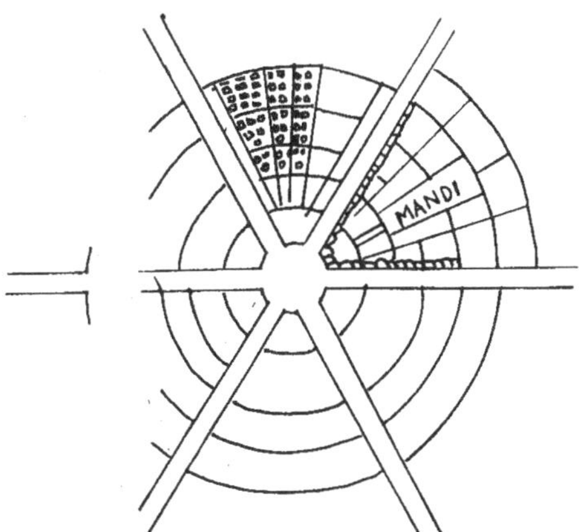

RADIAL ROADS

© REETA GREWAL : Diagram Three.

The new colony towns were founded at specifically chosen *mandi* sites in the form of squares or rectangles. Within these the broad metalled roads were laid out in a grid of parallel roads cutting across at right angles, as in Sargodha or radiating from a central *chauk* as in Lyallpur.[30] These primary roads formed a system of blocks for both small industry and residential purposes. The *mandi* was a big square with shops on all sides. On the main roads were located the bazaars of the town. The government sold the sites for shops and houses by auction. Link roads connected the blocks to the main roads and were unmetalled at times. The main bazaars were also residential, while additional residences were located on the roads parallel to and behind the main ones. Residential blocks had two entrances and enclosed a spacious square with a wide lane around containing two rows of houses. There remained a caste or religious grouping in these blocks as in the *mohallas* of the old town. There was, however, much more of open spaces and gardens in the colony towns. The lower castes, as in the old towns, lived on the outskirts of the urban centre.[31]

The new towns too had their suburbs. The railway stations were a short distance away and near them were located the factories and mills. Civil stations as before were separate units close to the new town. The offices as well as residences of the officials were located in them. Various gardens and parks too were laid out within the towns. There were, however, no cantonment areas.

III

The functional zones of the urban centres are interlinked with their morphology and reflect a distinct pattern of land use. We find that the old indigenous towns had an overlapping land use while the new areas, namely the civil lines, cantonments, and the colony towns, showed a specific land use (diagram 4).[32]

The old city had its commercial area in the *chauk* bazaars or the main road which also served as a residential area for the well-to-do shopkeepers. Other residential areas were based on caste groups and formed

[30]The layout of these towns has been described in *DG Montgomery 1933*, Part A, 76-87; *Gazetteer of the Chenab Colony, 1904*, 151-53; and Prakash Tandon, *Punjabi Century;* 158-61.

[31]This is true for example of Lyallpur: *Gazetteer Chenab Colony 1904, Part A*, 151. See also, Imran Ali, *The Punjab under Imperialism, 1885-1947*, Oxford University Press, Delhi 1989 (Indian rep), 8-61.

[32]Based on information available in the *District Gazetteers*.

FUNCTIONAL ZONES IN TOWNS OF THE PUNJAB

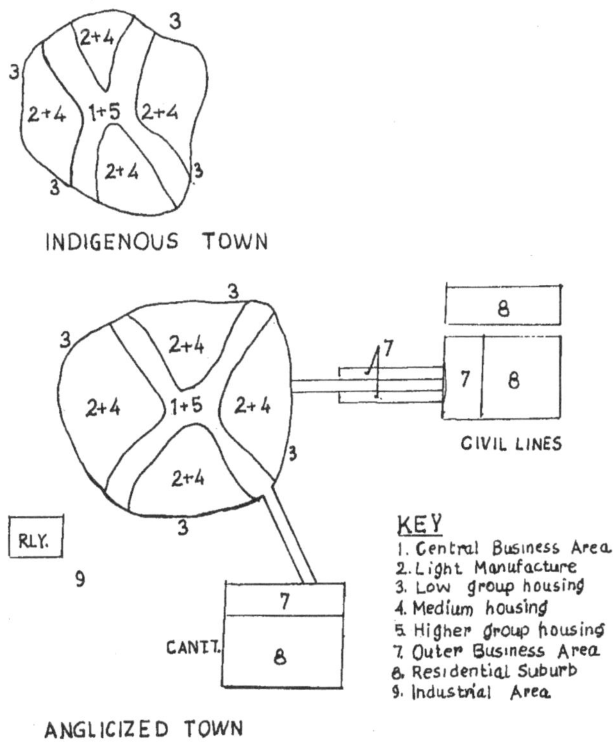

© REETA GREWAL : Diagram Four

separate *mohallas* in the areas located between the main crossroads. The *mohalla* also served as a small- scale industrial centre for the group. At the turn of the century, in many cases, industry and even trade was developed near the railway stations, as at Bhatinda, Amritsar and Sangrur, among others. Administrative offices were at times located in the old fort, as at Bawal, Nakodar and Jind; or in the *sarai* as was the case at Nurmahal and Talamba; or sometimes in the old palace as seen at Shujabad and Farrukhnagar. The fort was often the school house and post office as well. Open spaces and gardens were not given much area within the town and were often located on the periphery, as at Zira, Phul, Dhanaula, Kunjpura, Safidon and Haripur, among others. Kunja and Basi had gardens within the town but this was not a general rule. In some of the larger towns, such as Amritsar, the old *dhabs* or ponds of the indigenous town were filled up and utilised as parks and green spaces.[33]

We find therefore that the main business area was delimited by the main roads. Residential areas filled up the whole town though the well-to-do lived at the centre and the poor in the outer zone. Industrial units were scattered all over the town, and in some cases the factories came to be located in the suburbs outside the urban centre. Other structures such as offices, schools, hospitals, dispensaries and clubs and reading rooms were distributed over the town. In other words, though a main business area can be delimited, most areas in the old urban centres combined all functions and had a multiple land use pattern.[34]

In the 'anglicised' towns the business district extended along the Mall and Sadar Bazar.[35] The old areas in the indigenous town, however, also remained important commercially. In many places, such as Gujrat and Amritsar, shops catering to the Europeans were located inside one of the gates of the old town. The new residential areas in the civil lines and cantonments were independent of business or administrative pockets. The native upper classes moved to the civil lines area outside the old town and sometimes made their own colonies as in the case of the Model town

[33]*DG Amritsar 1892-93*, 160.
The Nichol Park in Amritsar was laid on one such filled *dhab*: Anand Gauba, *Amritsar 1849-1947: A Study in Urban History*, Ph.D. Thesis, Guru Nanak Dev University, Amritsar 1980, 70.

[34]A similar pattern is seen in the studies of Madras as well as Serampore: Susan M. Neild, Colonial Urbanism: The Development of Madras City in the 18th and 19th Centuries', *Modern Asian Studies*, 13, No.2, 1979, 217-46, and P. Ray, 'Urbanization in a Colonial Situation: Serampore', *Urban Sociology in India* (ed M.S.A. Rao), Orient Longman, Delhi 1974, 119-50.

[35]The functional zones of the 'anglicized' town can be seen in diagram above.

FUNCTIONAL ZONES OF THE COLONY TOWN

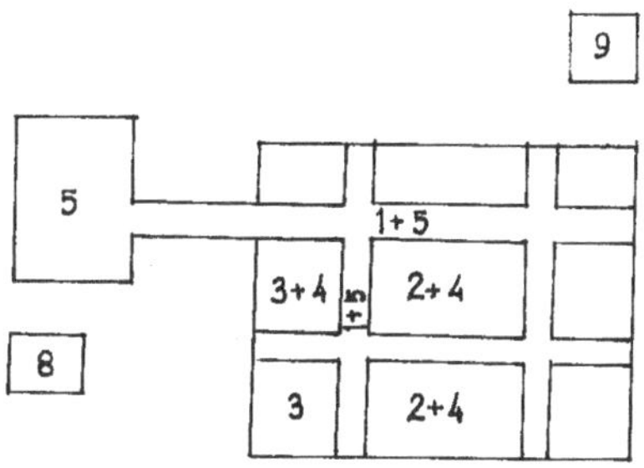

(a) GRID TYPE ROADS

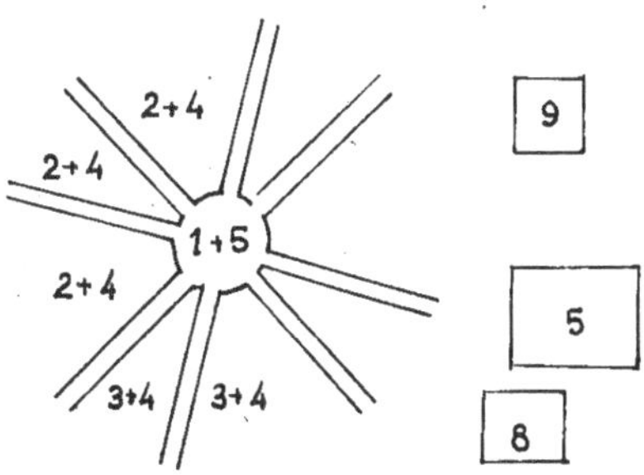

(b) RADIAL ROADS

KEY

1. Central Business Area
2. Light Manufacture
3. Low group housing
4. Medium housing
5. Higher group housing
7. Outer Business Area.
8. Residential Suberb.
9. Industrial Area.

at Lahore and the Indian station at Montgomery. There was no industrial zone in the civil lines and cantonments. Schools, mission buildings, dispensaries and hospitals had branches in the outer new areas as well or at times larger establishments were built in the 'anglicised' section as space was available. In the British settlements the residence and office zones were clearly demarcated. It is possible to trace linear extensions from the old town to the new suburbs in these centres.

In the new colony towns the business district followed the main roads again, and this was also the residence of the shopkeepers.[36] The blocks housing inhabitants by and large remained their workplace as well though larger industrial establishments were located at the new site near the railway line or away from the town. An industrial zone was therefore demarcated, while business and residences shared the same areas of the town. Open spaces, however, were found at more places within these new towns than the indigenous urban centres (diagram 5).

IV

To see how far the zonal distribution of land use within the three kinds of towns in the Punjab under colonial rule is similar to that of urban units in general, it would be helpful to compare them to models of land use patterns. These models are constructs of urban geographers and have been formed with western urban development in view.

There are three 'ideal' patterns of city structure, namely, the concentric zone theory, the sector theory and the multiple-nuclei pattern (diagram 6). In addition, a tri-level structure based on all three has also been put forth along with some other observations on the relation of physical form and functional growth of towns.

At the turn of the century, Richard Hurd observed that cities tended to expand in concentric circles and in axial spokes along the main transportation lines.[37] At that time little attention was paid to this aspect. In 1923, Ernest Burgess propounded what is referred to as the concentric zone theory.[38] He held that cities developed as five concentric rings around a central business core area. Outside this ring was a transition zone of low income group houses and extension of the business core. Zone three was medium-group housing, surrounded by a ring of higher-income group

[36]The 'Outer Business Area', indicated by No. 7 in the diagrams was not in existence in colony towns.

[37]Gerald Breese, *Urbanization in Newly Developing Countries*, 104.

[38]Jugendra Sahai, *Urban Complex of an Industrial City*, Chugh, Allahabad 1980, 50-51.

residences. The outer zone was of commuters and was along the transportation lines; this zone also had elite residences and specific suburbs interspersed with cultivated areas. These radiating centres moving outwards from the central business core were the result of the struggle between competing functions.[39]

The concentric zone hypothesis can be questioned on several points.[40] First, the core area is not necessarily a ring but may extend radially along the major routes or streets, as seen in the towns of the Punjab under British rule. Secondly, development of the subcentres of business areas was also noticed, for example in the Sadar Bazar and the Mall of the 'anglicised' town in colonial Punjab. Thirdly, industry was located not only within but also outside the zones close to the town as for instance near the railway suburb in the towns under study. Lastly, residential areas were not fixed but sprang up at any convenient location.

Homer Hoyt explains town structure and growth in terms of sectoral development 'along transport lines and paths of least resistance'.[41] According to him, different functional sectors cropped up around a core business area and residences arranged themselves like wedges along radial lines from the centre to the fringes. Low-grade residences would lie close to the core followed by medium housing.[42] This theory too does not encompass the growth of the suburbs around the town nor the existence of small industrial pockets within the residential areas or even combined with them.

In the mid forties Chauncy Harris and Edward Ullman theorised that land use patterns in a city developed around not one but several nuclei. These centres either existed previously near the town or were specifically developed for special land use.[43] The multiple nuclei pattern consists of a core area as well as several suburbs.[44] The core business area is surrounded by small manufacturing units and low-income housing on one side and medium income group residences on the other.[45] Residences of higher-income groups are located in the outer zone and have an adjoining business area as well. Heavy industry according to this

[39]See also Chauncy Harris, and Edward Ullman, 'The Nature of Cities', *Readings in Urban Geography*, Central Book Depot, Allahabad 1967, 282-83.

[40]Gerald Breese, *Urbanization in Newly Developing Countries*, 104.

[41]Ibid., 105; Harris and Ullman, 'Nature of Cities', *Readings in Geography*, 283.

[42]James Quinn, *Urban Sociology*, Eurasia, New Delhi 1967, 115-16, and Jugendra Sahai, *Urban Complex of an Industrial City*, 51-52.

[43]Gerald Breese, *Urbanization in Newly Developing Countries*, 105.

[44]For details See Harris and Ullman, 'Nature of Cities', *Readings in Urban Geography*, 283-85.

[45]James Quinn, *Urban Sociology*, 116.

MODELS OF URBAN LAND USE PATTERNS

(I) CONCENTRIC ZONE THEORY

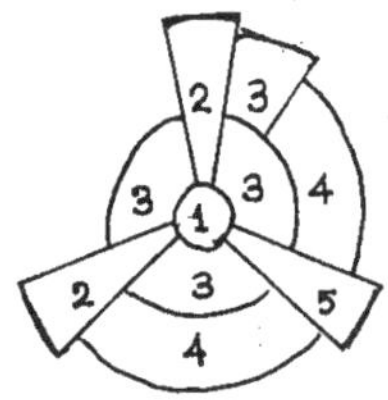

(II) SECTOR THEORY

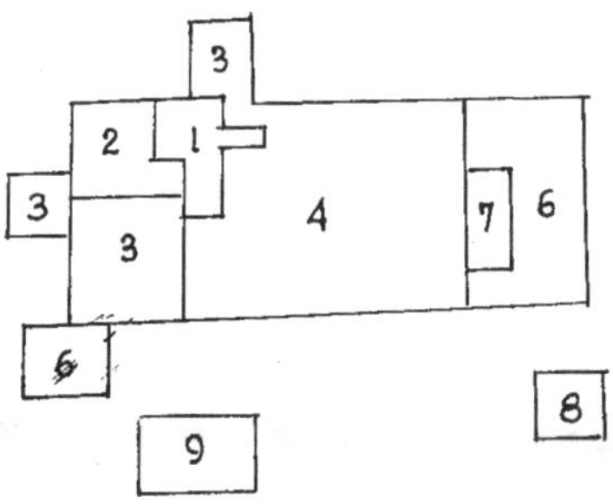

(III) MULTIPLE NUCLEI PATTERN

KEY

1. Central Business Area
2. Light Manufacture
3. Low grade residences
4. Medium residential
5. Higher grade residences
6. Heavy Manufacture
7. Outer business area
8. Residential Suburb
9. Industrial area
10. Commuters zone

Diagram Six.

theory also has a separate nucleus.

Another model of the colonial city describes it as 'dual' structured with its bazaar peasant economy juxtaposed with firm capitalist economy.[46] Gideon Sjoberg generalises in a very simplistic way that pre-industrial cities had 'a rich centre and a poor periphery'.[47] Mann emphasises that these models of city structure were not mutually exclusive and that the end result was a tripartite structure.[48] There is, however, no all-embracing model explaining city structure and physical growth universally.

The towns and cities of the Punjab do not strictly follow any of these distribution patterns of functional layout. In a way, the indigenous towns are close to Sjoberg's division, of a 'rich centre and poor periphery', but as already noted, this is a simplification and does not take into account growth over time. In fact, the indigenous towns had a linear core area comprising both the central business area as well as high-grade housing.[49] This was surrounded by areas of light manufacture and medium housing in the town, adjoining which was the poor-grade residential area. Over time these towns developed industrial, commercial and residential suburbs. They are, thus, close to the multiple nuclei pattern.

The 'anglicised' towns were also close to the multiple nuclei pattern though the core area differed. The central business area here too combined higher-income group residences, surrounded by small manufacture and medium-grade housing. Low-income groups remained on the periphery. With the establishment of the civil lines a high-grade residential suburb was added along with an outer business area and other residential suburbs. On another side of the urban unit an industrial suburb generally sprang up.

The new towns also had some similarities with the multiple nuclei pattern. The central business area and higher-income group residences were surrounded by the light manufacturing units and middle income group housing areas. Low-grade housing was on the outer zones of the

[46]This model is presented by McGee. One fails, however, to identify a 'firm capitalist type' economy in any of the towns in the Punjab. McGee also admits to an oversimplification and the possibility of 'intermediate' economy bases: T.G. McGee, 'Planning the Asian Cities: The Relevance of "Conservative Surgery" and Concept of Dualism', *The Outlook Tower* (ed J.V. Ferreira and S.S. Jha), Popular Prakashan, Bombay 1976, 269-72.

[47]V.L.S. Prakasa Rao, *Urbanization in India: Spatial Dimensions*, Concept, Delhi 1983, 173.

[48]Loc.cit.

[49]However, a dominant central business district is believed to be 'scarcely existent' in India: see 'John Brush', 'Morphology of Indian Cities', *Urban Sociology in India*, 224-36.

town. With the passage of time residential suburbs of the higher income groups and an industrial suburb was added to the new towns.

Thus, we find that the towns of the colonial Punjab were by and large close to the multiple nuclei pattern though their business zone areas were distinct with the additional element of a business-cum-higher income group residential zone. The industrial zone too differed in the sense that it was also a trading and commercial area for grain and cotton in addition to being the location of the various mills and factories.

V

Some generalisations about the internal spatial patterns in the urban centres in the Punjab under colonial rule may be attempted. The small centres tended to have a business area along the main streets, as in the indigenous towns; the smaller secondary commercial clusters developed away from this area with the growth of the town, as seen in the 'anglicised' towns. These secondary clusters sprang up at intersections or along transportation lines, like the grain *mandi* and the Sadar Bazar of the 'anglicised' towns. Factories in these towns tended to develop on the periphery of the town and near the railway station to be close to the line of transportation. The residential areas developed as socio-economic, cultural or racial clusters, broadly similar to those in the indigenous towns of the Punjab. The colony town also developed residential suburbs for the British administrators and higher-income groups away from the business area.

The general picture which emerges is of a combination or hybrid of the east-west urban pattern in the towns and cities in the Punjab. The indigenous town underwent few changes and remained the 'traditional Indian city' with a small suburb of colonial 'necessity'. In the 'anglicised' town the old city and the new western suburbs are distinct yet integral parts of one urban form. The principles of western urban planning were clearly evident in the colony towns which were wholly the product of colonial rule as far as physical form is concerned. The western concept was most visible in these new towns and in the modern areas of the old towns but failed to touch the features of the indigenous centres to any appreciable extent. Urban morphology under British rule thus saw varying elements of change coexisting with the old form, creating in the process a distinctive pattern of duality characteristic of colonial influence.

URBAN CULTURE IN MODERN INDIA WORLD OF THE LOWER CLASSES

NITA KUMAR

If we consider Indian cities and their populations, and we think beyond Bombay, Calcutta, Ahmedabad, Kanpur and a few other concentrations of factory labour, what we confront are millions of the urban poor engaged in domestic manufacture, petty trade, service and unorganised labour. Studies with urban lower classes in focus for social and cultural change are absent in the historiographical traditions in modern India. Even in the new social history, with its innovative treatment of familiar subjects and problems, the non-factory workers have been given negligible attention compared to the working classes with their political and economistic trade union activity, and also to the elite, whether seen in terms of caste, class, nationalist activists, social reformers, or self conscious organisers and searchers for new identities. This essay is concerned with expanding the agenda of urban studies to include the large, non-elite, often illiterate, mostly self-employed population of cities, and with emphasising the new sources for such studies and an interdisciplinary methodology, with a keener attention to cultural systems and fresh ways of conceptualising urban identities, urban lifestyles and socio-cultural change.

There are many reasons for the almost total neglect of urban lower classes and their culture. Organised labour, and specifically the question of the development of working-class consciousness, is seen as interesting by those historians who wish to reveal the workings of colonialism and capitalism in all their invidious detail. The development, or lack of development, of Indian industry is certainly a valid subject, including the social and human dimensions of the working conditions and politics of the workers. The analytical concepts of class conflict and exploitation come handy to those who find Marxism a compatible perspective to work with, like a great number of Indian historians. Unfortunately, as evidenced in some history writing, a basic readymade Marxism is available in the absence of a larger training in different theoretical perspectives.

As for the elite, they have long been the 'real' subject of history writing, and will continue to be so in the visible future. The prolific documentation they provide on themselves; government records of, for, and by them; and their comprehensibility to the average academic who comes from a comparable social class, all contribute to their maintaining the place of *cause celebre*.

I am not arguing for a 'proctological' history, one that would simply shift the weight of attention from the more privileged to the less privileged classes, but rather for the necessity of new, cultural perspectives. As Cohn has suggested, to understand the world of lower classes is, of necessity, to take into account those largely responsible for constructing it, namely, the rulers.[1]

The same combination of availability of resources (for studies of elite) and pre-defined considerations of importance of the economic aspects (for studies of the working classes) has produced among historians an indifference to the study of culture. With the exception of a Durga Puja here and a Ganesh Puja there, there is little historical research on everyday life in cities, on the celebrations, transactions, rituals, and public activities of ordinary people. These things are implicitly regarded as peripheral, if not also backward and obscurantist. My argument in this paper is that there is no dearth of sources for urban cultural history, that it is a methodologically viable project, and that from the perspective of the state of the art, it is a desirable one.

I

We need not draw, for our present purposes, a keen distinction between the study of urban 'society' and the study of urban 'culture', although certainly the distinction is a practicable one. For the kind of population we are considering, there are neither social histories nor cultural histories, and to emphasise their distinct subject matter is unproductive. In my

[1]Bernard Cohn, 'History and Anthropology: the State of Play', *Contributions to Studies in Society and History*, 22, No. 4 (1980), 597-625.

own research on the artisans of Banaras, I found, for example, that whereas what I wished to study was their cultural system in change, what I also had to include was a history of their industries, their systems of production, their economic and social relationships, their community structure, and so on.[2] There are no social histories of any such segment of urban population as the artisans. For a study of urban culture, we have to reconstruct social organisation and social process as well. The traditions we can turn to for such studies are: (a) that of working-class history; (b) that of the newly developing cultural history in the West, with its focus on everyday life and world views; (c) that of urban studies, particularly in the disciplines of sociology and anthropology, which seek to ascertain what makes this social and cultural life peculiarly urban. We should explore these traditions a little further.

In the West, the concept of 'urban lower classes' today is almost synonymous with working classes. Histories of the Industrial Revolution and the birth and development of these classes cannot help but be affected by a teleology based on this knowledge. We have to make a particular effort in the Indian case not to take American or English developments as a model and presume, what would be for us, an imaginary teleology. What we must focus on is our own lower classes, engaged in indigenous industry or other occupations. In so far as mechanisation and factorisation is a one-way process, we are justified in calling these lower classes, pre-industrial workers. But no detailed description of pre-industrial workers exists that will do justice to the social and conceptual structures of Indian artisans and labourers of modern (post-Mughal) times, certainly not the descriptions of American and European pre-industrial classes.

That is not to say that it is not instructive to note the questions asked in western history, particularly in the recent tradition of Marxist cultural history in England. The scope and approach of working-class history was broadened most dramatically by E.P. Thompson's classic work on the *English Working Class*.[3] It strove to question not only the omnipotence of capitalism in defining the nature of working-class life, but also the backgrounds of those who became factory workers, their aspirations, needs, and preferences, and the quality of their life. In pursuit of the understanding of class formation and the nature of working-class life,

[2]Nita Kumar, *Popular Culture in Urban India: the Artisans of Banaras, c.1884-1984* (cited hereafter as *The Artisans of Banaras)*,Ph.D. Thesis, University of Chicago 1984.

[3]E.P. Thompson, *The Making of the English Working Class*, *Pantheon* Books, New York 1963.

culture and ideas were given a recognition long overdue. Thompson's work has been followed by many others which seek to enrich our understanding of working classes in a more sympathetic way than formerly, primarily by giving importance to the aspects of their lives considered important by the workers themselves. Herbert Gutman, an outstanding example of this, brings out dramatically in his research that work ethic was not native to America, but had to be patiently nurtured, and that the working class did not arrive full blown but in fact underwent a rather painful and protesting development.[4] This movement in western history writing towards emphasis on experience and subjective meaning is accompanied lately by similar developments in Indian history, as witnessed by a number of recent writings.[5]

When we move on to the second tradition, that of cultural history, new directions become even more evident. Cultural history (the study of *mentalite*, world views, concepts, values) is almost a subdiscipline in western history writing now. Natalie Zemon Davis, Eugen Weber, and Theodore Zeldin for France; Keith Thomas, Thomas Reid, Robert Malcolmson, Hugh Cunningham, and Edward Thompson for England; and Eugen Genovese and Herbert Gutman for the U.S. have successfully shown the possibility and the value of studying culture historically.[6] Moreover, culture has been taken to be not the highest achievement in arts and letters – self-evidently of the elite – but the everyday world views, philosophies of life, and guiding principles of common people, whether expressed in ritual, in recreational activity, in attitudes to work, in religion, in fairs and festivities, in political activity, or in the routine of daily life. As these topics themselves suggest, cultural history requires learning from the disciplines of folklore, anthropology, and history of

[4] Herbert G. Gutman, *Work, Culture and Society in Industrializing America,* Alfred A. Knopf, New York 1976.

[5]Dipesh Chakaravarty, 'Conditions for Knowledge of Working Class Conditions: Employers Government and the Jute Workers of Calcutta, 1890-1940', *Subaltern Studies,* II (ed R. Guha), OUP, Delhi 1983, 259-310; G. Pandey, 'Liberalism and the Study of Indian History: A Review of Writings on Communalism', *Economic and Political Weekly,* 18, No. 42 (1983), 1789-94; Sandria Freitag, *Religious Rites and Riots: From Community Identity to Communalism in North India, 1870-1940,* Ph.D Thesis, University of California, Berkeley 1980.

[6]Natalie Zemon Davis, *Society and Culture in Early Modern France,* Stanford University Press, Stanford 1975; Theodore Zeldin, *France 1848-1945: Taste and Corruption,* Oxford University Press, Oxford 1977; Keith Thomas, 'Work and Leisure in Pre-Industrial Societies', *Past and Present,* 71 (1976), 76-101; R.W. Malcolmson, *Popular Recreations in English Society, 1770-1850,* Cambridge University Press, Cambridge 1973; Hugh Cunningham, *Leisure in the Industrial Revolution, c 1780-c1880,* St. Martin's Press, New York 1980; Edward P. Thompson, 'Patrician Society, Plebeian Culture', *Past and Present,* 38 (1967), 56-97.

religions, in terms both of their methodology and theory.

This combination of a broader definition of culture and an interdisciplinary approach in pursuing it is what we need for Indian urban history. The anthropology of India has successfully moved on to urban studies and some of our best statements on urbanism are from anthropologists. The questions for a social study of urban lower classes are fairly clear: questions regarding the degree and mechanics of caste and occupational mobility;[7] the meaning of community and neighbourhood;[8] the nature of kinship ties;[9] hierarchy of classes and interaction.[10] As we can see from these few available studies, historians have done some excellent work in these areas, but all these questions have to be explored further in their full historical context, with the kind of craft that historians practise, and their focus enlarged to include poorer and illiterate segments of the population.

For urban cultural history, no specific agenda has been laid out yet or is even silently accepted. What is the area to be covered and the questions to be asked? We may draw from anthropology, western cultural history, and Indian social history, in our efforts to propose an agenda.

For the elite and upper classes we have studies of reform movements and discussions of religion in relationship with caste, social reform and

Frank Conlon, 'Caste and Urbanism in Historical Perspective: the Saraswat Brahmans', *Urban India: Society, Space and Image* (ed R.G. Fox), Duke University, Durham 1970; Harold Gould, 'Lucknow Ricshawalas: the Social Organization of an Occupational Category', *International Journal of Comparative Sociology*, 6 (1965), 24-47; Robert L. Hardgrave, 'Urbanization and the Structure of Caste', *Urban India: Society Space and Image* (ed. R.G. Fox), Duke University, Durham 1970; Karen I. Leonard, *History of an Indian Caste: The Kayasthas of Hyderabad*, University of California Press, Berkeley 1978; Owen Lynch, *The Politics of Untouchability, Social Mobility and Social Change in a City of India*, Columbia University Press, New York 1969; Jim Masselos, 'Jobs and Jobbery: the Sweeper in Bombay under the Raj', *Indian Economic and Social History Review*, 19, No. 2 (1982), 101-14; Satish Sabarwal, *Mobile Men*, Vikas, New Delhi 1976.

[8] Leighton W. Hazlehurst, 'Urban Space and Activities', *Urban India: Society, Space and Image* (ed R.G. Fox), Duke University, Durham 1970; Meera Guha, 'The Definitions of an Indian Neighbourhood (Calcutta)', *Man in India*, 46, No. 1 (1966), 59-69; Richard Heitler, 'The Varanasi House-tax Hartal of 1810-1811', *Indian Economic and Social History Review*, 9, No. 3 (1972), 29-57; Jim Masselos. 'Jobs and Jobbery, the Sweeper in Bombay under the Raj', *Indian Economic and Social History Review*, 19, No. 2 (1982), 101-14.

[9] Mary Chatterjee, *Conjugal Rules and Social Organisation in an Urban Sweeper Community*, Ph. D. Thesis, Banaras Hindu University 1975; Sylvia Vatuk, *Kinship and Urbanization in North India*, University of California Press, Berkeley 1978.

[10] Gerald D. Berreman, 'Social Categories and Social Interaction in Urban India', *American Anthropologist*, 74 (1972), 567-86; Richard G. Fox, *From Zamindar to Ballot Box: Community Change in a North Indian Market Town*, Cornell University Press, Ithaca 1969; Carol Prindle, *Rank among Muslims in Chittagong, Bangladesh*, Ph.D Thesis, University of Chicago 1982.

nationalism.[11] If literature on reform movements and caste associations is relatively scarce for less privileged groups, the study of other phenomena such as religious riots is exceptionally important as a way of understanding mentality and organisation.[12] Other ways would be through studies of communal and political relations;[13] religious institutions;[14] and public performances, celebrations, and festivals.[15] Religious rituals, especially private, family-based ones, are probably difficult to recover historically, but public activities that are equally routine such as religious meetings, temple visits, and group ritual may be recovered from various sources. The kind of records that I have found useful in my own research are discussed in a later section.

My argument here is not in favour of a closed domain of 'religion among lower classes'. If lower classes, the poor, the masses, the 'subalterns' – or however we choose to characterise them – become our focus it is only because they and their culture have become residual categories for historians. The festivals, celebrations, and performances of ordinary people should not be regarded as quaint examples of a folk tradition, or more severely, as epiphenomenal and obscurantist, but rather as important social activities with a particularly rich symbolic content.

In the history writing of western working classes, attention is being progressively given to the lived-in experience of the people: their use of

[11]Charles H. Heimsath, *Indian Nationalism and Hindu Social Reform*, Princeton University Press, Princeton 1964; Kenneth W. Jones, *Arya Dharm*, University of California Press, Berkeley 1976; David Kopf, *British Orientalism and the Bengal Renaissance: The Dynamics of Indian Modernization, 1773-1835*, University of California Press, Berkeley 1969; Sushobhan C. Sarkar, *Bengal Renaissance and Other Essays*, People's Publishing House, New Delhi 1970.

[12]Dipesh Chakarvarty, 'Conditions for Knowledge of Working Class Conditions', *Subaltern Studies*, II; Sandria Freitag, *Religious Rites and Riots*, Ph.D. Thesis, University of California, Berkeley 1980; Gyanendra Pandey, 'Liberalism and the Study of Indian History', *Economic and Political Weekly*, 18, No. 42 (1983), 1789-94.

[13]N.G. Barrier, *Roots of Communal Politics*, Arnold Heinemann, Delhi 1976; Paul R. Brass, *Language, Religion and Politics in North India*, Cambridge University Press, New York 1976; Francis Robinson, 'Islam and Muslim Society in South Asia', *Contributions to Indian Sociology*, 17, No. 2 (1983), 185-203.

[14]Barbara D. Metcalf, 'The Madrasa at Deoband: A Model for Religious Education in Modern India', *Modern Asian Studies*, 12, No. 1 (1978), 111-34.

[15]Victor Barnouw, 'The Changing Character of a Hindu Festival', *American Anthropologist*, 56 No. 1 (1954), 74-86; Norvin Hein, 'The Ram Lila', *Traditional India* (ed Milton Singer), The American Folklore Society, Philadelphia 1959; *The Miracle Plays of Mathura*, Yale University Press, New Haven 1972; Jim Masselos, 'Change and Custom in the Format of the Bombay Mohurrum during the 19th and 20th Centuries', *South Asia*, 5, No. 1 (1978), 47-67; Jyotirmoyee Sarma, 'Puja Associations in West Bengal', *Journal of Asian Studies*, 28, No.3 (1969), 579-94.

time, rhythms of work and leisure, and attitudes towards both. Again, it is anthropologists in Indian studies who have at all studied the meanings of time, the relationships of people, activities, and seasons, and the conceptualisation of the calendar.[16] Whereas their studies are located in the countryside, my own work in Banaras city allows me to propose that these relationships and conceptualisations are worth studying as urban phenomena in urban locales. They will lead to a statement on Indian urban culture, and specially the lifestyle of the city, such as has not been made so far. Among the important questions we have to ask are: How does control over time vary with work patterns? How does the conceptualisaton of 'work' change with economic and technological changes? 'Modernisation', after all, assumes the development of a 'work ethic' even more than it does the change from ascription to achievement in occupation. We may well find, among urban lower classes, that the attitude towards freedom, time-discipline, and work and leisure divisions are among the best indicators of change.

None of the practices of urban lower classes may be dismissed as 'merely' survivals of folk traditions or customs imported from the countryside through migrants. There is a strong and viable indigenous urban system of activities which, surprisingly, has not been given any attention at all. These activities tell us of the fact of organisation, for example, *mohàlla*-level organisation into groups and 'clubs' such as *akharas* for music, poetry, and gymnastics; they are an expression of fundamental cultural concepts such as those of self-purification, dedication to art, discipline and balance in daily life, aesthetic standards, and so on; and they comprise contextual expression of economic and political experience. Central to all these questions of content is the question of change. Who have been the patrons of public music performances and wrestling matches, and who are the patrons now? What kind of social relationships have these activities been hinged on and what definition of social system have they presumed? What seemingly 'fundamental' cultural categories become markedly peripheral and isolated over time?

Together with the study of religious activities and celebrations, recreational activities must be approached in two related ways:

[16]Ruth S. Freed and Stanley A. Freed, 'Calendars, Ceremonies and Festivals in North Indian Village: Necessary Calendric Information for Fieldwork', *Southwestern Journal of Anthropology*, 2, No. 1 (1964), 67-9; Ralph Nicholas, 'The Bengali Calendar and the Hindu Religious Year in Bengal', *The Study of Bengal* (ed Peter Bertocci), Michigan State University, East Lansing 1982; Susan S. Wadley, 'The Rains of Estrangement: Understanding the Hindu yearly Cycle', *Contributions to Indian Sociology*, 17, No. 1 (1983), 51-55.

1. Sociologically, as activities that require organisation, interaction, and participation, all of which varies with political and community relationships over time.

2. As symbolic structures that depict a social world ordered according to certain cultural categories. What these categories comprise, in many instances, are 'first principles', attitudes to the body and the self, the understanding of nature, ideas about space and time, notions of the divine and of interpersonal relationship.

With all this we come to the question of cultural self-identification. Are towns and cities conglomerations of separate villages, like units, wards or *mohallas*, each of which is considered autonomous and definitive? Or is the city conceptualised as one whole, with a certain character and personality? Are activities based on kin and caste groupings? Or are there many cross-cutting levels of transactions, including those based on neighbourhood; commonality of teacher, taste, and talent; the tradition and history of the city? How do all these levels of transaction and association shift and change over the decades? My study of the indigenous popular culture of Banaras shows that formal and informal associations and 'clubs' are old, continuous, and multifarious, and that ties and parallelisms based on everyday activities cut across lines of caste and religion. What I cannot say with decisiveness is whether Banaras is exceptional in this respect. I suspect that all old (pre-colonial) cities with continuous traditions are rich in such intercommunity groupings and activities, but the whole subject of 'associations' beyond the British-inspired political and agitational ones has to be empirically investigated. I also suspect that each of these old cities has an identity which is expressed and articulated by its residents, among other things, in folklore literature, daily colloquialisms, styles of dress, food habits, leisure activities, and other aspects of lifestyle. The 'fact' of a Banarasi, a Mirzapuri, a Lakhnawi, a Hyderabadi, deserves more serious attention than the acceptance it gets as a tangential or peripheral (and perhaps outdated) mode of thinking. What precisely does this identification rest on? A pre-industrial lifestyle? Direct involvement and patronage of the city's elite in all aspects of public life? A pre-capitalist mentality that does not revolve around class and other socio-economic differentiations? A *communitas* that peaks at the largest festivals of the year? Or simply an Indian cultural proclivity to identify the person with the land and water that nourishes him? The nature of this identification, and the nature of it in the process of change, goes a long way towards making a very fundamental statement about Indian urbanism.

II

The published sources useful for a social history of urban lower classes will readily come to the mind of historians: census data; early ethnographies; Labour Commission Reports; Administration Reports; District Gazetteers; and publications and reports of business and commerce groups. Many of these are incomplete and inconsistent, but can at least confirm a presence or an absence, a general size, a direction, or even set one off with a problem to solve. Many others deal with the entrepreneur or the administrator, with little to say directly about the worker, but every little bit of information, statistical or impressionistic, counts. Then there are, of course, archival records, which again seem never to concern themselves with people on the ground, as I found in the case of Banaras. But at all three levels, the national, the state, and the local, they can be used rewardingly to construct a 'background' picture of industrial developments, urban conditions, municipal developments, and government measures in health and education. To complement them, we have the private records of institutions and associations, and less frequently, of families and individuals.

These are familiar sources to historians and have indeed been mined by scholars who study urbanisation and urbanism: Bayly, Chaudhuri, Gillian, Gupta, Heitler, Lewandowski, Naqvi, Oldenburg, Sinha, Spodek, among others.[17] I would rather like to spend some time in discussing three sources that I find invaluable in my own research and which have been relatively unused so far in Indian social or cultural history: local non-English newspapers and periodicals, police station régisters, and oral history materials.

In U.P., every large town or city has its Hindi and/or Urdu dailies and weeklies from the late nineteenth century onwards. They can be first looked up in the administrative reports of the province and perhaps in municipal reports. Some studies dealing with political movements and

[17]Chirstopher A. Bayly, 'Indian Merchants in a "Traditional" Setting: Benaras, 1780-1830', *Imperial Impact: Studies in the Economic History of Africa and India*, Athlove Press, London 1978; Richard Heitler, 'The Varanasi House-tax hartal of 1810-11, *Indian Economic and Social History Review*, 9, No.3 (1972), 239-57; Susan Lewandoski, *Migration and Ethnicity in Urban India: Kerala Migrants in the City of Madras*, New Delhi 1980; Veena Oldenburg, *The Making of Colonial Lucknow*, Princeton University Press, Princeton 1984; Pradip Sinha, *Calcutta in Urban History*, Calcutta 1978.

cultural policy describe selected papers.[18] In Banaras, for example, the *Bharat Jiwan*, and *Aj*; in Allahabad, the *Pradip;* in Kanpur, the *Pratap* and *Vartaman;* and several others in Lucknow and Agra, all date from between 1880 and 1920. They are likely, if extant, to be preserved on file in their respective offices, otherwise they may be found in a local library or university library, such as the Carmichael Library in Banaras or the Bharat Kala Bhawan in Banaras Hindu University; or on microfilm in a national library, such as the Nehru Memorial Museum and Library in Delhi. I am alluding chiefly to the most widely circulating and prestigious of these publications. There are scores of others in urban centres which lasted a few decades or a few years each and which may all be recovered from scattered depositories. In Banaras, there were thirty to fifty ephemeral and/or specialised publications now available (with proper formalities) at the collections of intellectuals such as Morarji Kedia and Raj Kumar, as well as at Bharat Kala Bhawan and Nagari Pracharini Sabha. In each urban centre there are likely to be professionals, including journalists, who were themselves involved, or whose forefathers were involved, with the publication of such ephemeral literature. These periodicals, incidentally, are being called less important by me not so much because of their specialisation or ephemerality (there may well be research projects seeking information on exactly the subject or the period of one of them) as because of their restricted circulation. They were all written by, for, and about the elite, and a study of urban lower classes is not going to benefit initially from their perusal. If part of the goal is to build a larger picture of the city, as focus or as background, or to talk of, say, municipal developments, social reform, or education in the city, they merit being searched through. I have been going by my experience of Banaras here. Suffice it to add that over the last century, Banaras was merely third, fourth or fifth, off and on, in the number of publications and position as publishing centre in U.P. Lucknow, Agra and Allahabad have usually been more important and it is time that their periodical literatures were explored for urban social history.

The second of the two sources I wish to emphasise, and the more original, are the records of police stations (*thanas*). These are of three types: festival registers, registers No. 8, and confidential registers. A festival register is maintained by every police station (at least in U.P.)

[18]Gyanendra Pandey, 'Mobilization in a Mass Movement: Congress "Propaganda" in the U.P. 1930-34', *Economic and Political Weekly*, 9, No.2 (1975) 205-26; Christopher King, *The Nagari Pracharini Sabha of Benaras, 1893-1914: A Study in the Social and Political History of the Hindi Language*, Ph.D. Thesis, University of Wisconsin 1974.

from , as far as I could discover, at least the end of the nineteenth century. It lists all the major and minor celebrations within the jurisdiction of the *thana,* with information on dates, numbers and constitution of participants (such as the names, addresses, and 'character' of organisers), as well as comments on possible threats to peace and the precedents for resolving these. It is like a diary of ongoing events kept by police station officers for the benefit of their successors. In my own research, I could trace the organisers (or their families) for all the major cultural activities, such as Ramlila and Muharram, for approximately a hundred years in this way. Indeed, I could barely scratch the surface: there are literally scores of activities and hundreds of activists detailed whom one can look up for different kinds of information. The other important data are on the festivals themselves. The festival registers preserve, for example, original correspondence between citizens and committees (such as those formed for *sringar* and *urs* celebrations) and police and administrative officers.

The second kind of police records are the so-called Village Crime Notebooks or Registers No. 8. These are individual registers for each *mohalla* of the area, beginning with an outline of the size, population, number and type of houses, main castes, *sardars*, and other important people. The registers are filled mostly with records of crime and indictments (a potential gold mine for those working on crime and order in the nineteenth and twentieth centuries); section IV has the kind of general information on social disputes, activities and leaders, that could be used for studies along the broad lines indicated earlier in this essay.

The third of the police records is the station officer's confidential register, which is again usually continuous from earlier years in the twentieth century to the present, and to disclose any part of which is strictly the discretion of the station officer. Entries include lists of 'bad characters', places of communal tension, chief *jatis* and their problematic characteristics, printing presses, important bazaars, and so on. Commentaries include cryptic ones on the 'political history' of the area, the causes of tensions, and the careers of some personalities. All three of those sources, of course, not only require local language expertise and the patience to decipher erratic handwritten styles, but also present certain other more unexpected difficulties. There is no established legitimacy to their use by the public, and they are likely to prove, at first try, unavailable. They are made accessible only through diplomacy, socialising, and, what should be kept strictly for the last resort, 'contacts' (permission from higher-ups). No letter, pass, or phone call should be expected to unlock doors automatically and may do exactly the reverse. No one, including their superiors, knows exactly what exists in a police station but the station officer and his *munshi*.

It is relevant to mention also that those who have the task of maintaining these registers, usually a *munshi* (clerk), or *diwan* (head constable), are educated and competent, but not dedicated to the proposition of aiding research. Consequently, the arrangement of entries has some scheme, but one that may take the researcher some time to discover. The entries are not consistent over time, since new people in charge have new preferences in record keeping. Those familiar with local archives in India are at least partially accustomed to the problem of inconsistency and disorganisation. I will only reiterate here that the rewards yielded by a struggle with police station records are greater than can be imagined.

A method little used by Indian historians so far is that of oral history. A recent article on south Indian weavers discussed the merits of using folklore and proverbs in complement with epigraphy.[19] It is interesting how historians find it compulsory to check and cross-check their orally recorded facts with more traditional sources, while sociologists or anthropologists for the same subject and the same period will provide a history based totally on oral materials. Historians have to be careful about using the discipline of their craft as indeed a discipline and not as an obstacle to imaginative expansion of their repertory of methods. Unless one is making a case for 'popular concepts of time and change' there is no doubt in my mind that the more the cross-checking possible, of any two or more kinds of sources, the more credible the conclusions.[20] Once we have the outlines of the Banaras silk industry for the last one hundred years, for example, we can, and indeed should, enrich our account with the more personal aspects of the matter. Memories of three generations are not difficult to explore, and provide a tale of up to seventy years. Much of this, even when vague and untrustworthy, gives important clues regarding what to look for further. The experience of the last two generations or forty-fifty years, is documentable in clear and verifiable terms. The emphasis should be on the recollection of specific bits of information. The question, for example, should not be, 'Did people weave different designs in the past than now?' but rather, 'When you first started weaving, what were the two or three designs you wove?' and many may remember. But, never may the interviewee be regarded as an

[19]Vijaya Ramasamy, 'Weaver Folk-Traditions as Source of History', *Indian Economic and Social History Review*, 19, No.1 (1982), 47-62.

[20]Akos Oster, *Culture and Power*, Sage, New Delhi 1984.

anonymous voice supplying 'facts' on the way things were. Each informant is a personality acting in a particular social context, and to pay attention to the context, as we do automatically with authors of written historical sources, is not an over-demanding procedure.

Whole papers could be written simply on the question of designing efficient interview approaches for oral history, but the point is a simple one. First, to use oral sources like any other source, that is not only for 'factual' information but as a comment on the speaker's intentions as imbedded in his presentation of it. Second, again, like any other source, to recheck it and evaluate it against at least one other, and, if possible, several other sources. These are both rather standard procedures for historians. Where there is more demand to be innovative is in displaying an alertness to accept the social universe not typically of interest to the historian. Two such aspects are geography and language. A city may itself be read as a document by the careful researcher. The remains of places, unused constructions, closed-up wells, rotting tanks, converted buildings, are all necessary and sufficient documentation of certain trends of change. Similarly, the implications of certain linguistic usage and the differentiation of the social world through categories of language are very sensitive media for insights into changes in conceptual and social systems.

Before closing the section on sources, a few words about the 'uses' of anthropology are in order. I have been speaking as if there was one kind of cultural analysis to be practised, one clear-cut methodology to be learnt, as it were, from a sister discipline. There is, fortunately or not, no consensus regarding what precisely constitutes 'culture' and which is the competent approach to it. My suggestion, as when I declined to emphasise the separation between 'social' and 'cultural', is that it is rewarding enough to learn from anthropology of certain important and 'problem' areas for research and thus expand our agenda. As I see it, it is equally important to be cognisant of the methodological perspectives being employed by anthropologists and others interested in these areas, but how far we ourselves wish to take our analyses is up to the individual historian, depending on his training and proclivities, to decide.

III

I do not mean to conflate my own topic with the whole of a cultural and social history. I have given specific instances of sources and hypotheses in the interest of being more concrete and suggestive. The relevance of turning to cultural perspectives, and specifically those relating to the masses, the ordinary people, or the lower classes, is undeniable, and may be summed up as follow:

1. For those interested in the non-elite and the historically marginal, as a good number of Indian social historians are, it is important to balance the growing number of studies of peasants and rural movements with studies of urban masses. Equally, working-class history should be seen to represent more than the organisational and prototypical rebel activity of an emerging proletarian consciousness. The latter work is not without its logic; but it leaves out of the debate the vast majority of the urban population for whom, as for the Banaras artisans, the experience of change has been different from that of factory workers. Most of all, as Thompson pleaded over a decade ago, a Marxist vision of people making their own history has to be fully developed to incorporate an attention to ritual, symbol and cultural practice, that is but a reflection of the priorities of their own life.[21]

2. Even more, there is need for a construction of the picture of the 'Indian city' and 'urban culture'. Our best historical studies of cities are either 'city biographies' or are based on literary data or are studies of aspects of colonialism in relation to cities. All these are valuable perspectives, but we yet have to come to grips with the 'nature' of Indian urbanism. More aggressively speaking, we have to break out of the paradigm of the 'pre-industrial city', and the 'folk-urban continuum', as is being done by Christopher Bayly, for example, and further, ask questions not only about social structure but about mentality as well.[22] What are the indigenous ways of thinking about, feeling about, and living in, cities? From my research in Banaras, I feel confident of the existence of an 'urban culture' that is both systemic and self-consciously identified with a place and a tradition as sources of meanings.

3. Social change is not a subject that can be understood by limiting its boundaries to familiar areas, such as kinship, caste and occupation, but rather by constantly being alert to new areas. For the mid-nineteenth, mid-twentieth centuries, 'modernisation' variously conceptualised, is the version of social change we are concerned with. This could be defined tentatively as tension between a faster developing technology (and 'modernist' national ideology) and a slower change in 'mental structure'. The study of cultural systems in urban areas illustrates this tension *par*

[21]E.P. Thompson, 'Folklore, Anthropology, and Social History', *The Indian Historical Review*, III, No. 2 (1977), 247-66.

[22]Christopher A. Bayly, 'Indian Merchants in a "Traditional" Setting: Benaras, 1780-1830'..

excellence. Because the technology and related apparatus become available to and are adopted first by dominant classes, one of the most telling aspects of change is the reversal in the position of the latter from that of patron and participant to one of withdrawal, condemnation, and reform.[23]

4. Changes based on technological developments, social movements, and even demographic developments, produce unwittingly profound redefinitions of very basic cultural concepts. These are observable in fundamental revisions in the notions of the desirable lifestyle, and the conceptualisation of the 'self' and the 'other'. Anthropologists generalise on these subjects which may be usefully researched historically, but are somehow considered out of bounds by professional historians. There is a fear of the lack, or difficulty of access, of source materials, of being involved in peripheral, unimportant subjects, and there is the fact of unfamiliarity with analytic concepts. Symbolic systems, as variously manifested, are being richly investigated by historians in Europe and America, and need to be accepted as agenda by the urban and social historians of South Asia.

[23]Peter Burke, *Popular Culture in Early Modern Europe*, New York University Press, New York 1978.

IMPACT OF COLONIAL RULE ON URBAN LIFE

KANCHAN JYOTI

New technology, new education and new administrative structure coming in the wake of British rule were so pervasive that they affected nearly all aspects of urban life. There were significant changes in the morphology of towns, their demographic profile and social structure; new industries came up and many of the old handicrafts declined; new means of communication altered the pattern of trade and facilitated migration to urban areas; the new educational system opened avenues for new professions and new ideas. Modern education also promoted rationalist thinking and instilled humanistic values which aroused concern for social reform and initiated simultaneously the processes of secularisation and communalisation among the educated Indians. The new politico-administrative framework and economic exploitation under colonial rule contributed towards the spread of Nationalism and growing politicisation of the people. Even women came out of seclusion to receive education and to make their presence felt in public life. Noticeable changes occurred also in the behavioural aspects of the people like food, dress, housing, amenities and articles of daily use as well as the means of recreation. At the same time, much that was old or traditional also continued. The present discussion relates particularly to the changes coming in response to colonial rule in the pattern of daily life as well as the institutional and collective aspects of life of the people of Jullundur, a medium-size town which, along with the surrounding Bist-Jullundur-

Doab in the Punjab, was annexed to the British Indian empire in 1846. Under the century-old British rule, Jullundur remained the headquarters of the district and division of the same name, also growing steadily in inhabited area and population to become a class I city in 1941.

I

The impact was more immediately noticeable in the day-to-day life in Jullundur. Within half a century of contact with Britain, there were significant additions in the articles of food and drink. By the end of the nineteenth century, potatoes and refined sugar, besides cigarettes began to be used in the town.[1] By about the same time, the educated and well-to-do Indians also began taking to tea, coffee, ice and soda water, besides liquor.[2] In the thirties, edibles like vegetable ghee, bread, biscuits and pastries were becoming part of the food of the well-to-do people in the town.[3] The staple food of the people, however, with wheat, pulses, vegetables and milk products by and large remained unchanged.[4]

Change was visible also in the eating habits of the people who were associated with the new administration and professions. Eating times were adjusted to the schedule of work in government offices, law courts and other institutions. The educated class, particularly the professional people and those holding middle-rung government jobs began to eat at tables. They also overcame the taboos concerning eating outside the home and began patronising hotels and eating places.[5]

Dress material and the style of dress too underwent change. The well-to-do of Jullundur as elsewhere in the province began using cloth imported from Great Britain, Japan and China.[6] Even the commoners,

[1]*Proceedings Municipal Committee, Jullundur,* 14 September 1892, Resolution 1. *Annual Report on the Working of the Municipal Committees in the Punjab 1890-91;* ibid, 1891-92. See also, Mohammad Hussain Khan, *A Few Phases of the Afghans in Jullundur Bastis*, Basti Nau, Jullundur nd, 164.

[2]Deputy Examiner of Accounts, Punjab Northern (State) Railway, 23 April 1878. See also, *Proceedings Municipal Committee*, 13 July 1889, Resolution 9; 14 September 1892, Resolution1; 21 October 1916, Resolution 291.

[3]*Punjab Government Gazettee Notification* No. 1289, 14 January 1933. See also, *The Tribune*, 20 September 1944.

[4]*Gazetteer of Jullundur District and Kapurthala State 1904-A* (cited hereafter as *DG*), Lahore 1908, 135-36.

[5]Upendra Nath Ashk, *Shahr Mein Ghumta Aina*, Neelabh Prakashan, Allahabad 1972, 168 and 181. See also, *Proceedings Municipal Committee*, 20 December 1938, Resolution 133.

[6]*Proceedings Municipal Committee*, 9 February 1889, Resolution 2; *The Tribune*, 19 May 1931. See also, *Report on the Working of the Department of Industries in the Punjab*, 1932, 384.

who generally used homespun, preferred the imported material for marriages and other festive occasions.[7] Clothes tailored on sewing machines and hosiery articles came into use in the early twenties.[8] Readymade garments also began to be worn in the first decade of the century.[9] The men, particularly of the educated professional class, started wearing hats, ties, bush-shirts and pants, besides watches.[10] The women in general continued to wear trousers (*shalwar*) and tunic (*kurta*) and shawl (*dupatta*), but *ghagra* or a longish skirt was going out of fashion.[11] The educated women, particularly those working in the professions or participating in public life, increasingly took to the saree as their dress.[12] Spectacles, sun glasses, celluloid combs and bangles came in use in the thirties.[13] The use of heavy gold and silver ornaments somewhat decreased by the end of the nineteenth century.[14] Leather boots and boot polish began to be used in the early decades of the twentieth century.[15]

By the beginning of the present century, the well-to-do and professionals started constructing properly ventilated and spacious bungalows outside the town wall.[16] These were seven-to-eight-room single-storeyed structures with covered verandahs placed in spacious lawns, with servants' quarters in one corner. In the Civil Lines each house was ordinarily to be built on an area of no less than 500 square yards or one *kanal*; three quarters of the compound was to be left clear of the buildings.[17] Many pleaders constructed their bungalows in the Civil Lines which had the

[7]*The Tribune*, 24 March 1935. See also, *File No. D-29*, Municipal Committee.

[8]*Proceedings Municipal Committee*, 14 September 1892, Resolution 1. See also, *Panchal Pandita*, August 1903, 5; *Punjab Mission Report 1909*, 28; *Punjab Government Gazette Notification No.* 27952, 16 December 1925.

[9]*Census of India, Punjab, 1911*, part I, 516.

[10]Mohammad Hussain Khan, *A Few Phases of the Afghans in Jullundur Bastis*, 18-20 and 78-79.

[11]*DG Jullundur 1904-A*, 137.

[12]Upendra Nath Ashk, *Shahar Mein Ghumta Aina*, 117 and 183.

[13]*Punjab Government Gazette Notification* No. 1289, 14 January 1933.

[14]*Punjab Administration Report 1881-82*, 105.

[15]*Proceedings Municipal Committee*, 2 April 1928, Resolution 1. See also, *Punjab Provincial Banking Enquiry Committee Report 1929-30*, Punjab Government Printing, Lahore 1930, I, 82.

[16]Note Recorded by Bhagat Ram, President of the Public Works Sub-committee, Jullundur Municipal Committee, *Report of the Punjab Sanitary Conference (August 1913)*, Punjab Government Press, Lahore 1913, 149. See also, Narayani Gupta, *Delhi Between Two Empires 1803-1931, Society, Government and Urban Growth*, Oxford University Press, Delhi 1981, 58-60.

[17]Public Works Sub-committee gave this suggestion on 30 April 1912, *File No.C-27/13*, Municipal Committee.

largest area and lowest density.[18] The common people, however, still continued with unplanned construction without proper arrangement for air, light and drains.[19]

Change also came about in the material used for house construction and the amenities provided in houses. Burnt bricks of a slightly bigger size came to be increasingly used for construction.[20] The use of glass for windows and ventilators became common.[21] In the thirties, hand pumps were being put up in the courtyards of houses as a source of water supply, but their number was relatively small: Jullundur had one hand pump per one hundred of its inhabitants. Piped water supply had not been introduced in the houses.[22] Electricity came to be used for lighting streets and houses in the twenties, yet till 1947, 80 per cent of the houses in Jullundur were without electricity.[23] Nevertheless, mustard oil lamps had been replaced by kerosene and gas lamps as well as wax candles.[24]

With the introduction of new technology, a change was visible in household articles. In the 1890s, glass bottles came to be used for storing oil in place of leather containers (*kuppi*).[25] Factory-made iron locks and trunks came to be used after 1900.[26] Iron buckets, tubs, iron stoves or *angithis* and vermicelli or *sewian* machines became locally available in the twenties. Factory-made metal utensils began also to be used, though they did not completely oust the clay pots.[27] By about this time, the drawing-rooms of many government servants and professional people

[18]Many of the pleaders of the town such as Badri Das Puri, Bhagat Ram Sondhi, Guru Datt Sehgal, Pandit Devi Chand, Hans Raj Sondhi, Shaikh Ghulam Dastgir and Nazeer-ullah Shah built their bungalows in the Civil Lines area: *Abadi Jo 1885 Se 1913 Tak Jullundur Shahr Mein Bani; File Nos. T 23/25; L-91*, Municipal Committee. See also, Reeta Grewal, *Urbanization in the Punjab 1849-1947*, Ph.D. Thesis, Guru Nanak Dev University, Amritsar 1988, 130.

[19]*File No. I-25*, Municipal Committee.

[20]*Proceedings Municipal Committee*, 10 March 1885, Resolution 18; 12 March 1884, Resolution 3.

[21]*DG Jullundur 1904-A, 50.*

[22]*Public Health and Sanitation Report, Municipal Committee Jullundur 1935,7.*

[23]*Report on the Working of the Department of the Industries in the Punjab*,1923, 2. See also, *Report on the Civic Survey Conducted by the Jullundur Improvement Trust, February to July 1950*, Jullundur 1950, 58-59.

[24]*Proceedings Municipal Committee*,12 September 1884, Resolution 3; 14 November 1892, Resolution 1.

[25] *Monograph on Pottery and Glass Industries in the Punjab*,1889, 22.

[26] *Indian Engineering Industries, 1944-45*, Engineering Association of India, Calcutta nd, 448-49.

[27]Ibid, 36, 55-90 and 448-49. See also, *Report on the Industrial and Agricultural Exhibition of the Punjab, North Western Province and Kashmir 1909-10*, Lahore 1910, 165.

came to be furnished with sofas.[28] Folding chairs were in use in the houses and offices in the early thirties,[29] but the common people still used low cane stools (*pirhas* and *muhras*).[30] By the early thirties, electric fans, electric irons, besides heaters were in use in the upper-class homes.[31] Battery cells came in use in the thirties.[32]

A change was noticed also in cultural life by the beginning of the twentieth century. People of all ages and both sexes visited parks for relaxation, initially in small numbers.[33] New games like cricket, football, hockey, tennis and volleyball were introduced in schools and colleges.[34] Horse races began to be held.[35] In the twenties, the silent cinema was becoming an important source of entertainment. People from the neighbouring villages too visited these cinemas because no other town in the district had provision for screening films.[36] Photography had been introduced in the second decade of the century.[37] In the thirties, the radio became another means of recreation and generating awareness.[38]

Public libraries added to the widening horizons of the people of Jullundur. The first library in the town was opened in the 1880s by the local Arya Samaj.[39] In 1896, the American Presbyterians started a

[28] *Census of India, Punjab, 1911*, Part I, 27.

[29] *The Tribune*, 24 July 1931.

[30] *DG Jullundur, 1904-A*,219.

[31] *Proceedings Municipal Committee*, 29 May 1926, Resolution 20; *The Tribune*, 3 March 1936. See also, *The Indian Association of Engineers*, 1944-45, 36-50, 54-90 and 365.

[32] *A Report on the Working of the Department of the Industries in the Punjab*, 1932,3.

[33] *Proceedings Municipal Committee*, 12 May 1920, Resolution 11. See also, *File No. 2-8*, Municipal Committee.

The ladies' and childrens' parks were separately earmarked. For public parks emerging as a new feature in the morphology of Jullundur, Kanchan Jyoti, *The City of Jullundur: A Study in Urban History (1846-1947)*, Ph.D. Thesis, Guru Nanak Dev University Amritsar 1988, 76-77.

[34] *Zilla Jullundur Gazette 1918*, 53; *The Tribune*, 30 July 1937; *Annual Administration Report,Municipal Committee 1938-39*, 552. See also, Satyadev Vidyalankar, *Lala Dev Raj: Kanya Mahavidyalaya Ki Suvarn Jayanti Ke Avsar Par*, Kanya Mahavidyalaya, Jullundur 1937, 19.

[35] *The Punjab Kesri*, 3 April 1982. It is a daily vernacular newspaper published from Jullundur.

[36] Letter dated 16 December 1925, received by the author from Gian Chand Soni, proprietor of the Krishna Theatre.

[37] *Zilla Jullundur Gazette 1918*. 17. See also, *Punjab Government Gazette Notification No*.27952, 16 December 1925.

[38] *The Tribune*, 3 March 1936. Radio station at Jullundur was started in November 1947: *Census of India, Punjab, 1951*, Part I, 77. See also, Upendra Nath Ashk, *Shahr Mein Ghumta Aina*, 313.

[39] M.R. Jambunathan (ed), *Swami Shraddhanand*, Bharatiya Vidya Bhavan, Bombay 1961, 79.

library.[40] The Salig Ram Memorial Library, opened by his descendants in 1916, had 504 books in 1944.[41] Another library was founded by Dr C.R. Swamy near the mausoleum of Imam Nasiruddin in 1936.[42] Local publications, besides the dailies like the English *Tribune*, Gurmukhi *Akali Te Pardesi,* the Urdu *Prabhat,* and the Hindi *Milap* were the people's favourite reading. The libraries were used mostly by the students and men of professional classes, particularly the retired.[43]

Some new fairs added to the cultural life of the town. Sodal fair, held at Jullundur since 1861, was attended by thousands from the town and neighbouring areas.[44] In 1875, Harbhallabh started a music conference on the death anniversary of Tuljagir, his teacher in music. Tola Ram, one of Harbhallabh's disciples, popularised this fair and founded the Shri Harbhallabh Sangeet Maha Sabha to manage it.[45] Thousands from far and wide attended this fair.[46] Christmas, Easter and New Year Day also came to be celebrated at Jullundur.[47]

Even the mode of celebrating traditional fairs and festivals like Id, Moharram, Diwali, Janmashtami, Dussehra, Ramlila and Gurpurab underwent changes.[48] Many public functions came to be held in public parks like Burlton Park.[49] Tournaments of wrestling, hockey and football were organised with some of the traditional festivals and fairs which were

[40] *Punjab Mission Report 1900*, 26.

[41] Salig Ram Sondhi of Jullundur worked as *zaildar, tahsildar* and honorary magistrate in the district at different times. He was the elected member of the Jullundur municipal committee and the district board in 1884. Salig Ram died in 1913: Ram Chandra Javed, *Arya Samaj Ke Maha Purush*, University Publishers, Jullundur 1964, 161. See also, *File No. L-161*, Municipal Committee.

[42] Gurdas Ram and Sant Ram Aggarwal, the local traders, donated 400 and 300 rupees, respectively for the library: *The Tribune*, 11 October 1942.

[43] *Punjab Mission Report*, 1900, 26; *File No. L-161*, Municipal Committee.

[44] Sodal fair is held in the memory of a child deity belonging to Chaddha sub-caste. The child is believed to have gone deep into the pond located at this place and reappeared in the form of snake and again disappeared: *Census of India, Punjab 1961*, Part VII, 40-41. See also, *File No. 0-292*, Municipal Committee.

[45] J.B. Goyal, *Shri Baba Harbhallabh: A Homage*, Shri Baba Harbhallabh Sangeet Maha Sabha, Jullundur 1978, 5-7. See also, H.S. Patel, *Directory of Cultural Organizations in India*, Indian Council for Cultural Relations, New Delhi 1975, 110. The Harballabh fair is continuing till today.

[46] *File No.B-1/41*, Municipal Committee.

[47] *Punjab Mission Report 1923*, 35.

[48] For more information on fairs and festivals, see C.H. Buck, *Faiths, Fairs & Festivals of India*, Asian Publication Services, India 1977 (reprint – first published 1917).

[49] *File Nos C-105; 0-306*, Municipal Committee; *The Tribune*, 24 May 1934; 27 May 1937; 23 April 1940.

attended even by people from the villages.[50] From the twenties loud-speakers and the brass band began to be used at public functions.[51] In the next decade, the use of gramophones became current.[52] Faster transport facilitated pilgrimages and the number of people from Jullundur visiting Kartarpur, Amritsar, Anandpur, Kangra and Hardwar increased considerably.[53] There is evidence of local Muslims making pilgrimages to the shrine of Sakhi Sarwar in Dera Ghazi Khan and going even as far as Mecca.[54]

Jullundur came to have literary and sports associations. In the thirties, Jagatjit Afghan Club was promoting sports.[55] There are references also to a Recreation Club and Youngmen's Muslim Association organising tournaments.[56] In 1931, Bazm-i-Iqbal came into existence to promote literature.[57] Doaba Punjab Kavi Sabha was arranging poetic meets in the forties.[58]

II

An altogether different element entered the socio-religious life with the arrival of the officially backed Christian missionaries. Soon after annexation, the American Presbyterian mission was established at Jullundur in 1846 under the charge of Golak Nath, a Bengali convert.[59] Conversions to Christianity aroused a fear in the minds of the leaders of

[50]*Proceedings Municipal Committee*, 4 June 1927, Resolution 135; *DG Jullundur 1904-A*, 145-46.

[51]Interview with Karam Singh Kirti on 5 April 1982 at Jullundur; *The Tribune*, 26 April 1935.

[52]*Proceedings Municipal Committee*, 4 June 1927, Resolution 135.

[53]*Lodiana Mission Report 1883*, 16; ibid, 1884, 34. See also, *Public Health and Sanitation Report, Municipal Committee* 1921, 256.

[54]*DG Jullundur 1904-A*, 125; *Proceedings Municipal Committee*, 29 January 1945, Resolution 90.

[55]Mohammad Hussain Khan, *A Few Phases of the Afghans in Jullundur Bastis*, 110.

[56]*Zilla Jullundur Gazette 1918*, 5; *Proceedings Municipal Committee*, 16 October 1936, Resolution 211.

[57]*Proceedings Municipal Committee*, 4 December 1944, Resolution 26. Iqbal died on 21 April 1938: S.P. Sen (ed), *Dictionary of National Biography*, Institute of Historical Studies, Calcutta 1974, II, 185.

[58]*The Tribune*, 29 May 1941.

[59]Golak Nath was the first Indian convert to the American Presbyterian church in 1837: C.H. Loehlin, 'Some Christian Leaders in the Punjab', *Proceedings of the Punjab History Conference*, September 1966, 205. Golak Nath was the first pastor of the Jullundur mission. He remained the sole in-charge of the mission for forty years. In 1885, foreign missionaries were stationed at Jullundur because of the old age of Golak Nath: H.C. Velke, *Survey of the Evangelistic Work of the Punjab Mission of the Presbyterian Church in the U.S.A.*, India Council, Lucknow 1929, 11.

Muslims, Hindus and Sikhs in the Punjab that their cultural identity, rather survival, was in danger.[60] The missionaries on the other hand had been openly and emphatically declaring that their goal was to gain converts from amongst the natives.[61] The methods they adopted were diverse. They would preach at some conspicuous place in the bazaar like outside the deputy commissioner's office.[62] In 1854, they constructed a chapel in Bazar Bansanwala to give sermons.[63] They preached also at the various fairs held at Jullundur [64] and themselves organised the Easter fair.[65] Biblical literature was sold or given away free of cost.[66] From the 1860s, the missionaries preached in the *zenanas* which evoked not merely the cry of 'religion in danger' but also of 'subversion in the home'.[67]

As a result of the missionaries' efforts, a microscopic Christian community came into existence in Jullundur. From no converted Christian in 1846, Jullundur came to have sixty-three communicants and 131 baptisms among Indians by 1930.[68] The Christian community included urbanites like the Bengalis, aristocrats like the royal house of the

[60]Kenneth W. Jones, *Arya Dharm:Hindu Consciousness in the 19th Century Punjab*, Manohar, New Delhi 1976, 10 and 66.

[61]John Newton, *Historical Sketches of the Indian Mission of the Presbyterian Church in the United States of America, from 1834 to 1884*, Allahabad Press, Allahabad 1886, 3 and 12. See also, E.M. Wherry, *Our Missions in India*, Stratford Company, Boston 1924, 4.

[62]*Lodiana Mission Report 1857*, 23; ibid 1875, 22; ibid 1883, 34.

[63]Ibid, 1854, 18.

[64]Ibid, 1857, 21; *Punjab Mission Report 1905*, 38.

[65]*Punjab Mission Report 1923*, 35; ibid., 1927, 47.

[66] In 1905, fourteen Bibles, forty-three New Testaments, 243 scripture portions and 1935 tracts were sold. In addition, 200 tracts were distributed free of cost: *Punjab Mission Report 1905*, 39.

[67]In 1880, missionaries were visiting seventy-eight *zenanas*: *Lodiana Mission Report 1880*, 69. See also, Kenneth W. Jones, *Arya Dharm*, 9.

[68]The following figures show the gradual increase in the number of the baptisms and communicants in Jullundur:

Year	*Christian Communicants*	*Baptisms*	*Increase*
1858	12	46	-
1860	27	59	13
1883	27	86	27
1918	60	121	35
1930	63	131	10

Sources: *Lodiana Mission Reports; Punjab Mission Reports*. The number of communicants and baptisms for the district as a whole was much larger, for example, 234 and 2602 in 1918.

Ahluwalias of Kapurthala, besides the so-called low-caste people.[69] The latter were allured as much by the prospects of employment as by the possibility of shedding the stigma of untouchability.[70] The so-called low castes formed three per cent of the population of Jullundur and were the reservoir from which the missionaries drew most of their converts.[71]

The converts persisted in observing the customs of their milieu.[72] In the early twentieth century, the Jullundur mission was getting stricter regarding the observance of the Christian social ceremonies by the converts.[73] Some of them were induced to adopt Christian rites, but till the end of British rule problems of adjustment remained evident.[74]

More than the actual number, the threat of conversions haunted the educated Hindus which led to the foundation of the Arya Samaj at Jullundur in 1877.[75] Regarded as the champion of the Hindus, it aimed at the revival of the ancient Hindu faith assimilating the progressive ideas of the West. The Aryas competed with the Christians in preaching

[69]Kali Charan Chatterjee, who worked for some time as the headmaster of the Mission High School, and Brij Nath Mittra, who became superintendent of the office of the Session's Court at Jullundur were some of the early converts. Among the Ahluwalias, Randhir Singh and his sons Kharak Singh and Harnam Singh were the early converts to Christianity: *Jullundur Mein Mission Ki Khidmat Ki Yadgar Mein Sadsala Jubilee*, Nagina Press, 1946, 2. See also, John C.B. Webster, *Christian Community and Change in the Nineteenth Century North India*, Macmillan, Delhi 1976, 76.

[70]In 1876, thirteen converts were in the employment of the Jullundur Mission: John C.B. Webster, *Christian Community and Change in the Nineteenth Century North India*, 76. The overtures of the missionaries like eating the food prepared by the low castes attracted them towards Christianity: *Punjab Mission Report 1909*, 24. Conversion removed at least the socio-psychological stigma these people suffered as outcastes and untouchables: Clarence O'MacMullen, 'Impact of Christianity on the Punjab', *Bulletin of the Christian Institute of Sikh Studies*, Batala, January 1985, 12.

[71]In 1931, the number of the persons from the low castes in Jullundur was 2,492: *Punjab Legislative Assembly Debates*, 30 November 1939; *The Tribune*, 14 June 1940.

[72]The *biradari* was assertive in performing social ceremonies. The niece of a Christian Chuhra of long standing was married to a non-Christian boy by the non-Christian rites because the *biradari* required it: *Punjab Mission Report* 1902,65. An old woman living with her son's Christian family died and the missionaries arranged to conduct the funeral. But she was buried by her relatives with Muslim rites an hour before the arrival of the missionaries: ibid, 1901, 65.

[73]Ibid, 1900, 52.

[74]Ibid, 1924, 34. Twelve marriages and eight betrothals were performed according to Christian rites in 1927: ibid, 1927, 6. See also, M.N. Srinivas, *Social Change in Modern India*, Orient Longman, New Delhi 1984, 60.

[75]The first Arya Samaj was founded at Bombay in 1875: Kenneth W. Jones, *Arya Dharm*, 35-38.

through *kirtans* and *kathas*.[76] Challenges were thrown for debates with the missionaries.[77] By the end of the century, the membership of the Jullundur Arya Samaj reached three hundred.[78] In 1921, it rose to 1,089.[79]

The Arya Samaj came in conflict with the Sanatanists or the Hindu orthodoxy who did not approve of its modernised and de-Brahmanised rituals and rejection of idolatry and Puranic scriptures.[80] Eight years after the foundation of the Arya Samaj, the Sanatan Dharam Sabha was founded at Jullundur to neutralise the former's activities and to spread the Puranic Hindu religion.[81] By the end of the nineteenth century, it had gathered nearly two hundred members.[82] In the twenties, a branch of the Hindu Maha Sabha was also working in Jullundur for the revival of Hinduism and uplift of the Hindus.[83]

To compete with the missionaries for converts, the Aryas too converted about a hundred *rahtias* or the low-castes in the two early decades of the twentieth century.[84] The leaders even dined with the newly converted Aryas from a low social background in 1922 in the annual anniversary celebrations of the Samaj.[85] In the thirties, Hans Raj Sondhi gave a stipend of thirteen rupees each to the depressed classes students of the Junior Anglo-vernacular class of the Normal school at Jullundur,[86] and the D.A.V. College, Jullundur, founded in 1918, granted them freeships.[87] Following this example, in the thirties, the government granted full fee concession to the depressed class students in schools as well as

[76] *Sat Dharm Pracharak*, 28 December 1888; 2 June 1889; 29 October 1889; 16 November 1889; 8 March 1890. See also, N.B. Sen (ed), *Punjab's Eminent Hindus*, New Book Society, Lahore 1944, 300.

[77] M.R. Jambunathan (ed), *Swami Shraddhanand*, 78.

[78] *Punjab Administration Report 1898-99*, Statement No. 62.

[79] *Register Abadi Dehat, Mardumshumari Sal 1921, Zila Jullundur*.

[80] *Sat Dharm Pracharak*, 17 August 1889; 21 September 1889; 9 November 1889; 14 December 1889; 28 December 1889.

[81] *Punjab Administration Report 1888-89*, Statement No. 63.

[82] Sanatan Dharm Sabha had 145 members in 1894-95 and 188 in 1900-01: ibid, 1894-95, Statement No. 62; ibid, 1900-1, Statement No. 62.

[83] *File No. D-29*, Municipal Committee; *The Tribune* 2 June 1932. Punjab Hindu Sabha was founded in 1907: Kirpal C. Yadav, *Elections in the Punjab, 1920-1947*, Manohar, Delhi 1987, 132. Hindu Maha Sabha was founded to protect the interests of the Hindus when the government introduced communal electorate by the Morley-Minto Reforms of 1909: Indu Banga 'Emergence of Hindu Consciousness in Colonial Punjab', *Self-Images, Identity and Nationality*(ed P.C. Chatterjee), Indian Institute of Advanced Study, Shimla 1989, 201-17.

[84] Prakash Chand Bahri, *Jullundur Arya Samaj Ka Sankshipat Parichay*, Adda Hoshiarpur, Jullundur nd, 4; Kenneth W. Jones, *Arya Dharm*, 202-3.

[85] Prakash Chand Bahri, *Jullundur Arya Samaj Ka Sankshipat Parichay*, 4.

[86] *The Tribune*, 15 March 1936.

[87] *The Tribune*, 16 May 1934.

in professional institutes.[88] In 1938, seven depressed class persons trained in Patwar School at Jullundur entered government service.[89] Gurbanta Singh, a Chamar, worked as a teacher in Sain Das High School, Jullundur,[90] and was a member of the Jullundur District Board for eighteen years.[91] In 1946, Sant Ram, a Chuhra by caste, was a member of the Punjab Legislative Assembly.[92] It is not surprising therefore that in 1940, on the demand of the Arya Samaj, Sanatan Dharm Sabha and the depressed classes, the government opened twenty-nine municipal wells for the low-castes.[93]

The Muslims viewed as a threat to their existence the proselytising activities of the Christians and of the Aryas, besides the advancement of the Hindus in education and public service.[94] This led to the foundation of the Anjuman-i-Islamia at Jullundur in 1883 and Anjuman-i-Himayat-i-Islam in the 1880s as elsewhere in the province. The Anjumans worked for the religious, educational and cultural welfare of Muslims.[95]

In 1891, a Singh Sabha was founded at Jullundur.[96] It aimed at saving the Sikhs from conversions to Christianity, defining their identity distinctly from the Hindus and regenerating the Sikh society. The Singh Sabha propagated the reformed Sikh religion, popularised the Punjabi language and sought to spread modern education.[97]

The voluntary associations initiated a number of activities for social welfare and social reform. The missionaries pioneered the movement to be followed by the native organisations and individual philanthropists.

[88] *Report on the Progress of Education in the Punjab 1935-36*, 89; *Punjab Legislative Assembly Debates*, 5 December 1939, Qestion 1384.

[89] *Punjab Legislative Assembly Debates*, 31 March 1938, Question 2341.

[90] *Golden Jubilee Commemoration Volume of Sain Das Anglo-Sanskrit High School, Jullundur* 1949, 2.

[91] *The Tribune*, 27 July 1977.

[92] Diwan Jagdish Chandra, *The Punjab Today*, All India Press, Ludhiana 1956, 128. Sant Ram was appointed private parliamentary secretary to the finance minister of the Punjab.

[93] *Punjab Legislative Assembly Debates*, 27 February 1940, Question 5218.

[94] Ikram Ali Malik, 'Muslim Anjumans in the Punjab', *Journal of Regional History*, V, Guru Nanak Dev University, Amritsar 1984, 97. See also, Prem Raman Uprety, *Religion and Politics in the Punjab in the 1920s*, Sterling, Jullundur 1980, 200.

[95] *The Punjab Administration Report*, however, gives 1896 as the year of the foundation of the branch of the Anjuman-i-Islamia at Jullundur and in this year it had 100 members: ibid., 1896-97, Statement No. 62. The Anjumans were established under the influence of the Aligarh movement initiated by Sayed Ahmad Khan which aimed at the regeneration of the Muslim society: Ikram Ali Malik, 'Muslim Anjumans in the Punjab', 97-99 and 103-5.

[96] The first Singh Sabha was founded at Amritsar in 1873 and the next at Lahore in 1879: Teja Singh, 'The Singh Sabha Movement in the Punjab', *The Panjab Past and Present*, VII, Part I, 1984, 35-36. See also, *Punjab Administration Report 1898-99*, Statement No. 62.

[97] N. Gerald Barrier, *The Sikhs and Their Literature*, Manohar, Delhi 1970, xiv.

Health care was one of the main features of the social welfare programme. The missionaries started allopathic and homeopathic dispensaries at the mission compound in 1886 and 1939, respectively; they opened an allopathic dispensary also in Bazar Bansanwala in 1915 for outdoor patients.[98] Medical aid was given through home visits too.[99] Dr Orbison, a foreign missionary, carried a mobile dispensary with him.[100] The Mahabir Dal, a Hindu paramilitary organisation, and the Hindu Sewak Sabha helped the authorities in combating epidemics.[101] In the thirties, the marketing committee of Mandi Fenton Ganj was also running a dispensary.[102] Salig Ram Sondhi, and later his descendants, ran a dispensary starting in 1907 and in the 1930s, Balak Ram and Nabi Bux too opened charitable dispensaries.[103] Sant Ram Aggarwal opened the Gurdas Ram Maternity Hospital in 1936. [104]

The Christian missionaries also set up a poor house in 1858 which could provide shelter to about forty persons at a time.[105] More than 10,000 paupers received meals annually from this poor house.[106] Religious instruction was also given to the recipients of the poor relief, [107]but conversions from the poor house were rare.[108] There is, however, a reference to conversions from amongst the persons who got famine relief during the scarcity of 1897. This induced the Jullundur Aryas to start an orphanage for girls in 1898.[109]

[98]If needed, indoor patients could also be accommodated. In 1917 and 1918, 10,398 and 15,000 patients in total, respectively, were treated in these clinics: *Lodiana Mission Report 1886*, 24; *Punjab Mission Report 1917*, 31; ibid., 1918, 28; *Proceedings Jullundur Mission*,19 August 1939.

[99]In 1918, 512 patients were treated through home visits and among them sixty-four cases were operated upon: *Punjab Mission Report 1918*, 26.

[100]Ibid., 1911, 11-12. Jullunder periodically suffered from the epidemics of smallpox, cholera,, influenza and the plague, among others. For a discussion of their effects, Kanchan Jyoti, *The City of Jullundur*, 99-115.

[101]Mahabir Dal and Hindu Sewak Sabha were the organs of the Hindu Maha Sabha and came in existence in the twenties: Prem Raman Uprety, *Religion and Politics in Punjab in the 1920's*, 78; *Public Health and Sanitation Report, Municipal Committee 1936*, 8.

[102]This hospital attended to about 20,000 and 29,000 patients in 1937 and 1938, respectively: *Proceedings Municipal Committee*, 21 February 1941, Resolution 189.

[103]Ibid., 2 April 1931, Resolution 103; *File No. C-113*, Municipal Committee.

[104]*File No. C-19*,Municipal Committee.

[105]*Lodiana Mission Report 1858*, 23; ibid, 1860, 49-50.

[106]In 1866 and 1890, 18,000 and 14,000 persons, respectively got meals from the poor house: ibid, 1866, 21; ibid., 1891, 38.

[107]Ibid., 1860, 49-50.

[108]One person was converted in 1866 and three in 1867. The missionaries lamented that the poor went away as soon as the scriptures began to be recited: ibid., 1866, 21; ibid., 1867, 38.

[109] John C.B. Webster, *Christian Community and Change*, 182.

The orphanage functioned as a part of the Kanya Mahavidyalaya, the well-known girls' school and later a college, founded by Lala Munshi Ram in 1886. In the beginning, orphan girls came from Madhya Pradesh.[110] The girls from Bengal were given shelter in 1906 and 1943 when it was stricken by famine.[111] In 1935, orphan girls were brought from Quetta when it was affected by a severe earthquake.[112] The orphans were fed, clothed, housed and educated free of cost.[113] The Jullundur Arya Samaj also arranged the marriages of about a hundred orphan girls.[114]

The question of the welfare of the widows too was taken up. The opening of a primary school for the widows by the American Presbyterian missionaries made the condition of widows a matter of public debate and concern.[115] The Aryas in 1908 began providing free board and lodging as well as education to widows.[116] The widows were lodged on the campus of the Kanya Mahavidyalaya and their number increased from eleven in 1908 to twenty-three in 1930-31.[117] In 1912, Savitri, a widow, was teaching at Jas Kaur girls' school at Jullundur.[118]

The Arya Samaj from the beginning concerned itself with the remarriage of widows. In 1900, Sumitra, an Arya widow, was married to Guru Datt in spite of opposition even from the Aryas.[119] Ralla Ram of Tanda married a widow on the persuasion of Munshi Ram.[120] In 1922, the Vidhwa Vivah Sahayak Sabha of Jullundur started its programme of the remarriage of widows. In less than a decade, hundreds of widows were married at its initiative.[121] The particulars of the aspirants for marriage

[110] Prakash Chand Bahri, *Jullundur Arya Samaj Ka Sankshipat Parichay*, 3.

[111] *Panchal Pandita*, July 1906, 22. See also, *The Tribune*, 13 September 1943.

[112] *The Tribune*, 23 June 1935.

[113] In December 1901, expenditure on food and clothing for twenty-six girls was 663 rupees 14 annas: *Register Karvahi Antarang Sabha, Jullundur Arya Samaj*, 3 January 1901. See also, *Kanya Mahavidyalaya Ka Vivarn Patra*, Maha Devi Onkar Press, Jullundur, Sambat 1992,3.

[114] *Register Karvahi Antarang Sabha, Jullundur Arya Samaj*, 1 August 1901; 16 November 1901. See also, Prakash Chand Bahri, *Jullundur Arya Samaj Ka Sankshipat Parichay*, 4.

[115] *Lodiana Mission Report 1882*, 22.

[116] Bhimsen Vidyalankar, *Arya Samaj Ka Sachitra Itihas: Arya Pratinidhi Sabha Ki Ardh Shatabadi Ke Uplaksh Mein*, Arya Pratinidhi Sabha, Lahore, Sambat 1992, 100.

[117] Satyadev Vidyalankar, *Lala Dev Raj*, 121.

[118] *Panchal Pandita*, June 1912, 27.

For a discussion of the spread of modern education in Jullundur, see Kanchan Jyoti, *The City of Jullundur*, 237-77.

[119] Shraddhanand Sanyasi, *Kalyan Marg Ka Pathik*, Gian Mandal Yantaralaya, Kashi 1924, 163.

[120] Ibid., 175.

[121] *The Tribune*, 15 December 1937.

with widows were published in the *Vidhwa Hitaishi*, a monthly journal started by the Sabha in 1936.[122] The issue of *Vidhwa Hitaishi* of September 1940 carried the matrimonials of eleven men, eight of them widowers and three bachelors.[123] This issue also published the matrimonial advertisements of seven widows, amongst whom three each were Aggarwals and Brahmans and one Khatri, with their age varying between 15 and 32 years.[124]

The programme of women's welfare included raising their age of marriage. Staying longer in educational institutions also saved them from the evil of child marriage.[125] Jullundur Arya Samaj made special efforts in this regard. In 1901, by a resolution, the Arya Samaj made it compulsory for its members not to marry their daughters below the age of sixteen.[126] Ved Kumari, the daughter of Munshi Ram, and her sister were married at this age.[127] The girls at the orphanage of Kanya Mahavidyalaya were also married after sixteen.[128]

The Aryas made a beginning towards simple marriage rites and intercaste marriages.[129] The marriages began to be ceremonised without fireworks, dancing girls and obscene songs.[130] Ved Kumari writes that in 1901 her sister was married even without dowry.[131] Another instance of such a marriage was reported in 1938 when despite opposition from the *biradari*, the bridegroom refused to take dowry.[132] In 1900, Sumitra, an Arya girl, was married outside her caste. It was perhaps the first intercaste marriage in Jullundur. Ved Kumari's sister and her brothers,

[122]Vidhwa Vivah Sahayak Sabha was established at the initiative of Mulraj Sharma: Shadi Ram Joshi, *Ek Samarpit Jivan: Pandit Mulraj Sharma*, Mulraj Sewa Ashram, Jullundur nd, 41.

[123] Five amongst these men were Brahmans, two Khatris, and one each belonged to Aggarwal, Arora, Jat and Labana castes. As regards their educational level, three had passed matric, two middle and the others had got elementary education. Their monthly income varied from 20 to 300 rupees: *Vidhwa Hitaishi*, September 1940, 34.

[124] Ibid., 12.

[125] *Punjab Administration Report 1918-19*, 37.

[126]*Proceedings of the Arya Samaj Jullundur*, 17 February 1901.

[127]Ved Kumari, *Mere Sansmaran*, Shukal Printers, Bombay 1966, 18.

[128]*Proceedings of the Arya Samaj Jullundur*, 1 August 1901.

[129]*Sat Dharm Pracharak*, 11 May 1889; 8 June 1889. Indra Vidyavachaspati, *Mere Pita*, np, Delhi 1957, 289. See also, Dharm Dev Vidyavachaspati, *Amar Dharm Vir Swami Shraddhanand*, Sarvadeshik Arya Pratinidhi Sabha, Delhi 1950, 12.

[130]*Proceedings of Arya Samaj Jullundur*, 30 June 1901. See also, Bhimsen Vidyalankar, *Arya Samaj Ka Sachitra Itihas: Arya Pratinidhi Sabha Punjab Ki Ardh Shatabadi Ke Uplaksh Mein*, 32.

[131]Ved Kumari, *Mere Sansmaran*,18.

[132]The Tribune, 22 July 1938.

Harish and Indra, that is, all the children of Munshi Ram, also were married outside the caste.[133]

Through these measures, the Aryas tried to reorient women's role in the family in particular and society in general. Ved Kumari referred to the miserable condition of women in the late nineteenth century: No care was taken of their health, not to talk of educating them; playing outside the house was unheard of; girls even one year old were married and the child widows were left to lead a miserable life.[134] A battle was fought by the social reform organisations on various fronts to pull the women out from the whirlpool of misery. By the early twenties, many of them had discarded the purdah and some even participated in civic and public life, though their number remained small.

In the early twenties, during the non-cooperation movement, the girls of the Kanya Mahavidyalaya, including Lajjavati who later became its distinguished Principal, participated in the Congress session held at Amritsar in 1919, immediately after the Jallianwala Bagh tragedy.[135] In 1929, in the Lahore session of the Indian National Congress, seventy girls of the Vidyalaya participated as volunteers under her leadership.[136] In the civil disobedience movement in the early thirties, Sushila Devi Khanna, Lal Devi Sondhi, Amar Kaur and Rajinder Kaur propagated the use of Khadi and even picketed the foreign cloth and liquor shops.[137] Sushila Devi was imprisoned and fined 400 rupees.[138] In 1941, Lal Devi Sondhi became the first woman satyagrahi in the province to participate in the individual satyagraha programme started by Gandhi.[139]

The press made a significant contribution to the programmes of education, social welfare and social reform. The press also created political and national consciousness which led to the people's participa-

[133]Ved Kumari, *Mere Sansmaran,* 19 ; Indra Vidyavachaspati, *Arya Samaj Ka Itihas,* Sarvadeshik Arya Pratinidhi Sabha, Delhi 1957, I, 289. Dharm Dev Vidyavachaspati, *Amar Dharm Vir Swami Shraddhanand,* 32.

[134]Ved Kumari, *Mere Sansmaran,*5-10.

[135]Shadi Ram Joshi, *Kanya Mahavidyalaya,* Kanya Mahavidyalaya, Jullundur nd, 192.

[136] Shadi Ram Joshi, *Satya Ki Manzil: Sewa Ki Rah,* Vishveshevaranand Vedic Research Institute Press, Hoshiarpur 1976, 62.

[137]*The Tribune,* 17 May 1930 ; 26 June 1930.

Mrs Sushila Devi was the wife of Daulat Ram Khanna, a businessman and Congress worker and Mrs Lal Devi Sondhi was the wife of Hans Raj Sondhi, a pleader.

[138]Ibid., 25 January 1932.

[139]Ibid., 13 December 1940; 12 April 1941; 6 May 1941.

tion in politics and in the freedom struggle.[140] The journalistic activity in Jullundur as in other big urban centres in the province was concerned mainly with the publication of periodicals and books.[141]

The first printing press at Jullundur appears to have been established in the late 1870s or the early 1880s.[142] Another printing press was set up in 1888-89 by Munshi Ram.[143] By 1927, Jullundur had eleven printing presses.[144] Institutions and individuals took to publishing books, journals and newspapers.

The Arya Samaj was the first institution to publish its journal in 1889-90. *Sat Dharm Pracharak,* an Urdu weekly brought out by Munshi Ram, discussed social and religious matters. Its circulation increased from 200 copies in 1890 to 600 in 1892.[145] In 1897, Kanya Mahavidyalaya published a Hindi monthly entitled, *Panchal Pandita,*which wrote, among other things, on the education and rights of women.[146] The monthly journal *Vidhwa Hitaishi* started in 1936 also discussed national issues.[147]

Jullundur was in fact emerging as a centre of publishing industry, bringing out books on education and religion. During the quarter ending on 30 September 1925, ten books were written at Jullundur. Out of the total of twelve books written or published at Jullundur, six were in English, four in Hindi and two in Urdu. Ten books were for educational and two for religious purposes. Most of these books were written by those

[140]N. Gerald Barrier, *Banned Controversial Literature and Political Control in British India 1907-1947,* Manohar, Delhi 1976, 9.

[141]See Emmett Davis, *Press and Politics in British Western Punjab, 1836-1947,* Academic Publications, Delhi 1983, 116.

[142]Jullundur does not figure in the list of printing presses in the Punjab given in *Home Department, Public B,* June 1873, Proceedings 216-17; June 1874, Proceedings 346-47, National Archives of India, New Delhi. The district gazetteer, however, does refer to the establishment of a printing press in the town: *DG Jalandhar* 1883-84, 23.

[143]*Report on the Vernacular Newspapers Published in the Punjab, 1890,* Statement No. 14.

[144] Incidentally, in 1927, seven printing presses at Jullundur were owned by Hindus, four by Muslims and one by a Sikh: *The Standard Indian Commercial Directory,* Standard Publicity Co., Lahore 1927, 537.

[145]*Report on the Vernacular Newspapers Published in the Punjab, 1890,* Statement No. 14; ibid, 1892, Statement No. 14.

[146]In 1920-21, the place of *Panchal Pandita* was taken by *Bharti* and in 1922 its name was changed to *Jalvid Sakha:* Satyadev Vidyalankar, *Lala Dev Raj,* 62.

[147]Shadi Ram Joshi, *Ek Samarpit Jivan: Pandit Mulraj Sharma,* 90-92.

associated with the Arya Samaj or the Presbyterian Mission.[148]

Several periodicals were published from Jullunder. In 1890, an Urdu fortnightly *Safir-i-Hind* was published by Barkat Ali from the Aftab-i-Hind Press.[149] In 1892, *Bharat Sewak* another Urdu monthly, was started by Gujar Mal Khatri, a *sahukar* of Muhalla Purani Katcheri. *Bharat Sewak* discussed religious and social matters, besides giving general news.[150] *Doaba*, an Urdu weekly published from 1929 to 1932 by Mulraj Sharma, discussed national issues.[151] *Desh Sewak*, a weekly, and *Dukhi Dunia*, an annual publication in Gurmukhi published by Kabul Singh, a Congress worker, represented the Sikh viewpoint.[152] The government attempted to curb the nationalist literature by banning and confiscating it, besides demanding security from the publishers concerned.[153]

III

Increasing awareness through education and the press and the clash of interests with administration over various issues of local, regional and national importance infused political consciousness among Indians who began to make a distinction between the 'alien' and the 'native' rule. The new professional and business classes of Jullundur as well as some members of the landed aristocracy identified themselves with the

[148] Three books were written by Dev Raj, manager of Kanya Mahavidyalaya, two by Mela Ram Verma of D.A.V. College, two by Keshav Chandra Handa of Handa Printing Press and one each by Panna Lal Jain, Jangu Ram Chopra and the headmaster of Mission High School. Eight of these books were published at Jullundur and two at Lahore: *Supplement to Government Gazette, Punjab and its Dependencies*, Part II, 1926, 14-41.

[149] In 1890, 300 copies of *Safir-i-Hind* were published: ibid., 1890, Statement No. 14.

[150] In 1892, 200 copies of *Bharat Sewak* were in circulation: ibid., 1892, Statement No. 14.

[151] Shadi Ram Joshi, *Ek Samarpit Jivan:Pandit Mulraj Sharma*, 93.

[152] *Akali Te Pardesi*, 31 October 1923; 24 May 1924. See also, *Punjab Legislative Assembly Debates*, 24 October 1939, Question 4739; *The Tribune*, 21 July 1936. In 1924-25, 1000 copies of *Desh Sewak* were in circulation: K.L. Tuteja, *Sikh Politics 1920-1940*, Vikas Publications, Kurukshetra 1984, 222.

In 1934, *Al Jehad*, a daily in Urdu with 500 copies' was also in circulation: *Punjab Legislative Council Debates*, 24 October 1934, Question 3629.

[153] In 1924, a biography of Master Mota Singh of the *Comagata Maru* fame written by Gyani Gurmukh Singh was banned: N. Gerald Barrier, *Banned Controversial Literature and Political Contorl in British India*, 198. In 1924, 300 copies of *Desh Sewak* were confiscated: *Akali Te Pardesi*, 21 May 1924. In 1931 and 1934, security of 5,000 and 500 rupees, respectively was demanded from the publishers of *Desh Sewak* and the security of 1,000 rupees was imposed on the publishing of *Dukhi Dunia* in 1936 and 1937: *The Tribune*, 2 April 1931; 2 July 1936; *Punjab Legislative Council Debates*, 22 February 1934, Question 3080; *Punjab Legislative Assembly Debates*, 24 October 1939.

political movements at all-India level.[154] Their responses however varied not only in accordance with the party affiliation, but also with their particular social background and communal identity.

As early as the 1880s, members of the Arya Samaj at Jullundur expressed concern for the propagation of Swadeshi and the programme of the Congress. In 1883, Dev Raj, an Arya *rais* spoke on 'Nationalism and Arya Samaj' at the local Arya Samaj *mandir* and laid emphasis on the use of Khadi.[155] In 1888, on 24 May, on the birth anniversary of Queen Victoria, a branch of the Indian National Congress was established at Jullundur at the initiative of the two Aryas – Balak Ram Khatri, a *rais* and Munshi Ram Khatri, a pleader.[156] In 1888, the fourth annual session of the Congress held at Allahabad was attended by four pleaders from Jullundur.[157] Munshi Ram addressed the Congress session at Amritsar in 1893.[158] The Congress did not, however, get the support of most of the Muslim inhabitants of the town. In fact, parallel to it, a branch of the 'Aligarh Party' was founded in 1888 at Jullundur by the local pleaders.[159]

The outbreak of World War I in 1914 brought about a change in the people's general attitude towards government. Initially, the people of Jullundur as elsewhere in the Punjab helped the British in the war-effort because they asserted that they were fighting for the right of 'self-determination and equality of nations'.[160] The services of the people were

[154]For a discussion of the nationalist politics in urban areas, see Ravinder Kumar, 'The Role of Urban Society in Nationalist Politics', in the present volume.

A few amongst the pleaders who participated in the national struggle were Bhagat Ram, Devinder Lal Sondhi and Hans Raj Sondhi, Labhu Ram Khatri, Munshi Ram Khatri, Naubat Rai Sehgal, Piara Lal Sondhi, Som Datt Bahri and Sayyid-Ata-ullah-Shah. A few teachers of the town, such as Kabul Singh and Mulraj Sharma, also participated in the struggle for freedom. The businessmen such as Brindaban Sondhi, Daulat Ram Khanna, and Hari Singh too were in the forefront of the freedom struggle.

[155]Satyadev Vidyalankar, *Lala Dev Raj*, 23-24.

[156]The resolution for the foundation of the Congress was moved by Khan Bahadur Fazal Karim Khan, a *rais* and vice-president of the Jullundur municipal committee seconded by Harbhaj Rai, honorary magistrate and president of the Sanatan Dharm Sabha: Shraddhanand Sanyasi, *Kalyan Marg Ka Pathik*, 153-54.

[157]The members who attended the Congress session were Sohan Lal and Madan Gopal Khatris, Sheo Narain and Devi Chand Brahmans: *Fourth Annual Session of the Indian National Congress at Allahabad December 1988*, 369-72.

[158]J.T.F. Jordens, *Swami Shraddhanand: His Life and Causes*, Oxford University Press, Delhi 1981, 25 and 29.

[159]Shraddhanand Sanyasi, *Kalyan Marg Ka Pathik*, 153-54.

[160]H.D. Watson, *War History of the Jullundur District, 1914-1918*, Civil and Military Gazette Press, Lahore 1921, 6-12. See also, *Indian Annual Register, 1914*, 130-31.

acknowledged at the thanksgiving functions held at Jullundur.[161] The Montagu-Chelmsford declaration of 1917, however, turned out contrary to the people's expectations. The Rowlatt Act of 1919 further aroused anti-British feelings.[162] On the call of Gandhi, a peaceful *hartal* was observed at Jullundur against the Rowlatt Act on 6 April 1919. There was a qualitative change in the situation after the brutal massacre of the unsuspecting and unarmed people at the Jallianwala Bagh at Amritsar on 13 April.[163]

After the Jallianwala Bagh tragedy, the government adopted a stern attitude towards the people of Jullundur as in other parts of the province. The local authorities became hostile towards the members of the reception committee of the Punjab Provincial Conference which was still to be held at Jullundur in April 1919. This was evident from the following: the cancellation of the licences of Baijnath and Brindaban for the sale of kerosene oil; discontinuance of the orders for doing printing work for the government to Hari Singh; and confiscation of a *jagir* given to Qazi Mahbub Alam for his service during World War I.[164] But these measures did not discourage the people. In December 1919, the Congress session at Amritsar was attended by 237 delegates from the Jullundur district and seventy-one among them belonged to the town of Jullundur. Most of them were Hindu businessmen and pleaders, besides some government

[161]Thanksgiving *durbars* were held at Jullundur on 28 January 1918 and 19 February 1919 by the lieutenant-govemor of the Punjab and the commissioner of the Jullundur division. Amongst the lawyers, Badri Das Puri and Bhagat Ram Sondhi got the title of *Rai Bahadur* and Pandit Devi Chand that of Member of the British Empire. Amongst the landlords, Dalip Singh was awarded the title of Member of the British Empire and Qazi Mahbub Alam and Nizamudin Arain of *Khan Sahib:* M.S. Leigh, *The Punjab and the War*, Government Printing Press, Lahore 1921, 149. See also, *War History of the Jullundur District 1914-1918*, 6-12.

[162]*The Indian Annual Register 1919*, 123-24.

[163]Bhagat Ram Sondhi, a lawyer and member of the Punjab Legislative Council from Jullundur, had told Michael O'Dwyer, the lieutenant-govemor of the Punjab on 7 April that the *hartal* at Jullundur was peaceful due to the 'soul force' of Mahatma Gandhi. On this Michael O'Dwyer said to Bhagat Ram: 'Rai Sahib, remember, there is another force greater than Gandhi's soul force'. This was an indication of the use of force intended by the government which had its full play at Amritsar in the Jallianwala Bagh: *Report of the Committee Appointed by the Sub-committee of the Indian National Congress*, Lahore 1920, I, 31-34.

[164]*Report of the Commission Appointed by the Punjab Sub-Committee of the Indian National Congress*, I, 31 and 34. See also, V.N. Datta, *New Light on the Punjab Disturbances*, Indian Institute of Advanced Study, Shimla 1975, I, 356.

servants.[165] Shraddhanand's resolution, seconded by Bhagat Ram exhorted the people to participate in the peaceful agitation for the freedom of the country.[166]

On the call of Gandhi, the people of Jullundur participated in the Khilafat and non-cooperation movements against the British.[167] Non-cooperation continued for two years starting from August 1920 to February 1922.[168] The Punjab Provincial Conference, held at Jullundur on 2 April 1920, exhorted the people not to cooperate with the government.[169] Picketing of liquor and foreign cloth shops, boycott of foreign cloth, besides giving up titles formed part of the non-cooperation movement. Bhagat Ram Sondhi gave up the title of 'Rai Sahib' and Dev Raj Sondhi his honorary magistrateship. Kalyan Singh A.S.I. left the police service.[170] On Gandhi's visit to Jullundur on 8 March 1921, the municipal committee presented him with a welcome address thus incurring the displeasure of the government.[171] In 1922, the Prince of Wales visited Jullundur cantonment and a *hartal* was observed in the town as a part of the programme of non-cooperation, though the government

[165] The Hindu delegates who attended the Congress session included twenty-eight businessmen, eighteen pleaders, eleven government servants, three each doctors, artisans and landlords, one each a teacher and a clerk. The Muslims included two Rajput agriculturists and one *rais*: *Report of the Amritsar Session of the Indian National Congress 1919*, 124-37.

[166] S.C. Mittal, *Feeedom Movement in the Punjab (1905-29)* Concept, Delhi 1977, 146-47. See also, S.L. Malhotra, *Gandhi and the Punjab*, Panjab University, Chandigarh 1970, 56.

In 1917, Munshi Ram became a *sanyasi* and renamed himself Shraddhanand. In 1918 he made Delhi his headquarters: Ram Chandra Javed, *Punjab Ka Arya Samaj*, Arya Pratinidhi Sabha, Punjab, Jullundur 1964, 47-48. See also, Ragunath Prasad Pathak, *Amar Hutatama Swami Shraddhanand Ka Jivan Parichay*, Sarvadeshik Press, New Delhi, Sambat 1976, 5.

[167] By non-cooperation with the government, Gandhi aimed at paralysing the institutions of British rule in the country, namely, those of the administration, the judiciary and education: Ravinder Kumar, 'The Role of Urban Society in Nationalist Politics'. See also, *Punjab Mission Report 1921*, 6; *Punjab Administration Report 1920-21*, 13. Besides others, Sayyid Atta-ullah Shah was a Khilafat leader: Ruchi Ram Sahni, *Struggle for Freedom in Sikh Shrines*, Sikh Itihas Research Board, S.G.P.C., Amritsar 1965, 139.

[168] Tara Chand, *History of the Freedom Movement in India*, Publication Division, Ministry of Information and Broadcasting, Delhi 1967, II, 495. See also, S.P. Sen (ed), *Dictionary of National Biography*, Institute of Historical Studies, Calcutta 1974, IV, 187.

[169] Hans Raj Sondhi, a barrister from Jullundur was the chairman of the reception committee: *The Indian Annual Register 1921*, 89-92.

[170] Satyadev Vidyalankar, *Lala Dev Raj*, 58. See also, 'Material on Who's Who of Freedom Fighters Relating to Outstanding Personalities', *File No. I*, Punjab State Archives, Patiala.

[171] *The Collected Works of Mahatma Gandhi*, XIX, 455; *The Tribune*, 9 March 1921; 20 August 1921; 21 September 1921.

denied their connection.[172] The government nevertheless responded to the movements with repression. The Seditious Meetings Act of 1909 was enforced in Jullundur on 25 January 1921 and it remained effective throughout the year.[173] Moreover, among others, Hans Raj Sondhi, a barrister, Karam Singh Kirti, an industrialist, and Labhu Ram Khatri, a pleader, were arrested while picketing at liquor shops.[174] Subsequently, as a part of the constructive programme of the Congress, the Charkha Sangh was set up in Jullundur in 1925 aiming at popularising the use of Khadi.[175] In 1928, Hans Raj Sondhi and Labhu Ram participated in the demonstration against the Simon Commission and the former bore *lathi* blows along with Lajpat Rai.[176]

The people of Jullundur had also been active in the Akali movement.[177] Even the non-Sikhs, like Labhu Ram and Lajjavati, participated in the Guru Ka Bagh *morcha*.[178] Many of the participants suffered imprisonment.[179] The government continued with its repressive policy towards the Akalis. For instance, in October 1923, the government banned the sale of railway tickets for Jullundur to prevent the people from attending an Akali political conference to be held in the town.[180]

The people of Jullundur were even more active in the civil disobedience movement launched by Gandhi in 1930-31 which included the preparation of salt and boycott of foreign cloth and liquor.[181] The national flag was hoisted at Jullundur for the first time on 26 January 1930 at

[172] L.F. Rushbrook Williams, *The History of the Indian Tour of H.R.H. The Prince of Wales, 1921-22, Confidential*, Superintendent Government Printing, India, Calcutta 1922, 181. See also, *The Tribune*, 10 October 1921, 26 August 1922.

[173] *Punjab Government Gazette Notification* No.2373, 22 January 1921; *The Tribune*, 22 April 1921, 26 November 1921.

[174] *The Indian Annual Register 1922*, 71. See also, 'Material on Who's Who of Freedom Fighters'.

[175] *The Tribune*, 17 April 1925. See also, Shadi Ram Joshi, *Pandit Mulraj Sharma*, 32.

[176] 'Material on Who's Who of Freedom Fighters'. See also, S.P. Sen (ed), *Dictionary of National Biography*, II, 382.

[177] An Akali *Jatha* was formed at Jullundur in 1912: *The Tribune*, 30 November 1937.

[178] Guru Ka Bagh near Amritsar was one of the major *morchas* launched for freeing the Gurdwaras from the control of the government-supported *mahants*. For detail see Khushwant Singh, *A History of the Sikhs*, Oxford University Press, Delhi 1977, II, 203-4; *The Tribune*, 22 September 1922; S.P. Sen (ed), *Dictionary of National Biography*, II, 382.

[179] Deva Singh suffered one year's imprisonment, Hari Singh nine months', Jowala Singh seven months', Niranjan Singh, Buta Singh and Piara Singh suffered four months' imprisonment: Fauja Singh (ed), *Who's Who of Punjab Freedom Fighters*, Punjabi University, Patiala 1972, I, 250 and 350. See also, 'Material on Who's Who of Freedom Fighters'.

[180] *Akali Te Pardesi*, 24 October 1923.

[181] Shadi Ram Joshi,'K.Lajjavati', *Sat Prerna*, Jullunudur 1985, 12.

Gandhi Mandap near Kishenpura in the presence of 4,000 persons.[182] Hans Raj Sondhi made salt at Gandhi Mandap on 17 April and the historic scene was witnessed by about 20,000 people.[183] The cloth dealers pledged not to import foreign cloth and the medical practitioners and chemists boycotted medicines made in Britain. Foreign cigarettes and liquor were also boycotted.[184] Bhagat Ram resigned from his membership in the Punjab Legislative Council.[185] The government reacted to the civil disobedience movement with its usual policy of repression.[186] When Gandhi was arrested in 1930, a protest meeting was held at Jullundur on 5 May at Gandhi Mandap. The government arrested two hundred volunteers, six of whom died in police action.[187]

Anti-British feeling got intensified as a result of Ramsay MacDonald's Communal Award of 1932 and the Government of India Act of 1935. The local Congressmen criticized the Communal Award in their meeting on 28 September 1932 at Gandhi Mandap and on 19 October at Qilla Muhalla.[188] *Hartal* was observed at Jullundur on 1 April 1937, the day of the inauguration of the Government of India Act of 1935.[189] The Government again followed a repressive policy against the agitators. On 17 June 1937, Master Kabul Singh, a local teacher and Congress worker, was prohibited from making speeches in the province. [190] The police raided the office of the district Congress committee and searched the house of Mulraj Sharma, another teacher and Congress worker, in his absence.[191]

The outbreak of World War II and India's entry into the war without

[182] *The Tribune*, 28 January 1930.

[183] *The Tribune*,19 April 1930. At Lahore, the salt law was broken on 11 April 1930 and the highest bid to buy a packet of salt was 25 rupees which was given by Hans Raj Sondhi of Jullundur: ibid., 13 April 1930. *The Tribune* gave full-page photographs showing the salt being prepared at Jullundur: ibid., 27 April 1930.

[184] Ibid., 1 May 1930; 26 June 1930.

[185] Ibid., 1 June 1930.

[186] The police raided the houses of Atma Ram, Chiranji Lal Khosla, Des Raj Sud, Hans Raj Sondhi, Hari Singh, Prem Nath Sondhi and Labhu Ram. The house of Goverdhan Lal, a student of the D.A.V. College, Jullundur was also searched: ibid., 18 February 1930; 1 April 1930.

[187] Hans Raj Sondhi, president of the Jullundur district Congress committee, and Hari Singh were given one year's rigorous imprisonment. Even the deputy commissioner of Jullundur condemned the police action: ibid., 7 May 1930; 30 May 1930; 17 June 1930.

[188] *The Tribune*, 30 September 1934; 24 October 1934.

[189] Ibid., 2 April 1937.

[190] Ibid., 18 June 1937

[191] Ibid., 7 October 1937; 20 October 1937.

the concurrence of its leaders gave a fillip to the anti-British feeling.[192] The Congress launched the individual Satyagraha and Quit India movements respectively in 1941 and 1942. District and tahsil Congress committees were changed into Satyagraha committees.[193] Naubat Rai Sehgal resigned his post as *zaildar* and *lambardar* in protest against the pressure of the authorities to collect recruits.[194] Bansi Dhar Bahri, Som Datt Bahri and Dwarka Das resigned from the membership of the Jullundur Municipal Committee.[195] The government came out to suppress the movement. Provincial and district Congress committees were declared unlawful associations.[196] Darbara Singh, Karam Singh Kirti, Labhu Ram, and Mulraj Sharma were arrested.[197] The Akali Sikhs and the Muslim residents of Jullundur, however, by and large stayed away from these Congress-sponsored programmes.

At the end of the war, the three communities came together on the issue of the trial of the prisoners of the Indian National Army.[198] The INA trials elicited considerable response from all sections of the people of Jullundur who felt proud that among the three INA prisoners chosen by the British for exemplary punishment–Dhillon, Sehgal and Shahnawaz – Sehgal belonged to Jullundur.[199] The people demanded the release of the trio and the greeting 'Jai Hind' became popular in Jullundur.[200] The release of the INA prisoners was celebrated with illuminations in the city.[201]

IV

Growing political awareness in the country also aroused interest in the elections. The people got their early training in electoral politics through

[192]Hans Raj Sondhi expressed the feelings of Indians at large that India was declared belligerent without her consent. India had nothing to do with the war: *The Tribune*, 12 December 1939.

[193]*The Tribune*, 7 May 1940.

[194]Ibid., 17 March 1941.

[195]Ibid., 18 April 1941.

[196]*Punjab Government Gazette Notification* No. 10,456, B.D.S.T., 21 August 1942.

[197]*The Tribune*, 11 September 1942; 27 October 1942; 13 January 1943.

[198]For detail on the activities of Subhash Chandra Bose and the Indian National Army, see K.K. Ghosh, *The Indian National Army; Second Front of the Indian Independence*, Meenakshi Prakashan, Meerut 1969.

[199]Prem Nath Sehgal was the son of Achchru Ram Sehgal, an Arya Samajist lawyer at Jullundur: *The Tribune*, 23 November 1945; 24 November 1945; 20 December 1945.

Incidentally, the other two – Dhillon and Shahnavaz – happened to be Sikh and Muslim, respectively.

[200]*The Tribune*, 5 January 1946.

the municipal elections. The first municipal elections were held in 1884. In the 1880s, members were returned unopposed.[202] Even in 1894-95, one candidate appeared for each of the four vacancies occurring in the municipality of Jullundur.[203] But gradually, the contest became keener. From the twenties, elections at Jullundur were fought on party basis, with the contest usually remaining between the Congress and the Muslim League.[204] The local Congress fought elections on the question of Hindu-Muslim unity and the Muslim League for securing more rights for the Muslims.[205]

In the municipal elections of 1920-21, the people of Jullundur voted for the Congress as they had been impressed with its taking up the issue of Khilafat.[206] Again in 1930, the civil disobedience movement left the field open for the Congress in the elections.[207] In the municipal elections of 1933, 50 to 60 per cent of the votes were polled.[208] Interest in .he municipal elections was rising also in the province as a whole.[209] In 1936, in Jullundur, fifty candidates appeared for twenty-two seats in twelve wards. The *Tribune* noted in 1936 that there was stiff competition amongst the candidates for tickets. Cars and tongas were used for taking the voters to the polling stations.[210] In the municipal elections of 1936, however, the Congress was defeated by the Muslim League. This was perhaps due to the undecided stand of the former towards the Communal Award,[211] but it could also have been an early indication of the growing support for the Muslim League among the urban Muslims. In the last municipal elections held in 1939, the All India Congress Committee and the Provincial Congress however took considerable interest and the Congress party won.[212]

[201]Ibid., 7 January 1946; 8 January 1946.

[202]*File No. W-1*, Municipal Committee.

[203]*Review of the Divisional Reports of the Municipal Administration and Accounts for the Year 1894-95*, para 4.

[204]A branch of the Muslim League was founded at Jullundur in 1906 : Lal Bahadar, *Muslim League, Its History, Activities and Achievements*, Agra Book Store, Agra 1954,75.

[205]*The Tribune*, 23 March 1939; 24 March 1939; 28 March 1939.

[206]*Report on the Working of the Municipal Committees in the Punjab 1920-21*, 1.See also *Punjab Administration Report 1921-22*, 13.

[207]*Report on the Working of the Municipal Committees in the Punjab 1930-31*, 3.

[208]*File No.19/18*, Municipal Committee.

[209]FIn the elections of 1925-26, in the sixteen municipal committees in the Punjab, 70 per cent votes were polled: R. L. Khanna, *Municipal Government and Administration in India*, Mohindra Capital Publishers, Chandigarh 1967, 29.

[210]*The Tribune*, 15 March 1936; 25 April 1936.

[211]Ibid., 19 October 1935; *Punjab Administration Report 1934-35*, 2; *Annual Administration Report 1937-38*, 393.

[212]*The Tribune*, 23 March 1939;24 March 1939; 27 April 1939.

The elections for the Punjab Legislative Assembly evoked even greater response from the people, polling more than 60 per cent of the votes. Generally, the Congress candidates from Jullundur won in the general elections as well. In 1923, Bhagat Ram Sondhi, bar-at-law and in 1926 his brother, Hans Raj, also a bar-at-law, won the elections from urban-non-Muhammadan constituency. Hans Raj resigned in 1929, and in his place was elected Pandit Mehar Chand. In the elections of 1936, Seth Sudershan, a trader, won for the Punjab Legislative Council. In 1946, Master Gurbanta Singh, a scheduled caste, won the election on the Congress ticket. In these elections Sant Ram also won on the Unionist party ticket.[213]

For the Central Legislative Assembly also around 60 per cent of the votes were polled. In the ten general and by-elections from 1923 to 1945, the Congress candidates, Hans Raj Sondhi or his brother, alternatively won five times.[214]

V

Like any other city of the Punjab, Jullundur too was swept by communalism.[215] Heightened emphasis on self-awareness segmented on the lines of religion created unhealthy competition amongst the communities in asserting their distinctiveness and superiority.[216] Communalism in Jullundur usually concerned the Muslims and Hindus, the two major communities residing in the town.[217] The number of the Sikhs being small the controversy whether the Sikhs were Hindus did not have its impact in Jullundur.[218]

One major source of communal thinking were denominational educational institutions. Through the teaching of the tenets of their particular

[213]Kirpal C. Yadav, *Elections in the Punjab 1920-47*, 46,54,66,84,94 and 108.

[214]Ibid., 27, 30-31 and 34.

[215]Bipan Chandra defines communalism as a belief that the followers of one religion constituted a community with its own socio-economic and cultural interests distinct from other communities: *Communalism in Modern India*, Vani Educational Books, New Delhi 1984, 1.

[216]Kenneth W. Jones, *Arya Dharm*, 18-20.

[217]The ratio of Muslims and Hindus in the town ranged between 67.11 and 31.79 per cent respectively in 1868 and 65.37 and 25.26 per cent in 1941. The Sikhs were 0.93 per cent in 1868 and 2.60 in 1941: Kanchan Jyoti, *The City of Jullundur*, Table XI.

[218]Bhai Kahn Singh of Nabha wrote a book, *Ham Hindu Nahin* in 1899 in response to the *Sikh Hindu Hain* by Thakar Das written in 1888-89. The former book ran into five editions. Recently, it has been reprinted by the Shiromani Gurdwara Prabandhak Committee, Amritsar 1981: Bhai Kahan Singh's '*Ham Hindu Nahin*: Polemic or a Social Document?', paper read by Joginder Singh at the Indian History Congress, Burdwan 1983 (seen in typescript).

religions while imparting education, these institutions encouraged the students to think in terms of their respective religious identities and not as Punjabis, let alone Indians. Even the municipal committee provided separate schools for Muslims and Hindus, with even Muslim and Hindu servants for students of the respective communities.[219]

The government intensified the growing inter-communal rivalry by its divisive policies. Its intent was to curb the growing political consciousness of the people.[220] The census entries were based on religious identity. Greater attention began to be focused on demographic trends in terms of religious composition.[221] For instance, on the publication of the census report of 1901, *Panchal Pandita* warned the Hindus against conversions to other religions because the percentage increase of the Hindus in the Punjab was less than that of the other communities.[222] This concern was heightened after the demand for Pakistan was made in 1940.[223] The municipal records show that in the early forties all the communities were concerned with the swelling of their numbers through the manipulation of figures.[224]

The introduction of the element of election in the late nineteenth century created an arena for comunal competition. The major communities fought for the control of the new structures.[225] For instance,in the 1890s, in the municipal elections in Rasta Muhalla Ward, Muslim-Hindu tension mounted.[226] The Indian Councils Act of 1909 and the Government of India Act of 1919 introduced communal electorate in the municipal committees and provincial and central legislative councils.[227] Rights became synonymous with numerical strength and majority rule.

[219]*Proceedings Municipal Committee*, 24 January 1924, Resolution 120.

[220]Bipan Chandra, *Communalism in Modern India*, 245.

[221]Kenneth W. Jones. 'Religious Identity and Indian Census', *The Census in British India, New Perspective* (ed N. G. Barrier), Manohar, Delhi 1981, 80-81.

[222]*Panchal Pandita*, July 1901, 21.

[223]In March 1940, the Lahore session of the Muslim League had passed the Pakistan resolution proclaiming the achievement of an independent Muslim state as the immediate Muslim League goal: Satya M. Rai, *Legislative Politics and Freedom Struggle in the Punjab, 1897-1947*, Indian Council of Historical Research, New Delhi 1984, 270.

[224]The Muslims and the non-Muslims complained that the enumerators manipulated population figures in favour of their respective communities: loc cit. See also, *File No. W-I*, Municipal Committee.

[225]Kenneth W. Jones, *Arya Dharm*, 63-64.

[226]*File No.W-I*, Municipal Committee.

[227]N. Gerald Barrier, 'Muslim Politics in the Punjab 1870-1890', *The Panjab Past and Present*, vol. V-I, April 1971, 91. See also, A.C. Kapoor, *Constitutional History of India: 1765-1975*, S. Chand & Co., New Delhi 1976, 178.

In 1919, the Hindus demanded the allocation of seats in the municipal committee on the basis of the voting strength against the Muslim demand to base it on population.[228] In 1921, the Muslim-dominated Unionist ministry came into power in the province.[229] It insisted on the distribution of seats in the municipal committee in proportion to the population of the communities.[230] Consequently, in 1924, allocation of seats in the Jullundur Municipal Committee was done on this basis.[231] This policy benefited the Muslim middle class. The Hindus, who so far had equal or more representation, opposed the system which now made the election of Muslim presidents certain.[232] The Hindus also alleged that bogus claims had been put up to swell the number of Muslim voters.[233]

Community-wise representation in jobs particularly after 1919 also fostered communalism. The government proposed larger employment of the Muslims in the services. In 1919, the Muslims and the Hindus were to get 40 per cent each and the Sikhs 20 per cent of the jobs.[234] In 1938, under the Unionist government the proportion of jobs was increased by 10 per cent in favour of the Muslims at the cost of the Hindus.[235] The Sikhs too felt that they were underrepresented in jobs.[236] Despite the fixed communal proportion, however, more Hindus continued to get jobs because their proportion was higher among the educated.[237] Conse-

[228]*Proceedings Municipal Committee*, 21 June 1919, Resolution 2.

[229]Out of the total of seventy-one elected members in the Council, thirty-five happened to be Muslim, nineteen Sikh and fifteen Hindu: Prem Raman Uprety, *Religion and Politics in the Punjab in the 1920s*, 29.

[230]The Punjab Government asked the municipal committee to allocate its membership on communal basis by its letter No.4767, 3 October 1922: *File No. W-I*, Municipal Committee.

[231]*Proceedings Municipal Committee*, 4 June 1927, Resolution 27.

[232]*Proceedings Municipal Committee*, 14 July 1919, Resolution 3; 9 November 1929, Resolution 221. *File No. W-I*, Municipal Committee. See also, *Punjab Government Gazette Notification No.*252, 4 May 1868; Satya M. Rai, *Legislative Politics and Freedom Struggle in the Punjab, 1897-1947*, 108-9.

[233]The executive officer of the Municipal Committee wrote about it on 4 August 1945: *File No. W-I*, Municipal Committee.

[234]Satya M. Rai, *Legislative Politics and the Freedom Struggle in the Punjab*, 106-7; Prem Raman Uprety, *Religion and Politics in the Punjab in the 1920s*, 39.

[235]*Punjab Government Gazette Notification No.*7929-I- 2643-SG-38/33386, 8 October 1938.

[236]See for example, Satya M. Rai, *Legislative Politics and Freedom Struggle*, 346-47.

[237]For instance, in 1924, only one government school had a Muslim headmaster out of the eleven existing in the Jullundur division. In addition, in 1932, in the deputy commissioner's and divisional commissioner's office at Jullundur, the Muslims had only 17.4 per cent of the posts of superintendents and head clerks and 39.2 per cent of clerks:*Punjab Legislative Council Debates*, 14 November 1924, Question 924: ibid., 11 November 1932, Question 1741.

quently, debates in the Legislative Assembly usually centred around the question of the relative representation of the communities in services.[238] In professions too Hindus far outnumbered the other communities in the town.[239]

During the last two or three decades of colonial rule, the Hindu-Muslim tension manifested itself in various ways. In 1927, for instance, the *Tribune* reported that the Muslims did not allow the Hindus to sell their wares in the fair of Shah Sikander.[240] Some disturbance was caused in 1935 when Ramlila was being staged.[241] Between 1931 and 1938, sixty communal riots were reported from various places in the Punjab which had their fallout in Jullundur too.[242] The situation worsened in the forties.[243] The Muslim population of Jullundur responded enthusiastically to the demand for Pakistan, while the Hindus and Sikhs of the city were vehemently opposed to it.[244] In 1942, Mohammad Ali Jinnah, President of the All India Muslim League, reiterated at Jullundur his demand for Pakistan.[245] Communal riots beginning in the early forties got intensified in 1946-47. The *Tribune* reported the outbreak of communal riots at Jullundur many times during 1946-47.[246] Public meetings were

[238] *Punjab Legislative Council Debates*, 13 January 1922, Question 1211; 9 March 1925, Question 1526; 11 November 1932, Question 1741. See also, Satya M. Rai, *Legislative Politics and Freedom Struggle*, 109.

[239] For instance, in 1946, out of 278 pleaders in the city, the number of the Hindus and Muslims was 152 and seventy-five, respectively, besides forty-six Sikhs: In 1943, out of twenty M.B.B.S. doctors in Jullundur, the Hindus and Muslims were ten and eight, respectively, besides two Sikhs: *A List of Legal Practioners in the Punjab as it Stood on 1st January 1946*, Superintendent Printing, Lahore 1947; *Punjab Government Gazette*, Part III, 1943, 539-40.

[240] *The Tribune*, 13 September 1927.

[241] Ibid., 20 April 1935.

[242] These figures were reported by the government in 1939: *Punjab Legislative Assembly Debates*, 13 March 1939.

[243] In 1946, Some disturbance was caused during the Sodal fair: *The Tribune*, 11 September 1946. In the same year members of the Muslim National Guards, the militant wing of the Muslim League, picketed at the cinema houses owned by the Hindus and dissuaded the people from seeing the movies there: ibid., 16 November 1946.

[244] For a discussion of the opposition of the Sikhs to the demand for Pakistan, see Indu Banga, 'The Crisis of Sikh Politics (1940-1947)', *Sikh History and Religion in the Twentieth Century* (eds Joseph T.O' Connell et al.), Centre for South Asian Studies, University of Toronto, Toronto 1988, 233-55.

[245] In 1942, in a gathering of about 50,000 persons at the Burlton Park, Mohammad Ali Jinnah reiterated, 'We want Pakistan. Demand it with one voice'. We will get Pakistan: *The Tribune*, 15 November 1942.

[246] Ibid., 16 September 1946; 26 February 1947; 7 March 1947; 8 March 1947; 12 March 1947.

often banned and curfew was clamped frequently.[247] But all these seemed half-hearted attempts by the government to establish communal peace. It could not win the confidence of the minority communities, the Hindus and the Sikhs.[248] Mutual suspicion, fear and rioting eventually led to partition and the movement of population across the international border. Consequently, the structure of the population of Jullundur changed significantly, giving it the character of a Hindu-majority city whose Sikh population also increased its proportion from 2.60 per cent in 1941 to 22 per cent in 1971.[249]

[247]Ibid., 8 December 1946; 27 October 1946.

[248]Ibid., 2 September 1946; 25 March 1946.

[249]Trilochan Singh, *Economic Conditions of the Displaced in East Punjab*, No.10, Board of Economic Enquiry, Punjab, I, Ludhiana 1949, 11. See also, *Census of India Punjab*, 1971, Part X-C, 98-99.

THE CHOICE OF A CAPITAL : LUCKNOW UNDER THE BRITISH

KUSUM PANT-JOSHI

Lucknow provides the example of a city which during British rule retained and even furthered its position as an urban centre of importance. Taking the retention and addition of certain urban institutions to be indicators of a city's urban development, this paper attempts to make Lucknow its focus of attention between 1877,when it ceased to be a provincial capital,and 1921,when it was well on the way to becoming for all practical purposes the headquarters of the government of the United Provinces.

Ever since the commencement of British rule in Awadh in 1856,except for a brief interlude during the 1857-58 disturbances, Lucknow received special considerate treatment from the rulers. After annexation, the kingdom of Awadh,of which Lucknow was the capital, was converted into a non-regulation province with a chief commissioner as its head and a judicial commissioner in charge of the Awadh judicial administration. Both these officers had their headquarters in Lucknow which began to serve as the capital of the chief commissionership of Awadh.[1]

[1]Details of administration of judicial arrangements in Awadh (we shall use the Anglicised 'Oudh' only when unavoidable) after annexation are from W.C. Benett, *A Gazetteer of the Province of Oudh*, II, Allahabad 1877, 383; GOI Home Public 'A', August, 1877, 160-61, Minute by the Lieutenant-Governor of the North-Western Provinces (NWP) and Chief Commissioner of Oudh (hereafter abbreviated as the Minute by the Lieutenant Governor), 6 July 1877, National Archives of India (NAI); and J.L. Hill, *Congress and Representative Institutions in the United Provinces*, unpublished Ph. D. Thesis, Duke University, 1966, 8.

After a lapse of about twenty years, an official move which could have affected Lucknow's position adversely was taken in 1877. This was the announcement of the amalgamation of Awadh with the neighbouring North-Western Provinces and of the decision that the seat of the amalgamated areas was to be Allahabad. Frightened at the prospect of Awadh losing its identity by merger with the North-Western Provinces and of Lucknow being ruined by the capital being placed in Allahabad, a vigorous anti-amalgamation agitation was launched.[2] Though it claimed general public support from all over Awadh, the anti-amalgamation movement was centred in Lucknow and was spearheaded by the *talukdars* of Awadh who were above all else afraid that amalgamation would injure their privileged position and high social status.[3]

The fears of the anti-amalgamation agitators were unfounded, for the British in 1877 and in the years that followed gave ample evidence of their concern for Awadh, the *talukdars* and Lucknow. Although the memorial presented to the Secretary of State by the Raja of Mahmudabad on behalf of the agitators urging that amalgamation be annulled, was rejected,[4] the government took care to give assurances that amalgamation would not ruin Lucknow, affect the powers and privileges of the *talukdars* or destroy the identity of Awadh.[5]

These assurances were not a mere subterfuge because the amalgamation of 1877 turned out to be in reality only a nominal one. Awadh remained, as George Couper, its Chief Commissioner and Lieutenant Governor of the North-Western Provinces wrote in 1877, 'to all intents and purposes a separate province, with separate laws and a separate administration of her own, except in a few departments. . . .'[6] Moreover, though Allahabad was declared to be the capital of the amalgamated areas, Lucknow's position remained unaffected. It became the capital of the 'Province of Oudh' as the officials continued to refer to the Awadh

[2]*Selection from Vernacular Newspapers published in the Punjab, NWP, Oudh and Central Provinces* (1877) 131, 135, 428, 471, 607, 646, 712; and GOI Home Public 'A', August 1877, Minute by the Lieutenant Governor, Memorial presented by the Rajah of Mahmudabad Amir Hasan Khan to the Secretary of State (SOS) against the amalgamation of Oudh with the NWP, 3 May 1877, NAI.

[3]GOI Home Public 'A', August 1877, 160-61, Minute by the Lieutenant-Governor.

[4]Ibid., Letter from the Secretary of State for India to the Governor-General of India-in-Council, 31 October 1877.

[5]Ibid., Minute by the Lieutenant-Governor.

[6]Ibid.

area.[7] 'Before the recent amalgamation of Oudh with the North-Western Provinces', wrote settlement officer Benett, 'Lucknow was the residence of the Chief Commissioner and his staff. It still is the headquarters of offices whose authority extends over the province'.[8]

In the post-amalgamation years new offices were added to Lucknow's already impressive civil establishment.[9] In the early twentieth century, Lucknow was also the chief military station of Awadh and served as the headquarters of the government for a part of the year annually.[10]

Official concern for Awadh and for Lucknow was due to the importance the British began to give to the Awadh *talukdars* in the post-1857 period. The *talukdars* were viewed as props to British rule and ample care was taken to avoid official measures which might antagonise them. Since the *talukdars* expressed anxiety for the retention of the separate identity of Awadh, and the special position of Lucknow which they had made their base after1857, the British also tended to fall in line.[11]

The most conspicuous of the supporters of the pro-*talukdar* and hence pro-Awadh and pro-Lucknow official group was Harcourt Butler. In 1904, as secretary to the United Provinces government, he was reportedly the prime mover of an official secret plan which, as the United Provinces government then admitted, had the potential to convert Lucknow into the capital of the province.[12] The scheme proposed was that as a 'final settlement' of the government's intention to introduce much-needed judicial reform in Awadh, the judicial amalgamation of the

[7]In government publications and official correspondence of the post-1877 period, British officers used the term 'Province of Oudh' when referring to the Awadh area and described Lucknow as the 'capital of Oudh' as though despite amalgamation, Awadh still had a separate identity (see, for example, *Lucknow District Gazetteer*, 1901, 200). This anomaly of the separateness of Awadh in spite of its formal amalgamation was pointed out by two members of the Legislative Council in 1921: *Uttar Pradesh Legislative Council Proceedings* (cited hereafter as *UPLCP) 1921;* 3, 454-55 and 461.

[8]W.C. Benett, *Gazetteer of Oudh*, 383.

[9]Loc. cit.; *Lucknow District Gazetteer*, 1901, 110.

[10]*Lucknow District Gazetteer*, 1901, 110.

[11]For post-1857 British relations with Awadh *talukdars*, Veena T. Oldenburg, *The Making of Colonial Lucknow*, Princeton 1984, 182-83 and 259.

[12]The following statement in the press, for example, could have meant no one but Harcourt Butler when it wrote regarding the High Court question when it cropped up in 1906:'... If a regard for propriety did not prevent us from giving out the name of the chief mover we could easily do so. It is enough to say that the person happens to be a highly placed official and it is not difficult to discover his identity': *The Indian People* (Allahabad), 6 May 1906, 2. For other such veiled references to Butler and his associates, ibid., 7 June 1906, 3; extract from *Allahabad Law Journal* in *The Indian People*, 5 July 1900, 4; ibid., 15 July 1906, 1.

North-Western Provinces and Awadh should be immediately carried out, and a single High Court for the two areas should be established in Lucknow.[13]

Judicial amalgamation, though accepted as the solution to Awadh's judicial ills since the 1880s, had presented problems which neither the provincial government nor the Government of India had been able to solve.[14] While the officials concluded that the shift of the High Court from Allahabad to Lucknow would harm the interests of Allahabad and its residents, they were at the same time informed that any decision to bring Awadh under a High Court placed in Allahabad would undoubtedly be opposed in Awadh 'from the highest talukdar to the lowest peasant'.[15] Consequently, judicial amalgamation, though accepted as highly desirable, was kept in abeyance. This position continued for another two decades, when, setting aside all former precedents, the United Provinces government came forward with its 1904 proposal outlined above asking the Government of India to sanction what was then described by Lord Curzon in his characteristic style as 'a revolution that has been consistently vetoed for a period of more than twenty years'.[16]

Unfortunately for Butler and his supporters, the Government of India unanimously rejected the 1904 proposal. Recording his disapproval in an official note and criticising the bias that had inspired the scheme, Lord Curzon expressed doubts whether 'it would be to the good of the whole Province that the influence either of the Oudh talukdars as a body of landholders, or of the city population of Lucknow, as an urban centre, should become greater with the local government than they already are'. 'The individual of Oudh', he added, 'has a value and a charm. But I do not think it should be allowed to dominate the interests of the remainder of

[13]GOI Home Judicial 'A' February 1905, 177-80, Confidential letter from S.H. Butler, Secretary to the Government of the United Provinces (GUP) to the Secretary, Government of India (GOI) Nainital, 1 August 1904.

[14]For details of correspondence on the question of judicial reorganisation of Awadh up to 1920 see GOI Home Judl. 'A' Sept., 313-33; Home Judl. 'A' Feb. 1905, 177-80, and GOI Home Judl. 'A' September 1920, 215-17. For a short resume of the question up to 1915 see *Annual Report of the Committee of the Upper India Chamber of Commerce*, 1915 Allahabad 1916, 67-77.

[15]These were the words used by Justice Syed Mahmud who was one of the persons whose views the government had sought and to whose opinion the officials seem to have given much credence. For Justice Syed Mahmud's opinion see GOI Home Judl. 'A' September 1887, 303-14, Note by Justice Syed Mahmud Officiating Puisne Judge NWP High Court, dated Allahabad, 20 April 1886.

[16]GOI Home Judl. 'A' February 1905, 177-80, Official Note of Lord Curzon, 22 December 1904.

the province, or provinces under the Lieutenant-Governor'.[17]

Though the Government of India foiled their 1904 scheme, the government of the United Provinces with *talukdar* support was able in 1905 to acquire a medical college for Lucknow, an important educational institution and the first of its kind in the entire province. The idea of establishing a medical college had been first discussed in 1870 and again in 1902. On both occasions, the provincial government had expressed its opinion to the Government of India, that Allahabad was 'the best centre for the College'.[18] Contrary to this view, the United Provinces government in 1905 suddenly favoured a scheme to set up the provincial medical college in Lucknow. Even at the time, the Secretary to the Government of India had said that in supporting the claims of Lucknow for the medical college, 'it may be though that the United Provinces government may have been influenced by the desire to strengthen the case for an ultimate transfer of the headquarters of the Government to that place'.[19] Even had this charge been baseless, the liberal donations already made by the *talukdars* and their promises of further subscriptions[20] provided sufficient ground to the provincial government to build a strong case in favour of Lucknow. The positive attitude of the *talukdars* had thus enabled the Lieutenant-Governor to convince the Government of India that the Awadh *talukdars* were 'the only class of the community with the combination of means and public spirit requisite to finance a large scheme of this kind, that it is better to have a medical college at Lucknow than to have none at all for... to ask the talukdars to subscribe to a college at Allahabad would be of course out of question'.[21]

Hopeful that the *talukdars* would fulfil their promises and that the provincial government was in 'a position to exercise considerable pressure on them' to do so,[22] the Government of India finally gave its approval to the medical college scheme.

As the National Movement gathered momentum in the United Provinces in the second and third decades of the twentieth century and

[17]Ibid.

[18]GOI Home Medical 'A' December 1905, 24-28, Note of J.C. Fergusson, Under Secretary to the GOI, dated 22 November 1905 regarding letter of S.H. Butler, Secretary, GUP to Secretary to GOI, Home Dept., 17 November 1905.

[19]Ibid., Note of H.H. Risley, Secretary to GOI, 25 November 1905.

[20]For *talukdar* support to the scheme see ibid., Proceedings of a public meeting held at Baradari, Kaiserbagh, Lucknow on 7 November 1905.

[21]Note of H.H. Risley, 25 November 1905.

[22]Ibid.

Allahabad began to show signs of vigorous political life,[23] the pro-Awadh inclinations of the United Provinces government became more pronounced. In many ways, Lucknow had a far more congenial atmosphere for serving as a centre for an imperial power, then on its last legs, than Allahabad. With its modern institutions such as a well-established university, the High Court, civil secretariat and its newly emerging residential localities for lawyers, teachers and government employees,[24] Allahabad was clearly a city dominated by the new middle class. It was, moreover, the headquarters of the United Provinces Congress organisation and had a number of nationalist newspaper presses. In the period between 1922 and 1930, for instance, Allahabad was producing five important nationalist periodicals, which was the highest number for any city in the province, and was far ahead of Lucknow which brought out only one, that is, the *Indian Daily Telegraph*.[25] In sharp contrast to Allahabad, Lucknow was the former *nawabi* capital and had after 1858 become the centre of the feudal landlords or *talukdars* of Awadh. Here it was members of this group, whom the British regarded as a landed aristocracy and as the natural leaders of the people, who enjoyed social precedence over all others. Though not completely devoid of national political activity,[26] Lucknow, unlike Allahabad, was a city where the British had the advantage of having a group whose members with rare exceptions, were ready to lend support to them in return for governmental protection of their conservative landed interests. Ensconced in their palatial city residences, the Awadh *talukdars* by their ostentatious display of wealth, extravagant lifestyle and lavish hospitality and entertainment enlivened the atmosphere of Lucknow making it a far more attractive place in the eyes of an imperial power than Allahabad with its politically conscious middle-class gentry and its nationalist periodicals.

The contrast presented by the ethos of the two cities did not remain

[23]For the political scene of Allahabad in this period see C.A. Bayly, *The Local Roots of Indian Politics: Allahabad, 1880-1920*, Clarendon Press, Oxford 1975, 245-70.

[24]For some details of the city's development see Ujagir Singh, *A Study in Urban Geography*, Varanasi 1966, 44; *The Leader* (Allahabad), 10 September 1921, 8 and GOI Home Public 1921, File No. 131, serial Nos. 1-5; Letter to GUP No. 131-F of 30 July 1921.

[25]Figures calculated from 'Statement of Important Nationalist Periodicals in U.P., 1922-1930' in G. Pandey, *The Congress in Uttar Pradesh, 1926-1934*, Oxford 1978, 78 and 'Mobilization in a Mass Movement: Congress "Propaganda" in the United Provinces 1930-34', *Modern Asian Studies*, 9, No. 2 (1975), 208.

[26]In Lucknow, national political activity was muted and checked by the presence there of the *talukdars* of Awadh who as a group were generally pro-British and right from the days of the early Congress remained almost consistently hostile to Nationalism.

unnoticed by the people of those times.[27] In 1921, the '*talukdar*ophile' Harcourt Butler, for instance, called Allahabad the 'intellectual capital' and Lucknow the 'social capital' of the province.[28] At about the same time, a contemporary newspaper referred sarcastically on the one hand to the repelling impact on the British psyche of 'the pestilential influences in Allahabad of agitators and demagogues for whom despots have a holy horror', and on the other to the alluring charm for the rulers of 'the aristocratic and autocratic aroma and stifling and enervating atmosphere of talukdar-ridden Lucknow'.[29]

An additional factor which operated in favour of Lucknow was a change in the attitude of the Government of India towards matters concerning provincial governments in general. By the end of the first decade of the twentieth century, the controlling authority of the Government of India over the provinces was replaced by the principle of greater devolution of power to provincial governments in managing their affairs.[30] As a consequence, the United Provinces government, particularly from the time of the pro-Awadh Harcourt Butler[31] who became Lieutenant-Governor in 1918, took a number of measures which further advanced Lucknow's position.[32] Of these the one which produced the most profound impact on the city's urban growth was undoubtedly the plan to

[27]For some such view see *UPLCP*, 1921, Vol. 3, 458, 475 and 489; *UPLCP*, 1924, 197 and K.P. Kaul's Urdu article 'Lucknow ka ek Lateefa' in *Adbi aur Qaumi Tazkire*, Aligarh 1951, 119-30.

[28]From the speech of Butler in a public meeting held at Lucknow on 26 July 1918.

[29]*The Leader* (Allahabad), 20 October 1921, 3.

[30]In 1904, the Government of India which then exercised centralised control over the provinces, checked the pro-Talukdar inclinations of the government of the United Provinces by rejecting its scheme of shifting the High Court and the capital of the province to Lucknow from Allahabad. Among the reasons for its doing so was the fact that the provincial government had failed to dispel the old fear of the Government of India that 'Oudh retains far more of its native traditions than the rest of the United Provinces and that there is therefore a risk of political disturbances among its turbulent population': see GOI Home Judicial A, February 1905, Nos. 177-80, Confidential Letter from S.H. Butler, 1 August 1904. By the 1920s and 1930s, however, the move towards greater provincial autonomy had been initiated and the Government of India appears to have shifted to the viewpoint that the pro-*talukdar* government of the United Provinces should be given a free hand to deal with their problems in their own fashion so long as they were sure of being able to contain political discontent themselves: see GOI Home Public, 1933, File No. 231/233.

[31]For comments on Butler and 'Oudh Policy' in the early twentieth century, see T.R. Metcalf, *Land, Landlords, and the British Raj*, Oxford 1979, 197-99.

[32]Among these measures were the establishment of the Lucknow University in 1921, described by Butler as one of his 'early dreams', the formation of a Town Planning Committee under Sir Ludovic Porter which prepared a detailed report with proposals for the development of Lucknow for the next fifty years. Many of these were implemented with the help of the Lucknow Improvement Trust set up in 1919.

construct the new Council Chamber building in Lucknow.

Looking upon the Legislative Council as a necessary adjunct of the executive government and the hub around which official activity of the highest importance takes place, the people of Allahabad expressed fears that a Lucknow with the Legislative Council Chamber building lodged in it, would eventually draw all government offices to itself and usurp the position of Allahabad as the capital of the province.[33] They founded a Capital Retention Committee and launched a strong protest movement.[34] Despite these efforts, and despite determined resistance from the opposition benches, the proposal for a Council Chamber in Lucknow was brought before the Legislative Council in August 1921 and carried with the help of official votes and those of the Lucknow-based Council members.[35]

The construction of the building of the Legislative Council at Lucknow accelerated its growth as an urban centre. As predicted by some people of Allahabad, the location of the Council Chamber was followed by a gradual but steady shift of government offices from Allahabad to Lucknow in the avowed interests of efficiency and economy. Despite loud protests from the people of Allahabad,[36] this process of the aggrandisement of Lucknow at the expense of Allahabad continued in the twenties and thirties. The growing importance of Lucknow also prompted the Pioneer Press, an old and important private institution of Allahabad, and also called its 'Big Gun', to move to Lucknow.[37]

Thus, by the thirties, Allahabad, forsaken and sacrificed at the altar of British imperialist aims and Indian conservative landed interests,

[33]For views of the opponents of the proposal for a Council Chamber in Lucknow see GOI Home Public File No. 131, serial 1-5, letter of Tej Bahadur Sapru to GUP dated 30 July 1921, and *UPLCP*, 1921, Vol. 3, 454-55 and 461.

[34]*The Leader* (Allahabad), 22 July 1921, 5 and 9.

[35]For discussion on this issue in the Legislative Council see *UPLCP*, 1921, Vol. 3, 446-96. It had been openly alleged by some leading public men and supporters of Allahabad's claims for the Council Chamber such as Tej Bahadur Sapru, Hriday Nath Kunzru and Rai Sita Ram Sahib that the government whip had been used to influence voting in the Legislative Council in favour of a Council Chamber for Lucknow.

[36]For list of offices transferred in the post-1921 years see GOI Home Public, 1933, File 231/233, Memorial of residents of the Province of Agra to His Excellency the Viceroy and Governor General of India-in-Council, dated 9 June 1933.

[37]Santosh Mahajan Singh, 'The Pioneer Comes to Stay', in *The Pioneer Centenary Souvenir*, Lucknow, 21.

became, as a contemporary described it, a 'ghost town'.[38] On the other hand, Lucknow, backed by the Awadh *talukdars* and the pro-*talukdar* and hence pro-Awadh and pro-Lucknow inclinations of some British officials, acquired for itself the position of the *de facto* capital of the province and its foremost urban centre.

[38]Desmond Young, 'A Former Editor looks back', ibid., 17.

OF RAJAS AND PRAJAS: LEADERSHIP IN A COLONIAL TOWN

INDRANI GANGULY

This paper deals with patterns of leadership in Burdwan, a small town in Bengal, from the mid-nineteenth till the mid-twentieth century. In considering this question I have restricted myself to what might be called the elite groups. The neglect of what many contemporary historians now call the subaltern groups stems not from an unwillingness to recognise the capacity of these groups to produce their own leaders but simply from expediency: of looking where the light is. At this stage of my research I do not have enough data to be able to present a detailed and coherent picture of the non-elite sectors of the urban population.

Sociologists have tended to characterise the colonial period in India as one in which were created new structures of opportunity which weakened traditional barriers to social mobility and allowed men of relatively humble origin to acquire wealth and influence. There has also been a tendency to assume that the rise of one group or class necessarily leads to the demise of another. This assumption is most clearly evident in the body of studies dealing with what have come to be called the 'middle classes'. The assumption about the middle classes can be thus summarised: With the introduction of western education in the early nineteenth century and the growth of new professional and commercial activities, there was gradually created a new class which in occupation, lifestyle and intellectual and cultural orientation became westernised. By the end of the nineteenth century this class had come to constitute a new elite which took upon itself the task of providing social and political leadership for the indigenous population.

Many valuable insights have been provided by these studies. They have, however, failed to take adequate account of the continuity and importance of the pre-British forms of leadership, such as the rentier aristocracy. The latter is generally portrayed as a parasitic, predominantly loyalist class which managed to function as leaders of the pre-colonial style till about the middle of the nineteenth century. Relations between this group and the burgeoning middle classes were never easy and they became increasingly strained as the prestige and influence of the former was whittled down by the latter. By the early twentieth century this rentier aristocracy had been almost entirely eclipsed as leaders of indigenous society.

One of the reasons for this bias could be that most of the studies were conducted in the larger urban centres, the nerve centres of colonial rule, where most economic growth occurred, allowing for the growth of a large enough middle class with sufficient resources to operate independently of the landed aristocracy to establish institutions for expressing opinions and marshalling support through the press and voluntary organisations and to utilise control over municipal resources to buttress wider political networks. Although not much work has been done on the smaller urban centres, the few studies that exist show that the landed aristocracy continued to wield much local influence until after independence, when the estates which were the basis of their power were broken up.[1]

The case of Burdwan, which functioned as the headquarters of a wealthy and powerful *zamindari* family both in pre-colonial and colonial times, serves to illustrate these general observations. In this paper we examine how, while Burdwan participated in the general economic and political processes that led to the growth of those professional and commercial groups from whose ranks the new elite were drawn, it witnessed the continued importance of the *zamindars* with whom it had been for long associated.

The elite of Burdwan were identified through tapping a variety of sources. These included lists of those entitled to attend official *durbars* and other gatherings;[2] lists of honorary magistrates and the memoranda on individuals to be consulted in the event of the outbreak of 'communal

[1]Lauren A. Corwen, *Urban Life in a Rural Town: The Role of Provincial Elites in Bengali Society*, Ph.D. Thesis, University of Michigan, 1974.

[2]These gatherings were held in the West Bengal State Archives, H.P. Confidential Section.

rioting',[3] sundry accounts of those involved with the local press, voluntary organisations, the municipality and political parties.

I

Burdwan is the name of a town, a sub-district and a district.[4] The name *Bardhamana* in the vernacular is a corruption of the Sanskrit *Vardhamana* and implies 'the increasing' or 'the prosperous'. The town which lies on both banks of the Banka river, is located about seventy miles north-east of Calcutta. The immediate hinterland of the town is a wide alluvial plain that has been known for centuries for its fertility, and is enclosed by the rivers Ajay, Bhagirathi and Damodar on the north, east and south respectively. In the west it tapers into a strip of rocky, undulating land that forms the present subdivision of Asansol.

The origins of Burdwan remain unknown. Attempts have been made to identify it with the capitals of various Hindu kingdoms but no conclusive proof to this effect has been presented. Rather more reliable are the brief accounts of it given in works by historians of the medieval period. Burdwan under the pre-colonial rulers, however, never evolved into as important a political-administrative centre as Dacca or Murshidabad. The *nawabs* and *subadars* of Bengal have left only a few signs of their association with the town. Most of the landmarks of Burdwan, its palaces, tanks and recreation grounds, have been the creation of various members of the Burdwan Raj who were intimately associated with the town for nearly three centuries.

The Burdwan Raj, which constituted one of the 'little kingdoms' described by Bernard Cohn,[5] was a deliberate creation of Mughal official policy, which promoted its growth as a means of bringing the area under central control. According to tradition, the original founder of the house was one Sangam Rai, a Kapur Khatri from Kotli in Lahore, who, on his way back from a pilgrimage to Puri, was attracted to Baikunthapur, a village near Burdwan town, and settled down there devoting himself to commerce and money-lending. The family gained a foothold in the town during the time of his grandson Abu Rai who was appointed *chaudhari*

[3]*Bengal General Proceedings*: Misc. Br., 5-R, Progs. 1-6, December 1911, *Miscellaneous Annual Report of the Burdwan Division for the year 1910-11*; also ibid., 5-R, Proceedings, 1-4 November 1912, *Miscellaneous Report for the Burdwan Division for the year 1911-12*.

[4]Henceforth, unless otherwise indicated in the context, Burdwan refers to the town.

[5]Bernard S. Cohn, 'The Initial British Impact on India: A Case Study of the Benaras Region', *Journal of Asian Studies*, XIX, No. 4 (August 1960), 422-24.

and *kotwal* of Rekabi Bazar in Burdwan in 1657. The family prospered. Being an upcountry immigrant Khatri with no local military base, it was deemed worthy of trust by the *nizamat* which used it to destroy refractory principalities. By the end of Kirtichand's rule (1702-40), the Burdwan Raj had come to possess the premier *zamindari* in Bengal, paying the highest revenue among all Bengal *zamindars*. During this process successive heads of the house of Burdwan received increasingly grandiose titles. Krishnaram Rai was given the title of *zamindar* and *chaudhari* of Burdwan by Emperor Aurangzeb.[6] By Tej Chand's time (1771-1832) the head of the house was entitled to be addressed as *maharaj adhiraj*,[7] a title the family retained even under the British.[8]

Apart from some highly eulogistic passages by the eighteenth-century poet Bharatchandra, we have no extended descriptions of the physical layout of pre-colonial Burdwan. It was undoubtedly a highly prosperous urban centre. The various sources speak of the many commodities offered for sale in its markets and of the merchants who came from as far upcountry as Delhi and Agra to trade in these commodities. Under the patronage of the Maharajas, Burdwan also evolved as a minor centre of culture and learning.

[6]*Farman* given to Krishnaram by Emperor Aurangzeb dated 24th Rabi-ul-awwal Akhar in the thirty-eighth year of the reign, 1104 Hijri, confirming him as *zamindar* and *chaudhari* of *pargana* Burdwan etc. Original (courtesy P.C. Mahtab).

[7]*Farman* to Tej Chand granting the rank of Panch Hazari Zat with 3000 troopers and the title of *maharaj adhiraj* and a *jhalardar palki* and mare and *nagara* by Emperor Shah Alam dated 10th Shawwal, 1184. Original (courtesy P.C. Mahtab).

[8]Letter from Lord William Bentinck to Maharani Kanwal Kumari of Burdwan conferring the title of *maharaj adhiraj* on her adopted son Mahtab Chand Bahadur. Original (courtesy P.C. Mahtab). The genealogical tree of the Burdwan Raj is given below:

Sangam Rai
Banku Bihari
1. Abu Rai
2. Babu Rai
3. Ghanashyam Rai
4. Krishnaram Rai (1651-96)
5. Jagatram Rai (1692-1702)
6. Kirti Chandra (1702-40)
7. Chitra Sen Rai (1740-44)
Mitra Sen
8. Tilak Chandra (1744-71)
9. Tej Chandra (1771-1832)
10. Mahatab Chand (1832-81)
11. Aftab Chand (1881-85) (Adopted)
12 Bijoy Chand (1885-1940)
13. Uday Chand (1940-)

Source: Original (courtesy P.C. Mahtab).

In 1760 Burdwan district was ceded to the East India Company. Since Burdwan was easily accessible from the Presidency, the Council did not immediately send European officers to reside there. Their hope was that they would be able to leave nearly the whole of the administration in the Maharaja's hands. The latter however proved unwilling to cooperate. There were several armed skirmishes between the two parties in which the Maharaja was defeated. The English decided to administer the district directly.

A substantial curtailment of thc Burdwan ruler's power and authority ensued with the establishment of the British collectorate in his headquarters. In 1767 the size of his household troops was reduced. On the eve of the decennial settlement his household corps was totally abolished and only a part of the former military establishment remained under the *zamindar*.[9] Even this force was only nominally under the Maharaja; it was the collector who actually deployed it for the purpose of revenue collection and peace-keeping. With the establishment of a regular police force in Burdwan, the Burdwan Raj lost its police functions as well.[10]

With the enactment of the Permanent Settlement in 1793, the Maharaja was also faced with the possibility of having his estate broken up. Unlike many other *zamindari* families, the Burdwan Raj survived, largely because it was fortunate to have a series of extremely clever administrators who fought off the pressure of British land revenue policy by inventing a variety of ingenious techniques. The most successful of these was the letting out of portions of the *zamindari* in perpetual leases or *patnis*. The measures devised by the Raj were so successful that in the twentieth century the estate, which extended over several districts in Bengal, was found to be not only intact but paying much of the revenue in the district.[11]

The Burdwan Raj also consolidated its position by an adroit shift in its political attitudes. By the mid-nineteenth century we find the initial hostile reaction to the British replaced by active cooperation. At the time of the Santal rebellion in 1855, Maharaja Mahtab Chand aided the military authorities by forwarding and supplying stores and means of

[9] *Bengal Revenue Proceedings*, 3 April 1787, No. 4, to BR from Governor-General-in Council, 30 March 1787.

[10] *Bengal Revenue Proceedings*, 8 June 1787, No. 25 to BR from Collector of Burdwan, 1 June 1787.

[11] L.A.L. Hill and Phanindra Kumar Banerjee, *Final Report on the Survey and Settlement Operations in the District of Burdwan 1927-1934*, Bengal Secretariat Book Depot, Calcutta 1940, 20.

transport.[12] During the Mutiny in 1857, he did everything in his power to strengthen the hands of the government. The British reciprocated by appointing the Maharaja an additional member of the Viceregal Legislative Council and by granting honours and privileges to his successors.[13]

II

Colonial rule led to the decline of many indigenous urban centres either because their political influence was usurped by the new towns or because their economic base was destroyed by the inroads of the colonial economy. Burdwan however survived the initial impact and continued to prosper. The evolution of Calcutta as the political centre of the region had little negative impact on Burdwan, for its political influence had in any case been localised. Furthermore, the British decided to develop it as the district headquarters. The district of Burdwan continued to be one of the most productive parts of Bengal, 'yielding fine and plentiful crops of rice, sugar, potatoes, indigo, oilseed, tobacco... and some others of less importance'.[14] Burdwan town served as an important distribution centre for these commodities as well as 'coarse silks, hides, horns, lac and timber'.[15]

The changes which came in the subsequent period came from most unexpected sources. The lack of adequate communications had been a nagging problem in Burdwan for some time. It would seem that this problem had been partly resolved by the opening of the railway line from Hooghly to Raniganj through Burdwan in 1855.

The railways however brought not additional prosperity but the dreaded 'Burdwan fever', a particularly malignant form of malaria. The natural drainage system of western Bengal had for some time been undergoing serious disorganisation with the degradation of many rivers into stagnant pools. The railroad, which was built with an inadequate number of culverts, obstructed even the passage of monsoon waters. On one side of the railway the embankment was made especially strong to avoid the least possible breach of the railway even by abnormal floods. Several other parallel embankments were created such as the high roads and the Eden Canal. All these effectively shut out the flood waters of the various rivers and led to the proliferation of stagnant pools which were

[12] *Burdwan District Gazetteer*, 38-39.
[13] Home Political: Pol. Br. T-1, Progs., B1-2, August 1888.
[14] *Imperial Gazetteer*, Clarendon Press, Oxford 1907-8, 172.
[15] Loc. cit.

ideal breeding grounds for the anopheles mosquito, the carrier of malaria.

The immediate effect on Burdwan was devastating. In 1869 the population of Burdwan was estimated at 46,000. Three years later it was found to have fallen to 32,687, a decrease of over 30 per cent.[16]

There were also serious long-term effects. Malaria lent its weight to a host of other factors that led to the decline of the agricultural sector of Burdwan district.[17] There was little effort made by the colonial authorities to check this state of affairs. Eastern Burdwan was not a commercially important area for the British. Their major source of income from this area was land revenue and this issue had been settled on a permanent basis in 1793. There was consequently little economic development in the area which would help Burdwan town recover from the ravages of the notorious fever. Although the worst of its effects had been overcome by the end of the nineteenth century, population growth was extremely slow, as there was little to encourage large-scale immigration into the town.

The functional importance of Burdwan thus derived very largely from its being the district headquarters and the headquarters of the Burdwan Raj and to a much lesser extent to its being a commercial and redistributive centre for the eastern part of the district. Since urban social structure is closely linked up with urban functions, it is not surprising that, apart from the Burdwan Raj, the indigenous elite consisted of three main groups: the old gentry, the professionals and the commercial groups.

III

Most members of this group were Punjabi Khatris who had emigrated to Burdwan from a number of places in north India such as Lahore, Sarhind and Awadh. Like the Raj family, the other Khatris of Burdwan had abandoned their traditional calling and maintained themselves on income derived from estates received from the ruling family.

Many other old and well-known families, for whom details are available, seem to have come to the town attracted by prospects of employment in the Raj estate and gradually built up their own estates by both gift and purchase.

All of these families had two things in common: they were of non-Bengali Hindu origin and their position dated back to pre-colonial times.

[16] W.W. Hunter, *A Statistical Account of Bengal:IV*, D.K. Publishing House, 1973 (reprint), 55.

[17] Rajat Ray, 'The Crisis of Bengal Agriculture, 1870-1972', *Indian Economic and Social History Review*, 10, No.3 (1973), 244-79.

The educated professionals, however, were a feature of colonial period. In the late nineteenth century the district townships were developing into administrative and educational centres as a more unified system of administration, law courts and English schools came to be established throughout the Presidency. Consequently, towns outside Calcutta began to attract small nuclei of educated and professional men. As the *bhadralok's* income from rents grew smaller and their holdings shrank through subdivision, more of them were moving to the towns for education and employment.

Burdwan did not fail to participate in this process. As with many other towns of Bengal the most prominent of the modern professional groups were the lawyers. The establishment of medical and educational institutions led to the growth of the professional groups attached to these.

In many urban centres, the most important and affluent group of people after the nobility were the big bankers and merchants. Even under the British, there are instances of their continuing to occupy a central role in the local economy; their influence was often reinforced by their relationship with government and the British residents of the civil lines.[18] In Allahabad, for example, the big commercial families also came to occupy an important position in local society and politics.[19]

In Burdwan there were no large banking houses like that of Jagat Seth, nor do we hear of any individual merchants rising to the prominence of, for example, Virji Vohra of Surat. There was little development in the town to draw long-distance migrants and so, even on the commercial stage it was the Bengali rather than the ubiquitous Marwari who played the lead role. Most of the commercial families of Burdwan for whom we have any details had been settled for generations in the western suburb of Kanchannagar, shifting to the centre of the town around the middle of the nineteenth century.

At the apex of indigenous society in Burdwan was the Raj family. Although only a *zamindar*, the head of the family had the privilege of being addressed as *maharajadhiraj bahadur*. They adopted many of the insignia of royalty, such as a distinctive coat of arms, and conducted large and lavish *durbars*.[20]

The Raj family was also the most important patron of civil institutions in Burdwan. A large proportion of the Raj's income was devoted to the

[18] See Kenneth L. Gillion, *Ahmedabad*, Australian National University Press, Canberra 1969.

[19] C.A. Bayly, *The Local Roots of Indian Politics*, Clarendon Press, Oxford 1975, 72.

[20] E.A. Waley Cohen, *A Young Victorian in London*, London 1857.

support of Hindu temples and to the performance of Hindu rites and festivals.[21] Their patronage was not however guided by narrow sectarian barriers; although devout Hindus, they managed a Muslim shrine in Burdwan.[22] They had also encouraged the Brahmo Samaj to establish a branch in Burdwan.[23]

The Raj family also supported many fairs. These fairs were important from several points of view. They were the 'meeting grounds of many religions and many cultures, crafts and motifs from far and near, of ideas and . . . of trends of the future and vanishing practices of the past'.[24]

The Maharajas had been traditionally looked to for help and leadership during natural calamities. The river Damodar is given to flash flooding. One of the duties of the *zamindars* under the Mughal administration had been the protection of the embankments. They continued to hold this responsibility until 1855 when the British government decided to take over this role, each landlord being debited with a portion of the cost.

The Maharajas made no effort to introduce any economic innovations in the town. They did however support several educational institutions. The estate maintained both a modern Anglo-vernacular school and a Sanskrit *chatuspathi*, a Hindi *pathsala* and a *maktab*.[25] There were also several scholarships awarded, not only to students in the institutions maintained by the family, but to others as well.[26]

Several of the recreational facilities and activities in Burdwan were also dependent on the support of the Maharajas. The zoological gardens attached to the Rajbari were one of the principal places of interest in Burdwan.[27] Various members of the family took a keen interest in diverse cultural, intellectual and sporting activities in the town.[28]

[21]*The Bengalee*, 30 January 1904, 5; also, 3 March 1904, 4.

[22] George Herbert Risley Papers, MSS, EUR E295/Nos. 899, File 32, Paper No. 29, A Short Note on certain points regarding the History and Character of Mohammedans of Burdwan called for by the Superintendent of Census, Bengal.

[23] Benoy Ghosh (ed), *Samayikpatra Bulara Samajcitra*, Bengal Publishers, Calcutta 1903, 507.

[24] Ashok Mitra, *Fairs and Festivals in West Bengal*, Government of West Bengal Development Department 1953, 2.

[25] *Report on the Administration on Ward, Attached and Trust Estates in the Presidency of Bengal*, 1938.

[26] *Bengal District Gazetteer, Burdwan*, 181.

[27] Ibid., 101.

[28] *Proceedings of the Eighth Bengali Literary Conference*, 1320 B.S. 1-2; *the Bengalee*, 3 September 1914, 2.

The financial resources of the Raj family thus enabled it to be involved in many aspects of the social life of Burdwan and to create the illusion of a little kingdom as of old, where, as a local resident was moved to remark, it seemed that it was the Raja who was everyone's 'mother and father'.[29] The Maharajas themselves succumbed to this illusion from time to time. Bijoy Chand caused a great deal of amusement in 1905 by declaring that his relations with the British government were still friendly,[30] a remark that only a full sovereign can make in relation to foreign powers.

Other men also tried in their own way to contribute to the development of social institutions in the town. Thus the Burdwan Town Hall and the cremation grounds were funded by the Nandeys, a wealthy landed family. Wealthy merchants supported the construction of temples;[31] yet others ran private charitable homes. None of these however operated on a scale to rival that of the Maharajas.

A noticeable and oft-remarked-upon feature of late nineteenth-century Bengali society was the attempt by men to acquire social power and prestige through 'modern' institutions such as voluntary associations and the press. Among the voluntary associations established in Burdwan, the Burdwan Muhammadan Association, the Ugra Kshatriya Samaj, the Lawyers' Association and the Merchants' Association deserve mention. These associations did not however function on a very regular and organised basis.

From the data available there seems to have been little effort to build up a stable press. Most of the local newspapers that sprang up from time to time were sponsored by various men involved in nationalist activities and these were understandably short-lived phenomena.[32]

IV

It is often contended that of all the resources that in one way or another penetrated urban communities in colonial India, the composite whose elements constituted 'administrative reform' seemed to have the greatest effect in altering the parameters of local politics. The municipal system introduced certain new elements in Burdwan as in other towns. It differed from the Mughal system in that instead of vesting all power in the *kotwal*,

[29] Phakirchandra Ray, *Shadhinata Aandoloner Patabhumikay*, Writers' Forum, Calcutta 1978, 74.

[30] *The Englishman*, 9 March 1918, 3.

[31] Interview, A.N. Mukherjee.

[32] Dasarathi Ta, 'Shangbadiktay Bardhamaner Abadaan', *Lokbharati*, III: 1, 1383 (B.S.), 1-2.

it made provisions for including the inhabitants as participants, first by nomination and later by election. It would seem then that valuable political resources of money and status were thus made available to local men.

In many towns which were characterised by the overwhelming presence of a local magnate, the latter himself or members of his family joined the municipal board in an effort to gain additional local power. In Burdwan, however, apart from a brief period between 1928 and 1934 when Maharaj Kumar Uday Chand joined the board as a nominee of the government, no member of the Raj family itself attempted to secure a seat in the municipality.

The development of the municipal system did not however lead to a total undermining of the Maharajas' position as 'natural leaders' of the town, for their aid and counsel was elicited by government officials as well as the citizens of Burdwan. The Maharajas were not unwilling to support causes that could be accommodated within the framework of the empire. Thus they supported the move of the citizens of Burdwan in 1873 to have the elective principle extended to Burdwan. British officials claimed that barely a tenth of the rent payers had signed the petition and that it was the name of the Burdwan Maharajas which had given weight to the cause.[33]

The Maharajas also contributed substantially to the development of major civic facilities such as a modern waterworks and hospital in Burdwan.

The Raj family did not however exercise any authority over the actual distribution of urban services which remained very much under the control of the municipal commissioners themselves, especially after the introduction of the Ripon reforms. The municipal commissioners in Burdwan were drawn overwhelmingly from the ranks of lawyers although there was also a small proportion from amongst the commercial men and landed gentry in Burdwan. For these men a municipal commissionership, apart from being a valuable source of status and power within the town, was also a route to added prestige, the honours list of the Raj, and what were potentially even greater powers beyond the municipality. A municipal commissionership could help to make the unknown pleader known, get a man an honorary magistracy or higher honours such as a Rai or a Khan Bahadurship, and from 1909 onwards it was the first step to a seat in the provincial council. Not surprisingly, much of the history of the

[33]Tarakumar Mishra, 'Bardhaman Paur Sabhar Itibritta' *Bardhaman Paur Satabar Satabarsiki Smaranika*, Burdwan 1965. 14.

Burdwan municipality was marked by increasingly keen struggles for control over its administration.

The municipal system thus created an arena of status and power that was largely outside the orbit of the Burdwan Raj. Since, however, the commissioners rarely challenged the privileges of the latter,[34] this development did not directly lead to the expected competition and tension between the two parties.

A much greater threat was posed by the development of what is popularly known as the nationalist movement, for this challenged the legitimacy of the colonial system itself on which the Burdwan Raj's existence also depended. The Burdwan Raj however was not either speedily or easily dislodged. Burdwan remained under the shadow of the Maharajas right until independence.

V

No formally constituted political organisation managed to strike root in Burdwan until 1920. The only events of note during this period were the two provincial conferences of the Bengal Congress, the first in 1899,[35] the second in 1904.[36] As in municipal politics, the lawyers were in the fore. Their leader was Nalinaksha Basu, locally dubbed as the 'grand old man' of the Burdwan Bar and the most successful and oft-elected chairman of the municipal board. Both the provincial conferences were substantially funded by him. He also played host to visiting political figures and sometimes undertook to defend those accused of political crimes.

The low-key tone of Burdwan's political life did not lull the Maharajas into any false sense of complacency. Bijoy Chand Mahtab, whose reign as Head of the House overlapped very largely with the growth of the nationalist movement in Burdwan was especially assiduous in his attempts to keep the latter at bay. Like many other public figures Bijoy Chand was wont to arouse conflicting sentiments in different quarters. Some parties were inclined to ridicule him as a 'ponderous and portentous' figure[37] over-inclined to fawn on the government for favours[38] and

[34] There were reports of friction between the two parties on such occasions as when the commissioners attempted to impose the water tax on the Raj family. The latter also expressed resentment at what it considered to be over-valuation of its holdings in the town. These do not, however, seem to have created a permanent rift between the two parties: ibid., 52.

[35] Bolai Deb Sharma, *Bardhamaner Itihas*, Bardhan Press, Calcutta 1959, 52.

[36] *The Bengalee*, 30 January 1904, 5.

[37] Ibid, 9 April 1909.

[38] *Reports on the Newspapers of Bengal Province*, week ending 11 June 1908, 1289.

to exaggerate his own importance.[39] Others lauded him as a 'natural leader of the people'[40] and a model landlord.[41] The British, recognising his position as first in wealth and importance among Bengal *zamindars* considered it prudent to confer public recognition on his status. Bijoy Chand was also able to establish close ties with various governors of Bengal both on a personal level and in gubernatorial conferences.

There was little ambivalence as to where his political sympathies lay. In a letter to Lord Curzon, Bijoy Chand had quite clearly stated that he considered the administration of India to be a sacred duty of England. He also stated his conviction that in a country like India it was a 'mistake' to allow too free a circulation of western ideas of liberty, equality and fraternity.[42]

The Maharaja did not attempt to establish or even espouse any political institution in the town. This does not mean however that he did not attempt to influence the political life of Burdwan. Students were a part of the population considered to be especially vulnerable. Bijoy Chand issued a letter to the parents and guardians of the students of the Raj College asking them to discourage their wards from participating in political demonstrations. While inaugurating the debating club of the Raj College and the collegiate school he instructed the heads of the two institutions not to allow debates on 'unhealthy' and 'polluting' subjects.[43]

Bijoy Chand was also sometimes able to prevent flagrant displays of nationalist fervour by other bodies such as the Burdwan municipality. Around this time other municipalities were tentatively beginning to express their sympathy with nationalist sentiments. A common way of doing so was by boycotting receptions organised for visiting members of the government. The Earl of Ronaldshay had been refused a welcome by both the district board and the municipality at neighbouring Bankura when he visited it in 1918. The Maharaja told the commissioners of the Burdwan municipality that he would not wish them to behave likewise when Ronaldshay visited Burdwan; his wishes seemed to have carried some weight for no open act of defiance was noted in Burdwan.[44]

Again in 1920, Abul Kasem, a prominent local supporter of the Congress, sought permission to erect a small pillar on the Town Hall

[39] *Foreign and Political (Intelligence)*, May 1880-81. Part B, 1905.
[40] *The Bengalee*, 30 January 1904, 5.
[41] *Amrita Bazaar Patrika*, 20 February 1905.
[42] B.C. Mahtab, *Studies*, Simpkin and Co, London 1904, 66.
[43] *The Englishman*, 2 May 1911, 8.
[44] Phakirchandra Ray, *Shadinata Andoloner Patabhumikay*, 73.

grounds in memory of the victims of the Jallianwala Bagh tragedy. The municipality was at this time under government control. The chairman approached the Maharaja and asked him for advice. Bijoy Chand replied that as the matter was a political one the municipality should have nothing to do with it. The pillar was never erected.[45]

Local politics underwent several changes during the years from 1920 to 1936. The most important development in Burdwan was of course the establishment of the Burdwan District Congress in 1921. Muhammad Yasin, a well-known local lawyer and one-time chairman of the Burdwan municipality, was elected president. A patron was found in the person of Durlabh Kishore Mishra, the sole heir of an affluent family in Burdwan. He established the Sadhana Press which published the first journal of the Burdwan Congress, the *Shakti*. The role of the editor was filled by Bolai Deb Sharma, a local journalist.[46] From the mid-1920s, the Congress also began to recruit more outsiders to help organise its ranks.

The other organisations that were established around this time did not make a very noticeable impact on local politics. Although many Muslims from Burdwan had joined the Muslim League the latter had not assumed a militant form in the town. Nor were the more radical groups active in the town. The Congress thus remained the major vehicle for most of Burdwan's politically ambitious Hindus and Muslims.

But even the Congress was far from being able to dispel the shadow of the Maharajas. The year 1935 provided two major opportunities which could have been capitalised upon and turned into important political resources. The Congress leadership proved itself woefully inadequate to make use of either. In August 1935 Burdwan was devastated by severe floods. Both the Maharaja and the government formed committees to render aid to those affected. To the surprise of various parties the Congress made no effort at all in this direction.[47]

The post-war period had not been an economically prosperous one for Burdwan. The *Bengal Administration Reports* carry numerous accounts of the high prices of foodstuffs and shortages of essential goods. The serious popular discontent that was beginning to crystallise as a result of the depressed economic state of the region was fuelled further by the Bengal Development Act of 1935 and the tax imposed thereunder. Here again the Congress failed to capitalise on the political development that

[45] *Proceedings of the Burdwan Municipality*, 24 February 1920.
[46] Dasrathi Ta, 'Shangbadiktay Bardhamaner Abadaan', 1-2.
[47] Home Political (Conf), File No. 974/35, 1935.

these factors gave rise to the movement popularly known as the Damodar Canal Satyagraha.

In an earlier section we have briefly outlined how the establishment of the railways had inadvertently led to the silting up of the rivers and the decline of agriculture in Burdwan district. In an effort to compensate the people who were affected by this, the government had opened the Eden Canal in 1881. A second scheme, the Damodar Canal Project was sanctioned in 1921 by the Secretary of State.

The project was not favourably viewed by either the Maharaja or the general public in Burdwan. Many of them had landed interests in the canal area and would be considerably affected by the government levy that would undoubtedly be imposed to cover the cost of the project. Shortly before the Bill was actually passed the citizens of Burdwan formed the Burdwan District Raiyats' Association and organised a meeting in the Burdwan Town Hall. A more informal discussion was also held in the Burdwan Raj palace. The Maharaja suggested that a protest meeting should be held with his heir Uday Chand as the president to formulate the grievances of the parties concerned and to place them before the government for consideration.[48] The Congressmen once again remained aloof from these general developments. This proved to be a source of embarrassment when they canvassed for votes in the 1936 elections.

The electorate for the Bengal Provincial Council was divided into several constituencies. Of these, the Landholders' Constituency had been the traditional stronghold of the Burdwan Raj family. In 1935, Bijoy Prasad Singh Roy, a member of the well-known *zamindari* family of Chakdighi, and a close associate of the Burdwan Raj family, expressed his desire to contest the elections. It was agreed that he would contest the Landholders' Constituency and the Raj candidate Uday Chand, the Rural Burdwan Sadar Constituency. [49]

The Congress was placed in a dilemma as to who should be its candidate for the latter constituency. Jadabendranath Panja, a resident pleader who also belonged to one of Burdwan's leading merchant families, was eventually nominated. When news of this reached the palace, the Raj family immediately set about trying to eliminate this challenge. Consultations with several high-ranking government officials revealed that Panja had been jailed and fined for some minor breach of the law in 1932. He had however been unable to pay the fine. The

[48] *Vardhaman Varta*, 17 July 1936.

[49] B.C. Mahtab, *Studies*, 280.

provincial government decided that he was a legal offender and debarred him from contesting the elections for two years.[50]

The Congress next settled upon Bijoy Kumar Bhattacharya who had been called in from his base in Hooghly to help build up the Burdwan Congress. But, although Bijoy Kumar was well-regarded for his efficiency and devotion to Congress affairs, he was not well known to the Burdwan public. Men like the Congress editor Bolai Deb Sharma expended much time and energy going to the rural areas and delivering speeches exhorting the voters to support the Congress. This was a shortcoming that was difficult to overcome.

The Congress had little to show in the way of contributions to tackling the needs of Burdwan. The Maharaja's supporters on the other hand could point to the temples and the educational, medical and charitable institutions funded by the Raj estate; they could also contrast the aid and support rendered by the Maharaja during the events of 1935, against the total lack of involvement by the Congress. The elections placed the voters of Burdwan in a quandary. Some tried to resolve this dilemma by working for the Maharaja within the Sadar area and for the Congress outside the Sadar. The Congress lost. An effigy of Bolai Deb Sharma was burnt outside the Congress office by jubilant members of the Maharaja's party.[51] The Raj family had once more shown that it was capable of holding its own.

It was only in the final decade before independence that the Congress was able slowly, albeit haltingly, to gain control in Burdwan. From 1935 onwards it was generally able to command a majority in the municipal board. In 1940 the Congress was also able to fulfil a long-cherished ambition when its candidate ended the long reign of the Burdwan Raj candidate, Raja Moni Lall Singh Roy, as chairman of the district board.[52]

The death of Bijoy Chand in 1941 removed a formidable opponent. His successor, Uday Chand, was much less closely involved in local activities in Burdwan, spending much time overseas and correspondingly cutting a less commanding figure than his father.

The Congress however was still not able to obliterate the aura of the Maharajas. Communal tension is often regarded as a sort of controlled experiment for gauging changes in the lay of local influence.[53] Bijoy

[50]Home Political: Poll Department, 2P-128 of 1935, Proceedings 828-32, January 1936, Conviction of J.N. Panja under section 17(2) Indian Criminal Law Amendment Act.

[51]Rajat K. Ray, 'The Crisis of Bengal Agriculture', 270-71.

[52]Interview, S. Shahedullah.

[53]C.A. Bayly, 'Local Control in Indian Towns – The Case of Allahabad 1880-1920', *Modern Asian Studies* 5, No.4 (1971), 289-311.

Chand had been regarded as a key figure in the maintenance of peace between the Hindus and the Muslims in Burdwan. His successor Uday Chand also often took the initiative to try and ease tension between the two communities.[54]

Possibly the degree to which the Congress continued to labour under the shadow of the Maharajas can be indicated by the fact that while it continued to stage demonstrations against the government there was never any move to organise demonstrations against the Maharaja.

The deluge came only after independence with the break-up of the *zamindari* estates. Uday Chand gave the palace away to the West Bengal government, and accepted monetary compensation for the rest of his property and gardens, which today, together with the palace, form the campus of the present University of Burdwan. The memory of the Maharajas still lingers in this and in the names of some of the thoroughfares, the main monument and other institutions in the town, but undoubtedly, the *zamindari* has given way to the ballot box.

VI

In the colonial context the role of such families as the Burdwan Raj may be likened to that of a banyan tree which affords shade to many but allows nothing to grow underneath it.

According to scholars like Howard Spodek, the relations between landholding and the professional and business groups were generally marked by great hostility and tension.[55] The case of Burdwan serves to illustrate that the situation was not so simple and one-dimensional. In a way the situation in Burdwan approximated the model suggested by Musgrove:[56]

> The estates were not simple or even complex systems of deference with power concentrated at one point in them but rather they were diffuse organisations, with no level, even the lowest entirely lacking in power. Far from the landlord dominating the area which fell under his nominal control, he was dependent for his position in society on the cooperation of the 'important' men within his

[54]Interview, Sri Kumar Mitra.

[55]Howard Spodek, 'Urban Politics in the Local Kingdoms of India: A View from the Princely Capitals of Saurashtra under British Rule', *Modern Asian Studies*, 7, No. 2 (1973), 253-75.

[56]P.J. Musgrove, 'Landlords and Lords of the Land: Estate Management and Social Control in Uttar Pradesh, 1860-1920', *Modern Asian Studies*, 6, No.3 (1972), 274-75.

estates. But as in all political systems, the summit was never entirely without resources, the landlord never entirely at the mercy of his subordinates. The estate worked not because of the overwhelming power and dominance of the landlord, or the passivity of the tenants but rather because at all levels of society men found it useful within their local political and social context to have good relations with the estate, its bureaucracy and in particular the whole series of resources possessed by them which could be brought in to bear in the struggles and rivalries of the little community.

THE ROLE OF URBAN SOCIETY IN NATIONALIST POLITICS

RAVINDER KUMAR

Over the past two decades there has grown in modern Indian history a substantial corpus of literature on the rural classes which were drawn into the nationalist movement of the late nineteenth and twentieth centuries. To some extent the agrarian bias of historical inquiry into the nationalist movement is understandable. India was and very largely remains an agricultural society, and no political phenomenon in the subcontinent can be termed truly significant unless it also reached out to the social classes which reside in the villages. The British government, too, knew full well that whosoever controlled the villages controlled India; and it was only when the nationalist movement, in the decades after 1920, drew increasingly upon the rural social classes that the government decided to surrender control over India to the nationalist leaders.

Yet in all this the role of cities and of the urban classes remained a pivotal role, whose exploration is likely to add substantially to our understanding of nationalist politics in the subcontinent. That nationalism as an ideology first transformed the consciousness of certain urban social classes – particularly the urban notables and professional men; that the first organised expressions of nationalism took root in the cities, and from there spread to the towns and *qasbas* (of which we shall have more to say later); that the artisan classes of the traditional cities as well as the working classes of the new industrial cities made a very substantial contribution to the nationalist struggle; all these are phenomena that are well known to historians of modern India. What we lack, however, is an integrated view of the place of cities and urban society in the structure and dynamics of nationalist politics. What was the texture of British authority over India? How did this texture relate to the matrix of urban society? How was this authority challenged by those classes within the urban realm which participated in the nationalist struggle? These are some of the questions to which the historian of modern India can profitably address himself in order to discern the role played by the urban classes in the struggle for political independence.

I

Before we examine the texture of British authority over India, particularly as it related to urban society, it may be profitable to analyse the spatial distribution and the social structure of cities in the subcontinent as they were linked to each other and to rural society.

In a recent essay on this theme, I have referred to three interlinked categories of urban settlements in the country.[1] Urban society, at the basal level, was made up of modest settlements called *qasbas*, which were the market centres for small groups of villages whose consumer needs were partially met by these markets, and whose surplus produce was syphoned off by them to larger markets within the country and overseas. Above the *qasbas* and linked to them were towns of intermediate size which provided administrative, commercial and political coherence to a number of *qasbas* and their hinterlands. Superior still to such towns in their population and social complexity were urban settlements which we can describe as cities, and which presided over the constituents of urban society in a region. This three-tiered pyramid of urban society rested upon tens of thousands of villages whose agricultural activity sustained the economy as a whole.

Our portrayal of the fabric of urban society, with the three tiers of the city, the town and the *qasba*, is brief to the point of caricature. But it is essential to convey some idea of this social fabric if we are to explore the part played by the urban social classes in nationalist politics. The social ecology of urban settlements in the coastal region, particularly in the late nineteenth and early twentieth centuries (which is the period with which we are concerned here), was different from those of urban settlements in

[1]R. Kumar, 'The Changing Structure of Urban Society in Colonial India', *Indian Historical Review*, V, Nos. 1-2 (July 1978-January 1979), 200-15.

the interior, and this difference related to the distinct economic roles which these settlements performed in the larger context of the social order. The coastal cities were industrial centres, as well as the ports of entry for industrial products from overseas, and ports of exit for the agricultural produce of India to markets across the seas. In these cities, therefore, resided substantial elements of an industrial proletariat, drawn from the rural areas, and involved in the production of goods under the control of private owners of capital. The industrial bourgeoisie was the next most significant class in these cities, a class holding a position in urban society out of proportion to its numbers, but related to the concentration of economic power in its hands. Between the owners of industry, on the one hand, and the working classes, on the other, stood powerful communities of merchants as well as the professional bourgeoisie, whose education and culture, over and above their material interests, conferred on them a seminal role in the development of the nationalist struggle in India.

The urban settlements of the interior had a different structure from the urban settlements of the coastal region. The cities of the interior lacked centres of industrial activity within their social matrix. The predominant economic activity in such settlements was of a mercantile character; and this activity related to the distribution of consumer goods, which entered the country through the port cities, or were fabricated through indigenous industrial enterprise. Again such urban settlements could also act as conduits for the transmission of the agrarian surplus to overseas markets through the mediation of the port cities. Quite often, also, the cities of the interior housed artisan classes, whose craft activity met the consumer requirements of the regions in which they were located. Over and above this, the cities of the interior housed professional classes – men employed in the civil service, or in vocations like law, medicine, journalism and teaching – though it is important to remember that the professional classes of the interior lacked that access to western ideas which shaped the world view of their peers in the coastal cities.

As the literature on the history of modern India reveals, there were two parallel and mutually reinforcing channels which upheld the authority of British government over India. At one level, the government had built a system of informal alliances with certain classes in society – the most obvious examples being the landed magnates in rural society and the urban notables who performed a variety of roles in the cities – which extended powerful support to the Raj in return for the protection of their special interests.[2] This system of informal alliances was in turn underpinned by a military presence, which ensured that any challenge to imperial authority would be crushed expeditiously. The spatial distribution of military power, as the supportive constituent of a system of class collaboration, to which we have already referred, broadly followed the spatial structure of urban society outlined above. Most of the important cities were not only centres of administrative, industrial and commercial power, but they also housed very substantial cantonments or military stations, discreetly set apart from the civil areas of the city, yet present as a grim reminder of the ultimate sanction behind British rule over India. The administrative and judicial institutions of British rule fanned out from the cities, through towns of intermediate size, to the *qasbas*, and they were buttressed by a number of military stations, big and small, which ensured that all challenges to British authority would be effectively met very early in their career. Broadly speaking, the structure of military authority and its spatial distribution had taken firm shape by the first quarter of the nineteenth century, though the Uprising of 1857, on which we shall dwell briefly hereafter, encouraged the British government to bring about some changes in the racial composition of the army in India and in the military technology that was entrusted to native contingents of this army.

II

Even though the Uprising of 1857 does not form a part of the nationalist movement, as defined for the purposes of the present essay, we can gain an appreciation of the texture of British military authority, its distribution in space as well as its linkage with urban society, if we explore the mechanisms by which British power collapsed in the Gangetic plain, in the space of a few weeks in the summer of 1857. The 'mutiny' broke out initially in the cantonment city of Meerut, which was located in close proximity to the former imperial capital of Delhi. From Meerut the 'mutiny' spread to Delhi, and it was the revolting sepoy regiments of Meerut who marched to the erstwhile Mughal capital and persuaded their fellows in Delhi to rise against British authority and confer upon the ageing Mughal emperor the shadow of imperial authority over the

[2]This view has been expressed in a number of scholarly studies. The two classic statements of this position from the 'elite' and the 'class' view, respectively, are: (a) A. Seal, *The Emergence of Indian Nationalism*, Cambridge 1968 and (b) A.R. Desai, *The Social Background of Indian Nationalism*, Bombay 1959.

country as a whole. From Delhi the seeds of discontent spread to the neighbouring district towns, each of which housed the administration (executive and judicial) of the district officers, in addition to modest contingents of the British army. The initiative in staging an uprising was in each case taken by the sepoys stationed in the district towns, who attacked administrative and judicial offices after eliminating their British officers. In the next stage, the revolting sepoys were joined by substantial sections of the urban population, often led by downwardly mobile landed magnates resident in the city. It was only in the final stage that the spirit of revolt against the imperial authority spread out to the villages, affecting, as some detailed studies have shown, different classes of rural society, some of which were wholly or partially stripped off their possessions under the British Raj, while others perceived in its institutional and legal framework a threat to their social identity.[3]

The mechanism of revolt which we have sketched above for the Delhi-Meerut region, urban and rural, also indicates how British authority crumbled in 1857 throughout the Gangetic plain. In the North-Western Provinces, as they were then constituted, cities like Bareilly and Aligarh were the regional centres of revolt. In Awadh, which stood distinct from provinces which had experienced direct British rule for substantial periods, the pattern of revolt was basically similar. The same was true of Bihar, where Patna and some other urban centres, which were equally the basis of military and administrative power, were the first to witness localised uprisings, and it was only thereafter that the social classes of the smaller towns, and of the villages, raised the banner of revolt against the British government.

A portrayal of the manner in which British authority over the Gangetic plain crumbled in 1857 substantiates our contention that urban settlements, big and small, were the true bases of British military authority over India. It is equally true, as we have suggested earlier, that this authority provided an underpinning to the informal political alliances which the government had contracted with powerful sections of Indian society, like the landed gentry and the urban notables, to mention only two. It needs to be emphasised in this context that the political alliances which sustained British rule were very fragile alliances, at least in the first half of the nineteenth century, and it was only because they were backed by military power, distributed through an intricate network of cantonments and military stations over the subcontinent, that British

[3]See, for instance, the essays on this theme in E. Stokes, *The Peasant and the Raj*, Cambridge 1978.

authority appeared so formidable. The moment British military power disintegrated through the tensions which had accumulated within the army over half a century, the Raj stood exposed as a paper tiger, with little capacity to survive as a purely political phenomenon or administrative organisation.[4]

III

The manner in which the British government in India rebuilt its military and administrative infrastructure after 1857 has been spelt out in a number of scholarly studies.[5] Here we can do no more than refer in passing to the findings of such studies before we resume our analysis of the role of the urban classes in the national movement. At the political level, the system of alliances which the government had attempted to build before 1857, with important classes within Indian society, was reinforced through extending concessions to the ruling princes and the landed magnates, on the one hand, and the peasant proprietors, adversely affected by the market economy introduced under colonial aegis, on the other. Besides, for the first time the British government tried to set up, at the imperial level in Calcutta, as well as at the provincial level, mechanisms for political consultation in the form of embryonic legislative institutions, through the induction of individuals drawn from the landed classes, who were regarded as the natural leaders of the people. Over and above this, the government also attempted to create within the cities institutions of civic activity, which would draw the rapidly growing educated and professional classes into a framework of politics that would link them in bonds of sympathy to British rule over India. Such changes in political strategy were accompanied by a radical overhaul of the military system in India. This overhaul was directed much more at the social composition of the army than at its spatial distribution, in contingents big and small, in the urban network to which we have referred earlier. Briefly, the British component of the army was reinforced in a substantial way. In addition, the recruitment base for Indian soldiers was completely transformed, particularly so far as the Gangetic plain was concerned. The pre-1857 armies had been largely drawn from the upper-caste village *zamindars* – Thakurs, Brahmans and Bhumiyars – of the

[4]The best factual account of the Uprising of 1857, which spells out clearly the mechanisms of the upsurge, still remains S.N. Sen's *Eighteen Fifty-Seven*, New Delhi 1957.

[5]For changes in civil and military policy after 1857 see: T.R. Metcalf, *The Aftermath of Revolt: India 1857-1870*, Princeton 1965 and H.L. Singh, *Problems and Policies of the British in India (1859-1898)*, Bombay 1963.

middle regions of the Gangetic plain. Thereafter, the Indian army was recruited from the more humble peasant proprietary classes of the Punjab and the border regions. Finally, the artillery units were made an exclusive preserve of British officers and men. Through such a strategy, which, on the one hand, reinforced British military power over India, and on the other, established a new framework of consultation between the colonial state and powerful classes within Indian society, the British attempted to place their domination over the subcontinent on a firm and enduring basis.

IV

Our examination of the part played by the urban classes in the nationalist movement, which became so significant a political phenomenon in India towards the closing decades of the nineteenth century, can best be conducted in the context of the bases of British military and political power which we have sketched above.

Although the professional classes in the cities had been allocated a role of considerable significance in the political system which the British government conjured into existence after 1857, it would be a mistake to imagine that their newly awakened political consciousness, a consciousness which encouraged them to redefine the political identity of India in terms of a 'nation state' on the western model, was fully contained within the framework devised by the Raj. Even the narrow sectional interests of the professional bourgeoisie could not be fully satisfied by the structure of politics which the government had created in the closing decades of the nineteenth century. A number of scholarly works reveal, however, that the professional classes looked upon themselves as a supra-class social group, exercising responsibility for the 'nation' as a whole-although this national interest was perceived within the framework of the market economy and the capitalist order.[6] Within the confines of a vision shaped by such a social system, the educated classes, particularly those based in the cities of Calcutta, Bombay and Madras, expressed themselves through a politics which refused to acqiesce in a role strategically subordinate to that of British government over India. Within a few decades of the uprising of 1857, therefore, the professional classes within the urban domain, were able to create for themselves political

[6] The argument that the intelligentsia sought to articulate the interests of the 'Nation' as a whole is succinctly put forward by B. Chandra, *The Rise and Growth of Economic Nationalism in India*, New Delhi 1966.

institutions which articulated their newly discovered consciousness, and they conceived in the Indian National Congress an organised movement for the realisation of the destiny of the 'Indian nation'.

Although the political strategy of the professional classes was never clearly spelt out in the first few decades after 1857, it is clear that their leaders (a) looked upon the Indian National Congress as an embryonic parliament of the people of India, and (b) gradually envisaged the transfer of political power from British into Indian hands. In spelling out such a strategy, the educated classes apparently believed that the destiny of the Indian nation, as they conceived it, could be decided by them in a dialogue with the British government without reference to the social classes residing in the villages. This was so despite the fact that some leaders of the Indian National Congress tried to reach out to the peasantry, or the tenantry (depending upon whether they were located in a *ryotwari* or a *zamindari* region), and relate their grievances as well as their social activism to the nationalist struggle.[7]

Although the social base of organised nationalism in the nineteenth century was confined to the professional classes within the cities, the political strategy outlined above did not exhaust the ideological resources of these classes. We are referring here to the revolutionary movement of the first two decades of the twentieth century, which sought to overthrow British rule through militant action, of a terrorist variety, rather than through constitutional means. In this context it is important to remember that, with the possible exception of the Punjab, the cadres of the revolutionary movement were drawn from a lower stratum of the educated classes. These social groups rejected the constitutional strategy held out by their peers in the Indian National Congress, and sought to overthrow British authority through violent means. There is little evidence to suggest that the urban classes dedicated to the violent overthrow of British rule had any links with the rural classes in their respective regions. Despite the absence of such links, however, their theory of revolutionary action envisaged a scenario in which they would, through heroic acts of terror (like the assassination of key British officers), destroy the psychological hold of the British government over the rural classes and encourage them to rise in an insurrection against their alien rulers. This was a theory of political action which had found formal

[7] For an attempt on the part of the Poona intelligentsia to reach out to the ryots of western India, see R. Kumar, *Western India in the Nineteenth Century*, London 1968, 174-75. For similar attempts by the Bengali intelligentsia around this time, see Seal, *The Emergence of Indian Nationalism*, 222-24.

expression in Tzarist Russia, in the late nineteenth century, where the intelligentsia not only dreamt of triggering off a successful revolution through acts of violence, but backed their strategy by 'going out to the rural people' in a bid to raise their level of political consciousness.

V

When Gandhi entered nationalist politics in the second decade of the twentieth century, the political consciousness of the urban classes – professional, petty bourgeois and working – acquired a new militancy in the context of the dialogue between nationalism and imperialism within India. Gandhi applied to nationalist politics the strategy of militant non-violence, as a strategy particularly well suited to the needs of the anti-imperialist struggle in India. In the first instance, it is important to remember, the organisational instruments which Gandhi created (the Satyagraha Sabhas) or usurped (the Home Rule League) for the promotion of his movements were largely urban in social character.[8] As a recent scholarly critique suggests, the Rowlatt Satyagraha, the first nationwide agitation to be launched under the aegis of Gandhi, was confined in the main to the cities and towns, big and small, in the subcontinent. Here, too, the intensity of the agitation against the Rowlatt Act varied greatly from region to region, and city to city, depending upon the character of the local discontents which Gandhi was able to draw into his moral crusade.[9] The scale of the agitation, however, as well as the manner in which it sought to paralyse the imperial government, were novel, and it was this combination of scale and novelty (of agitation technique), which provoked the authorities into brutal acts of repression, more particularly in the province of the Punjab and in the city of Amritsar.

When we look at the non-cooperation movement of 1920-22, which Gandhi launched close on the heels of the Rowlatt Satyagraha, the role of the urban classes in the new style of nationalist politics popularised by Gandhi becomes even more crucial than before. The tactics adopted by Gandhi were designed to paralyse through militant yet non-violent action, some of the seminal institutions of British rule over the country, namely, those of the administration, the judiciary and education. The professional and commercial classes were expected to play a key role in the paralysis of British commerce in India. Gandhi hoped to draw the

[8] See H. Owen, 'Organising for the Rowlatt Satyagraha of 1919', in R. Kumar (ed), *Essays on Gandhian Politics*, Oxford 1971.

[9] See 'Introduction' by R. Kumar in *Essays on Gandhian Politics*, Oxford 1971.

urban classes solidly into his agitations, and he believed that if they refused to extend cooperation to British imperialism in India, the British Raj would collapse like a house of cards.[10] Only in the final stages of the onslaught were the rural classes to be drawn into the fray, through their refusal to pay to the government the taxes which were due to it. For reasons connected with facility of organisation and dissemination of political values, the Gandhian programme, so far as it concerned the urban classes, and the institutions of government resting within the cities, was set in motion with devastating consequences for British rule in 1920 and 1921. Gandhi thus largely depended on the urban classes, in the first instance, to win the battle which he was waging against the British government. While it is true that the message of the Mahatma went beyond the cities and towns, big and small, to transform the consciousness of the rural classes, it is also true that Gandhi was extremely cautious about drawing such classes into the nationalist struggle. So far as the *ryotwari* regions were concerned, the position was a relatively straightforward one, since the peasant-proprietors in such regions were involved in a direct economic relationship with the government. But in the *zamindari* areas, the rural social structure was more complex, and there was every 'danger' of a *no-tax* campaign being transformed into a *no-rent* campaign, thus triggering off a species of class warfare which Gandhi was anxious above everything else to avoid. Paradoxically, therefore, although Gandhi has gone down in the history of the freedom struggle as the leader who took the struggle against British rule from the cities to the villages, it is also true that the danger of class warfare in rural society prevented him from making use of the rural classes in the anti-imperialist struggle in same manner in which he made use of the urban classes.[11]

Even within urban society, the Gandhian agitations against the government were mounted with great circumspection. Thus, although Gandhi had acquired considerable experience as a leader of the working classes in the course of the Ahmedabad textile workers' strike, and although he had propounded a full-blown theory of Capital-Labour relations, as the basis of non-violent action by the working classes, it is beyond dispute that the working classes were not drawn in any significant measure into the non-cooperation movement of the 1920s, or even the

[10]See *Collected Works of Mahatma Gandhi*, Vol. XXI for Gandhi's position in this regard.

[11]See Kapil Kumar, *Peasants in Revolt: Tenants, Landlords, Congress and the Raj in Oudh*, Manohar, New Delhi 1984, 'Conclusion', 213-33.

campaign for civil disobedience which he waged in the 1930s.[12] Why this was so is not difficult to discern. Gandhi knew full well that individuals, no less than social classes, needed a substantial measure of education before they could be drawn into the Satyagraha mode of political action. Apart from the workers residing in Ahmedabad, Gandhi had not been able to influence their fellows in any significant measure with his political ideology, in contrast to the influence he exercised over the commercial classes, the professional classes and the *petit bourgeois* in the cities of India. Because of this, Gandhi was reluctant to draw a volatile class, acutely conscious of its organised power, into a nationalist struggle which could very easily transform itself into class warfare within Indian society. We have reason to believe that the working classes were involved to a limited extent in movements like the non-cooperation campaign of 1920-22, but such participation came about under the influence of Khilafat leaders, or 'socialist' leaders, who took the initiative in joining the nationalist struggle in the hope of securing through such participation their distinctive objectives.

It would, in this context, be a mistake to imagine that the classes politicised by Gandhi exhausted the list of those who participated in the nationalist struggle so far as urban society was concerned. In the decade after World War I, the working classes in industrial centres like Bombay, Ahmedabad, and Calcutta (among others) were organised in powerful trade unions, and were as conscious of the conflict between nationalism and imperialism as they were of their class interests. This movement had three ideological facets: the workers of Ahmedabad organised themselves along Gandhian lines, though they were unique in this respect. In Bombay, in Calcutta and in other industrial centres, the trade union movement was either dominated by a socialist leadership, which sought to radicalise nationalist politics, or it was controlled by a liberal leadership, which believed that the working class should keep away from the political struggles that characterised the contemporary scene.[13] During the nationalist movement of 1920-22, working class organisation was at a relatively undeveloped stage, and the members of this class did not feature very significantly in the agitations of these years. Within a decade, however, the working-class movement had acquired considerable organisational strength and political consciousness, largely under

[12]See R. Kumar, 'Nationalist Politics in the City of Bombay, 1920-32', in D.A. Low, *Congress and the Raj*, New Delhi 1977.

[13]R.K. Newman, *Labour Organisation in the Bombay Cotton Mills, 1918-1929*, Ph. D. Thesis, University of Sussex, 1930.

socialist leadership. When the leadership of the Indian National Congress, under Gandhi, sought to launch a campaign of civil disobedience against the British, the organised working class seemed capable, jointly with other classes, urban and rural, of delivering a death blow to British rule over India. The reaction of the government to the threat of united action on the part of the professional and the working classes is revealing. We have spoken earlier of the manner in which the informal alliances which the British had contracted with certain social classes were backed by the military power of the garrisons and cantonments distributed in the cities and towns of the subcontinent. In the case of any renewed nationalist assault on British institutions, comparable to the assault launched in 1920-22, the British were confident of their capacity to frustrate the designs of Gandhi and the leadership of the Indian National Congress. This confidence rested, however, upon the assumption that the nationalists would be unable to destroy the communication system which linked the principal cities of the subcontinent to each other, and also linked each city to the townships and *qasbas* within a region. The prospect of a non-violent struggle, that would not only paralyse institutions like the administration, the judiciary, and schools and colleges, but would also undermine the communication system (since the railway workers had been unionised under radical promises) greatly alarmed the government. Such a fusion of bourgeois and radical nationalism within urban society, even if it did not reach out to the villages, could spell the end of British rule over India. Hence, in the late 1920s, the government struck with great force at the socialist movement in India, which controlled a substantial proportion of the workers in the factories as well as in the railway system, by incarcerating the leaders of this movement in the remote city of Meerut.[14] With the Marxist leaders removed from the scene of action, British officials in Delhi as well as in the provincial capitals were confident that they would be able to defeat the Gandhian movement, whose lineaments they had come to recognise so well through the encounters of 1920-22.

It would be interesting to speculate whether a paralysis of the institutions of government in the cities could by itself have destroyed British rule over India. It is difficult to make any categorical assertion in this regard, because the Gandhian campaigns of the twenties and the thirties rested upon social support from urban society which varied greatly from region to region and from city to city. The historical

[14] See Note Section of File No. Home Political 18/XXVI of 1928, NAI (National Archives of India).

literature on nationalism assumes that the participation of the rural classes was essential to the success of the nationalist cause. It would be difficult to reject this perception wholly. Yet it would also be difficult to deny that a paralysis of the institutions of urban society, particularly if accompanied by a breakdown of communications between different regions, and within different regions, could seriously endanger imperial authority over India. Perhaps the erosion of imperial authority in the cities by *itself* was insufficient to deliver the *coup de grace* to the British government. At the same time, an urban uprising was an *essential* precondition to such a consummation, if only for the reason that the institutions, civil and military, through which the Raj could re-establish its hold over rural society were largely located in the cities. All this is exemplified by the Uprising of 1857, to which we have already referred. It is also exemplified by the uprising of 1942, when the breakdown of British authority in the cities, towns and *qasbas*, within the Gangetic valley (and in some regions outside the Gangetic valley) was as striking a phenomenon as it was in 1857. Perhaps the role of the urban classes in the nationalist movement, as we have sketched it out, was crucial in two respects. In any attempt at revolutionary change, the initial responsibility for organisation and politicisation inevitably falls upon the urban classes. The participation of the urban classes is also necessary to ensure the success of a revolutionary movement. Yet by themselves, both these preconditions may not suffice in bringing about a revolutionary transformation. Over and above what men, and social classes, can do in the cities, they need the cooperation of their fellows in the villages, before they can mount a successful attack on established authority within a political system.

SELECT BIBLIOGRAPHY*

Acharya, P.K. 'Villages and Towns in Ancient India', B.C. Law Volume, II, Poona 1964.

Ahmad, A., 'Towns in the *Ain-i-Akbari*', *C.R.D. Papers*, Jawaharlal Nehru University, New Delhi 1972.

Ahmad, E., 'Origin and Evolution of the Towns of U.P.', *Geographical Outlook*, Jan. 1956, 38-58.

Aiyer, C.P., *Town Planning in Ancient Deccan*, Law Printing and Publishing Co., Madras 1916.

Alam, Shah Manzoor, 'Masulipatam: A Metropolitan Port in the Seventeenth Century A.D.', *Indian Geographical Journal*, July-Dec. 1959,33-42.

Albuquerque, Teresa, 'Christian Impact on Nineteenth Century Bombay', *India*, Vol. 20, 1983.

Altekar, A.S., *A History of Ancient Towns and Cities of Gujarat and Kathiawad*, Bombay 1926.

Amarnath, *Development of Local*-Self Government (1849-1900), Monograph 8, Punjab Government Records, Lahore 1929.

Arasaratnam, Sinnappal, *Merchants, Companies and Commerce of the Coromandal Coast, 1650-1740*, Oxford, Delhi 1986.

Argal, R.M., *Municipal Government in India*, Agarwal Press, Allahabad 1954.

* For additional entries on urban studies the reader may refer to the *News-letters* of the Urban History Association of India.

Arora, R.C., *Delhi: Imperial City*, Unique Publishing, Aligarh 1935.

Attwood, D.W., 'Why Some of the Poor Get Richer: Economic Change and Mobility in Urban Western India', *Current Anthropology*, 20, 3, Sep. 1979, 459-508.

——,M. Israel and N.K. Wagle (eds), *City, Countryside and Society in Maharashtra*, Centre for South Asian Studies, University of Toronto, Toronto 1988.

Azmi, A.A., 'The Decay of the City of Lucknow, 1840-1870', *Proceedings Indian History Congress*, New Delhi 1970, 168-72.

Bachan Ram, *Demographic Aspects of Urbanization in Bihar, 1901-1971*, Unpublished Ph.D. thesis, Patna 1979.

Bajpai, Gita , 'A Brief Review of Aspects of Agrarian and Urban Economy of British Gujarat, 1860-1900', *Proceedings Indian History Congress*, Dharwad 1988, 470-77.

Ballhatchet, Kenneth and John Harrison(eds), *The City in South Asia: Pre-Modern and Modern* ,Curzon Press, London 1980.

Banerjee, Prajanananda, *Calcutta and its Hinterland: A Study in Economic History of India, 1833-1900*, Progressive Publishers, Calcutta 1975.

Banga, Indu, 'Agrarian Roots of Urbanization', *Proceedings Indian History Congress*, Bodh Gaya 1981.

——(ed), *Ports, Port Cities and their Hinterlands in India, c 1700-1950*, Nehru Memorial Museum and Library, New Delhi in association with Indian Institute of Advanced Study, Shimla and the Urban History Association of India (forthcoming).

Baqir, Muhammad, *Lahore: Past and Present*, Punjab University Press, Lahore 1952.

Barr, F., *Imperial City: The Story of Delhi and Her Royal Rulers*, Times Press, Simla 1902.

Basu, Dalip K. (ed), *The Rise and Growth of the Colonial Port Cities in Asia*, Monograph Series No. 25, Center for South and South East Asia Studies, University of California, Berkeley 1983 (rep).

Bayly, C.A., *The Local Roots of Indian Politics: Allahabad, 1880-1920*, Clarendon Press, London 1975.

——*Rulers, Townsmen and Bazaars: North Indian Society in the Age of British Expansion, 1770-1870*, Cambridge University Press, Cambridge 1983.

Bhattacharya, B., *Urban Development in India* (since Pre-historic Times), Shree, Delhi 1979.

Boman-Behram, B.K., *The Rise of Municipal Government in the City of Ahmedabad*, Bombay 1937.

Bose, Ashish, 'A Note on the Definition of 'Town' in the Indian Census', *The Indian Economic and Social History Review,* Vol. I, No. 3, Jan.-March 1964.

——*Urbanization in India – An Inventory of Source Materials,* Academic Books, New Delhi 1970.

——*Studies in India's Urbanization, 1901-1971,* Tata Mcgraw-Hill, New Delhi 1974.

——*India's Urbanization, 1901-2001,* Tata McGraw Hill, Delhi 1980.

Bose, Nirmal Kumar, 'Calcutta: Premature Metropolis', *Scientific American,* Sept. 1965, 91-102.

Bose, N.S. (ed), *Calcutta: People and Empire,* Calcutta 1975.

Briggs, H.G., *The Cities of Gurjarashtra: Their Topography and History,* Bombay 1849.

Broeze, Frank (ed), *Brides of the Sea: Port Cities of Asia from the 16th to 20th Centuries,* New South Wales University Press, Australia 1989.

Busteed, H.E., *Echoes from Old Calcutta,* Calcutta 1897.

Carthill, Al, *Madampur;* William Blackwood, London 1931.

Chakrabarti, Dilip Kumar, *Early Urban Centres in India,* Unpublished Ph.D. thesis, Calcutta 1972.

——'Concept of Urban Revolution and the Indian Context, *Purattatva,* No.6, 1972-73.

——'Some Theoretical Aspects of Early Indian Urban Growth', *Purattatva,* No. 7, 1974.

Chakrabarty, Dipesh, 'Trade Unions in a Hierarchical Culture: The Jute Workers of Calcutta, 1920-50', *Subaltern Studies III,* Writings on South Asian History and Society (ed Ranajit Guha), OUP, Delhi 1989, 116-52.

Champakalakshmi, R., 'Urbanisation in South India: The Role of Ideology and Polity', Presidential Address Ancient Indian Section, *Proceedings Indian History Congress,* Srinagar 1986.

Chandra, J.P., *Delhi: A Political Study,* Metropolitan, Delhi 1969.

Chandra, Satish, 'Some Aspects of the Growth of the Money Economy during the 17th Century', *Indian Economic and Social History Review,* Vol III, No. 4, 1966.

——*The Indian Ocean : Explorations in History, Commerce and Politics,* New Delhi 1987.

Chandrabai, M., *Changes in Status, Attitude, Choice and Aspirations of Hindu Urban Women,* Unpublished Ph. D. thesis, Madras 1979.

Chattopadhayaya, B.D., 'Trade and Urban Centres in Early Medieval India', *Indian Historical Review,* I, 1974, 203-19.

Chaudhuri, K.N., 'Some Reflections on the Town and Country in Mughal India', *Modern Asian Studies,* Vol.12, Pt. I, Feb. 1978, 77-97.

Chaudhuri, M.K. (ed), *Trends of Socio-Economic Change in India,* Indian Institute of Advanced Study, Shimla 1969.

Chauhan, Brij Raj, *Towns in the Tribal Setting,* National, Delhi 1969.

Chauhan, D.S., *Trends of Urbanization in Agra,* Allied, New Delhi 1970.

Chawla, I.N., 'Urbanisation of the Punjab Plains', *Indian Geographer,* Dec. 1958, 29-48.

Chettiar, C.N.L., *Coimbatore: Its Past and Present,* Indian Chamber of Commerce, Coimbatore 1958.

Childe, V. Gordon, 'The Urban Revolution', *Town Planning Review,* XXI, 1950, 3-17.

Chopra, Prabha (ed), *Delhi – History and Places of Interest,* Delhi Administration, Delhi 1970.

Cohn, B.S. 'The British in Benaras: A Nineteenth Century Colonial Society', *Comparative Studies in Society and History,* 1962, 169-208.

Conlon, Frank F., *A Caste in a Changing World: The Chitrapur Saraswat Brahmans, 1700-1935,* University of California, Berkeley 1977.

——'Caste, Community and Colonialism: The Elements of Population and Urban Rule in British Bombay, 1665-1830', *Journal of Urban History,* Vol. II, No. 2, Feb. 1985, 181-208.

Cornish, V., *Great Capitals: A Historical Geography,* Metheun, London 1980.

Costa, Frank J. *et al.* (eds), *Asian Urbanization : Problems and Processes,* Gebrü der Borntraeger, Stuttgart 1988.

Cotton, Harry Evan Auguste, *Calcutta: Old and New,* New Man & Co., n.p., 1907.

Cousens, H., *Bijapur and Its Architectural Remains,* Bombay 1916.

Da Cunha, J.H. Cerson, *Origin of Bombay,* Royal Asiatic Society, Bombay 1900.

Dani, Ahmed Hasan, *Dacca: A Record of its Changing Fortunes,* Dacca 1962.

Das Gupta, Ashin, *Indian Merchants and the Decline of Surat,* Wiesbaden 1979.

——*and M.N. Pearson (eds), India and the Indian Ocean 1500-1800,* Calcutta 1987.

Datta, V.N., *Amritsar: Past and Present,* Municipal Committee, Amritsar 1967.

David, M.D., *History of Bombay, 1661-1708,* Bombay 1973.

Davis, Kingsley, 'The Origin and Growth of Urbanization in the World',

American Journal of Sociology, IX, 1955, 429-37.

Deshmukh, Cynthia, *Bombay Cottons on--A Case Study of the Economic Revolution in Bombay 1850-1914*, Bombay n.d.

——'The Bombay Plague, 1896-1897', *Proceedings Indian History Congress*, Dharwad 1988, 478-83.

Dey, S.K., *Nilokheri*, Asia, Bombay 1962.

Dhabariya, S.S., 'Evolution of Cultural Landscape in Udaipur City', *National Geographical Journal of India*, 1964, 92-99.

Dikshit, K.R., 'Evolution of Cities in Maharashtra: An Analysis of the Phases of Urbanization', *Indian Geographical Journal*, 1970, 53-64.

Dobbin, Christine, *Urban Leadership in Western India: Politics and Communication in Bombay City 1840-1885*, Oxford University Press, London 1972.

Dodwell, Henry, *Nabobs of Madras*, London 1926.

Dossal, Mariam, *Imperial Designs and Indian Realities: The Planning of Bombay City, 1845-1875*, Oxford University Press, Bombay 1990.

Dutt, Ashok Kumar 'Evolution of Jamshedpur City: A Historical Approach to Urban Geography', *Indian Geographical Journal of India*, Jan.-June 1966, 19-28.

Dutt, B.B., *Town Planning in Ancient India*, Thaker Spinks, Calcutta 1925.

Dwyer, D.J., *The City as a Centre of Change in Asia*, Hong Kong University Press, Hong Kong 1972.

Edwards, S.M., *Rise of Bombay*, Bombay 1902.

Fanshawe, H.C., *Delhi: Past and Present*, Murray, London 1902.

Fauja Singh (ed), *Sirhind Through the Ages*, Punjabi University, Patiala 1972.

——(ed), *The City of Amritsar*, Oriental Publishers, New Delhi 1978.

Fauja Singh and R.C. Rabra, *The City of Faridkot*, Punjabi University, Patiala 1976.

Feldman, Herbert, *Karachi Through A Hundred Years: A Centenary History of the Karachi Chamber of Commerce and Industry, 1860-1960*, OUP, Karachi 1960.

Fonseca, R., 'The Walled City of Delhi', *Ekistics*, 1971, 72-80.

Forde, C. Daryle, 'The Ancient Cities of the Indus', *Geography*, 1932, 183-92.

Forrest, C.W., *Cities of India: Past and Present*, London 1903.

Fox, Richard G., *From Zamindar to Balltot Box: Community Change in North Indian Market Town*, Cornell University, Ithaca 1969.

——(ed), *Urban India: Society, Space and Image*, Programme in Comparative

Studies on Southern Asia, Monograph 10, Duke University, Durham 1970.

Ganguly, Indrani, *Social History of a Bengal Town, 1872-1947,* Himalaya, New Delhi 1987.

Gauba, Anand, *Amritsar (1849-1947): A Study in Urban History,* ABS Publishers, Jalandhar 1988.

Geeta Rani, *The Municipal Committee of Ludhiana* (1849-1947), M. Phil dissertetion, Department of History, Guru Nanak Dev University, Amritsar 1989.

Ghosh, A., *Calcutta: The Primate City,* Manager of Publications, Delhi 1966.

——*The City in Early Historical India,* Indian Institute of Advanced Study, Shimla 1989 (rep).

Ghosh, Bijit, 'Jaisalmer: Urban Form and Pattern of a Medieval Indian Town', *Urban and Rural Planning Thought,* Jan. 1968, 5-55.

——'Oh Calcutta', *Hindustan Times Weekly Review,* 8 March 1970.

——and K.C. Srirangam Mago, 'Urban Form and Pattern of an Ancient Indian Town', *Urban and Rural Planning Thought,* 14, 2, April 1971, 9-128.

Ghosh, Binoy, 'Colonial Beginnings of Calcutta : Urbanization without Industrialisation, *Economic Weekly,* July-Dec. 1960, 12-60.

Ghosh, Murari *et al., Calcutta: A Study in Urban Growth Dynamics,* Firma K.L. Mukhopadhyay, Calcutta 1972.

Ghosh, S.L., *Urban Morals in Ancient India,* Calcutta 1944.

Ghurye, G.S., *Cities and Civilization,* Popular Prakashan, Bombay 1962.

Gillion, Kenneth, L., *Ahmedabad, A Study in Indian Urban History,* New Order Book Co., Ahmedabad 1968.

Gokale, B.G., *Surat in the Seventeenth Century : A Study in Urban History of Pre-Modern India,* Scandinavian Institute of Asian Study, Monograph Series No. 28, Curzon Press, London 1979.

——, 'Some Urban Commercial Centres of the Western Deccan in the XVIIth Century', *Images of Maharashtra: A Regional Profile of India* (ed N.K. Wagle), Curzon Press, London 1980.

——*Poona in the Eighteenth Century,* OUP, Bombay 1988.

Gosal, G.S., 'Urbanization in Punjab (India), 1921-61', *Tijdschrift Voor Economische en Sociale Geographic,* Vol. 57, No. 3. 1966, 104-22.

——'Urbanization in Punjab (India) 1881-1961', *Research Bulletin (N.N). Panjab University,* June 1966, 1-26.

——'Agricultural Development and the Urbanisation Process–A Case Study of Punjab (1901-81)', *Urbanisation et Organisation Regionale,*

CEGET, CNRS, France, No. 53, Nov. 1985, 68-78.

Gould, Harold A, 'Who got a piece of the action? A Century of Urban Politics in Faizabad Municipality', *Contributions to Indian Sociology* (New Series), 16, 1, 1982, 97-124.

Grewal, J.S., *In the By-Lanes of History: Some Persian Documents from a Punjab Town*, Indian Institute of Advanced Study, Shimla 1975.

——(ed), *Calcutta: The Foundation and Development of a Colonial Metropolis*, Urban History Association of India, 1990.

——and Indu Banga (eds), *Studies in Urban History*, Guru Nanak Dev University, Amritsar 1981.

Grewal, Reeta, 'Polity, Economy and Urbanization: Early 19th Century Punjab', *Journal of Regional History*, Vol. IV, 1983, 56-72.

——'The Pattern of Urbanization in the Punjab Under Colonial Rule', *Journal of Regional History*, Vol. V, 1984, 69-82.

——*Urbanization in the Punjab, 1849-1947*, Ph. D. thesis, Guru Nanak Dev University, Amritsar 1988.

Guha, M., 'The Development of Urban Functions of Calcutta', *Journal of Social Research*, March 1962, 91-96.

Gumperz, Ellen McDonald, 'English Education and Social Reform in late Nineteenth Century Bombay', *Journal of Asian Studies*, Vol. 25, 1966, 453-70.

Gupta, Giri Raja (ed), *Urban India (Main Currents in Indian Sociology-VI)*, Vikas, New Delhi 1983.

Gupta, Iswar Prakash, *Urban Glimpses of Mughal India: Agra, the Imperial Capital* (16th and 17th Centuries), Discovery Publishing House, Delhi 1986.

Gupta, Narayani, 'Military Security and Urban Development : A Case Study of Delhi: 1857-1912', *Modern Asian Studies*, 1971, 61-77.

——*Delhi Between Two Empires 1803-1931, Society, Government and Urban Growth*, Oxford University Press, Delhi 1981 (2nd ed 1986).

Hall, Kenneth R., *The Nagaram as a Marketing Centre in Early Medieval South India*, Ph.D. thesis, Department of History, University of Michigan, 1975.

Hambly, Gavin, *Cities of Mughal India*, BSPO, Delhi 1968.

Hasan, M. Fazlul, *Bangalore Through the Centuries*, Historical Publishers, Bangalore 1970.

Havell, E.B., *Benares: The Sacred City*, Thacker Spinks, London 1905.

Hazlehurst, Leighton W., *Entrepreneurship and the Merchant Castes in a Punjabi City*, Monograph I, Commonwealth Studies Centre, Duke University, 1966.

Hurliman, Martin, *Delhi, Agra and Fatehpur Sikri*, Thames and Hudson, London 1968.

Hussain, I., 'Some Afghan Settlements in the Gangetic Doab–1627-1707', *Proceedings Indian History Congress*, New Delhi 1970, 173-81.

Indra Devi, *'Growth and Development of Vizag City and Region'*, Ph. D. thesis, Deptt. of Geography, Andhra University, Waltair 1978.

Irfan Habib, 'Non-Agricultural Production and Urban Economy', *Cambridge Economic History of India*, Vol. I (eds Tapan Raychaudhuri and Irfan Habib), Cambridge University Press, London 1982, 76-92.

Jagmohan, *Rebuilding Shahjahanabad : The Walled City of Delhi*, Vikas, Delhi 1975.

Jain, Kailash Chand, *Ancient Cities and Towns of Rajasthan : A Study of Culture and Civilization*, Delhi 1972.

Jain N.G., 'The Emergence of Urban Centres in the Eastern Districts of Vidarbha', *National Geographical Journal of India*, Sept-Dec 1964, 146-63.

Jasdip Kaur, *Kartarpur: Some Aspects of its Social and Economic History* (1849-1947), M. Phil. dissertation, Dept. of History, Guru Nanak Dev University, Amritsar 1990.

Jauhari, A.S., 'Trend of Urbanization in the Punjab Plain', *National Geographical Journal of India*, Sept.-Dec., 1957, 125-36.

——'Growth of Urban Settlements in the Sutlej-Yamuna Divide', *National Geographical Journal of India*, March 1962, 1-24.

——'Urban-Settlement of the Sutlej-Yamuna Divide, circa 647 A.D.-1947', *The National Geographical Journal of India*, June 1962, 114-35.

Jayaswal, S.N.P., 'Bindki-A Study in the Evolution of a Trade Centre', *National Geographical Journal of India*, 1963, 187-200.

Jindal, Rajendra, *Culture of a Sacred Town: A Sociological Study of Nathdwara*, Popular Prakashan, Bombay 1976.

Johnson, G., *Provincial Politics and Indian Nationalism: Bombay and the Indian National Congress, 1880-1915*, Cambridge 1973.

Joshi, C.B., 'Historical Geography of the Islands of Bombay', *Bombay Geographical Magazine*, December 1956, 5-13.

Jyoti, Kanchan, *The City of Jullunder : A Study in Urban History (1846-1947)*, Unpublished Ph.D. thesis, Guru Nanak Dev University, Amritsar 1988.

Kale, B.D. 'Growth of Towns in Mysore State', *Journal of Institute of*

Economic Research, July 1967, 47-67.

Kamlesh Kumari, *Gurdaspur Municipality in the Punjab, 1920-1947,* M. Phil. dissertation, Dept. of History, Guru Nanak Dev University, Amritsar 1986.

Kanwar, Pamela, 'The Changing Image of Shimla', Occasional Papers Series: 10, Urban History Association of India, 1989.

——, *Imperial Simla: The Political Culture of the Raj,* Oxford University Press, Delhi 1990.

Karim, Abdul, *Dacca: The Mughal Capital,* The Asiatic Society, Dacca 1964.

Kerr, Ian, J., 'Urbanization and Colonial Rule in the 19th Century', *Punjab Past and Present,* Vol. XIV, Part I, April 1980, 88-126.

Khan, Masood Ali, *Social Change Among the Muslims of Aurangabad City,* Unpublished Ph.D. thesis, Marathwada University, Aurangabad 1980.

Khan, Muhammad Ishaq, *History of Srinagar 1846-1947: A Study in Socio-Cultural Change,* Amir Publications, Srinagar 1978.

Kidwai, Atiya Habeeb, *Characteristics and Process of Urbanization in Colonial India : A Case Study of Calcutta and its Hinterland, 1872-1921,* Unpublished Ph.D. thesis, JNU, Delhi 1979.

King, Anthony D., 'India's Urban Past', *Quarterly Review of Historical Studies,* Vol. VIII, No. 4, 1968-69.

——, *Colonial Urban Development : Culture, Social Power and Government,* Routledge and Kegan Paul, London 1976.

——, 'Conceptualizations about Colonial Cities', *Colonial Cities : Essays on Urbanism in a Colonial Context,* Leiden 1985.

Klein, Ira, 'Urban Development and Death: Bombay City, 1870-1914', *Modern Asian Studies,* Vol. 21, Pt. 4, Oct. 1986, 725-55.

Kosambi, Meera, *Bombay and Poona : A Socio-Ecological Study of Two Indian Cities, 1650-1900,* Department of Sociology, University of Stockholm, Printed Ph.D. thesis, 1980.

——, 'Commerce, Conquest and the Colonial City: Role of Locational Factors in the rise of Bombay', *Economic & Political Weekly,* Vol. XX, No. 4, 5 Jan. 1985, 32-37.

——, *Bombay in Transition: The Growth and Social Ecology of a Colonial City, 1880-1980,* Almqvist & Wiksell International, Stockholm 1986.

—— and John E. Brush, 'Three Colonial Port Cities in India', *The Geographical Review (U.S.A.),* Vol. 78, No. 1, Jan. 1988, 32-47.

Kulwinder Kaur, *The Town of Phillaur 1867-1947,* M.Phil. dissertation, Department of History, Guru Nanak Dev University, Amritsar 1989.

Kumar, Nita, *Popular Culture in Urban India : The Artisans of Benaras, c. 1884-1984*, Ph.D. thesis, University of Chicago, 1984.

Kumar, Radha, 'City Lives: Workers' Housing and Rent in Bombay, 1911-47', *Economic & Political Weekly*, Vol. XXII, No. 30, 25 July 1987, 47-56.

——, 'Family and Factor : Women in the Bombay Cotton Textile Industry, 1919-1939', *Women in Colonial India: Essays on Survival, Work and the State* (ed J. Krishna Murty), *IESHR*, OUP, Delhi 1989, 133-62,

Kumar, Ravinder, 'Nationalist Politics in the City of Bombay, 1920-32', *Congress and the Raj* (ed D. A.Low), New Delhi 1977.

——, 'The Changing Structue of Colonial Society in Urban India', *Indian Historical Review*, Vol. V, Nos. 1-2, July 1978-Jan. 1979, 200-25.

——, 'The Rowlatt Satyagraha in Lahore', *Essays in the Social History of Modern India*, Oxford University Press, Calcutta 1986 (paperback), 148-212.

——, 'The Bombay Textile Strike', ibid., 213-39.

Kumar, Tej B., 'From Desolation to Over-Population: Delhi', *Civic Affairs*, Vol. 29, No. 8, Feb.1982, 17-26.

Lal, K., *Holy Cities of India*, Delhi 1951.

Lelyveld, Joseph, *Calcutta*, Perennial Press, Calcutta 1975.

Leng, James, *Calcutta in the Olden Times: Its Localities and its People*, Grantham, Calcutta 1974.

——, *Calcutta and its Neighbourhood: History of Calcutta and its People from 1690 to 1857*, Indian Publications, Calcutta 1974.

Leonard, John G., 'Urban Government under the Raj : A Case Study of Municipal Administration in the Nineteenth Century South India', *Modern Asian Studies*, Vol. 7, Pt. 2, April 1973, 227-53.

Leonard, Karen I., *The Social History of an Indian Caste: The Kayasths of Hyderabad*, University of California Press, Berkeley 1978.

Lewandowski, Susan J, 'Changing Form and Function in the Colonial Port City in India': An Historical Analysis of Madurai and Madras', *Modern Asian Studies*, Vol. II, Pt. 2, April 1977, 183-213.

——, *Migration and Ethnicity in Urban India: Kerala Migrants in the City of Madras, 1870-1970*, Manohar, New Delhi 1980.

Lietner, Georges Kristoffel, *Colonialism, Class and Nation : The Confrontation in Bombay Around 1930*, K.P.Bagchi, Calcutta 1984.

Love, H.V. *Vestiges of Old Madras*, 3 Vols.,New York 1968.

Lynch, Owen, *The Politics of Untouchability : Social Mobility and Social Change in a City of India*, Columbia University Press, New York 1969.

Masheswari, B.N., *Bombay City –Fifty Years Ago and Today: A History of Its Improvement and some Suggestions for its further Improvement*, Bombay 1940.

Malabari, Phiroze B.M., *Bombay in the Making, Being Mainly a History of the Origin and Growth of Judicial Institutions in the Western Presidency, 1661-1726*, T. Fisher Unwin, London 1910.

Maledina, M.H., *History of Poona Cantonment, 1818-1953*, Poona 1953.

Masani, R.P., *Evolution of Local Self Government in Bombay*, London 1929.

Masselos, J.C. 'Bombay in the 1870s : A Study of Changing Patterns in Urban Politics', *South Asia*, No. 1, 1971.

——, 'Aspects of Bombay City Politics, 1919', *Essays in Gandhian Politics* (ed Ravinder Kumar), Oxford 1971.

——, *'Public Association and Urban Politics in Western India*, Bombay 1975.

——, 'Social Segregation and Crowd Cohesion', Reflections around some preliminary data from 19th century Bombay City, *Contributions to Indian Sociology* (New Series), Vol. 13, No. 2, July-Dec. 1979, 145-67.

Massey, Montague, *Recollections of Calcutta for over a Half Century*, Thacker Spinks, Calcutta 1948.

Mathew, K.S., 'Masulipatnam and the Maritime Trade of India during the Seventeenth Century', *Proceedings of the Andhra Pradesh History Congress*, 1987.

Mathur, J.C. and Y. Mishra (eds), *Homage to Vaisali*, Muzaffarpur 1948.

McGuire, John, *The Making of A Colonial Mind –A Quantitative Study of the Bhadralok in Calcutta, 1857-1885*, Monographs in South Asia, No. 10, Australian National University, Canberra 1983.

Mehta, M.J., 'Some Aspects of Surat as a Trading Centre in the 17th Century', *Indian Historical Review*, Vol. I, No. 2, 1974, 247-61.

Mehta. S.M., *The Cotton Mills of Bombay*, Bombay 1934.

Michael, L.W., *The History of the Municipal Corporation of the City of Bombay*, Bombay 1902.

Mishra, Kamla Prasad, *Banaras in Transition, 1738–1795 : A Socio-Economic Study*, Munshiram Manoharlal, New Delhi 1975.

Mishra, V.S. 'Nature and Strength of Capitalist Class in Bombay City in the 19th Century', *Proceedings Indian History Congress*, Annamalainagar 1984.

Misra, R.P. (ed), *Million Cities of India*, Vikas, New Delhi 1978.

Misra, S.D., 'Note on the Socio-Historical Geography of Mathura', *National Geographical Journal of India,* December 1958, 189-99.
Mitchell, Nora, *The Indian Hill-Station : Kodaikanal,* Chicago 1972.
Mitra, Ashok, *Calcutta : India's City,* New Publishers, Delhi 1963.
——, *Internal Migration and Urbanizaion in India,* Part 1 : Text; Part II: Appendics, U.N. ECAFE Expert Working Group on Problems of Internal Migration and Urbanization, Bangkok 1967.
——, *Delhi : Capital City,* Thomson Press, New Delhi 1970.
——, *Functional Classification of India's Towns,* Institute of Economic Growth, Delhi 1974.
Monirul Huda, *Sibasagar Town : A Study in Urbanisation,* Unpublished Ph.D. thesis, Dibrugarh 1979.
Moorhouse Geoffrey, *Calcutta,* Weidenfield & Nicolson, London 1971.
Morris, Morris David, *The Emergence of an Industrial Labour Force in India: A Study of the Bombay.Cotton Mills, 1854-1947,* University of California, Berkeley 1965.
Mukherjee, N., *The Port of Calcutta : A Short History,* Calcutta 1968.
Mukherjee, Radha Kamal and Baljit Singh, *A District Town in Transition: Socio-Economic Survey of Gorakhpur,* Asia, Bombay 1965.
Mukherjee, S.N., *Calcutta: Myths and History,* Subarnarekha, Calcutta 1977.
Munshi, Sunil K., *Calcutta Metropolitan Explosion: Its Nature and Roots,* People's Publishing House, New Delhi 1972.
Murphy, Rhoads, 'New Capitals of Asia', *Economic Development and Cultural Change,* Jan. 1957, 216-43.
——, 'The City in the Swamp : Aspects of the Site and Early Growth of Calcutta', *Geographical Journal,* June 1964, 241-56.
——, 'Traditionalism and Colonialism - Changing Urban Roles in Asia', *Journal of Asian Studies,* Vol. 29, 1969, 67-84.
——, 'City and Countryside as Ideological Issues : India and China', *Comparative Studies in Society and History,* 14, 3, June 1972, 250-67.
Naqvi, Hameeda Khatoon, *Urban Centres and Industries in Upper India, 1556-1803,* Asia, Bombay 1968.
——, *Urbanisation and Urban Centres Under the Great Mughals,* Indian Institute of Advanced Studies, Shimla 1972.
——, *Mughal Hindustan: Cities and Industries, 1556-1803,* National Book Foundation, Karachi 1974.
Neild, Susan Margaret, *Madras : The Growth of a Colonial City in India, 1780-1840,* Ph.D. thesis, University of Chicago, Chicago 1977.

——, 'Colonial Urbanism : The Development of Madras City in the 18th and 19th Centuries', *Modern Asian Studies*, Vol. 13, No. 2, 1979.

Newman, R.K., *Labour Organisation in the Bombay Cotton Mills, 1918-1929*, Ph.D. thesis, University of Sussex, 1930.

Nigam, M.N., 'Evolution of Lucknow', *National Geographical Journal of India*, March 1960, 30-46.

Oldenburg, Veena Talwar, *The Making of Colonial Lucknow 1856-1877*, Princeton University Press, Princeton 1984.

Pandey, Gyanendra, 'Encounters and Calamities: The History of a North Indian *Qasba* in the Nineteenth Century', *Subaltern* Studies III, Writings on South Asian History and Society (ed Ranajit Guha), OUP, Delhi 1989, 230-70.

Pandeya, N.M., 'Growth Characteristics of South Gujrat Towns', *Journal of the M.S. University of Baroda*, 19, 2, July 1970, 79-86.

Panter-Downes, M., *Ooty Preserved : A Victorian Hill Station in India*, Hamish Hamilton, London 1967.

Parasnis, D.C., *Poona in Bygone Days*, Times Press, Bombay 1921.

Pearson, Gail, 'Reserved Seats - Women and the Vote in Bombay', *Women in Colonial India : Essays on Survival, Work and the State* (ed J. Krishnamurty), OUP, Delhi 1989, 199-217.

Pearson, M.N., 'The Port City of Goa : Policy and Practice in the Sixteenth Century', *Coastal Western India: Studies from the Portuguese Records*, Concept, New Delhi 1981.

Pearson, Roger, *Eastern Interlude : A Social History of the European Community in Calcutta*, Thacker Spinks, Calcutta 1954.

Piggot, Staurt, *Some Ancient Cities of India*, Oxford University Press, Bombay 1945.

Possehl, Gregory L. (ed), *Ancient Cities of the Indus*, Vikas, New Delhi 1979.

Prakasarao, V.L.S., *Towns of Mysore State*, Asia, Bombay 1964.

Prasad, B.R. and B.S. Rao, 'Growth of Cities of One Lakh and Above Population in Andhra Pradesh (1951-77)', *Civic Affairs*, Vol. 29, No.2, Sept. 1981, 17-19.

Prasad, Lalita, *Growth of a Small Town*, Unpublished Ph.D. thesis, Gorakhpur 1978.

Puri, B.N., *Cities of Ancient India*, Meenakshi Prakashan, Meerut 1966.

Rai, Jaimal, *The Rural-Urban Economy and Social Change in Ancient India*, Delhi 1974.

Rajagopalan, C. 'Towards a Theory of Urbanisaion and Social Change', *Dimensions of Social Change in India* (eds M.N. Srinivas, S. Seshaiah and V.S. Parthasarthy), Allied, Bombay 1977, 101-13.

Rajeshwar Singh, 'Evolution of Jabalpur City', *National Geographical Journal of India*, 19, 2, 110-23.

Ramesh. A., 'Origin and Evolution of Ootacamund', *National Geographical Journal of India*, March 1964, 16-28.

Rao, B.P., 'Evolution of Vishakhapatnam', *National Geographical Journal of India*, Dec. 1960, 242-59.

Rao, Ram Mohan, *Growth of Cities : A Case Study of Warangal*, Inter-India Publication, Delhi 1981.

Rao, S.R., *Lothal and the Indus Civilization*, Asia, Bombay 1973.

Rao, V.K.R.V. and P.B. Desai, *Greater Delhi : Study in Urbanization, 1940-57*, Asia, Bombay 1965.

Ray, Amita, *Villages, Towns and Secular Buildings in Ancient India*, Firma K.L. Mukhopadhayay, Calcutta 1974.

——, 'Urbanization in Bengal', Presidential Address: Ancient Section, *Proceedings Indian History Congress*,Goa 1987, 9-47.

Ray, Rajat K., *Urban Roots of Indian Nationalism: Pressure Groups and Conflict of Interests in Calcutta City Politics, 1875-1939*, Vikas, New Delhi 1979.

Raza, Moonis, 'Urbanization in Pre-Historic India', *The Geographer*, 4, May 1951, 15-29.

Reddy, N.B.K., 'Urban Evolution, Growth Pattern, and Urbanization Trends in Krishna and Godavari Deltas', *National Geographical Journal of India*, 1970, 270-87.

Reeves, P.D., F.J.A. Broeze and K.I. McPherson, *Ports and Port Cities*, Centre for South and South East Asian Studies, Nedlands, Western Australia 1982.

Rizvi, Saiyid Qamar Ahmad, *Urban Growth and Functional Morphology of Gorakhpur City*, Unpublished Ph.D. thesis, Agra 1979.

Robson, W.A., *Great Cities of the World*, George Allen and Unwin, London 1957 (2nd ed).

Ross, Robert and Gerard J., Telcamp (eds), *Colonial Cities: Essays on Urbanism in a Colonial Context*, Leiden 1985.

Roy, Ashin Kumar, *History of the Jaipur City*, Delhi 1978.

Roy, U.N., *Prachin Bharat Mein Nagar tatha Nagar-Jiwan* (Hindi), Allahabad 1965.

Rukobo, Andries Matenda, *Land Class and Dominance in North Western India : Social Structure, Agrarian Relations and Change in Muzaffarnagar*, Ph.D. thesis, J.N.U., Delhi 1980.

Rutnagar, S.M., *Bombay Industries: The Cotton Mills*, Bombay 1927.

Sabapathy, T.V., *Madurai City : A Survey of its Past and Present*, Diploma thesis, the School of Town and Country Planning, New Delhi 1957.

Sabarwal, Satish, *Mobile Men: Limits to Social Change in Urban Punjab*, Indian Institute of Advanced Study, Simla 1976 (2nd ed 1990).

Sankhdher, Brijendra Mohan, *Sambhal: A Historical Survey*, Kumar Brothers, New Delhi 1971.

Saraswati, Baidyanath, *Kashi: Myth and Reality of Classical Cultural Tradition*, Indian Institute of Advanced Study, Shimla 1975.

Sarkar, H., 'Growth of Cities in Andhradesa', Presidential Address, *Proceedings of the Andhra Pradesh History Congress*, Guntur 1986.

Sharar, Abdul Halim (tr and ed), *Lucknow: The Last Phase of an Oriental Culture*, Paul Elek, London 1975.

Sharma, Harish, 'A Note on Urban Artisans', *Proceedings Indian History Congress*, Burdwan, 1983.

Sharma, K.D., 'Evidence of Mohallas in the Reconstruction of Urban Morphogenesis', *Geographical Aspects*, 1980, 42-48.

Sharma, Raj Kumar, *The Town of Gurdaspur--An Urban Study (1825-1981)*, M. Phil dissertation, Dept. of History, Guru Nanak Dev University, Amritsar 1989.

Sharma, R.S. 'Decay of Gangetic Towns in Gupta and Post Gupta Period', *Proceedings Indian History Congress*, New Delhi 1973, 92-104.

——, *Urban Decay in India (c A.D. 300-c 1000)* Munishram Manoharlal, New Delhi 1987.

Sheppard, S.T., *Bombay*, Bombay 1932.

Singer, M. 'The Great Tradition in a Metropolitan Centre – Madras', *Journal of American Folklore*, July-Sept. 1958, 347-88.

Singh, Harihar, 'Evolution of the Townscape of Jaunpur City', *National Geographical Journal of India*, 1958, 35-46,

Singh, Kumud Kumar, 'Historical Study of Patna, Bihar', Paper for 21st Indian Geography Congress, Abstracts, 1968, 285.

Singh, Mahindra Pal, *Town, Market, Mint and Port in the Mughal Empire, 1556-1707*, Adam, New Delhi 1985.

Singh, Madhusudan, 'Evolution of Meerut', *National Geographical Journal of India*, 1965, 144-58.

Singh, R.L. and K.N. Singh, 'Evolution of the Medieval Towns in the Saryupar Plain of the Middle Ganga Valley–A Case Study', *National Geographical Journal of India*, March 1963, 1-11.

Singh, S.C. 'Evolution of Azamgarh', *National Geographical Journal of India*, Sep.-Dec., 1963, 175-86.

Singh Ujagir, 'Evolution of Allahabad', *National Geographical Journal of India*, Sept. 1958, 109-29.

——, 'The Origin and Growth of Kanpur', *National Geographical Journal of India*, Jan. 1959, 1-11.

——, 'Bombay : A Study in Historical Geography, *National Geographical Journal of India*, March 1960, 19-29.

——, *Allahabad : A Study in Urban Geography*, Varanasi 1966.

Singh, Vishwa Nath Prasad, 'Historical Development of Deogarh Town', *Indian Geography Congress*, Abstracts, 1968, 301.

Sinha, Pradip, *Calcutta in Urban History*, Calcutta 1978.

Sinha, Surajit (ed), *Cultural Profile of Calcutta*, Calcutta 1972.

Spodek, Howard, 'Urban Politics in the Local Kingdoms of India', *Modern Asian Studies*, VII, 2, 1973.

Srinivaschari, C.S., 'Stages in the Growth of City of Madras', *Journal of Madras Geographical Association*, Oct. 1927, 79-105.

Srivastava, A.K., *Urban Economic Life in Ancient India (700-1200 AD)*, Allahabad 1984.

Stein, Burton, *Peasant State and Society in Medieval South India*, Oxford University Press, New Delhi 1980.

——, *Vijayanagara*, The New Cambridge History of India, Cambridge University Press and Orient Longman, 1989.

Subramanian, Lakshmi, 'Capital and Crowd in a Declining Asian Port City: The Anglo Bania Order and the Surat Riots of 1795', *Modern Asian Studies*, 19, 2, 1985.

Swarn Lata, *Urbanization in the Punjab 1849-1947*, M.Phil dissertation, Dept. of History, Guru Nanak Dev University, Amritsar 1988.

Sullery, S.K., 'Cities and City Life During the Reign of the Chandellas', *Proceedings Indian History Congress*, Dharwad 1988, 145-50.

Surinder Singh, 'The Jesuits and their Activities in the City of Lahore', ibid., 249-56.

Tewari, A.K., 'Mathura : A Study in Site and Evolution', *National Geographical Journal of India*, March 1963, 48-59.

Thakore, M.P., 'Sixteen Sites of Delhi', *Indian Geographer*, Dec. 1963, 84-119.

Thakur, V.K., *Urbanization in Ancient India*, New Delhi 1981.

Tindall, Gillian, *City of Gold, A Biography of Bombay*, London 1980.

Torri, Michelguglielmo, 'Surat During the Second Half of the Eighteenth Century : What Kind of Social Order? - Rejoinder to Lakshmi

Subramanian', *Modern Asian Studies,* Vol. 21, Pt. 4, Oct. 1987, 679-711.

Toy, Sidney, *The Fortified Cities of India,* Heinemann, London 1965.

Trevelyan, G., *Cawnpore,* Macmillan, London 1894.

Tyagi, R.K. and R.B. Singh, 'Evolution of Land Routes and Growth of Four Towns in Western U.P., *Proceedings Indian Science Congress,* Abstract of Papers, 1970, 242.

Vaiyapuri, Pillai, 'Life in an Ancient Tamil City : Kaveripatanam', *Ceylon Historical Journal,* July-Oct. 1952, 5-7.

Viswanadham, Garimella, 'Ecological Organization of a Transitional City : A Case Study of Hyderabad', *Geographical Review of India,* Vol. 43, No. 4, Dec. 1981, 301-9.

Vicziany, Marika, *The Cotton Trade and the Commercial Development of Bombay,* Ph.D. thesis, University of London 1975.

Wacha, D.E., *Rise and Growth of Bombay Municipal Government,* Madras 1913.

——, *Shells from the Sands of Bombay : My Recollections and Reminiscences, 1860-75,* Bombay 1920.

Wheeler, J.T., *Madras in the Olden Times,* 3 Vols., Madras 1861-62.

Yadav,C.S., (ed), *Morphology of Towns,* Perspectives in Urban Geography, X, Concept, New Delhi 1987.

CONTRIBUTORS

R.CHAMPAKALAKSHMI: Professor of History at Jawaharlal Nehru University, New Delhi. With research interests in urban history, and religion and society in South India of the early historic and early medieval periods, she is also working on a historical atlas of Tamil Nadu upto A.D. 1300; her publications include *Vaishnava Iconography in the Tamil Country*, besides a number of articles.

SATISH CHANDRA: Formerly Chairman of the University Grants Commission and Professor of History, Jawaharlal Nehru University, New Delhi; at present, National Fellow of the Indian Council of Historical Research, New Delhi; done pioneering work in the history of India during the seventeenth and eighteenth centuries and in regional history; his well-known works include *Parties and Politics at the Mughal Court*; *Medieval India: The Village Society and the Crisis of Jagirdari System; The Eighteenth Century in Indian History : The Role of the Jats, Afghans, Sikhs and Marathas;* and *The Indian Ocean: Exploration in History, Commerce and Politics (ed).*

INDRANI GANGULY: Presently working in Brisbane, Australia; her Ph.D. work from the Australian National University, Canberra, was published in 1987 as *The Social History of a Bengal Town, 1872-1947.*

J.S. GREWAL: Formerly Professor of History and Vice-Chancellor, Guru Nanak Dev University, Amritsar; at present, Director, Indian Institute of Advanced Study, Shimla; areas of interest are philosophy of history, historiography, medieval India, regional history and history of the Sikhs; major publications include *Muslim Rule in India : The Assessments of British Historians; Guru Nanak in History; In the Bye-lanes of History : Persian Documents from a Punjab Town*; and *The Sikhs of the Punjab* in *The New Cambridge History of India* series.

REETA GREWAL: Lecturer in History, Panjab University, Chandigarh; a revised version of her doctoral work forthcoming as *Urbanization Under Colonial Rule : The Punjabi Century;* her published articles on urban history include 'Polity, Economy and Urbanization: Early 19th Century Punjab', and 'The Pattern of Urbanization in the Punjab Under Colonial Rule'.

NARAYANI GUPTA: Reader in History at Jamia Millia Islamia, New Delhi. The revised version of her doctoral thesis *Delhi Between Two Empires 1803-1931* was republished in 1986; her research interests include urban and architectural history. She is on the editorial board of *Urban History Yearbook* (Leicester) and of *Planning Perspectives* (Birmingham).

S. NURUL HASAN: Formerly Minister of Education, Government of India, Vice-Chairman, Council of Scientific and Industrial Research, and Professor of History at the Aligarh Muslim University and the University of Delhi; at present, Governor of West Bengal. Eminent among the pioneers of social and economic history, and methodology, in Indian historiography and the author of several articles and monographs of seminal character, best reflected in the *Thoughts on Agrarian Relations in Mughal India.*

KANCHAN JYOTI: Till her sudden passing away in August 1990, she was heading the Postgraduate Department of History at the G.N. College, Banga (Punjab). Her doctoral work on *The City of Jullundur : A Study in Urban History, 1846-1947,* was submitted to Guru Nanak Dev University in 1988. Author of several articles on aspects of the history of Jullundur, she was engaged in the revision of her doctoral work for publication at the time of her pre-mature death.

ATIYA HABEEB KIDWAI : taught at the Department of Architecture and Regional Planning, Indian Institute of Technology, Kharagpur; at present, Associate Professor, Centre for the Study of Regional

Development, Jawaharlal Nehru University, New Delhi. Her current research relates to the process of urbanisation in the Third World and to history of urbanisation in colonial India. She is a member of the International Geographical Union's Commission on Third World Development.

NITA KUMAR : Presently at the Brown University, Providence, RI, USA; obtained her doctorate from the University of Chicago in 1984 on *Popular Culture in Urban India : The Artisans of Banaras, c. 1884-1984;* subsequently researched in India as a social anthropologist at the American Institute of Indian Studies, Centre for Arts and Archaeology, Varanasi.

RAVINDER KUMAR : Formerly Professor of History at the University of Allahabad and the University of New South Wales, Sydney, Australia; at present, Director, Nehru Memorial Museum and Library, New Delhi. Besides several articles on social history of modern India, his published work includes *Western India in the Nineteenth Century; Essays In The Social History Of Modern India; The Making Of A Nation : Essays in Indian History And Politics; Essays in Gandhian Politics (ed); and Philosophical Theory and Social Reality* (ed).

S.C. MISRA : Professor and Head of the Department of History at the M.S. University of Baroda from 1959 to 1984. Before his pre-mature passing away he was engaged in path-breaking studies of Akbar and Gandhi. Besides several articles and edited works on source materials throwing fresh light on the social history of medieval India and regional history, his major publications include *The Rise of Muslim Power in Gujarat,* and *The Muslim Communities in Gujarat.*

KUSUM PANT - JOSHI : Formerly lecturer in History at the Allahabad University and a Visiting Fellow at Oxford; her doctoral thesis on Kashmiri Pandits submitted to the Sydney University, Australia, was published in 1987; researched in India and in London on the history of Lucknow during the colonial period as a Post-Doctoral Fellow of the Indian Council of Historical Research from 1985 to 1988.

ALOKA PARASHER: Reader in History at the University of Hyderabad; at present, UGC Career Awardee working on the 'Social and Economic History of Early Deccan - A Source Book'. Besides several articles on the social and economic history of ancient India, her doctoral work submitted to the University of London is being published as the *Mlecchas in Early India.*

G.D. SHARMA: Professor of History at the M.S. University of Baroda till his sudden passing away in May 1990. In his short-lived but active career, he wrote several articles and edited important source - materials like *Hakumat - Ri - Bahi*, *The Vakil Reports* and *The Bakshi Documents*. His *Rajput Polity* remains a valuable contribution to Indian historiography. He popularised scientific research on social and economic institutions of medieval India through the medium of Hindi.

R.S. SHARMA: Formerly Chairman of the Indian Council of Historical Research, and Professor of History at the Universities of Delhi and Patna; at present, National Fellow of the Indian Council of Historical Research, Delhi; has done pioneering work in the social, economic and administrative history of early India; his major publications include *Shudras in Ancient India; Aspects of Political Ideas and Institutions in Ancient India; Indian Feudalism c A.D. 300-1200; Ancient India; Perspectives in Social and Economic History of Early India; Material Culture and Social Formations in Ancient India*, and *Urban Decay in India (c A.D.300-c1000)*.